THE INNATE CAPACITY

THE INNATE CAPACITY

Mysticism, Psychology, and Philosophy

EDITED BY
ROBERT K. C. FORMAN

New York Oxford • Oxford University Press 1998

Oxford University Press

Oxford New York
Athens Auckland Bangkok Bogota Bombay Buenos Aires
Calcutta Cape Town Dar es Salaam Delhi Florence Hong Kong
Istanbul Karachi Kuala Lumpur Madras Madrid Melbourne
Mexico City Nairobi Paris Singapore Taipei Tokyo Toronto Warsaw

and associated companies in
Berlin Ibadan

Published by Oxford University Press, Inc.
198 Madison Avenue, New York, New York 10016

Library of Congress Cataloging-in-Publication Data
The innate capacity : mysticism, psychology, and
philosophy / edited by Robert K. C. Forman
p. cm.
Includes bibliographical references.
ISBN 0-19-511697-6
1. Mysticism—Psychological aspects.
2. Mysticism—Comparative studies.
I. Forman, Robert K. C.
BL625.I56 1998
291.4'22—dc21 97-1585

1 2 3 4 5 6 7 8 9

Printed in the United States of America
on acid-free paper

Good Friends, enlightenment (bodhi) and intuitive wisdom (prajna) are from the outset possessed by people of this world themselves. It is just because the mind is deluded that people cannot attain awakening to themselves. They must seek a good teacher to show them how to see into their own nature.

—Hui Neng, *Platform Sutra* ¶ 12

Preface

SOMETHING IMPORTANT IS happening in the study of religions and religious experiences that may have reverberations in every field.

For decades, social scientists and scholars of the humanities have been laboring under one dominant model. That model, constructivism, suggests that in one way or another, cultural training, social background, economic circumstance, and one's beliefs largely shape one's experiences, feelings, actions, and life. The idea is that, at least in part, we create our own reality. This "constructive" model has been enormously productive, especially in the study of human actions, hopes, and ideas. It has helped us understand a great deal about how people's behavior, beliefs, and experiences are shaped and conditioned by their backgrounds.

Constructivism has also been helpful when applied to the study of religion and religious experiences.[1] Just as all experiences are mediated or constructed, champions of this approach suggest, so, too, are mystical experiences. Mystical experiences, like other experiences, are in large part shaped, formed, or built by the concepts, expectations, hopes, and beliefs we bring to them. An extraordinary number and depth of connections exist not only between one's social situation and religious

1. In religious studies this notion has been outspokenly applied to mystical experience by several notable scholars: Steven Katz in his essays "Language, Epistemology, and Mystical Experience" in *Mysticism and Philosophical Analysis* and "The 'Conservative' Character of Mystical Experience" *in Mysticism and Religious Traditions*; Robert Gimello, Ninian Smart, Peter Moore, and the other contributors to Katz's two books; Wayne Proudfoot in *Religious Experience*: William Wainwright in *Mysticism*; and the philosophers represented in Richard Woods's *Understanding Mysticism*.

experiences but also between one's language and beliefs and the shape of one's mystical experiences.

Recently, however, a number of scholars in the humanities—and particularly those who study religious experiences—have begun to challenge this model. Certain mystical experiences may escape the ordinary constructive processes of language and belief. Sallie King, Donald Evans, Leon Schlamm, as well as my colleagues and I who contributed to *The Problem of Pure Consciousness* (Oxford University Press, 1990) have argued that some experiences—notably the silent mystical experience of pure consciousness—do not seem to be shaped or formed by the language system. Through a process akin to forgetting, one may be able to let go of one's concepts and conceptual baggage and come to an experience that is both nonconceptual and not shaped by concepts and beliefs.

While not duplicating those arguments, this book continues and expands the explorations into this new, nonconstructivist direction. *The Problem of Pure Consciousness* and articles by other writers have done much of the "destructive" work in exploring this avenue. It is now time, we feel, to attempt the much more difficult "constructive" academic work of putting forward a new hypothesis about the formative cause(s) of these experiences.

This volume began when several contributors to *The Problem of Pure Consciousness* suggested, either in their articles or in the correspondence leading to it, that, rather than being the product of a cultural and linguistic learning process, mysticism seems to result from some sort of *innate* human capacity. The book's principal questions, then, are: Do mystical experiences arise from a learned, socially conditioned constructive process, or are they the expressions of some sort of innate human capacity? If the latter, what is that capacity? How is it spoken of and understood? How can we make sense of an innate capacity for mysticism? How shall we understand it?

As this book has developed, several distinct but interconnected theses have emerged. First, while mysticism is conceived differently by different contributors, all agree that mysticism *is* the expression of an innate capacity. This capacity is spoken of and understood differently, however. Many writers conceive of it as an expression of our consciousness, awareness itself. Most who speak of it thus maintain that we should conceive of consciousness as separate from all sensation, perception, and thought—and thus separate from the culturally "trainable" aspects of human experience. Some suggest that consciousness should be conceived of as a built-in connecting link to the greater world—and that a mystical experience is an experience of that inherent connectedness.

Another frequently appearing thesis is that mystics come to this innate capacity through a process of letting go of the ego and the conceptual system. This is especially clear in William Chittuck's article on Ibn al-ʿArabī, the Sufi who teaches that it is but self-centeredness that "conceals the sun" of the innate character of the self—that is, God's own self manifestation within the self. Through the annihilation of the self, *fanā'*, "abandoning" our egocentricity or giving up our "delimited consciousness," we reveal the innate "sun" within.

Roger Corless suggests something similar: that the Buddhist *Lotus Sūtra*'s procedure leading to the Buddha Nature is one of "deconstruction"—the undoing of attachments. The key attachment to be deconstructed is that to Buddhist doctrines and procedures. The text itself, he shows, enables one to let go of the disciple's attachments to it.

Diane Jonte-Pace's fascinating study of the Rorschach responses of three spiritual masters makes an unexpected yet valuable contribution to these discussions. All three of her subjects had highly unusual, yet strikingly similar, responses to the tests. Each viewed the test patterns with a surprisingly consistent and cohesive set of responses, using the cards as an integrated teaching tool. The author maintains that their responses, which were not focused on the sensory world, show that they had in deep ways "dismantled" or let go of the ordinary perceptual structures. Her article tends to reinforce both claims: that (a) something cross-culturally consistent is being engendered in mysticism and that (b) it is achieved through a process of "letting go."

Finally, thanks go to each of the contributors to this volume. All responded with grace to the no doubt irritating shouts, pleas, and demands of their crotchety editor. Many waited patiently and with good humor—in some cases for years—for this book to reach publication. My thanks also to my colleagues at Hunter College, especially my wise department chair, Barbara Sproul, for the encouraging and supportive atmosphere she has created in our fine institution. My deepest thanks to Yvonne, Rosha, and Avram Forman for being the wonderful people that they are.

The Forge, Hastings-on-Hudson, NY R. K. C. F.
March 1997

Contents

Contributors xiii

ONE Introduction: Mystical Consciousness, the Innate Capacity, and the Perennial Philosophy 3
Robert K. C. Forman

PART I THE INNATE CAPACITY IN THE RELIGIOUS TRADITIONS

TWO Discriminating the Innate Capacity: Salvation Mysticism of Classical Sāṃkya-Yoga 45
Lloyd W. Pflueger

THREE Parables of Deconstruction in the *Lotus Sūtra* 82
Roger Corless

FOUR Between the Yes and the No: Ibn al-ʿArabī on *Wujūd* and the Innate Capacity 95
William Chittick

FIVE Mysticism, Mediation, and Consciousness: The Innate Capacity in John Ruusbroec 111
James Robertson Price III

PART II PSYCHOLOGY AND THE INNATE CAPACITY

SIX The Innate Capacity: Jung and the Mystical Imperative 123
John Dourley

SEVEN The Swami and the Rorschach: Spiritual Practice, Religious Experience, and Perception 137
Diane Jonte-Pace

EIGHT William James and the Origins of Mystical Experience 161
G. William Barnard

PART III THE PHILOSOPHY OF THE INNATE CAPACITY

NINE Innate Mystical Capacities and the Nature of the Self 213
Anthony N. Perovich Jr.

TEN Postconstructivist Approaches to Mysticism 231
R. L. Franklin

Contributors

G. WILLIAM BARNARD received his doctorate from the University of Chicago and teaches in the Religious Studies Department of the Southern Methodist University. He is the author of *Exploring Unseen Worlds: William James and the Philosophy of Mysticism* and more than ten articles on the philosophy of mysticism and the psychology of religious experience.

WILLIAM C. CHITTICK is professor of comparative studies at the State University of New York at Stony Brook. He is the author and translator of some fifteen books and numerous articles.

ROGER CORLESS is professor of religion at Duke University. He is a specialist in Pure Land Buddhism and Buddhist-Christian dialogue and is the author of four books, including *The Vision of Buddhism* (1989), and about fifty articles, of which "Idolatry and Inherent Existence: The Golden Calf and the Wooden Buddha" in *Healing Deconstruction: Postmodern Thought in Buddhism and Christianity*, edited by David Loy (1996), is relevant to the discussion in the present essay.

JOHN P. DOURLEY is professor in the Department of Religion, Carleton University, Ottawa, Canada. He is a Jungian analyst (Zurich, 1980) and has written widely on Jung and religion. He is the author of seven books, including *Psyche and Sacrament* (1980) and eighteen articles on psychology and religion.

ROBERT K. C. FORMAN received his doctorate in religion from Columbia University and is an associate professor in the Program in Religion at the City University of New York's Hunter College. He is the author of more than thirty articles and six books, among which is the much discussed *The Problem of Pure Consciousness* (1990). He is the founder and executive editor of the *Journal of Consciousness Studies* and the founder and director of the Forge Institute for Spirituality and Social Change, and he was the founder and chair of the mysticism group at the American Academy of Religion. He lives in a 250-year-old house with his wife, two children, a dog, and a turtle.

RICHARD L. FRANKLIN was born in 1925 in Melbourne, Australia, where he practiced as a lawyer until he decided that philosophy was his true love. He received his Ph.D. in philosophy from the University of Western Australia. He became a professor in and head of the Department of Philosophy at the University of New England. He has practiced the stilling of the mind in meditation for some twenty-five years and is a lay reader in the Anglican Church. His attempts to relate philosophy to such issues as mysticism include many articles and his latest book, *The Nature of Understanding* (1995). He is an Emeritus Professor who now finds himself increasingly attracted to the view, found in many cultures, that wisdom increases with age.

DIANE JONTE-PACE received her doctorate from the University of Chicago and is an associate professor in the Department of Religious Studies at Santa Clara University. Her publications have focused on two major areas in the field cf religion and psychological studies: (1) religion and the Rorschach test, and (2) religion, psychoanalysis, and feminist theory. She is currently writing a book on Freud, gender, religion, and modernity. She serves as chair of the editorial board of the *Religious Studies Review.*

ANTHONY N. PEROVICH JR. received his doctorate from the University of Chicago and teaches at Hope College in Holland, Michigan. He is the author of a number of articles dealing with the philosophy of mysticism and German idealism.

JAMES ROBERTSON PRICE III has taught religion at Georgia State University and Catholic University of America and is now with the Shriver Center, University of Maryland, Baltimore County, Baltimore. He has written several books about philosophy and mysticism and Christian spirituality.

LLOYD PFLEUGER is assistant professor of philosophy and religion at Truman State University. He has his Ph.D. in religious studies from the University of California at Santa Barbara with specialties in South Asian religion and philosophy and theories of religious behavior. Pflueger's book on Indian theism and yoga, *The God Within: The Lord of Worship and the Lord of Meditation in Ancient India*, is forthcoming. He lives by a small lake outside Kirksville, Missouri, with his Tibetan terrier, Rosco.

THE INNATE CAPACITY

ONE

Introduction

Mystical Consciousness, the Innate Capacity, and the Perennial Psychology

ROBERT K. C. FORMAN

You can't know it, but you can be it
at ease in your own life
Just realize where you come from:
This is the essence of wisdom.[1]

Mysticism, Constructivism, and Decontextualism

It is commonly observed that many, if not most, seminal religious leaders have undergone some form of mystical experiences. Less commonly known is how surprisingly widespread such experiences are; summarizing several large-scale studies, David Hay, in *Religious Experience Today*, concludes that nearly *half*—43 percent of all Americans and 48 percent of all British people—have had one or more mystical experiences. These experiences are not confined to the uneducated; more than half of all college graduates have had such experiences.[2] Though most keep their tales of these extraordinary experiences largely private, many of this near majority have oriented vital aspects of their lives around them.

Despite the extensive and significant nature of this phenomenon, scholars have reached little consensus about the causes and character of such extraordinary moments. Within philosophy and religious studies over the past twenty years, two fundamental interpretations, called "constructivism" and "decontextualism" (in which camp I place myself), have been propounded. In this article I first describe these two approaches, showing in particular how the decontextualists (I prefer the term perennial psychologists,[3] for reasons I explain shortly) have responded to the first group, the constructivists. Then I describe several conceptual problems that we perennial psychologists have left unanswered and suggest how they might be answered. Finally, I explore a few of the implications of my proposed answer.

ONE GOOD WAY to grasp the constructivist and the perennial psychologist approaches is to see how each might look at a mystical passage.[4] Let us look at a passage from the fairly late Hindu Upaniṣad, Maitri 6:18–19.

> To the unity of the One goes he who knows this. (18) The precept for effecting this [unity] is this: restraint of the breath (*prāṇāyāma*), withdrawal of the senses (*pratyāhāra*), meditation (*dhyāna*), concentration (*dharana*), contemplation (*tarka*), and absorption (*samādhi*). Such is said to be the sixfold Yoga. . . .
>
> (19)Now it has elsewhere been said, "Verily when a knower has restrained his mind from the external, and the breathing spirit (*prāṇa*) has put to rest objects of sense, thereupon let him continue void of conceptions. Since the living individual (*jīva*) who is named "breathing spirit" has arisen here from what is not breathing spirit, therefore, verily, let the breathing spirit restrain his breathing spirit in what is called the fourth condition (*turya*).[5] For thus it has been said:
> That which is non-thought, [yet] which stands in the midst of thought,
> The unthinkable, supreme mystery!—
> Thereon let one concentrate his attention
> And the subtle body (*liṇga*), too, without support.[6]

This is a passage that touches upon many of the themes commonly seen in mysticism: (1) it is obviously concerned with some nonordinary experience; (2) it mentions meditation; (3) it suggests that something ineffable is involved ("the unthinkable, supreme mystery"); (4) it implies an experience of unity ("the unity of the One").

While I have read no other analyses of this specific passage, it is clear that because the constructivist claims that one's background, beliefs, and expectations shape both a text like this and the experience it describes, constructivists would begin by analyzing our passage's background. They might note that the Upaniṣads are generally placed at c. 600–200 BCE in the newly posttribal Aryan context and that our text describes the results of meditative techniques that were themselves shaped and influenced by their context.[7] To understand a passage like "the breathing spirit has arisen here from what is not breathing spirit," they would correctly point to highly ramified terms like *prāṇa* (breath) and "the One" (i.e., Brahman). They might also point to the formative character of such antecedent Vedic texts as *Ṛg Veda* 10:129, in which the world arises out of "the One" that first breathed, the well-known Puruṣasūkta, *Ṛg Veda* 10.90, which suggests a proto-monistic doctrine of the world emerging out of a primeval sacrifice, or to the possible influence of earlier Upaniṣadic passages about the world's emergence from *prāṇa* (breath). In their analysis of the background of this text, the constructivists would be, I believe, both correct and helpful.

But constructivists do not stop with merely analyzing a text. They go on to claim that such a passage is describing an *experience* that was *itself shaped* by previously learned notions of *ātman*, the self, and *brahman*, the world-essence.[8] Steven Katz,[9]

Robert Gimello,[10] Hans Penner,[11] and Wayne Proudfoot[12] have argued that, like all experiences, a mystical experience like ours is subject to the formative and constructive processes of the subject's language and culture. *All* of our thoughts and experiences, they argue, are shaped, conditioned, and in part constructed by our background of beliefs and concepts; hence, mysticism, being an experience, is also so constructed. For example, when Professor Katz writes about the background causes of a mystical experience, he suggests that it is shaped much as Claude Monet's famous paintings of Rouen were shaped.[13] In those paintings, Rouen's arches were depicted with the vaulted points of Gothic arches, despite the fact that the real arches bore the rounded Romanesque crests. Monet's expectations, Katz plausibly suggests, which were based on his expectations about Gothic churches, shaped his visual experience—thus, he *mis*perceived and hence *mis*painted the arches. Similarly, Katz continues, mystics bring their expectations—not visual but religious—to bear on their experiences and thus shape or construct their experiences on the basis of their traditions' mystical models:

> As a result of his process of intellectual acculturation in its broadest sense, the mystic brings to his experience a world of concepts, images, symbols, and values which shape as well as color the experience he eventually and actually has.[14]

> The experience itself as well as the form in which it is reported is shaped by concepts which the mystic brings to, and which shape, his experience.[15]

Wayne Proudfoot argues similarly: the key fact in a mystical experience is the identification of it "under a particular description."[16] Were I to have a mystical experience, I would identify it "as" Brahman or "as" Buddha Nature or "as" Christ Consciousness. Bound up with these terms is the full range of my background of concepts, images, symbols, values, and so on. Thus, the terms with which I identify a mystical experience, in significant ways, determine and shape my experience.

Let us name the mystic who is being described in our Upaniṣadic passage "Śvetaketu Aruneya," who was, according to *Chāndogya Upaniṣad* 6:8, the son of the great guru Uddālaka Aruni.[17] Were Śvetaketu to have a mystical experience, he would no doubt encounter it "as" *ātman*, "as" the Self, or "as" *brahman*, as his father and his culture no doubt would have taught him. Thus, his experience naturally would be shaped, constructivists maintain, by these terms and by the background of beliefs and expectations that made them what they were.

Because his experience would have been shaped by his Hindu background, Śvetaketu's experience would necessarily differ from a Christian's or a Muslim's. For the experiences of people from different cultures are always pluralistic, constructivists say; our backgrounds, cultures, eras, and training lead us all to see and experience differently. After all, they cogently observe, the Upaniṣads never spoke of "Yahweh" but talked instead of *ātman* and *brahman*. Nor did the Hebrews write psalms or have experiences of the glories of *ātman*. The point is, constructivists conclude, that we experience what our language, background, concepts, culture, dreams, and dreads shape for us. As the Buddhologist Robert Gimello puts it, "mystical experience is simply the psychosomatic enhancement of religious beliefs and values."[18] Or, as H. P. Owen said about Christian mysticism, "Christian forms of mystical experience are shaped by antecedently held beliefs."[19]

The other recent school of thought has been called variously "decontextualism," "deconstructivism," and "postconstructivism." I prefer the more suggestive "perennial psychology," as I explain later. Adherents of this position, including myself, maintain that while the texts and statements of mystics may be shaped by background, it is wrong to say that an experience like Śvetaketu's is necessarily conditioned by the same sorts of processes that condition Monet's observing Rouen.[20] Here are a few of our reasons, though for the interested reader I commend *The Problem of Pure Consciousness* and articles by William Barnard, Jonathan Shear, James Price, Louis Nordstrom, and others.[21]

First, no constructivist has ever justified drawing a parallel between *seeing* some sensory object and having a *mystical* experience. It is not clear that these two are in fact epistemologically parallel structures. What, for example, is playing the role of the visual *object* in mysticism? Our passage directly says that in order to do the procedure correctly, Śvetaketu, our theoretical Upaniṣadic mystic, is supposed to "restrain his mind from the external, and [his] breathing spirit [is to] put to rest objects of sense." That sounds like he is being instructed *not* to look at or smell *any*thing. If he does in fact "restrain his mind from the external," he will then see and hear *no* intentional object. The purported parallel is, primae facie, falsely drawn.

Second, it is not clear just how language and concepts are involved in a mystical experience. Our passage says that Śvetaketu is to "continue void of conceptions." If he does so, he will not be thinking in words, entertaining any concepts, or identifying his experience with words, visual images, linguistic thoughts, beliefs, or even background ideas. In other words, no constructivist has ever plausibly explained how language and its background actually are active in mystical experiences like these.

Third, mystical texts rarely assert that mystics learned about mystical experiences *before* they had them. For example, it is in no way clear in our Upaniṣadic passage that the purported subject must necessarily have heard about mystical experiences *before* becoming "void of conceptions." The text just does not say. Clearly, if our subject did not hear of *ātman* before having his first mystical experience, then we would say that Śvetaketu's background knowledge could *not* have formed the experience. And indeed, there are many cases on record in which mystical experiences came before the subject learned of them. For example, the Zen Master John Daido Sensei Loori, head of the Rivers and Mountains Lineage and abbot of the Mountain Tremper Zendo, told me that he had his first mystical five years before he ever took up Zen Buddhism or meditation of any sort.[22] His experience *led* him to explore Zen, not the other way around.[23]

Fourth, even if our Śvetaketu did hear of *ātman* before he had an experience "of" it, no one has ever established that his prior hearing actually shaped his experience.

Merely because we learn about something before we experience it doesn't mean that our experience is thereby *caused* by that prior learning. I had heard that Indian food makes people's throats burn long before I had Indian food; yet my hot throat was caused not by that knowledge but by the spices.[24] When Steven Katz or Wayne Proudfoot writes as if the mere existence of prior knowledge implies that the experiences were shaped by that knowledge, they commit the fallacy of *post hoc ergo propter hoc* (if B comes after A, B is therefore caused by A). Other causes may be at work.

Finally, we have suggested a new model for experiences like this passage's, the so-called forgetting model. Notice how our passage says "*restrain* the breath," "*withdraw* the senses," "*put to rest* objects of sense," and "let the breathing spirit *restrain* his breathing spirit." Mystical texts nearly always use such language: one should "forget" or "lay aside" or "cease thinking" or "restrain the mind" or "put behind a cloud of forgetting" or come to *vergezzenheit* (the state of having forgotten). Taking such expressions seriously, we have suggested that the key process in mysticism is not like a construction process but more like one of unconstructing. Meditative procedures encourage one to gradually lay aside and temporarily cease employing language and concepts.[25] If one truly forgets all concepts and beliefs for some period, then those concepts and beliefs cannot play a formative role in creating the mystical experience(s). This forgetting model shows how at least some forms of mysticism—that is, the pure consciousness event (PCE), a wakeful but objectless consciousness—should be viewed as *decontextualized*.[26]

These, then, are some of the reasons we believe that, however well suited to explain our sensory experiences and our thoughts, constructivism is ill suited to account for such mystical experiences.

Two obvious questions surface. First, if culture is not shaping these quiet mystical events, then what *does* explain the features of this form of mysticism? What factors *are* responsible for their peculiar "shape"?

One might answer, well, nothing, for during the pure consciousness event one encounters nothing whatsoever and, thus, no "shape." The problem with this response is that these experiences are not quite blank: one does not simply recall nothing. One recalls, many have asserted, the merest being awake inside: "I know I wasn't asleep," or "I was awake."[27] One just knows that one wasn't "gone," dead, blacked out. Paradoxically, such reports assert that one knew both something (that one was awake, that there was a continuity of awareness throughout the event) and nothing—that one had no mental or sensory objects.

This leads us to our second question. One emerges out of a PCE knowing somehow that one's awareness had been unbroken. Usually I can assert that I was awake, say, fifteen minutes ago, on the basis of the fact that I remember something or other: walking up the steps, typing, thinking about this article. But in the quiet PCE there is purportedly no content to one's mind, and yet one knows that one has been aware continuously for some time—a few seconds, a minute, or however long the PCE lasted. How can I know that my awareness has been continuous for the (indeterminate) duration of a PCE without remembering at least some content, words, or images?[28] In short, how do I remember being awake during and after a pure consciousness event?

Claims of Innateness in Mystical Texts

We start with the first question first: If culture does not shape these phenomena, then what *is* responsible for them? Let us begin by looking at what a few thoughtful mystics have said about the philosophical character of their experiences, for I believe that it is they who, driven in part by the peculiarities of their own experiences, have been motivated to dig most deeply into questions like these.[29]

Any one familiar with the Upaniṣads knows that, while it does not use the term, our passage is speaking of an experience these texts call *turiya*, the fourth, which is an expression of an "encounter" with *ātman*, the "highest" within the human. Our passage suggests that by letting go of sensory input ("the external") and thoughts and images ("conceptions"), one will come to the experience. Furthermore, it suggests that "the living individual (*jīva*) who is named 'breathing spirit' has arisen here from what is not breathing spirit." This suggests that there are two distinct aspects of the human spirit—one of which "has arisen" and the other of which has not—that is, was present *ab initio*.

The implications of these suggestions were brought out most clearly by the great Hindu Advaitan philosopher Śankara. He suggests that attachments to thoughts and external things cause the individual to be in bondage, hiding or clouding the *ātman* within.

> Liberation is not an effect—it is but the destruction of bondage, not a created thing. . . . Production, attainment, modification and purification are the functions of [rituals and] work. In other words, work can produce, or bring within reach, or modify, or purify something, it has no other functions besides these. . . . And liberation is not one of these; we have already seen that it is simply hidden by ignorance.[30]

One's *ātman* cannot be "produced" or "attained," for it is already present. *Ātman* is the *natural* condition of the human spirit, he tells us. The activity that seems to bring about the experience of it does so only by destroying the bondage that had hidden it. We are only revealing what had been present all along but hidden: *ātman*. The mystic's techniques are not "producing" something new but "revealing" something preexistent: "Though Ātman is an ever present reality, yet because of ignorance It is unrealized. On the destruction of ignorance, Ātman is realized. It is like the case of [searching for] the ornament on one's neck."[31] Discovering *ātman* is like finding a necklace hanging on one's neck: it has always been present and is indeed available, just overlooked. This image emphasizes that *ātman*, and with it the possibility of its realization, is already present to one. It is, in a word, *innate*. Thus, as our benchmark passage says, we need only to "restrain [our] minds from the external" and "continue void of conceptions" to reveal what has been present all along.

Claims that in some forms of mysticism one is encountering something innate are found in mystical texts from many traditions. While the present article focuses primarily on two traditions, the rest of the book offers examples from many other traditions. For example, in his article in the present volume, Roger Corless describes a set of stories from the Mahāyāna Buddhist *Lotus Sūtra*, the most famous of which is the parable of the lost heir. A young man leaves home and wanders penniless for many years throughout his land, ultimately returning to his native village. There he meets his father, who recognizes him. The son does not recognize his father, however, for he seems a very rich and powerful man. The father, hoping not to shock the now poor son, offers him a lowly job. The son works hard and, as he can handle greater and greater responsibility, the father slowly promotes him to positions of greater and greater authority. Eventually, the father even adopts the son, bestowing on him his own name and ultimately granting him complete equality with himself. As the father nears death, he reveals the truth to his son, that the father's great riches and name really *are* the son's by birth. The riches thus have been the son's all along; he had only to realize it.

Obviously, the *Lotus Sūtra* is suggesting that each of us is somehow like the son and that we are to come to our "Buddha Nature" in a similar manner. Several morals can be drawn. First, in order to come to the realization of our own Buddha Nature, we must undergo a transformation process. Like the son's, this process involves an expansion of our capacity: we must become capable of perceiving more and bearing greater responsibilities, thus allowing us to bear more and more of our own true nature. Second, this transformative process does not involve accumulating something external, like wealth or knowledge about the world, but rather involves realizing something about ourselves—that we ourselves, like the son, are inherently grand, noble beings. Third, we have always been this noble being: the son had been wealthy from the start. We are not to take on some new wealth, some new gift, but rather to come to psychically own, as it were, that which is innate. What we are inherently, the Buddha Nature, has been present in us all along, even though we have not realized it.[32] It is not something to be appropriated from outside but rather is something that we must realize about ourselves, with our father's (i.e., a Buddha's) help, by *removing* certain mistaken perceptions.

The famous fourteenth-century Dominican Christian mystic Meister Eckhart also suggests that something which is encountered in mysticism has been present all along. Eckhart speaks of a *Geburt*, the birth of the Son (or Word) within the soul, suggesting that each human being carries something of the same spiritual "power in the soul" with which Jesus himself had been endowed.[33] It is ours from the moment we come alive. We are blessed with

> a power in the soul which touches neither time nor flesh, flowing from the spirit, remaining in the spirit, altogether spiritual. In this power, God is *ever* verdant and flowering in all the joy and all the glory that He is in Himself. There is such heartfelt

> delight, such inconceivably deep joy as none can fully tell of, for in this power the eternal Father is *ever* begetting His eternal Son without pause.[34] (Emphasis mine)

To Eckhart this spiritual power, the Birth of the Son in the soul, is the locus of our spiritual connection with God. And it is present within human beings at all times, whether or not we are cognizant of it. As a result of the fall, however, we have become attached (*eigenschaft*) to "this and that," the things of the world, thus losing our awareness of this inherent internal power. By relinquishing (*gelâzen*) those attachments, we can become aware of the "spiritual light" that has been at our core all along. That is, we can become overtly conscious of the "Birth of the Son" within. The Birth itself, as well as the capacity to experience it, is, therefore, *innate*. If one simply releases the attachments that hide it, God's preexisting presence within us becomes manifest.[35]

Again, three claims jump out. First, a *transformation process* is suggested. We begin attached to things of the world, and we must somehow let go (*lâzen, gelâzen*) of those attachments. Second, when one has let go sufficiently, one comes to discover something *about the self itself*—that we ourselves have the Birth "going on" within us. We enjoy a direct contact with God, be it conscious or not. Third, this spiritual contact with the infinite is not something one has to learn or acquire through books; rather, it is *innate* within each of us. Although it takes a transformation process to "forget" (*vergezzen*) that which conceals it, it is, as it were, built into the machinery of being human.

According to Lloyd Pfleuger's contribution to this volume, the classical Hindu Sāṃkhya-Yoga mystical/philosophical system suggests a different division than Śankara's. Whereas Advaita holds to a single innate reality (*brahman*), Sāṃkhya proposes a dualism. There are two innate and independent realities, *puruṣa* (which Pfleuger reasonably defines as "consciousness itself") and *prakṛti* (material reality). This dualism should not be confused with the traditional Western distinction between body and soul, for Sāṃkhya includes within the material side of the world most of what our tradition would categorize as soul: it parses the material side into twenty-four fundamental principles (*tattvas*), "*prakṛti*" plus the so-called twenty-three evolutes: intellect (*buddhi*), ego (*ahaṃkāra*), mind (*manas*), the five sense and the five action capacities (the *indriyas*), the five subtle elements (the *tanmātras*), and the five gross elements (the *mahābhūtas*).[36] All twenty-four, Sāṃkhya says, are distinguished from *puruṣa*, consciousness itself. *Puruṣa* here is the sheerest awareness; it watches, sees, or witnesses my thinking and acting. "*Puruṣa*," says Pfleuger, "is the knower, bereft of all intentionality, all content."[37]

Note that what we typically think of as psychological elements (e.g., thinking, cognitive functions) Sāṃkhya includes under "the material." Both my thoughts and my chair are thus part of *prakṛti*, the material world. Not only thoughts but sensations and mental activities are part of *prakṛti*. On the other side, however, only *puruṣa* (consciousness) itself stands over against the material—or perhaps we should say "intentionally encountered"—world. *Puruṣa* is thus utterly distinct from the mental and material processes. Yet it is necessary, for without it the play of thoughts and sense perceptions could not be experienced. Without *puruṣa,* thought or activity would not be conscious.[38] Awareness makes a thought or a perception an experience: we can have no experience without being conscious of it. *Puruṣa,* sheer awareness, is thus *innate*, part of the essential machinery of having any experience.

As does our Upaniṣadic passage, Sāṃkhya declares that through a meditative process, it is possible for the yogi to relinquish any and all intentional objects, ultimately "extinguishing" the operations of *prakṛti*[39] and thus isolating consciousness itself. Then, says the *Yogasūtras* (1:3), "[the seer] abide[s] in [his or her own] essential nature"—that is, within *puruṣa* itself.

Again we can draw three conclusions. Sāṃkhya—like the Upaniṣads, Śankara, Eckhart, and the *Lotus Sūtra*—suggests that the key element of the mystical realization results not from mental activities or, by implication, from a culturally mediated learning process. All learning would fall, we noted, under the "material" side of Sāṃkhya's dualism. Rather, it is only by relinquishing mental activities that one can come to experience *puruṣa* in the silent meditative experience it calls *kaivalya*. Thus, there is a transformation process at work here. Second, what is encountered as a result of this process is not something acquired from outside, learned, or even thought, for these would all be elements *(tattvas)* within prakṛti. Rather, what is encountered in *kaivalya* is *puruṣa*, which is inherent *within the self itself. Puruṣa* is a feature of our selves, not of our external world. Finally, the *puruṣa* that is encountered in *kaivalya* is innate, an inherent feature of being human.[40]

IN SUM, THE CONSTRUCTIVISTS argued that mysticism results from a process akin to constructing. Out of their social, linguistic, and religious background, the mystics construct and shape their experiences. Because each culture constructs differently, members of different cultures shape and build different experiences. But the mystics we have discussed all suggest that mysticism results from relinquishing such constructive, linguistic process and coming to something that is innate within the human being.

By this these mystics apparently refer to something originating in or inherent in the constitution of the person rather than derived from culture or experience. The claim here is that key aspects of certain mystical experiences are not constructed from language, learning, personality, or culture acquisition but come from something inherent or prelinguistic within us.

According to these mystical thinkers, the process leading to mysticism is not like one of constructing images but more like a process of removing what we have "seen" or "constructed" until the subject persists alone. We are dropping away the twenty-three *tattvas* of *prakṛti* or dropping the soul's attachments *(eigenschaft)* and external "powers." The mystic thereby reveals something intrinsic about his or her own fundamental nature—his or her inherent Buddha Nature, *puruṣa,* or *ātman*. Meditation removes or deconstructs something, revealing only the most basic "equipment" of being human.

It seems to me that the suggestions of these mystics and the others described in this volume should serve as a strong counterbalance to the tendency to simply assume—largely on the basis of ill-defended presuppositions about the constructed character of experience in general that are themselves based on a dubious analogy with ordinary experience—that all mystical experiences are linguistically constructed. But the case is far from settled. The question still comes up: Does the claim of innateness make sense? Should we take seriously the thoughts of these mystics about the cause of their experiences, or should we merely write them off as ill-justified faith statements?

Approaching Consciousness

In what sense can mystics mean that they are experiencing something innate? Clearly, the capacity to encounter mysticism is not innate in the sense that all people undergo it, as all breathe or even hiccup. Just the reverse is true: many human beings have never had mystical experiences.[41]

It seems to me that the mystics we have just examined are suggesting, rather, that there is something *about* the mystical experiences that is innate. What?

Our Upaniṣadic text points us to "That which is non-thought, [yet] which stands in the midst of thought." This suggests that when thinking stops, there is something that yet remains that is in the "midst of thought." Elsewhere in the same Upaniṣad it is stated that what remains is the "understander of understanding, the seer of seeing." By this, it is generally agreed, the Upaniṣads are speaking of consciousness or awareness itself.[42]

The claim that mysticism is an encounter with consciousness itself is surprisingly common in a wide range of mystical traditions.[43] According to William Chittick's excellent article in the present volume, it is seen in Islam's Sufism. Ibn al-ʿArabī, Chittick notes, suggests that what is at hand in his mysticism is consciousness or mere awareness. He says that even though only a "small minority of human beings" ever attain to the experiences of *fanā'* and *baqā'*, the mystic experiences "utter undifferentiation, pure unity, sheer consciousness."[44]

According to the modern Hindu teacher Maharishi Mahesh Yogi, the sine qua non of the spiritual path is an experience of "transcendental consciousness," which he defines as an experience of one's own consciousness devoid of any content: "Through transcendental meditation [TM], the attention is brought from gross experience to subtler fields of experience until the subtlest experience is transcended and the state of transcendental consciousness is gained. . . . This state of transcendental pure consciousness [is] also known as Self-consciousness, Self-awareness [or] *samādhi*."[45] According to Maharishi, this "transcendental consciousness" is an encounter with the very same consciousness that we employ during ordinary experience. Maharishi maintains that transcendental consciousness is an experience of this consciousness in an unmixed or pure form, uninvolved with perception and thought.

In the previous section, we observed that the examples of mysticism we have seen are not gained from learning or from contact with something outside but rather result from an uncovering or revealing of something innate and internal. The two mystics just discussed are adding that that which is within us from the start and which is encountered in these quiet times is *consciousness*, or *awareness itself.* Indeed, that we are, in some unmixed way, "encountering" consciousness itself may be the marker of these events. In different ways and with differing emphases, these mystics are suggesting that what is encountered in these mystical events is the subject's sheerest awareness itself. Apparently this is the selfsame consciousness by means of which one has always been conscious, but here it seems to be unalloyed with the usual intentional content.

How can we make sense of these assertions that one is encountering awareness or consciousness itself? This is no easy matter, since "consciousness" is, as is well known, one of the most perniciously difficult terms to define, in part because it has such a multiplicity of uses and meanings. Ralph Barton Perry pointed this out as early as 1904:

> There is no philosophical term at once so popular and so devoid of standard meaning. How can a term mean anything when it is employed to connote anything and everything, including its own negation?[46] One hears of the object of consciousness and the subject of consciousness, and the union of the two in self-consciousness; of the private consciousness, the social consciousness, and the transcendental consciousness; the inner and the outer, the higher and the lower, the temporal and the eternal consciousness; the activity and the state of consciousness. Then there is consciousness-stuff, and unconscious consciousness, called respectively mind-stuff for short, and unconscious physical states or subconsciousness to avoid a verbal contradiction. This list is not complete, but sufficiently amazing. Consciousness comprises everything that is, and indefinitely much more. It is small wonder that the definition of it is little attempted.[47]

Without denying the polyvalence of "consciousness," I will attempt to characterize what seems to me the sense of the term that is, I believe, being harnessed by mystics. I believe this is the most fundamental sense of the term. Unfortunately, it is also the most difficult to define, principally because that to which it points resists clear and precise analysis or definition. This difficulty of definition occurs in part because consciousness in the sense I mean can never be an object of analysis by itself, for it is the agent *of* any analyzing and so resists definition.

Because the word "consciousness" so resists definition or analysis, I do not propose to define it but rather, à la John Wisdom, offer several "clues" to what I believe the mystics mean when they use this term. I am not trying to be coy in so doing; instead, I am trying to be as true as possible to the idiosyncrasies of that to which this term points. I believe that we know what it is to be conscious by virtue of our own experience of being conscious; I can only offer clues so that you know which aspect of your experience I mean. For, as Sir William Hamilton observed, "Nothing has contributed more to spread obscurity over a very transparent matter than the attempts of philosophers to define consciousness. Consciousness cannot be defined; we may be ourselves fully aware what consciousness is, but we cannot, without confusion, convey to others a definition of what we ourselves clearly apprehend."[48] Except for the fourth and fifth, all my clues point to experiences everyone has of being conscious; the two exceptions refer to experiences that meditators are more likely to have had, though nonmeditators should readily be able to relate to them.

1. "Conscious" generally implies either *feels* or *is aware of* something.
2. Think about the change that comes over you as you come out of chloroform or wake up from a dreamless sleep. As John Wisdom said, "You know quite well the kind of change I mean. That kind of change I call 'becoming conscious.'" By this, Wisdom tells us, he means not the physiological changes but rather the "kind of change which you immediately thought of when I spoke of the change from sleep or chloroform."[49]
3. While it usually implies it, to say that "Sally is conscious" does not necessarily imply either that (a) "Sally is conscious of her environment" or that (b) "Sally is conscious of herself." We might point to dreams as an example of being conscious without being aware of one's environment. When deeply focused on a math problem, we often lose awareness of our external environment.[50] In deep meditation one also often loses consciousness of one's social identity, one's physical positioning, and the environment.
4. During meditation there is a difference between being awake without thoughts and being blacked out. There is a difference between being dead, being asleep in dreamless sleep, being blacked out, and being conscious. The difference is more fundamental than that I perceive objects and think thoughts in one state and not the other. The difference is that in one I have been conscious and in the other I have not.
5. One thing that initially surprised me about my own pure consciousness experiences was that there is no felt-difference between being conscious during such thoughtless moments and being conscious at other times. Though objects may drop out of my attention, what it is like to be conscious does not change.
6. If I am not conscious of a perception, I would say, "*I* did not perceive that." Even if I was in the room when something happened but was not conscious of it, I would say "Oh, I didn't notice that." I must be conscious of a perception for it to be mine.

These clues to what I mean by "consciousness" are slightly different than those of many other people. According to most Western philosophers, consciousness is understood as always and inevitably intentional—that is, always focused toward or on something. "We can no more eliminate [conscious content] and be conscious without being conscious of something than we can separate a dog's bark from the dog."[51] Any claim that consciousness can be contentlessness is therefore a mistake. As Donald Evans maintains, "a person cannot be conscious without its being true that he is either perceiving, or having thoughts, emotions, etc."[52] After all, philosophers have observed, in any introspection all one ever comes across is the content or objects of consciousness, never consciousness itself. In a famous passage, Hume stated: "For my part, when I enter most intimately into what I call myself, I always stumble on some particular perception or other, of heat or cold, light or shade, love or hatred, pain or pleasure. I *never* can catch myself at any time without a perception, and *never* can observe anything but the perception."[53] Because consciousness is always attending *to* some content, such philosophers hold, a definition of "consciousness" might plausibly be "awareness of anything at all."

But this definition is unjustly restrictive. To understand this, let us think about the kind of definition we should be seeking. Most definitions are of the "formal" ("bachelor" means an unmarried male) or of the "prescriptive" or "stipulative" type (let's agree that in the future we will call this device a "fax machine"). But in a situation like ours, we need what is called a "recursive" definition—one that typically lists examples of the class of phenomena we want to represent with the term and then identifies the patterns in those examples. In a recursive definition, the test for an adequate definition is that it is complete enough to include all the examples that we have or are likely to include in the class.

Suppose that someone has defined the term "feeling" as "the emotion of joy or sadness." Even before we could come up with our own alternative definition, we would respond, "No, 'feeling' includes a whole lot more. We use the term for jealousy, fear, love, hate, hot, rough, and many other emotions and sensations, not just for happy or sad. Sometimes we use 'I feel' to cover hunches, attitudes, and judgments. This definition is too narrow." The reason we can say that is that we use the term "feeling" to point toward more than just happiness or sadness. Any adequate recursive definition must include all the phenomena for which we use the term.

Furthermore, let us think about a "feeling" that I personally have not had. For example, someone, say Counselor Troy, tells me that she is empathic and can feel precisely what someone else is feeling. Even though I have never experienced such empathy, she is using the term "feeling" in a way I can understand intuitively. Thus, any recursive definition of the term "feeling" should be inclusive enough to include phenomena that, even though we may not personally have encountered them, we would naturally or intuitively subsume under that term. Similarly, with reference to "consciousness," our recursive definition of that term should include all phenomena for which we would naturally use the term, whether or not we ourselves have experienced them.

Although people like Hume and Moore use "consciousness" only to describe their awareness of intentional objects and thoughts, we have just seen that many mystics apply "consciousness" to that which they "encounter" when they are devoid of intentional content. Thus, I believe we should expand our recursive definition of the term to include that which seems intuitively natural: consciousness is what persists when the human being persists without content. Thus, a synonym of consciousness should not be something like "awareness of anything at all" but perhaps "awareness per se, which *can* become aware of anything at all."[54] This characterization is wide enough to include the sense of "consciousness" that is evoked in our mystical passages.

But, the reader may plausibly ask, although mystics use the term thus, perhaps they are making a mistake. After all, as we have just seen, many Western philosophers have denied this possibility, claiming that consciousness can "never be" encountered without content. As G. E. Moore stated, "the moment we try to fix our attention upon consciousness and to see what, distinctly, it is, it seems to vanish: it seems as if we had before us a mere emptiness. When we try to introspect the sensation of blue, all we can see is the blue: the other element is as if it were diaphanous."[55]

We should, however, take note of the peculiar status of consciousness and the peculiar nature of a recursive definition. Although philosophers like Moore, Hume, and Evans, whom we have quoted, are making philosophical assertions, their understanding of consciousness is, at heart, grounded in their empirical observations. Hume makes the perfectly cogent observation that whenever *he* enters into himself, he stumbles on perceptions. When he says he never can catch himself without a perception, he is merely generalizing from the fact that experientially *he* never has. Similarly, when Moore tries to fix his attention on consciousness and finds that it vanishes when he does so, he, too, is describing *his* experience. Both men are making empirical observations and extrapolating philosophically from what they know of *their* experiences of consciousness.

It should be clear that on empirical matters, the statements of philosophers have no legislative force. No matter how many Humes, Moores, or Hamiltons observe that they cannot catch themselves devoid of perceptions, this tells us little about what a Hindu monk, Dominican friar, or Sufi adept might experience after years of yoga, Jesus Prayer, or Sufi dancing. Indeed, many mystics *do* report that they have undergone something quite unique.

Probably a Hume or Moore tried to "catch" himself without a perception on two or three quiet, furtive attempts. Furthermore, those attempts would have been elements within their philosophical projects. Thus, probably without being aware of the experiential implications of their attitude of "trying to see something about consciousness," they could hardly have allowed themselves to "drop away" completely. Who is to say whether one of them might have achieved a silent consciousness after some years of meditation practices, visualizations, or other practices that were not saddled with such an ulterior agenda? Who is to say what Professor Moore might have "seen" in his sensation of blue had he performed twenty years of Tantric visualizations of blue mandalas?[56] These are *empirical* matters, not logical or presuppositional. There are enormous differences between ordinary empirical attempts to "introspect the sensation" of consciousness and a transformative meditative path; the former does not impose logical limits on the latter.

What is empirically possible for a human being is not something we can answer a priori, with assertions based on what we *have* experienced so far, any more than we can rule out the possibility of Counselor Troy's feeling someone else's feelings because no one I know, so far, has.

In short, philosophical mystics such as Maharishi, Sāṃkhya Karika thinkers, and Ibn al-'Arabī suggest that the data of mysticism point toward expanding our sense of the term "consciousness" enough to leave room for the possibility of an experience of an "awareness per se." And we have shown that it makes good sense to expand our characterization in that way. Even though the reader may not personally have experienced his or her awareness per se directly, we still want to leave room for those who may have done so. We should not rule out, strictly for definitional or empirical reasons, the possibility of an unmixed encounter with awareness per se.

I should point out that expanding our definition thus has no insignificant implications for psychology and the philosophy of mind. If we accept it, we can no longer rule out, on strictly definitional grounds, the idea that awareness itself is always intentional or that it cannot be distinguished from its function of processing content in some sense. This runs counter to virtually every theory of mind propounded since Immanual Kant's *Critique of Pure Reason.*

Yet despite the general currents of Western philosophy, I believe it makes sense to think of consciousness as distinguishable from content, even with reference to ordinary experiences. After all, as Kant, Strawson, and others have argued, there must be some awareness that ties together diverse and temporally successive experiences.[57] As Kant said, if I could not tie together perceptions into one consciousness,

> there might exist a multitude of perceptions, and indeed an entire sensibility, in which much empirical consciousness would arise in my mind, but in a state of separation, and without belonging to a consciousness of myself. This however is impossible. For it is only because I ascribe all perceptions to one consciousness (original apperception) that I can say of all perceptions that I am conscious of them.[58]

That we must tie all percepts and thoughts together Kant calls the "supreme principle of understanding." If he is correct, then we must leave room for a consciousness that is *not* part of intentional thoughts and perceptions so that it can tie them together.[59]

Second, if we collapse the distinctions between content and consciousness, then successive perceptions must belong to successive worlds of experience. If this were true, we could not distinguish successive mental states within a single coherent stream of experience. But this is absurd.

Third, let us reverse this and say that consciousness is *indistinguishable* from its intentional objects. Then consciousness must be indistinguishable from some object. We could then talk about an object, but we could not also talk about consciousness of that object. Were consciousness not distinguishable from content, we could not conceive of the thesis of intentionality, which is, as Sartre put it, the notion that we are "confronted with a concrete and full presence *which is not consciousness*."[60]

Thus, even with reference to ordinary experience, I believe it makes sense to think of consciousness as discrete from its intentional content.

Defining consciousness as intentional is parallel to defining a radar system as "something that responds to the presence of airplanes." But this definition, it seems to me, is too restrictive. Whether or not an airplane is flying by, a radar system remains what it is. Would it not be more accurate to define a radar system as "a mechanism that has the *capacity* to respond to the presence of airplanes in certain ways?" For even if there are no airplanes within its range, if the machinery is turned on, the radar dish is "poised," as it were, ready and able to receive radar reflections. It has the immediate capacity to receive and process appropriate incoming data without undergoing any structural changes.

Similarly, if we define consciousness in a way that includes its object, we are improperly including its objects within its definition. Like the radar system, awareness per se undergoes no structural changes between being contentless and having content.[61] That is, to be merely aware and to be aware of something requires no transformation in the continuity of awareness but merely the addition of content. Thus, we should hold that consciousness remains consciousness, whether or not there are objects.

Do not mistake what I am saying: consciousness usually does involve intentional objects, just as radar systems usually do involve airplanes. And certainly it makes sense to analyze consciousness as such when appropriate. All I am arguing is that it does not make sense to rule out plausible capabilities of consciousness by definition, as have so many Western philosophers.

Of Knowledge by Identity

To recapitulate: several mystics have suggested that mysticism is an encounter with one's own consciousness. We have noted that to understand their statements we must expand the definition of "consciousness" to include awareness per se. I would now like to consider their assertions by asking how a mystic might be able to encounter his or her own consciousness—and to know that he or she has done so. To answer this, let us think about how, in ordinary experience, we know our own awareness. And how in general do we know that we have been conscious for, say, the past fifteen seconds?

Here it is important not to begin on the wrong foot. Many philosophers have based their thoughts about how we know ourselves on an analogy with how we know other people. Certainly we learn some things about ourselves by drawing analogies with what we see of other people. I probably learned my name is Robert by hearing it repeated over and over, much as I learned Bruce's and Martha's names. I learned that the growling in my belly is called "hunger" by hearing other people talk about the growling in their bellies and seeing them go to the pantry.

But the key question is whether we learn what it is to have a consciousness by seeing what it is for someone else to have a consciousness. Not at all! In fact, it goes the other way: I *assume* I know what it is like for you to have an awareness by projecting from my own intimate and subjective sense of what it is for me to have an awareness. If I didn't know what it was to be conscious by virtue of being conscious, all the assertions of another person's consciousness wouldn't help me a whit.

The importance of this difference—between my first-person acquaintance with my own consciousness and my acquaintance with others and with the world—cannot be overestimated. As John Searle said,

> It would be difficult to exaggerate the disastrous effects that the failure to come to terms with the subjectivity of consciousness has had on the philosophical and psychological world of the past half century. In ways that are not at all obvious on the surface, much of the bankruptcy of most work in the philosophy of mind and over a great deal of the sterility of academic psychology over the past fifty years, over the whole of my intellectual lifetime, have come from a persistent failure to recognize and come to terms with the fact that the ontology of the mental is an irreducibly first person ontology.[62]

My knowledge of being conscious is connected with a firsthand familiarity with it. This can readily be seen by thinking about how we might set about teaching what it means to be conscious to something that is not conscious—say my Compaq 386 computer. Even before we begin the attempt, it is clear that this will be a hopeless enterprise, since what I mean by "conscious" seems available only to some person or entity that knows what it is to be conscious by virtue of being conscious. Even if my computer were to flash the words "Aha! I know what it is to have a consciousness," I would not believe that it really did know what I meant.

Like John Wisdom, I can define "consciousness" only by using clues to refer the reader (or computer) toward that consciousness with which he or she already has an intimate familiarity, the sort of familiarity that can come only from "having" a consciousness.[63] Note that he said, "You know quite well the kind of change [from being under chloroform to being conscious] I mean" and that it is "the kind of change you immediately thought of." He is suggesting something that is precisely correct about consciousness: we do not come to an acquaintance with consciousness by virtue of someone else's consciousness or some ostensive definition. I can't hand you a consciousness as I might a kiwi and say, "Here, this is what I mean by one of these." Rather, we know what it means to be conscious *by virtue of being conscious*. That is, we know it through our own direct and intimate firsthand familiarity with being conscious.[64]

Let us reverse this and think about how we ourselves might come to understand something new about the subjective experience of consciousness. Say someone proposes a theory of consciousness—for example, that all consciousness is blue. How will I check it? I will not turn to some other theory of consciousness, say Hume's,

Moore's, or Dennett's, that I believe to be true. Rather, I will check it against my own experience of being conscious. I might think, "Nah, I can't see how my consciousness is blue. That's wrong!" The final arbiter of any theory or so-called fact of consciousness is my own intimate acquaintance with what it is to be conscious.[65]

To clarify the kind of acquaintance we have with our own consciousness, let us turn to William James's epistemological distinction between "two kinds of knowledge":[66] *knowledge-by-acquaintance* (which he sometimes calls knowledge-of-acquaintance) and *knowledge-about.*[67] Knowledge-by-acquaintance generally involves direct sensory contact; it is operative when we taste a kiwi or see the color blue. Knowledge-about is conceptual or representational, operative when we name the fruit or compare it conceptually with other fruit, analyze its hereditary relationships, and so on. It is the more constructed kind of knowledge, clearly involving language, memory, conceptualization, and so on.

Even though it is inevitably laced with knowledge-about, James says, knowledge-by-acquaintance provides us with a qualitatively different sort of information:

> In training institutions for the blind they teach the pupils as much about light as in ordinary schools. . . . But the best taught born-blind pupil of such an establishment yet lacks a knowledge which the least instructed baby has. . . . A blind man may know all about the sky's blueness, and I may know all about your toothache conceptually. . . . But so long as he has not felt the blueness, nor I the toothache, our knowledge, wide as it is, of these realities, will be hollow and inadequate.[68]

We generally gain knowledge-by-acquaintance through direct sensory impressions; we gain knowledge-about through thinking about something or comparing or contrasting it to something else. According to Gerald Myers, in James's conception, "feelings are the vehicles of acquaintance and thoughts the vehicles of knowledge."[69]

James's distinction between knowledge-by-acquaintance and knowledge-about may be more a theoretical distinction between ideal types than a sharp chasm. When I taste a kiwi, for example, the word "kiwi" may be present in my experience. So, too, I will compare and contrast its taste with that of other fruits, which suggests knowledge-about. In other words, there is a great deal of knowledge-about infused even in direct sensory contact, in which I gain knowledge-by-acquaintance. Conversely, knowledge-about is generally grounded in some knowledge-by-acquaintance contact. In short, the two are generally found intertwined.

We might want to say that these two form a continuum: some experiences seem nearer to the knowledge-by-acquaintance pole, whereas others seem nearer to a knowledge-about pole. Yet, James reminds us, there is a "difference between the immediate feltness of a feeling, and its perception by a subsequent reflective act."[70]

It should be obvious that both knowledge-about and knowledge-by-acquaintance are intentional in structure, involving a subject that is aware of some object, be it sensory, thought, or feeling. Furthermore, in any intentional knowledge three distinct elements must be involved: the knower, the object of knowing, and the epistemological process(es) involved in that knowing. In the case of my knowledge-by-acquaintance of a kiwi, the object is clearly distinct from the subject, and I know it largely through the sensory processes. Similarly, in knowledge-about, I know something that is distinct from my own consciousness through some thinking processes. In both, the complex mediating or constructing epistemological processes referred to by the constructivists are clearly involved. This is so even in the case of most self-knowledge, in which some aspect of the personality or ego, a disposition, or a self-concept serves as an intentional object. Here, too, all the constructive activities of the mind are once again operative.

But the intentional structure of both of these forms of knowledge makes them particularly ill suited to account for the knowledge I have of my own awareness. For in any contact with my own consciousness, the subject is not distinct from the object. I just have "contact" with "my" awareness,[71] or perhaps we should say, "I am it."

Because it is so sharply unlike either of James's binary epistemological division, I propose that our knowledge of our own consciousness represents a third major form of knowledge. I call it *knowledge-by-identity*.[72] In knowledge-by-identity the subject knows something by virtue of being it. I know what it is to be conscious, what it is to have "my" consciousness, because and only because I am or have that consciousness.[73] I am acquainted with "my" consciousness not through a conceptual knowledge of something but because being conscious carries within itself a noninferential sense of what it is to be that consciousness. It is a reflexive or self-referential form of knowing. I *know* my consciousness, and I know that I am and have been conscious simply because I *am* it.

Knowledge-by-identity is similar to knowledge-by-acquaintance because each is not, in theory, known linguistically.[74] As in the (ideal type of) knowledge-by-acquaintance, my knowledge of my own consciousness is, in a real way, direct and "intuitive": it is known not through analysis or thinking but just by some kind of direct "contact." Again, as in knowledge-by-acquaintance, my knowledge of it may or may not demand that I name it.

But knowledge-by-identity is also different in important ways from knowledge-by-acquaintance. First, as James emphasized, knowledge-by-acquaintance is inevitably involved with knowing-about in some way. An actual experience of tasting a kiwi inevitably is bound up with the knowledge of what other fruits are like, the word "kiwi," the idea of tasting, and so on. Yet I have "knowledge" of my consciousness whether or not I am thinking about it, or things like it, or am even using a term like "consciousness."

Second, knowledge-by-acquaintance can generally be grounded on an ostensive definition. I can hand you a kiwi and say, "Here, taste this." But this is not true of knowledge-by-identity. I cannot hand you your own consciousness and say, "Here, this is what I mean." I must count on the fact that you know what it is to be conscious in the same direct and reflexive way that I do. If I am to teach you the term, you must have a prior acquaintance with your own awareness to which I can refer you, perhaps via clues.

Third, knowledge-by-acquaintance is transient. No matter how spectacular its taste, eventually I will lose the immediate flavor of a kiwi. Over time I may even forget its taste altogether. But unless I die or go into a coma, my "contact" with my own awareness does not change or disappear. It is, in this sense, permanent.[75]

Finally, and most obviously, knowledge-by-identity is not intentional in structure: I can not know my own awareness as an object. It is, first and last, subjectivity.

Other than the knowledge I have of my own awareness, I know of no other cases of knowledge-by-identity. The acquaintance I have with my own awareness and the knowledge that I am and have been aware is, in other words, unlike any other, sui generis.

Knowledge-by-identity seems to be a direct or immediate form of knowledge. Both knowledge-about and knowledge-by-acquaintance come through a complex set of epistemological processes involving memory, expectation, language, and concept use. However, the knowledge-by-identity that I am and have been conscious is a, and perhaps the only, form of knowledge that is *not* "processed through" these "extremely complex epistemological ways."[76] The knowledge that I am aware and have been aware for the last few seconds is not a matter of language, nor does it stand on the back of prior experiences. I *just know* directly and without complex reasoning that I am and have been aware. And I know it simply by virtue of being aware.

Nor is awareness per se itself constructed or formed by language. While an understanding *that* I am conscious is certainly linguistically formed, clearly understanding *that I am conscious* and *being* conscious are not the same thing. The acquaintance someone has of what it means to be conscious cannot be articulated without knowledge of a language system, including the term "consciousness" (or a synonym). A nonspeaking woman's acquaintance with her own consciousness may remain mute, but in order for her to come to know intellectually what it is to be conscious, she must be able to capitalize on her primary and direct knowledge-by-identity. To learn the words "conscious" or "consciousness," she will ground those terms on her own consciousness in exactly the same way as anyone else—that is, she will capitalize on her own direct acquaintance with consciousness. She will not gain an acquaintance with consciousness by virtue of learning the term "consciousness," but vice versa.

A Wittgensteinian may object that "consciousness" is a word, like any other, whose meaning is learned through language and acts. We come to identify "consciousness" by projecting from "public" behavior and utterances; for example, we may have learned it when we heard our mother say, "Oh, good morning. I see you are conscious now," and we project to what it is to be conscious.

But there is a difference between learning to use the word "conscious" in a sense that derives from movement and activity and learning the meaning of the word "aware," which is not behavioral. A robot may move without awareness, and we all know the difference. The term "awareness" does not refers to feelings such as anger or pleasure, which have behavioral correlates. It is present amid all feelings and behavior. We cannot project to some specific behavior to pick it out.

Indeed, consciousness itself is not linguistically formulated. Just the reverse is true. This can be seen very simply. For a child to learn any language at all, he or she must be conscious. Being aware, or having a consciousness, is presupposed by language acquisition, not the other way around. Awareness per se must be present not only before someone can learn the word "consciousness"; it must be present before one can learn the meaning of any word at all. For it is only by virtue of being conscious that we have the capacity to understand any speech acts at all.

I do not infer my acquaintance with being conscious from the fact that I have been thinking over the past while. Although I cannot be absolutely certain exactly what I was thinking or perceiving half a minute ago, I am absolutely certain that I was conscious. That is, the continuity of my awareness and my certainty that I have been conscious is a fact more fundamental than any facts from which I might infer my past consciousness. Yet I have not the foggiest notion of how I *do* know that I have been conscious. It just comes with being conscious. I know it by virtue of being conscious.

Thus, to the question How do I know this continuity of consciousness, I think we should say I know it not because I have learned about it through words or analysis but because I am directly acquainted with it by virtue of being it. I know my awareness per se as a unity, tying itself together as it ties memories and thoughts together with present stimuli *because I do this*. I know it as a unity that can become aware of any thought, perception, or what have you because I *am* this unity.

But I know absolutely nothing about the mechanics of how I do this, how I hold myself together through time, or how I know my own awareness per se. Such matters are beyond what I *can* know. I do not know about the mechanics of recalling my own being awake for the past thirty seconds, since my ability to recall anything at all is directly grounded in this self-recollective ability. Nor do I know about the epistemological processes involved in the fundamental act of tying myself together through time in a single awareness, since any epistemological processes are "for" or "by" it. As the *Bṛihadāraṇyaka Upaniṣad* says, "Lo, whereby would one understand the understander?"[77]

Malcolm quotes Wittgenstein as saying in a lecture that in philosophy it is important to know when to *stop*.[78] If ever there was an instance of knowing when to stop, it is in speculating how we know that we are conscious and have been conscious for the past few seconds and that the unbroken continuity between these two is a single consciousness.

While we cannot tease out any constituent elements within an awareness per se, we can analytically assert one or two things about it. First, because I do not have access to how I know my own awareness, this knowledge-by-identity is *simple* in the sense of being utterly without complexity or plurality. As Śankara says, "The *ātman* which is the object of knowledge is without parts."[79] I cannot phenomenologically tease out its constituent parts or elements; any parts or elements would be known only *by* consciousness. At best, I can *hypothesize* about its features and abilities, but I cannot experience them as I might experience the layers of flavor in a fine wine.

Second, to have an awareness involves tying together what, in intentional experience, we call past and present. That is, consciousness involves a kind of recollection, one that does not *think* past and present but rather simply includes past and present within something like one large present/past/now. It does not involve a sense of a particular temporal period; that involves the concept of time, a clock, and so on. Rather, awareness per se simply ties past and present together as one single continuous awareness. It transcends our time experience.

Third, there seems to be a kind of knowledge-about implicit in having an awareness. If we were to tie ourselves together over time and not at some unspoken level know that what is being tied together is a single thing, a single me, then we would not be able to hold the present perception as being encountered by the same awareness as was the past one. This begins to sound like linguistic knowledge, which it cannot be. But we can say that to be a single awareness over time must include some immediate "remembering" that it was single and continuous over time; this form of remembering, however, "remembers" itself only as a single unity.

Remembering Pure Consciousness Events

We are now in a position to better understand mysticism, I believe. Some mystics, we said, write that during certain experiences they are experiencing their own consciousness, without additional content. How is this possible that we can *know* that we have done so?

The answer is, *I do not know how* I know I have been aware in a pure consciousness event. I just know by means of knowledge-by-identity that I was continuously awake. And that's all.

But ignorance here is the only plausible answer. For in order to answer this question, I would have to be able to know the answer to the same question with reference to ordinary experience—that is, to say how, in general, I know that I am and have been conscious a moment ago, that there has been an unbroken continuity of awareness between a few moments ago and now, and that I have an awareness per se at all. But, as we have just seen, *I cannot say how I know any of this* because such matters are beyond the purview of conceptual knowledge in general and beyond what knowledge-by-identity can reveal.

In general, the mechanics of how a consciousness knows itself or ties itself together continuously through time is something we *cannot* possibly know. We just tie ourselves together continuously through time, that's all. And we simply emerge from a PCE with the certainty that we have tied ourselves together, as usual. But we are precisely as in the dark about how we do this during mystical (nonintentional) experiences as we are about how we do it during ordinary (intentional) experiences. In short, there is no special paradox in not knowing how I recall being awake in PCE. I just know through knowledge-by-identity that I was awake during that (blank) period in just the same sui generis way as always!

The most obvious alternative to this view is that mysticism is a moment of knowledge-by-acquaintance. This is most powerfully argued by William Barnard in what we might call the Barnard-James thesis of mysticism. Accepting William James's version of knowledge as bipolar (knowledge-about and knowledge-by-acquaintance), Barnard observes that when mystical techniques strip away the thoughts and memories that constitute knowledge-about, the mystic shifts along the scale from "largely knowledge-about" toward "largely knowledge-by-acquaintance."

This Barnard-James approach has several advantages. It allows Barnard to make reasonable sense of mystical experiences that seem to involve some dimly perceived language and to understand subtle differences between several similar-sounding experiences. Barnard also seems to be able to explain what W. T. Stace called "extrovertive experiences," those mystical experiences that involve a new relationship with the world. For Barnard they become a combination of both knowledge-by-acquaintance and knowledge-about. Barnard writes:

> The knowledge-by-acquaintance aspect of [a mystical] experience does not appear alone, but rather, comes into consciousness fused with the mystic's knowledge-about, and structured by the mystic's cultural and psychological categories. Furthermore, this mystical experience is not a static moment frozen in time, but rather, it shifts and reforms, with different "percentages" of these two types of knowledge prevalent at different moments in the process.[80]

But the Barnard-James approach fails when we look closely at common mystical experiences. Let us think about experiences of both the pure consciousness type and the extrovertive or unitive variety, in which a subject perceives him- or herself to be in unity with the perceptual "object."[81] Here is an example of that unitive form of experience, particularly clearly described by the German idealist Malwida von Meysenburg: "I was alone upon the seashore. . . . I felt that I . . . return[ed] from the solitude of individuation into the consciousness of unity with all that is, [that I knelt] down as one that passes away, and [rose] up as one imperishable. Earth, heaven, and sea *resounded as in one vast world* encircling harmony. . . . I *felt myself one* with them"[82] (emphasis mine). Von Meysenburg sensed in some sort of immediate or intuitive manner a connection with the things of the world, as if she were a part of them and they part of her. It is as if the membranes of her self, her own consciousness, became permeable, and she flowed in, with, or perhaps through her environment. In short, the object is encountered as fused with the self itself.

But this means that, unlike knowledge-by-acquaintance, neither this form of experience nor the PCE of which I wrote earlier is intentional in structure.[83] In other words, though more sensitive to mysticism's peculiar structures than most, Barnard and James have nevertheless, like so many others, based their thoughts about how we know ourselves in mysticism on the model of how we know the sensory world and other people. They have used intentionality as the model for nonintentionality.

Indeed, Barnard seems to recognize the inadequacy of his own account. After suggesting that mysticism should be viewed as an example of a "nearly pure" knowledge-by-acquaintance, Barnard offers the following caveat: "However, to describe what remains during these non-dual experiences as knowledge-by-acquaintance is perhaps philosophically imprudent, since the category of knowledge depends upon an implicit duality of the knower and the known, and it is this very duality which has purportedly disappeared during unitive mystical experiences."[84]

It seems to me that it makes more sense to classify the kind of encounter the mystic has in a PCE as an instance of *knowledge-by-identity*. For the mystic is instructed to let go not only of his thoughts and concepts but of his sensory input as well. Our Upaniṣadic passage teaches that its mystical experiences will arise if and only if one has "restrained his mind from the external, and the breathing spirit (prana) has put to rest objects of sense, thereupon let him continue void of conceptions." Hence, the intentional trinities of subject-perceiving-object and the subject-thinking-thought is abolished. Rather than rely on a knowledge-by-acquaintance, one is instructed to let go of intentional knowledge altogether and to come to rest "in" or "through" one's awareness alone. Removing both conceptual knowledge, knowledge-about, and sensory contact, knowledge-by-acquaintance, in *turiya* one comes to employ knowledge-by-identity alone. "That" which we know when we know we are aware is *all* that we recall after we have continued "void of conceptions."

This idea, that mysticism is a sui generis example of knowledge-by-identity in which the subject knows only itself reflexively, is seconded by D. T. Suzuki's account of the Zen Buddhist's experience of sūnyatā.

> Sūnyatā is to be experienced and not conceptualized. To experience [sūnyatā] means to become aware of, but not in the way in which we become aware of the world of sense-and-intellect. In the latter case, we always have a subject that is aware of something and an object of which the subject is [intentionally] aware. . . . To be aware of sūnyatā, according to Zen, we have to transcend this dichotomous world in such a way as not to be outside it. Sūnyatā is to be experienced in a unique way. This unique way consists in sūnyatā's remaining in itself and yet making itself an object of experience to itself. This means dividing itself and yet holding itself together. . . . Sūnyatā is experienced only when it is both subject and object. . . . "Knowing and seeing" sūnyatā is sūnyatā's knowing and seeing itself; there is no outside knower or spectator; it is its own knower and seer.[85]

When Suzuki suggests that sūnyatā is known as the subject serves as both subject and object, thus knowing and seeing itself, he is not suggesting that there are two. Rather, he is drawing an analogy with ordinary seeing and suggesting that, despite remaining a single subject, the subject reflexively serves the role of the object. In this sense, he is also holding to a doctrine of the subject "knowing" itself through being itself, or knowledge-by-identity.

I might observe that this thesis, that the mystic encounters the PCE and the unitive or extrovertive mystical experience through knowledge-by-identity, has the same advantages as the Barnard-James hypothesis. It too enables us to make reasonable sense of mystical experiences that seem to involve some dimly perceived language or some sensory contact and to understand subtle differences between several similar-sounding experiences. For in such experience, consciousness is aware of itself through knowledge-by-identity and simultaneously is perceiving thought or language intentionally. Furthermore, "extrovertive experiences" can be understood as a life in the world in which knowledge-by-identity does not disappear even while other epistemological structures are active. In such a phenomenon, one would continue to know the self reflectively simultaneously with seeing, acting, thinking, and so on.

MANY MYSTICS HAVE SAID that in their experience of a pure consciousness event, they have encountered their own consciousness. And they have observed that to bring about such an event, one needs to forget or slough off the intentional processes involving language, concept use, and other cognitive functions. Those constructivists who have suggested that remembering a PCE necessarily signifies that one was using language, thinking thoughts, or remembering something in particular were wrong. They have misunderstood the nature of awareness's self-recollection. While we often employ these processes to think about ourselves, awareness's merely tying itself together through time is of a wholly different order—and it is that other order that is tapped by these apophatic mystics. The self-recollection of awareness in mysticism taps into what is arguably the most fundamental human capacity, one that is innate: the ability to be aware at all and to tie one's awareness together with one's past awareness.

A Perennial Psychology

We are suggesting that some mystical experiences tap into a fundamental human psychophysiological structure. Not created by culture, this structure—consciousness itself, its ability to tie itself together through time, and the intimate but nonconceptual acquaintance we each have with it—comes with the machinery of being human. In consciousness itself and in the way it encounters the world intentionally, we may have something that transcends cultures and eras. That is, I assume that a fourteenth-century Dominican friar must have been aware and have tied together his own awareness through time just as I do, and also in precisely the same way as did an eighth-century Korean. Because we each have an awareness, we must all remember it without any mechanics of self-recall, in just the same uncomplex and unmediated way. Though the content of our minds is no doubt profoundly different, in order to gain a PCE we must all be able to temporarily let go of the contents of our own minds, whatever they may be, similarly. This utterly human pattern implies several things.

Based on these parallels in both the structure of being human and the deconstructive processes involved in bringing about mystical experiences, it makes sense to do cross-cultural comparative work in the philosophy of mind, cognitive psychology, mysticism, spirituality, and religion. If we can say that there are some such phenomena that are common to humans from a variety of ages and cultures, then it not only makes sense but it behooves us to look at a variety of human experiences, especially the experiences of the world's mystics, as speaking about similar processes.[86]

I propose that this school should not be called the "deconstructivists," which reveals nothing but what we aren't. Rather, I propose calling ourselves the "Perennial Psychologists," for what mysticism and the above arguments reveal is a *psychologia perennis*, a *Perennial Psychology*.[87] This is not a claim of a perennial *philosophy* as Huxley, Watts, or Otto formulated it.[88] Their claim was that across cultures there are deep similarities in metaphysical and philosophical claims about reality and other aspects. That position has been justifiably criticized.[89] The claim of the Perennial Psychology is not that there exists a commonality of philosophical claims but rather that in the human psyche there are certain deep and consistent psychological structures. (In suggesting this term, "Perennial Psychology," I do not mean to assert that this is a proven case. Rather, I offer it as a developing hypothesis. As Diane Jonte-Pace suggests later in this volume, I see it as a call for further research into the reason that we see cross culturally consistent psychological patterns. Her work, like the other articles in the present volume, is an admirable example of such research.[90]) As I see it, the hypothesis of the *psychologia perennis* implies several general claims:

1. Awareness is virtually always present to the human; it is usually intentional; it serves to tie together content and itself through time; it is transcendental to any content.
2. There are at least two and possibly more experience modalities, or perhaps "states of consciousness." They have markedly different cognitive or epistemological structures.
3. Mystical experiences show reasonably consistent structures across cultures and ages. The PCE, the unitive mystical state, and possibly other experiences show remarkable similarities across time and space. These states exhibit similar phenomenological characteristics, and probably similar physiological attributes as well, though data is scarce.
4. The transformative processes that bring about mystical states of consciousness have a similar structure, notably the key process of undoing, forgetting, or deconstructing.
5. Awareness itself and mystical experiences that tap into it are not learned but result from certain innate human capacities.

I have focused on several of these points already, so I now focus on the way these points bear on mysticism.

Two Capacities, Two Experience Modalities

There are at least two epistemological modalities, or states of consciousness, available to the human being: ordinary and mystical. Ordinary experiences, thoughts, emotions, sensations, perceptions, and the like are intentional. Objects are encountered as distinct from the self. Their content is constantly changing. We are active in building and in part constituting or constructing them in terms of our expectations, beliefs, and concepts. Such experiences share a tripartite epistemological structure: (1) the subject is aware of (2) some intentional object by means of (3) some process of knowing or perceiving. One recalls them by means of intentional memory.

Mystical experiences of the PCE type (and perhaps aspects of others) are, by contrast, nonintentional. One encounters or rests within awareness per se itself, however it is understood. The consciousness encountered therein is "experienced" as unchanging. Epistemologically, "that" which is encountered is known through knowledge-by-identity.

This account is in perfect accord with the distinction between two kinds of experience and knowledge described by the Upaniṣads:

> Where there is a duality, as it were, then one sees another; one smells another; one tastes another; one speaks to another; one hears another; one thinks of another; one touches another; one understands another. . . . That self (*ātman*) is not this, not that (*neti, neti*). It is unseizable, for it cannot be seized; indestructible, for it cannot be destroyed; unattached, for it does not attach itself; it is unbound, it does not tremble, it is not injured.[91]

> When cease the five sense knowledges, together with the mind, and the intellect stirs not—that they say is the highest course.[92]

The Upaniṣads here make a distinction between intentional knowledge or perception ("one sees another," "the five sense knowledges," "thought") and nonintentional acquaintance with the self itself ("the five senses," "intellect stirs not," the "unthinkable"). And when one stops employing the one experiential modality—that is, stops using the intentional epistemological structure—the other becomes available.

Śankara evokes a similar distinction between two kinds of knowledge. The first, *vyāvarāharika* or lower knowledge, includes all the sublevels of appearance and thought and is dualistic (intentional). Any and all sensory and mental experience or any experience of a self who has not attained ultimate reality are known through *vyāvarāharika*. The second form of knowledge, *pāramārtika*, represents "pure spiritual identity; the experience wherein the separation of self and non-self, of ego and world, is transcended, and an experience of pure oneness."[93] It finds its most perfect expression in *nirvikalpa samādhi*, samādhi without seed or contentless consciousness, in which one gains self-realization nonconceptually.[94]

The distinction between intentional knowledge and knowledge-by-identity is also in accord with Meister Eckhart's two modes of experience, which express the two different kinds of powers or epistemological modalities.[95] By means of the first "power" we are aware of images, creatures, sensations, and so on. Here we have images of people and objects, and we create those images by means of our cognitive and sensory "powers."[96] The other power—which is responsible for *gezucket*[97]—is the spiritual one: "There is a power in the soul which touches neither time nor flesh, flowing from the spirit, remaining in the spirit, altogether spiritual."[98] Eckhart names this power the place in which God "gives birth" to his son or word in the soul. When one is able to "draw in all your [intellectual and sensory] powers to a unity and forget all those things and their images which you have absorbed," then the other power becomes accessible.[99]

> [That place within the soul] is a strange and desert place, and is rather nameless than possessed of a name, and is more unknown than it is known. If you could naught yourself for an instant, indeed I say less than an instant, you would possess all that this is in itself. But as long as you mind yourself or anything at all [viz. intentionally], you know no more of god than my mouth knows of color or my eye of taste.[100]

I have argued elsewhere that the ninth-century Buddhist Yogācārin Paramārtha also differentiates two distinct epistemological structures, which again involve constructed knowledge of the external world and nonintentional "knowledge" of śunyata, emptiness.[101] This sort of common epistemological claim across cultures suggests this epistemological dualism as an element of a perennial psychology.

Movement between the Two Types

According to the Perennial Psychology, it is possible to move from one experience modality to another. Through various transformative means, some shift is possible from ordinary experience to the second modality. Furthermore, mystics are generally optimists: it is possible, they uniformly claim, to "move" from one to the other. Humans, they hold, are not ultimately stuck.

Furthermore, the general outlines of the transformative process are reasonably consistent across cultures. The key feature of the transformative process is stripping or letting go of concepts, attachments, and pictures of one's self and others.[102] This allows one to separate what is inherently "within" from what is not. By this means one can shift from the constructed modality into something closer to the utterly unconstructed one.[103]

It is commonly observed that in an extraordinary number of cultures and eras, mystics have employed an enormous number of metaphors involving paths, roads, journeys, which suggest a transformation process. Buddha suggests that the mystic's way is like crossing a river or walking down a path.[104] Journey imagery permeates Meister Eckhart. It is possible, according to him, to move from using the one power to tapping the other, more inward, one. Eckhart instructs his listeners to *"withdraw* from the unrest of external activities then flee and hide from the turmoil of inward thoughts":[105] "'To achieve an interior act, a man must *collect* all his powers as if into a corner of his soul where, *hiding away* from all images and forms, he can get to work.' Here he must *come* to a forgetting and an unknowing. There must be a stillness and a silence . . . " (emphasis mine).[106] Because he holds that a transformation is both possible and desirable, Eckhart often speaks of the religious life as a developmental process: "We are wholly transformed . . . and changed."[107] He also capitalizes on images of increasing "light": "The divine light breaks forth in the soul, more and more."[108] Such passages clearly imply that one can and should move from a status of "darkness"—our ordinary, imagistic, epistemologically intentional world—toward a different state, wherein one comes to persist as that which is *innately* suffused with the divine "light."

Even if such movement is sometimes presented as a "pathless path," as Zen often does, many mystics have suggested that there is some sort of transformative path involved in their teachings.

The "Advanced" State(s) Result from Something Innate

When mystics speak of pathways and transformation processes, this may be thought to imply that the meditative practices and techniques themselves are responsible for the "advanced" state(s). But many mystics suggest that these experiences are not the direct *effects* of these techniques but rather are like uncovering something they have *been all along*. The essays in the present volume show this more thoroughly than I can here.

To add just one more nail to this evidence, we can see this claim in Śankara's famous commentary on the *Vedanta Sūtras*: "As *Brahman* constitutes a person's Self, it is not something to be attained by that person. And even if *Brahman* were altogether different from a person's Self, still it would not be something to be attained; for as it is omnipresent it is part of its nature that it is ever present to everyone."[109] For Śankara the realization of the Self is a realization of awareness itself, *ātman*. This has been present all along, for it "constitutes" our self. Indeed, it is the critical part of our own innate nature. When we let go of the illusory self (the *jīva*, which is produced by *māyā*) and gain the mystical experience of *samādhi*, what we "encounter" there is not caused, brought about, or engendered by some temporal practices or teachings. We come to that which we have always been, our innate nature. After all, I have been conscious throughout my life; the mystical experience is only a coming to an uncompounded experience of that.

The Zen Master Huang Po makes a similar claim that the mystical experience he calls "being one with the Buddha" is a realization of that which one has always been: "That there is nothing which can be attained is not idle talk; it is the truth. *You have always been one with the Buddha*, so do not pretend you can attain to this oneness by various practices."[110] Again, this kind of agreement suggests a common pattern in human psychological structure.

A Nonpluralistic Phenomenon

This last point should be apparent from the foregoing, but it is worth emphasizing. While languages all over the world differ in ways great and small, and while our language for consciousness and awareness per se differ, being conscious and having immediate knowledge that "I am conscious" is one phenomenon, possibly the only one, that seems utterly and precisely shared by virtually all human beings.[111] I have suggested that there is no discernible difference between the awareness per se of a Hindu and a Christian or between a Chinese woman and a French peasant. I stated earlier that I can't teach a computer what it means to be conscious, since the knowledge of being conscious seems available only to someone who knows consciousness by virtue of being conscious. That is, we each know what it is to be conscious by means of knowledge-by-identity. And this familiarity is part of, if not the *principal* element of, what it means to be human. No matter what our language and conceptual system may be, we are each as privy to this knowledge-by-identity as any other human.

We argued in *The Problem of Pure Consciousness* that pure consciousness events are remarkably consistent from culture to culture. Our insights about consciousness and about the epistemological character of an encounter with consciousness may help illuminate why this observation makes sense. Having an awareness per se is not pluralistic. It is because this is so, and because mysticism taps into human awareness itself, that it makes sense that certain mystical phenomena should be nonpluralistic.

In addition to accounting for the commonalties of mystical experience, this model also accounts for the variation we see in descriptions of mystical experiences. Some experiences are directly related to certain words. My experience of the rectangular brown object before me includes the word "desk." To describe my experience correctly, we must include the word "desk" or a synonym: "I was looking at my desk when . . ." But a thorough description of a German speaker's experience of her desk will include the term *das Pult*, not "desk." That is, these experiences must differ, since different languages necessarily lead to experiences that are, at least in part, different.

But our knowledge-by-identity of awareness is nonlinguistic and nonconceptual. No words are part of my acquaintance with my own consciousness. Since it does not necessarily involve any particular language, that acquaintance remains open to an indeterminate number of terms, theories, and modes of descriptions. Today I may encounter my own awareness using the term "awareness"; two years from now, if I choose to adopt the Upaniṣadic lexicon, I may think of it as *ātman*. Then I may take on the Zen vocabulary and refer to it, emphasizing somewhat different aspects, as "no mind" or perhaps as *tathāta*.[112] And while these shifts represent deep changes in my understanding of the world and of consciousness, they change nothing of my direct acquaintance with awareness per se, for it is transcendental to any words or even conceptual scheme.

In addition, I have said that I will check any theory of what it means to be conscious, not against some theory but against my own intimate familiarity with my own consciousness. Thus, the only natural constraints on theories of consciousness is that they must be sufficiently in accord with our intuitive and direct sense to stand up to such an internal check. But many theories can meet this test; thus, theories of consciousness or of mystical awareness can, in principle, be widely diverse and yet be understood as talking of the same thing. A thirteenth-century Dominican friar may refer to this element as *das Funklein*, the spark, or as the highest "power" in the soul. Given a Dominican's context, it makes sense to say that consciousness is the highest "power," if we were to think of the human cognitive capacities as hierarchical. The author of *The Cloud of Unknowing* may say that consciousness is at the level of my being, since what it is to be is to be conscious.[113] A ninth-century Hindu may refer to consciousness as *vijnana* or as *ātman* and may speak of it as separate from the *upādhis* (individualizing personality features), and as a witness (*sākṣin*). A twentieth-century philosopher of mysticism may speak of "a knowledge by identity" with the continuity of awareness per se. Finally, the Buddhist may say that the awareness per se is *śunyata* in the sense that it is devoid of the subject/object distinction and of any content or specifiable shape. Given their context, each of these accounts makes sense of what we know as consciousness.

Despite these differences, it is perfectly plausible that these theorists are all referring to the very same consciousness per se that we each know through knowledge-by-identity. It makes sense to think that mystics could be talking in a variety of languages—applying different beliefs and background claims—about the same phenomenon and experience. In awareness, and in our direct experience of it, we may have the beginnings of an answer to the postmodern problem of incommensurability. Mysticism and awareness per se are, in important respects, nonpluralistic.

Concluding Remarks

Despite the assumptions of neo-Kantian or Wittgensteinian constructivists, the mystical experiences we have analyzed are not the psychological realization of expectations or concepts or the expression of the background of experience. Rather, mystics may be correct when they suggest that it is an encounter with, or a bringing out of, consciousness itself. Answering the first question we posed at the beginning of this essay, the PCE occurs when one "forgets" and lays aside language, image, and other content and arrives at what one had been all along. It is *consciousness* itself, then, peculiar and sui generis though it may be, that is responsible for the peculiar "shape" of the pure consciousness event.

Answering our second question, we know we have been in a PCE and remember having been so in precisely the same way that we remember our consciousness itself at any other time. And that is in a sui generis, knowledge-by-identity manner. We do not know consciousness in the same way we know another person, an apple, or even facets of our own personality. We know it through a familiarity so intimate, so without seams, that we have no way of teasing out its constituent parts, processes, or mechanics. We just have an immediate sense of it and know that it has been continuous through (what we know intellectually as) past and present. Our knowledge of our consciousness and our awareness that we have remained conscious is, in general, more fundamental than any thinking or perceiving. The nature of this immediate acquaintance, and with it the "knowledge" we have that we have persisted through ordinary experiences and through the PCE, must be distinguished from all other knowledge, just as our mystics have suggested.

The mystical encounter with awareness itself thus represents an innate capacity in several senses.

1. Consciousness itself is innate within each human being. To be fully human is to be conscious, in all cultures. Although there are countless differences among humans and among cultures, sheer consciousness, in the sense of that which perceives anything at all and ties past and present together, does not differ.
2. The acquaintance with consciousness we gain through knowledge-by-identity is not and cannot be taught. Rather, this acquaintance comes with the equipment of being human; it is innate in this sense.
3. One realizes consciousness unmixed with intentional content by means of a process of letting go, an emptying of self, a forgetting of language and sensation. Though the content that we "forget" differs, the capability to forget is innate. Thus it is that the processes of coming to mysticism are so strikingly similar from era to era. We have an innate capacity, through a process akin to forgetting, to encounter consciousness in its simplicity.
4. The capacity to rest solely within awareness itself in a pure consciousness event is also innate. That is, humans have an innate capacity not only to be conscious and to know things intentionally but also to remain conscious even when content drops away. This implies that human beings carry an innate capacity for some forms of mysticism.

Notes

1. Steven Mitchell, trans., *Tao te Ching* (New York: Harper, 1988), chap. 14 (no page number).
2. David Hay, *Religious Experience Today* (London: Mowbray, 1990), p. 79.
3. I will explain this name toward the end of the paper.
4. I had hoped that I could find representatives of both schools of thought who look at a single passage. But both schools are so young that, to my knowledge, no such pair exists. Thus, I offer what is, at best, a likely scenario.
5. *Turya* means fourth and denotes a state gained in meditation that later came to be known as *samadhi*. The first three mentioned in the Upaniṣads are the waking, dreaming, and deep

sleep conditions, or what we would call "states of consciousness." *Caturtha* is the regular form of the ordinal numeral adjective, but this state is more commonly named *turiya*. Later philosophical treatises more typically have the form *turiya*, which came to be the accepted technical term.

6. Robert Hume, *The Thirteen Principle Upaniṣads* (Oxford: Oxford University Press, 1921), p. 436.

7. While he does not discuss this passage, for a similar methodology in studying Christian mystical texts see H. P. Owen's "Experience and Dogma in the English Mystics," in *Mysticism and Religious Traditions,* ed. Steven T. Katz (New York: Oxford University Press, 1983), pp. 148–162. In the same volume, see Robert Gimello's excellent study of Buddhist mysticism in "Mysticism in Its Contexts," pp. 61–88.

8. As Steven Katz, "Language, Epistemology and Mysticism" in *Mysticism and Philosophical Analysis*, ed. Steven Katz (New York: Oxford University Press, 1978), Wayne Proudfoot, *Religious Experience* (Berkeley: University of California Press, 1986), and others, in fact, do.

9. Katz, "Language, Epistemology and Mysticism."

10. Robert Gimello, "Mysticism and Meditation," Gimello, in *Mysticism and Philosophical Analysis*, ed. Steven Katz (New York: Oxford University Press, 1978), as well as Gimello, "Mysticism in Its Contexts."

11. Hans Penner, "The Mystical Illusion," in Katz, *Mysticism and Religious Traditions.*

12. Proudfoot, *Religious Experience.*

13. Katz suggests that "Manet" painted "Notre Dame." With all due respect, I believe he was thinking of Monet, whose famous paintings were of the Rouen cathedral. Despite the possibility of confusion, I will use what I believe to be the correct names.

14. Katz, "Language, Epistemology and Mysticism," p. 46.

15. Ibid., p. 26.

16. This thesis permeates Proudfoot's entire *Religious Experience*, but see especially pp. 119–154.

17. These two are the main character is *Chāndogya Upaniṣad* 6:8. We know very little about Śvetaketu, who is presented primarily as a foil for his father. I use his name as archetype, not as portrait.

18. Gimello, "Mysticism and Meditation," p. 85.

19. Owen, "Experience and Dogma," p. 148.

20. The position has been most completely articulated in the eleven essays in Robert K. C. Forman, *The Problem of Pure Consciousness* (New York: Oxford University Press, 1990). See also Donald Evans, "Can Philosophers Limit What Mystics Can Do? A Critique of Steven Katz," *Religious Studies* 25: 53–60; Robert Forman, "Paramārtha and Modern Constructivists on Mysticism: Epistemological Monomorphism versus Duomorphism," *Philosophy East and West*, 39, no. 4 (October 1989): 393–418; and G. William Barnard, "Explaining the Unexplainable: Wayne Proudfoot's *Religious Experience*," *Journal of the American Academy of Religion* 60, no. 2 (1992): 231–256.

20. Robert K. C. Forman, "Introduction: Mysticism, Constructivism and Forgetting," pp. 1–49; Anthony Perovich Jr., "Does the Philosophy of Mysticism Rest on a Mistake?", pp. 237–253; Steven Bernhardt, "Are Pure Consciousness Events Unmediated?," pp. 220–236; Donald Rothberg, "Contemporary Epistemology and the Study of Mysticism," pp. 163–210; R. L. Franklin, "Experience and Interpretation in Mysticism," pp. 288–304; Norman Prigge and Gary Kessler, "Is Mystical Experience Everywhere the Same?," pp 269–287; and Mark Woodhouse, "On the Possibility of Pure Consciousness," pp. 254–268; all in Forman, *The Problem of Pure Consciousness.*

21. See again the articles in the philosophical section of Forman, *The Problem of Pure Consciousness*. See also Barnard, "Explaining the Unexplainable"; Michael Stoeber, "Constructivist Epistemologies of Mysticism: A Critique and a Revision," *Religious Studies* 28 (1992): 107–116; James R. Price, "The Objectivity of Mystical Truth Claims," *Thomist* 49 (January 1985): 81–98.

22. In 1991 I conducted an interview with Daido Sensei Loori, head of the Zen Mountain Monastery in Mount Tremper, New York. He told me that his first experience of what he calls "absolute *samadhi*" came during a photography workshop with Minor White, years before he had looked into Zen. He had been out on assignment, photographing this and that when he came on a tree, "which was basically just a tree, just a plain old tree like a hundred thousand other ones. But this one was very special for some reason. And Minor used to say, sit in the presence of your subject until you have been acknowledged. . . . So I set up my camera and I sat with this tree, and it was in the middle of the afternoon, and that's all I remember until it was dusk, the sun had gone down and it was cold. And I was feeling just totally elated, just wonderful." From the fact that he had started in the early afternoon and came out after dusk, when it was cold, he deduced that he had been there for roughly four hours. Yet he had no recollection of anything from that entire period. He states he hadn't thought anything odd had happened, by which I came to understand that he had not blacked out or lost awareness. He was certain he had not slept.

It wasn't until five years later that he learned the term *samadhi*, which he now believes most adequately describes this experience.

23. In fact, our passage says that Śvetaketu's experience would be "unthinkable" and a "supreme mystery"! Doesn't that mean that he will have no good language to describe his experience, that his experience will go beyond language and thought? This means that even if he had heard about the experience, he would have heard something that did not adequately describe the experience. Language would not be enough to truly foreshadow and shape the precise character of any subsequent experience.

24. For this argument I am indebted to William Wainwright's *Mysticism* (Ann Arbor: University of Michigan Press, 1982).

25. See here Daniel C. Matt, "*Ayin*: The Concept of Nothingness, " and Franklin, both in Forman, *The Problem of Pure Consciousness*. See also Daniel Brown, "The Stages of Meditation in Cross-cultural Perspective," in Ken Wilber, Jack Engler, and Daniel Brown, *Transformations of Consciousness: Conventional and Contemplative Perspectives on Development* (Boston: Shambhala, 1986).

26. Michael McLaughlin, *Lonergan and the Evaluation of Theories of Mystical Experience*, unpublished dissertation, University of St. Michael's College, University of Toronto, 1995.

27. Robert K. C. Forman, "Pure Consciousness Events and Mysticism," *Sophia* 25, no. 1 (1986): 49–58. Unpublished interview with DR, 1990.

28. This question has been asked in public by Steven Katz and Robert Gimello, American Academy of Religion Mysticism Group, November 1990. See also Gene Pendleton, "Forman and Mystical Consciousness," *Sophia* 27, no. 2 (July, 1988): 15–17; and Bagger's review article of *The Problem of Pure Consciousness*, *Religious Studies* 27 (1991): 400–413.

29. I believe thoughtful mystics have much to contribute to modern discussions, if we can only understand them. Mystical texts offer many things, among which are often descriptions of certain key experiences and transformations and reflections on them. This, by the way, is why it is so hard to explore those texts as if they are merely direct experience reports, as many modern analysts of mysticism are wont to do.

30. *Bṛhad Upaniṣad Śankara Bhāsya*, 3.3.i. Quoted in William M. Indich, *Consciousness in Advaita Vedanta* (Delhi: Motilal Banarsidass, 1980), p. 107.

31. Śankara, *Ātmabodha*, 44. Quoted in Indich, *Consciousness in Advaita Vedanta*, p. 107.

32. Roger J. Corless, "Parables of Deconstruction in the *Lotus Sūtra*," present volume. I am indebted to Dr. Corless for the substance of this paragraph.

33. See here my *Meister Eckhart: Mystic as Theologian* (Warwick, N.Y.: Element Books, 1992).

34. M. O'C. Walshe, *Meister Eckhart: Tractates and Sermons*, vol. 1 (London: Watkins, 1978), p. 74.

35. I have discussed these matters in greater detail in my *Meister Eckhart*, chaps. 6 and 7.

36. See Lloyd Pfleuger, "Discriminating the Innate Capacity: Salvation Mysticism of Classical Sāṃkhya-Yoga," present volume, for a more thorough explanation of these twenty-four features of prakṛti.

37. Ibid.

38. "Puruṣa exists because [it] must be an overseeing power [and because] of the need for an experiencer." Ibid.

39. The *Yogasūtras*, for example, suggest that the key of this meditative process is *Dharana, Dhyana,* and *Samādhi.*

40. It is interesting to think that Sāṃkhya has, in effect, come up with a religious doctrine based on the notion of intentionality parallel to Brentano and Husserl's. Space forbids me from launching into a full exploration of this fact. See my *Mysticism and Mind* (Albany, NY: SUNY Press 1997), chap. 4.

41. Fifty-seven percent, to be quite precise, if Hay's numbers are correct.

42. In the *Mandukya Upaniṣad*, for example, the waking dream and deep sleep states, along with the "fourth" (*turiya*) state, are identified as the four quarters of *ātman*, or pure consciousness. *Ātman* as consciousness is said to underlie the first three state and to remain unaffected as it moves through them. Furthermore, two of the great sayings (*mahāvakya*) state this directly: "*brahman* is consciousness" and "*ātman* is *brahman*" (*prajnanam brahma, Aitareya Upaniṣad* 3.5.3, *ayam atma brahma, Bṛhadarānyaka Upaniṣad* 2.5.19.)

43. Though I will not explore his claim here, D. T. Suzuki suggests that Hui Neng, the famed Zen Buddhist patriarch, may be teaching something similar. This, admittedly, is not commonly claimed. See "The Zen Doctrine of No-Mind," in *Zen Buddhism: Selected Writings of D. T. Suzuki*, ed. William Barrett (Garden City, N.Y.: Doubleday Anchor Books, 1956), pp. 157–228. Suzuki suggests that the Zen doctrine of No-Mind points toward what he calls an "Unconscious" "below" intentional consciousness. As I argued in "Zen and Reflexive Consciousness," a lecture at the University of Helsinki, Finland, October 1994, I understand this to mean the awareness per se, to which we are referring herein.

44. William Chittuck, present volume.

45. Maharishi Mahesh Yogi, *Bhagavad Gita, A New Translation and Commentary with Sanskrit Texts* (Baltimore: Penguin Books, 1971), p. 144.

46. Here Perry seems to be referring to the fact that sometimes we are "unconscious" of certain things that we know. This includes certain facts that have "slipped our minds," dispositional characteristics that we do not want to confront, and so on. These are conscious (as opposed to what they are to a rock or a corpse), but "unconscious" as opposed to a presently occurring mental state.

47. Ralph Barton Perry, quoted in C. O. Evans, *The Subject of Consciousness* (New York: Humanities Press, 1970), p. 282.

48. Sir William Hamilton, in Evans, *The Subject of Consciousness*, p. 45. When John Dewey defined the "phenomenon of Self," he used the concept of consciousness in a similar way: "The self not only exists, but may know that it exists; psychical phenomena are not only facts, but they are facts of consciousness. . . . What distinguishes the facts of psychology from

the facts of every other science is, accordingly, that they are conscious facts. . . . Consciousness can neither be defined nor described. We can define or describe anything only by the employment of consciousness. It is presupposed, accordingly, in all definitions and all attempts to define it must move in a circle." John Dewey, *Psychology, 3d ed.* (New York: Harper, 1886), p. 2.

49. John Wisdom, *Problems of Mind and Matter* (Cambridge: Cambridge University Press, 1934), p. 15.

50. Ibid., pp. 12–15.

51. David Ballin Klein, *The Concept of Consciousness: A Survey* (Lincoln: University of Nebraska Press, 1980), p. 36.

52. Evans, "Can Philosophers Limit What Mystics Can Do?," p. 49.

53. David Hume, *A Treatise of Human Nature*, ed. L. A. Selby-Bigge (Oxford: Clarendon Press, 1888), p. 252 (emphasis mine).

54. Such a synonym for consciousness may be read into Wisdom's fifth clue: "S[omeone] is conscious" need involve neither consciousness of self nor "environment." For to be conscious neither of environment nor self may be taken to imply the possibility of consciousness solo.

55. G. E. Moore, *Philosophical Studies* (London: Oxford University Press, 1960), p. 17.

56. I do not claim that a Hume or a Moore would have necessarily achieved a pure consciousness event had he only had the right technique. Not all meditators get all results.

57. See P. F. Strawson, *The Bounds of Sense* (London: Methuen, 1966) part 3, sect. 2. This is, of course, commentary on Kant's *Critique of Pure Reason*. For the substance of this paragraph I am indebted to Mark Woodhouse.

58. Immanuel Kant, *Critique of Pure Reason*, trans. Norman Kemp Smith (New York: St. Martin's Press, 1965) A 122, p. 145.

59. See William Bossart, "Sartre's Theory of Consciousness and the Zen Doctrine of No-Mind," in *The Life of the Transcendental Ego*, ed. Edward S. Carey and Donald Morano (Albany: SUNY Press, 1986), p. 129.

60. Jean-Paul Sartre, *Being and Nothingness*, trans. Hazel Barnes (New York: Philosophical Library, 1956), p. 48 (emphasis mine).

61. I would like to say "it undergoes no structural changes," but this can be confusing. The shift from nonintentionality to intentionality may be taken to change the "structure" of consciousness from solo to tripartite. What I have in mind is that there is no change in the structure of awareness per se; it remains aware without discernable mechanics.

62. John Searle, *The Rediscovery of the Mind* (Cambridge, Mass.: MIT Press, 1992), p. 95.

63. Again, I do not *have* a consciousness as I might "have" a bicycle. There is no ownership of consciousness.

64. Strictly speaking, "acquaintance" is a misleading verb. One is acquainted with another person, a color, a piece of music. These are one and all intentional contacts, the familiarity with things distinct from the self. Here my "acquaintance" is with something that is the self; there is no intentional structure. It is in part for this reason that I think we will be on firmer ground to propose a new term for this epistemological structure.

65. I may be shooting myself in the foot here. The reader may check my theory of an awareness per se against his or her own "acquaintance" with having an awareness and come to deny the possibility of a PCE or the plausibility of my thesis. Indeed, I suspect that this will be the real stumbling block to a heretical view like mine. My hope here, however, is that the reader may be willing to accept that some people, mystics, have had experiences of consciousness that are plausible but unlike their own.

66. For the discussion that follows, I am indebted to G. William Barnard's excellent dissertation, "Exploring Unseen Worlds: William James and the Philosophy of Mysticism," University of Chicago, March 1994, pp. 123–134.

67. William James, *Principles of Psychology*, p. 216. We might add to his division "knowing how" the knowledge of how to drive a car or follow a rule and to "formal knowing" the kind of knowledge we might have when we understand a mathematical equation. But when it comes to mysticism, neither is particularly relevant, for both are intentional and high level—that is, grounded on the more basic "knowledge-about" and "knowledge-by-acquaintance." So, to save space, I omit both in my discussion.

68. James, *Principles of Psychology*, p. 656. Quoted in Barnard, "Exploring Unseen Worlds," p. 125.

69. Myers, p. 275, quoted in Barnard, "Exploring Unseen Worlds," 125–126. These divisions are strikingly similar to Meister Eckhart's division between the knowledge gained by the "inner man," which centers on feelings, and that gained by the "outer man," which focuses on knowledge and understanding.

70. James, *Principles of Psychology*, p. 189.

71. Here language fails us: "contact" implies a dualism, which is absent here. "My" is also misleading, for again I do not "own" my awareness as I own a house.

72. I first came across this term in Franklin Merrell-Wolff, *Pathways Through to Space* (New York: Warner Books, 1976), p. 93–97. It is, however, undeveloped there and is used in inconsistent and confusing ways. Furthermore, Wolff is speaking exclusively of mystical experience. It is true that certain mystical experiences are known by means of a new epistemological structure, but so is consciousness in ordinary experience.

73. Here the terms "my" and "I" are again problematic. Consciousness is at once the subject of any first-person appellation; yet it is also unrelated to anything denoting personality, possession, and so on. Some would have consciousness as impersonal; some hold it to be personal. I note only that it is problematic to say either.

74. This is speaking of James's knowledge by acquaintance in its ideal sense. There are, however, absolutely no words in my acquaintance with my own awareness.

75. It is obviously not permanent in the sense of immortality.

76. These expressions are taken from Katz, though they permeate cognitive psychology.

77. *Bṛihadarānyaka Upaniṣad* 4.5.15. Translation from Robert E. Hume, *The Thirteen Principal Upaniṣads*, 2d ed. (Oxford: Oxford University Press, 1931), p. 147.

78. Norman Malcolm, *Ludwig Wittgenstein: A Memoir* (Oxford: Oxford University Press, 1958), p. 87.

79. Shankara *Brahma Sūtra Bhasya,* 4.1.2. Quoted in Indich, *Consciousness in Advaita Vedanta,* p. 15.

80. Barnard, "Exploring Unseen Worlds," p. 130.

81. Here Bernadette Roberts, *The Experience of No-Self* (Boulder, Co.: Shambala, 1984), is a good example. I put quotes around "object" to indicate that if some perceptual object is encountered as the self, then there is no experienced distinction between that object and the subject. Thus, the intentional experiential structure behind the intentional grammar is dissolved.

82. *Memoiren einer Idealistin,* 5th ed., (1900), vol. 3, p. 166. Quoted in James, *Varieties*, p. 395.

83. We have discussed this for the PCE most fully. While I do not have space to explore this in as much detail as it warrants, in the more extrovertive experience, the object is encountered as the self. If this is the case, then the object is not experienced as separate from the self, and thus there is no distinction between subject and object as there is in intentional

experience. I hope to develop a fully fleshed-out typology of mysticism that includes this form of experience.

84. Barnard, "Exploring Unseen Worlds," p. 131.

85. D. T. Suzuki, "Existentialism, Pragmatism and Zen," in *Zen Buddhism: Selected Writings of D. T. Suzuki,* ed. William Barrett (Garden City, N.Y.: Doubleday, 1956), pp. 261–262.

86. We may thereby tap into a rich lode of insights about the relation in general of consciousness to the world, to the self, and to itself. See my talk, "What Does Mysticism Have to Tell Us about Consciousness," delivered at the Conference "Towards a Science of Consciousness," Tucson, Arizona, 1996, and to be published by MIT Press. In this talk I suggest that cross-cultural patterns in mysticism have a great deal to tell us about the nature of human consciousness.

87. For the insight that this is the claim we are making, I am grateful to the careful reading and energetic correspondence of Barry Bushell.

88. Aldous Huxley, *The Perennial Philosophy* (New York: Harper Colophon Books, [1944] 1970). Virtually all of Alan Watts's huge corpus is on Zen and this theme; the most explicit is the introduction to his oft-neglected *Myth and Ritual in Christianity* (London: Thames and Hudson, 1983); Rudolf Otto, *The Idea of the Holy*, trans. John W. Harvey (New York: Oxford University Press, [1923] 1950). Also see Rudolf Otto's *Mysticism East and West*, trans. Bertha Bracey and Richenda C. Payne (New York: Macmillan, 1932).

89. See, for example, Katz, "Language, Epistemology and Mysticism" and Proudfoot, *Religious Experience.*

90. I am grateful to Diane Jonte-Pace, "The Swami and the Rorschach: Spiritual Practice, Religious Experience, and Perception," in the present volume.

91. *Bṛihadāryaṇyaka Upaniṣad*, trans. Hume, 4:5:15.

92. *Maitri Upaniṣad*, 6:30, trans. Hume.

93. Eliot Deutsch, *Advaita Vedanta: A Philosophical Reconstruction* (Honolulu: University Press of Hawaii, an East-West Center Book, 1973), p. 18.

94. Ibid., 19. See also M. Hiriyanna, *Essentials of Indian Philosophy* (London: Unwin, 1978), pp. 151–174.

95. Actually there are sometimes three "men" in Eckhart: the outer man, by whose means we know the external world; the inner man, by whose means we feel, think, and know ourselves; and the "innermost" man. But Eckhart makes it clear that the outer and the inner man have similar epistemological structures. See my *Meister Eckhart: Mystic as Theologian* (Rockport, Mass.: Element Books, 1991).

96. Walshe, *Meister Eckhart*, vol. 1, pp. 3–6.

97. See my "Eckhart, *Gezücken* and the Ground of the Soul," in Forman, *The Problem of Pure Consciousness,* pp. 98–120.

98. Walshe, *Meister Eckhart*, vol. 1, p. 74.

99. Ibid., p. 7. See my *Meister Eckhart: Mystic as Theologian,* pp. 95–132.

100. Ibid., p. 144.

101. Robert Forman, "Paramārtha and Modern Constructivists on Mysticism: Epistemological Monomorphism versus Duomorphism," *Philosophy East and West* 39 (1989): 393–418.

102. See articles by Forman, Rothberg, and Franklin in *The Problem of Pure Consciousness,* as well as Franklin's article in the present volume.

103. See my article "Of Deserts and Doors: Methodology in the Study of Mysticism," *Sophia* 32, no. 1 (1993): 31–44.

104. Buddhism called itself from very early times "The Middle Path." The metaphor of crossing a river, and the idea that the Buddhist *dharma* is like a raft, permeates Buddhism. References to the Path of the Arhant, the Path of Nirvana, the Pathless Path, and so on also permeate its writings.

105. Walshe, *Meister Eckhart*, vol. 1, p. 7.

106. Ibid., p. 20.

107. Walshe, *Meister Eckhart*, vol. 2, p. 135.

108. Walshe, *Meister Eckhart*, vol. 1, p. 273.

109. *The Vedanta Sūtras of Badarāyāna*, trans. G. Thibaut (New York: Dover, 1962). Quoted in Ken Wilber, *Eye to Eye: The Quest for the New Paradigm* (Garden City, N.Y.: Anchor Books, 1983), p. 299.

110. John Blofeld, *The Zen Teachings of Huang Po* (New York: Grove Press, 1958), quoted in Wilber, *Eye to Eye*, p. 299.

111. I say "virtually all" to allow for exceptions such as people in comas or those people with neurological disorders, and so on.

112. D. T. Suzuki, "The Zen Doctrine of No-Mind," in *Zen Buddhism: Selected Writings of D. T. Suzuki*, ed. William Barrett (Garden City, N.Y: Double Anchor Books, 1956), pp. 157–226.

113. Here is a possible variation on Descartes: "I am conscious, therefore I am."

PART I

THE INNATE CAPACITY IN THE RELIGIOUS TRADITIONS

TWO

Discriminating the Innate Capacity

Salvation Mysticism of Classical Sāṃkhya-Yoga

LLOYD W. PFLUEGER

But when the sun has set, Yajñavalkya, and the moon has set, and the fire has gone out, and speech is hushed, what light does a person here have?

—*Bṛhad Āryaṇyaka Upaniṣad*[1]

I have never had any revelations through anesthetics, but a kind of *waking* trance—this for lack of a better word—I have frequently had, quite up from boyhood, when I have been all alone. This has come upon me through *repeating my own name* to myself *silently*, till all at once, as it were out of the intensity of the *consciousness of individuality*, individuality itself seemed to *dissolve* and fade away into *boundless being*, and this not a confused state but the *clearest*, the surest of the surest, utterly beyond words—where death was an almost laughable possibility—the *loss of personality* (if so it were) seeming *no extinction*, but the *only true life*. I am ashamed of my feeble description. Have I not said the state is utterly beyond words?

—Alfred, Lord Tennyson[2]

MYSTICISM OR MYSTICAL experience in world religions presents a varied set of phenomena. Those who would approach and attempt to analyze, classify, and understand such phenomena from their own perspectives, with their own intentions, methods, backgrounds, languages, and cultures, can perhaps agree on at least one aspect of their enterprise: in dealing with mystical experience, however defined or undefined, we are dealing with highly significant events that at the same time transcend ordinary experience. This transcendence of the limits of what is usual or paradigmatic for experience makes mysticism particularly valuable. At the limits of the ordinary we are likely to learn something new about religion and its study and about experience itself.

In the last ten years a debate about the nature of religious experience, especially with respect to mysticism, has become increasingly active. At issue is the role of the mind in mystical experiences. Are the creative activities of the mind, with its cultural shaping, training, and basic presuppositions, responsible for mystical experiences, or is something else responsible? It may depend on which experiences we are talking about. Katz and his colleagues represented in *Mysticism and Philosophical Analysis*,[3] the so-called constructivists, argue that the active building processes of the intellect, the constructive activities of language use, and the expectations generated by a life in a religious tradition are responsible. Sallie King, Donald Evans, and Robert Forman and his colleagues, whom we might call, as Forman does, Perennial Psychologists as represented in *The Problem of Pure Consciousness*, have argued that mystical experiences do not necessarily result from such a conceptual building process, but rather result from some other sort of process.[4] To wit, PCEs (Pure Consciousness Events),[5] they argue, do not show signs of being so shaped and may result not from a construction process but from a process of progressively *eliminating* conceptual shaping.

It seems like common sense to apply the same kind of analytic tools and perspectives to mystical experiences as we might apply to any other ordinary experience. The farther the actual experiences are from the ordinary, however, the more dubious such common sense becomes. Perhaps the farthest extreme from ordinary experience is the mysticism represented by the class of PCEs. In particular, the *kaivalya* experience described in the Sāṃkhya-Yoga philosophy of Hinduism stands out in the history of religions as an instructively clear example of a mysticism so beyond the framework of ordinary experience that, I believe, it has something to say to the present debate between constructivists and postconstructivists on the nature of mysticism.

The classical systems of Hindu philosophy known as Sāṃkhya and Yoga offer an outline of theory and practice to gain a particular mystical insight, known as "knowledge of the difference" (*viveka-khyāti*), which results in a salvific isolation (*kaivalya*) of consciousness from all other components of experience and from all suffering. The "liberation from suffering" demands the analysis and relinquishment of nothing less than the structure of ordinary experience. It demands the discrimination of *all* intellectual, cultural, linguistic, and personal elements of conscious experience from the consciousness itself. It demands the separation of all that is or can be constructed in experience from the simple capacity to be conscious at all. What's more, Sāṃkhya-Yoga philosophy not only describes and analyzes the PCE of *kaivalya* but also outlines methods to achieve it, bridging the conceptual gap between ordinary experience and salvific mystical experience. To be sure, cultural and linguistic means such as meditation are used to achieve *kaivalya*, but only because, as the Indian proverb goes, it takes a thorn to remove a thorn—*kaivalya* itself transcends constructed experience of any kind.

Sāṃkhya-Yoga employs meditative technique to examine progressively more subtle levels of mind until the full range of mind is experienced and discarded: all things (including all mental things) are in this analysis *material process*—both the process of knowing and the objects known. This insight into the nature of human experience reveals something else, something totally apart from material process: a pure innate capacity to know. The difference between the material process and consciousness itself is crucial not only to the dualistic system but also, I argue, to the correct understanding of our contemporary discussion on the nature and study of mystical experience. To elucidate the difference, in this essay we explore three main areas: the structure of reality in Sāṃkhya-Yoga philosophy; the significance of *kaivalya*, the isolation of the innate capacity of consciousness itself; and an analysis of a yogic meditation method for isolating consciousness from intellectual, cultural, and linguistic process.

The evidence suggests that at least in the case of *kaivalya* mysticism of classical Sāṃkhya-Yoga, the postconstructivists do well in their theory to make allowance for an experienced capacity of consciousness beyond cultural or linguistic programming (or reprogramming). Salvation experience in Sāṃkhya-Yoga assumes an impersonal and culture-free core of the human being, open to direct experience by all technically proficient investigators.

The Structure of Reality in Classical Sāṃkhya-Yoga

Of the various orthodox[6] systems of Indian philosophy, the oldest is generally acknowledged to be Sāṃkhya, "enumeration," a dualist system of which but fragments remain, represented chiefly by the *Sāṃkhya-Kārikā* (SK) of Īśvarakṛṣṇa and the *Yogasūtra* (YS) of Patañjali. The SK is a short summary (ca. 350–450 C.E.) of Sāṃkhya philosophy in verse.[7] It is the SK that today is our best source of Sāṃkhya in its classical form. The Sāṃkhya of the SK consists of a theoretical analysis that enumerates, categorizes, and characterizes the structure of reality. This knowledge is understood to be salvific, the antidote to the epistemological error (ignorance) responsible for the suffering inherent in human life.[8]

As the Sāṃkhya of Īśvarakṛṣṇa focuses on the correct salvific understanding of structure of creation, the contemporaneous Sāṃkhya of Patañjali, outlined in the aphorisms of the *Yogasūtra* (ca. 400 C.E.), focuses on the practical means, *yoga* (i.e., meditation, spiritual discipline), by which such saving knowledge becomes direct experience. Although there are some differences in emphasis, terminology, and other details, the two systems present, by and large, a complementary whole for apprehending the nature of the mystical salvation event both term *kaivalya*, "isolation."[9]

The Sāṃkhya Structure

To understand *kaivalya*, we must first gain an overall grasp of the Sāṃkhya-Yoga structure of reality.[10] Sāṃkhya enumerates the component principles that make up the universe from "inside out" and from subtle to gross.[11] In a view rather similar to that of modern physics, Sāṃkhya notes that reality involves a wide continuum of experience from subtle to gross, from invisible to visible, from unmanifest to manifest.[12] All component principles (*tattvas*) are considered open to perception. Unlike our modern scientific reliance on indirect perceptions furnished by the instrumentation of atom smashers, electron microscopes, and other sophisticated technology, however, Sāṃkhya relies on the experiential reports of saints and sages who are understood to have cultivated their *inner* perception to directly perceive what is invisible to our ordinary faculties.[13] Sāṃkhya outlines the perceived structure, from the most subtle, simple, and abstract components to the most gross, complicated, and concrete—something like a primordial "periodic table of elements"—twenty-five in all.

Even with twenty-five basic components, Sāṃkhya metaphysics, epistemology, and psychology posit a firm dualism. There are two irreducible, innate, and independent realities in our universe of experience:

1. consciousness itself (*puruṣa*)
2. primordial materiality (*prakṛti*).

These two are copresent and coeternal.

The Material World

On the *material* side, the world of experience is analyzed into twenty-four fundamental principles (*tattvas*), pure unmanifest primordial materiality (*prakṛti*, no. 2) and its twenty-three progressive evolutes.[14] Like a rope, the unmanifest materiality is composed of three "strands," called *guṇas*, in dynamic equilibrium; when the equilibrium between the three is disturbed, the "symmetry breaking" results in combinations of these three *guṇas* such that new successive principles manifest:

3. intellect (*buddhi*, *mahat*)
4. ego (*ahaṃkāra*)
5. mind (*manas*)

6–15. the ten sense and action capacities (*indriyas*) (hearing, touching, seeing, tasting, smelling, speaking, grasping, moving, excreting, procreating)
16–20. the five subtle elements (*tanmātras*) (sound, touch, form, taste, smell)
21–25. the five gross elements (*mahābhūtas*) (space, air, fire, water, earth)

The gross elements (the five *mahābhūtas*) combine to form the gross material objects (bodies, tables, bananas) of ordinary experience. Please note that the psychological machinery of experience—intellect, ego, and mind together with everything they can process external to themselves—are all seen as merely different forms of nonconscious matter.[15] This is *not* the garden variety mind/body dualism encountered in Western philosophy! Here both body and mind are seen as unequivocally material. Even so, Sāṃkhya-Yoga cannot reduce the universe of experience to the nonconscious permutations of matter alone.

For Sāṃkhya the most important element of experience is still unaccounted for: creation is not merely an intricate interweaving of basic material strands (*guṇas*), a tapestry blindly woven by accident, but a purposeful weaving, a dance (SK 59) before and for conscious observation.[16] Content, including its intellectual processing, is only half the equation of experience—our experience necessarily involves the element of consciousness. In addition to and independent of the twenty-four principles of matter is *puruṣa*, the principle of consciousness itself. SK 3, in four hemistichs (half lines), contrasts *prakṛti* and its twenty-three material evolutes (variously grouped: 7, 16) with *puruṣa*:

(I) Primordial materiality is ungenerated.
(II) The seven—intellect, and so forth—are both generated and ungenerated.
(III) The sixteen are generated.
(IV) Consciousness is neither generated nor generative.[17]

Thus, *prakṛti*, although uncreated, evolves dynamically to create from itself further material building blocks (seven, then sixteen), while *puruṣa*, also uncreated, remains static and uncreative. The difference is further elaborated in SK 10 and 11:

Puruṣa is similar to unmanifest *prakṛti* in being:

uncaused (*ahetumat*)
nontemporal (*nitya*)
nonspatial (*vyāpin*)
stable (*akriya*)
simple (*eka*)
unsupported (*anāśrita*)
nonmergent (*aliṅga*)
without parts (*anavayava*)
independent (*aparatantra*)

Puruṣa is different from all *prakṛti* in being:

without tripartite process (*atriguṇa*)[18]
differentiated (*vivekin*)
noncontent (*aviṣaya*)
uncharacterizable (*asāmānya*)
conscious (*cetana*)
unproductive (*aprasavadharmin*)[19]

In addition SK 19 summarizes *puruṣa*'s nature as:

a witness (*sāskṣitva*)
possessed of isolation or freedom (*kaivalya*)
indifferent (*mādhyasthya*)
a spectator (*draṣṭṛtva*)
incapable of activity (*akartṛbhāva*)

Thus, *puruṣa* is consciousness itself, without intention or process, the indifferent witness of all mental activity (thoughts, perceptions, feelings, etc.). The point here is that *puruṣa*, pure consciousness, is not the same as ordinary psychological awareness.[20] Ignorance itself, the underlying factor that opposes salvation, in Sāṃkhya-Yoga is equated with just this confusion[21] between the appropriated "light of consciousness" and the material content and processes it "illuminates": thoughts, sensations, processes—that is, mental activity of any kind.[22] In this dualistic perspective, our ordinary experience of the world, as we noted earlier, is an undistinguished combination of (1) subtle material processes (such as we might today call brain processes), the incessant permutations and interactions of the three *guṇas*, and (2) the principle that witnessing "illuminates" them as intentional objects (see Table 2-1).

Consciousness (*puruṣa*), on the other hand, is in itself completely inactive and unintentional—pure sentient presence without any contents, a "principle" but never a thing. In terms of Western typologies, Larson clarifies the Sāṃkhyan *puruṣa* in this way:

> Consciousness, in other words, is sheer contentless presence (*sāskṣitva*). Sāṃkhya philosophy thereby rejects idealism without giving up an ultimately transcendent "consciousness." It also rejects conventional dualism by reducing "mentalist" talk to one or another transformation of material "awareness"; and it modifies reductive materialism by introducing a unique notion of "consciousness" that is nonintentional and has nothing to do with ordinary mental awareness.[23]

Why does Sāṃkhya teach such a nonintentional consciousness? SK 17 clarifies the reasoning:

Puruṣa exists (*puruṣo'sti*)

a. because combinations [of the *guṇas*] exist for another's purpose (*saṁghātaparārthatvāt*)

b. because (this other) must be apart or different from the three *guṇas*[24] (*triguṇādiviparyayād*)
c. because [this other must be] an overseeing power (*adhiṣṭhānāt*)
d. because of [the need for] the existence of an experiencer (*bhoktṛbhāvat*)
e. and because [all] functioning [of the *guṇas*] is for the purpose of liberation (*kaivalyārthaṃ pravṛtteś ca*).[25]

For the Sāṃkhya system, it is not enough to say that matter functions in its various levels and forms: the evolutionary manifestation of *prakṛti* into twenty-three principles and all their combinations implies a purpose, a purpose that the material world, however complex, cannot supply. Matter is not conscious in itself; it has no sentient light in which to be seen. Without a conscious principle outside itself, it is blind, unknowing, and unknown.[26] Without *puruṣa*, even mental processes *know* nothing. Like the flickering arrays of electrical on and off switches within a computer, mental operations without a conscious principle are just material changes, not experience. Only the witness who observes the computer screen makes the readout *knowledge*. Larson captures the thrust of the arguments for *puruṣa* in SK 17 in this way:

> All of these arguments amount to one basic claim, namely, that the very notion of tripartite process itself becomes unintelligible in the absence of a distinct principle of sentience. In other words, tripartite process although a powerful intellectual synthesis or conceptualization, cannot stand alone in and of itself, for even the awareness of the concept presupposes a ground or basis, or perhaps better, a "medium" through which and for which the concept becomes meaningful. Otherwise what appeared to be a uniform, rational, and meaningful world "from Brahma down to a blade of grass" would finally show itself as an endless mechanical process in which the transactions of ordinary experience would amount to little more than occasional pleasurable respites from an endlessly unfolding tragedy. Or putting the matter another way, one would come upon the remarkable paradox that an apparently uniform, rational, and meaningful world is finally pointless.[27]

TABLE 2-1. Two Separate Realities

prakṛti	*puruṣa*
matter	consciousness itself
psychological faculties	alone
intellect, ego, mind, sense capacities, and action capacities	
subtle elements	
gross elements	
material objects	

Puruṣa *in Patañjali's YS*

Patañjali's Sāṃkhya formulation, the *Yogasūtra*, emphasizing meditative experience as the means of salvation, gives important corroboration to our understanding of the dualism of *prakṛti* and *puruṣa*.

The closest the YS comes to a definition of *puruṣa* comes in chapter 2, which echoes the salvation scheme of the SK. Having established (parallel to SK 1) that the "totality of experience is nothing but pain"[28] (YS 2.15), there is a logical resolve to avoid this suffering in the future (2.16). To do this, the cause and mechanics of suffering and liberation are succinctly presented. Although a wealth of synonyms for *puruṣa* and *prakṛti* are used (such as *seer* and *seen*),[29] the basic Sāṃkhyan theory is quite recognizable:

2.17 The cause [of future suffering] that should be avoided is the association (*saṃyoga*) of the seer (*draṣṭṛi*) and the seen (*dṛśya*).
2.18 The seen, disposed to illumination, activity, or inertia,[30] consists of the elements and the sense organs and functions for the sake of experience and liberation.
2.20 The seer is simply the seeing, [which] although pure sees the object.
2.21 The essential nature of the seen is to function for the sake of the seer.
2.23 Association is the cause of the apprehension of the essential nature of the owner (*svāmī,* i.e., *puruṣa*) and the owned (*sva,* i.e., *prakṛti*).
2.24 Ignorance (*avidyā*) is the cause.
2.25 From an absence of this [ignorance] there is an absence of association—the deliverance—this is the isolation (*kaivalya*) of seeing (*dṛśi*).
2.26 Undeviating perception of the difference (*viveka-khyāti*) is the means of deliverance.

We see in Yoga philosophy the same Sāṃkhya structure of reality and the same concept of salvation. The faculty of consciousness (*puruṣa*), which is *simply the seeing*, is erroneously associated (2.18), misidentified, with what is *seen* (*prakṛti*)—the thinking *process* of the mind complete with its *contents*—that is, what it thinks about. Both are watched, simply, indifferently watched by something else: *puruṣa*, the ultimate *watcher* or *seer*. Consciousness does not think. It only witnesses the thinking (2.20). Without the presence of pure consciousness, the mechanical play of thought and sense perception have no meaning. It is only through the seeming conjunction of two innate and completely independent realities that what humans know as experience comes to be (2.23). Experience is invariably painful (2.15). Salvation is afforded by breaking down the nature of ordinary experience into its dual and eternally distinct components: consciousness and matter, seer and seen, owner and owned (2.23). Ignorance is the ordinary overlap of the two in what seems to be unified experience of a person; liberation is the dissolution of personal experience. What is essentially conscious is separated from what is merely nonconscious (though dynamic) material. Ordinary experience is distilled, as it were, into its innate components; ignorant process is tricked into "deconstructing," dismembering, ignorance. The cognitive bubble bursts on inspection; what is conscious is isolated from the material process it seemed to animate. The result is *kaivalya*, isolated *puruṣa*, the Pure Consciousness Event (PCE). Anything cultural, linguistic, psychological, intellectual, or even sensory is eliminated in the final dismemberment of ordinary experience—the clear distinction between *puruṣa* and *prakṛti*.[31]

The Significance of Pure Consciousness

As we have noted, one of the big philosophical surprises of Sāṃkhya-Yoga dualism is that it analyzes our *psychological* faculties in terms of material principles and processes. Thus, the intellectual faculty (called *buddhi* or *mahat*), the ego structure (*ahaṁkāra*),[32] the sensory mind (*manas*), and the sense and action capacities (*indriyas*) are just so much mechanical hardware; they are no more conscious in their nature than the bones or toenails of the body or the gears and cogs of a motor. Sāṃkhya relegates all such faculties to the material side of life. They are not merely activities beneath the surface of ordinary consciousness, in modern terminology *subconscious* or *unconscious* processes; they are by their material nature the very opposite of consciousness. These faculties are all merely inert *objects of knowing*, incapable of being subjects or *knowers*.[33] Sāṃkhya-Yoga is unique in its subject-object dualism in that it classifies as matter not only the objects of the world but also everything knowable—including the most subtle inner objects of experience: thoughts, ideas, intuitions, and feelings, along with the whole process of cognition. If these are objective, material things, what, then, is left of personal subjectivity and the knower? In reality, *nothing* at all!

This *nothing*, pure nonobjectivity, *puruṣa*, is not a thing or the mere absence of a thing. It is the very opposite of matter; *puruṣa* can never be isolated in the same way material objects are discriminated one from the other. It cannot be known the way material things, subtle or gross, are known. It is the knower, consciousness itself, bereft of all intentionality, all content, a witness of the contents of experience that makes experience possible. It is the pure core of subjectivity—not subjectivity in the ordinary sense, which has mostly to do with thoughts, feelings, intentions, and conceptions (private mental content), but subjectivity in the most radical sense: the essence, the quintessential nature of the subjective act of thinking, feeling, intending, willing, and selfhood and the "seeing" or consciousness *of* all these things.

Sāṃkhya-Yoga directly tackles the profound philosophical problem of consciousness, which in our thinking is so often ignored. Consciousness in itself is philosophically and perceptually all too easy to ignore due to its transparency and to the subjective depth at which it is embedded in our nature, for it is the ultimate presupposition of all human thinking and being. To be a conscious being naturally entails a capacity of consciousness, the one common factor in all moments of awareness, the key to all and any knowing.

Words do not suffice here. Consciousness, as such, is not even a medium or background—that is to make it objective and material. It is more basic even than that—it is the knowing itself. In all human knowledge-events, whatever the object, is the common factor of *knowing*. Knowing in this sense does not mean the cognitive processing, the analysis and articulation in symbolic or formal structures. Knowing refers to the fact that contents of whatever kind are present to awareness. The conceptual, cultural, and linguistic frames that shape the contents of knowing from the Sāṃkhya-Yoga viewpoint are—must be—material. This means that any constructivist claim about mystical experience can only apply in Sāṃkhyan analysis to the material portion of experience. But there is more to experience, says Sāṃkhya, than material constructions.

Whereas *prakṛti* is internally complex, the knowing, the knowing-ness before which *prakṛti* evolves,[34] involves,[35] or maintains dynamic equalibrium[36] is utterly still, pure, and simple. This is *puruṣa*, the pure knowing core of the person, of personhood itself—the pure core of subjectivity.

Indian thought has shown a great interest in the bipolar nature of existence, subjective and objective. Its interest in isolating the pure core of subjectivity is exceptional and may leave Westerners, with the exception of a few mystics, behind.[37] The Sāṃkhya idea of consciousness (*puruṣa*, *cit*, *cetana*) is as subtle as it is bold. The question "What is consciousness?" already seems to presuppose that it is a "what"—something objective, something that ordinary language can deal with, rather than the immaterial knowing that, beyond language, knows language (though to qualify consciousness in subject/object language also goes too far).

Consider the difficulty. The word *know*, because it is a verb, may seem to imply some kind of action, but consciousness is actionless. For example, the verb *know* implies a subject/agent, some*one* who does the act of knowing—but calling consciousness a knower objectifies it, falsifies it. It is nothing, does nothing. Pure knowing no more requires an active agent/knower than being requires an active agent or a "be-er." The Sāṃkhya-Yoga *puruṣa* is the knowing, as light is illumination.[38] The process of knowing something, however, is not the *knowing* itself but always the object of *puruṣa*'s illumination. (*Puruṣa* knows mental processes and their products, but mental processes and products are not *puruṣa*.) Agency in Sāṃkhya is all on the side of the material knower, the intellect (*buddhi*), mind, and senses. Intellect, mind, and senses do something. The knowing (knowingness), *puruṣa*, is changeless consciousness. It spontaneously knows the material agency, the mechanical process of cognition and perception, and, through it, the material world.

If it were easy to articulate conceptually and isolate experientially, there would be no need for the Sāṃkhya-Yoga system, for in this philosophy nondiscrimination of pure consciousness is the very definition of the ignorance whose elimination is the system's only goal. The isolation of the factor of consciousness in human experience is the way to the salvation, the liberation from all forms of suffering.

The goal is not armchair speculation or knowledge for its own sake. Sāṃkhya-Yoga sees itself as the answer to a practical problem. This is important to recall because the issue is not speculation but experience. There are those who might say that all talk of consciousness itself is mere speculation, thereby denying the possibility of any actual PCE. It is instructive in Sāṃkhya-Yoga to see with what seriousness the *experience* of isolating consciousness itself is taken.

Salvation here is not a future event apprehended by faith but a particular experience beyond faith or any other mental construction.[39]

In Sāṃkhya-Yoga the object of consciousness can refer to three things:

1. The internal mechanical process of cognition (involving the subtle material agents known as intellect, ego, mind, and senses)
2. The internal mental operations of the intellect, ego, mind, and senses corresponding to what we would call thoughts, feelings, and sensations
3. The external objects that are perceived and processed. All three of these entities, as we know, are understood as *material* objects.

Suffering a toothache, for example, involves reception and processing of certain tooth and gum sensations. Both the sensations and the mental processing that categorizes them not only as suffering but as *suffering-to-someone* are to be understood as material events. The intellect (*buddhi*), the mental core of personhood, suffers so long as it takes itself to be a conscious *someone* experiencing pain. The true situation from the view of Sāṃkhya-Yoga is quite different, however. The capacity of consciousness is eternal, unchanging, untouchable consciousness—pure spirit. It is a silent witness[40] of mental operations. It is not those operations: it is not the ego's fear or insecurity, nor the intense sensation, nor electrochemical nerve impulses, nor the nerve, nor the tooth, nor the concepts associated with them. Consciousness is eternally free of such objects, infinite, immaterial, and awake. The sensations and judgments assembled by the intellect are mere permutations of matter, *prakṛti*, without consciousness of any kind.[41]

Pain (or pleasure for that matter) exists in this understanding only when the machinery that receives and conceptualizes the intense stimuli as "pain" also appropriates to itself the faculty of consciousness. By so doing, not only pain is born but necessarily *pain-to-someone*—personhood is born as well. Since, however, consciousness is eternally other than and actually unconnected with matter and its permutations, the human experiences of personal feelings (pleasure/pain/neutrality), personal selfhood (*ahaṃkāra*), together with personal awareness as a whole are generated by epistemological error—intellectual appropriation of consciousness.[42] According to Sāṃkhya-Yoga, the mistake of the intellect (*buddhi*) can be rectified by the intellect and the liberating truth of separate, eternal, free *puruṣa* can be realized, but not without finding out what the person[43] really is.

The eternal subject, the silent, inactive, sentient witness of all mental events, is not a personal subject. The personal or phenomenal subject is the functioning of what is called the "inner instrument" (SK, *antaḥkaraṇa*; YS, *citta*), mistakenly associated with the "light" of consciousness. The situation is somewhat similar to that of a mirror; neither the light nor the objects it represents are ever really "in" the mirror. The delicately perspicacious but seriously mistaken "*buddhi*-mirror" experiences *in ignorance* not only that it has "light" in it but that it is the very *source* of such illumination. When this mirror is "yogically polished," its culminating intuition is that the light is "other" than it. *Buddhi* is in itself not conscious, not spiritual—not the illuminator of "personhood" but only the illuminated "reflector." With respect to this inner consciousness, the *buddhi* must now (apologies to St. Paul) think "not me, but *puruṣa* in me."

This realization destroys all possibility of suffering and all possibility of taking phenomenal personhood seriously.[44] Behind the facade of a person knowing is the reality of a separate knowingness and a material personality known. After this realization there is no longer a personal consciousness around which the results of action, *karman*,[45] can collect; there is no one subjected to mental or physical states. The states come and go, but the real knower of the states is experienced as eternal and eternally free. Even these states continue only until the *karman* is exhausted, for, according to SK 67, the mind/body complex still continues by dint of remaining karmic impressions (as a potter's wheel continues to spin for a while after the pot is thrown). Self-conscious individuality is no longer a source of pain. The "toothache" has been fixed by "x-raying" the phenomenal knower and extracting the phenomenal person! In this spiritual dentistry, the tooth remains; *the person is pulled.*

The point for our discussion of mysticism is this: most mystical experience—for example, visions, auditions, perceptions or conceptions of unity with nature, and conversions—from the viewpoint of Sāṃkhya-Yoga, belong entirely to the material side of the equation. In fact, any kind of personal mystical experience would be seen as just another rearrangement of the material components of the world. As such, any personal mystical experience from the Sāṃkhya viewpoint is necessarily a constructed experience, dependent on the material world of physical and psychological faculties, and all that shape them, including culture, language, and belief. Even so, this does not preclude the possibility of a nonordinary experience, which, although it may be described, articulated, and even engineered in a constructed way, in itself *as experience* is not personal or in any way constructed. Though nonordinary, *kaivalya* in Sāṃkhya-Yoga is seen as experience and as as real.

Experience of Pure Consciousness

Consciousness itself in Sāṃkhya-Yoga is distinct from concepts or conceptual processes, including language and culture. Some might argue that as such it should be excluded from the concept of experience entirely. The argument is largely semantic. The effect of denying *kaivalya* the status of *experience* would merely deemphasize what the tradition insists upon—its practical reality. Whatever its final ontological status, it is truer to the Sāṃkhya-Yoga tradition to represent it as experience. In their sense it is the *only* truly spiritual experience, since it is the only experience that is of a principle other than matter. By nature it is nonordinary. It transcends the subject/object structure of ordinary experience. The *kaivalya* experience as the experience of consciousness alone in and of itself might as well be termed *pure* experience. Our language is not designed to handle the load of nonordinary realities. It is an event, but outside of time. It is an experience, but not in the continuum of ordinary experiences.

Our tendency, necessarily, is to emphasize the objective pole of ordinary experience: the various objects of experience, including our aversion or attraction (which as mental operations or thoughts are also objects). Consciousness is for us (on the ordinary phenomenal level) an abstraction—merely the common denominator to all experiences of objects. It is the one constant, the knowingness in all forms of knowledge. As such, it is necessarily transparent to us, just as the fish may know everything that floats in the ocean but never consciously know or notice water itself. Yet the water is real and important, overwhelmingly so.

To say that pure consciousness isn't experiencable or conscious falsifies the record of what Sāṃkhya-Yoga practitioners are clearly asserting. Though it is not ordinary experience, it happens and is valued as the greatest happening, transforming suffering into liberation.

Just as the issue is obfuscated by shrinking the realm of experience to ordinary experience, excluding pure consciousness, it also distorts the issue to make consciousness, pure subjectivity, into its *own object* to say that it *knows itself*. It is just knowingness in itself. That which is pure luminosity does not need another light to illuminate itself. This Sāṃkhya-Yoga consciousness should not be confused with the usual language of phenomenal (subject/object) awareness or with similar-sounding terms like *self-consciousness* or *consciousness of consciousness*, *unconsciousness*, or the Freudian *subconscious*, all of which would in Sāṃkhya understanding still involve phenomenal, conceptual cognition. Dealing respectfully with nonordinary experiences is full of semantic traps.

What is this pure consciousness? The question remains, perhaps very naturally, without a final or satisfactory conceptual answer. In Sāṃkhya-Yoga it is the one reality that is truly mysterious, for it cannot be captured in the play of matter, not even in thoughts or feelings. It appears most distinctly when matter, in the form of intellect, surrenders its claim to conscious personal identity. In Sāṃkhya, when the material faculty of intellect is led to the clear vision of itself as nonconscious, fulfilling its cosmic task, it dissolves into its unmanifest source. Yet consciousness remains.

The situation is in no way bleak. The greatest mystery is neither rare nor unavailable. *Puruṣa*, even if we miss it in its isolated purity, is not only transcendent but also immanent, innate to every experience, transparent ocean to (and in) every fish.

To approach even the concept of consciousness in itself is to distance oneself from the material element in experience, the element that for us is usually synonymous with experience. Though experience seems unitary, like a single ongoing motion picture, Sāṃkhya-Yoga views it as something like a sequence of frames, a sequence of objects of awareness: thoughts, feelings, and sensations. What we call life experience is but a sequence of such objects on the mind's screen. Not only our environment, our possessions, and our body are objects, but our personalities as well. Our very existence as distinct persons is also a constructed object. But in all ordinary experiences of objects there is something else, according to Sāṃkhya-Yoga, that makes the experience possible. Something "Wholly Other" (apologies to Otto), so other that it is not even a thing, but an ungraspable no-thing, a *presence* in which and for which objects appear. It is the mystery of conscious existence; to know it in its uniqueness is to be it and (in Sāṃkhya-Yoga) to be saved.

Isolating Pure Consciousness: A Yogic Method

As noted, Sāṃkhya-Yoga finds in the structure of experience two separate capacities: the capacity to know and the capacity to be known. On one side there is the capacity of consciousness[46] and on the other the capacity to be objectified[47] and to intellectually process objects.[48] The confusing or apparent mixing of these eternally separate realities is seen to be the source of all suffering. So, as we have seen, the unmixing, the discrimination (*viveka*) of the intellectual capacity (*buddhi*) from the consciousness capacity (*puruṣa*) brings about salvation from suffering.

As the SK painstakingly emphasizes the enumeration of twenty-four subtle material principles and their contrast with the principle of consciousness, the YS emphasizes the means of traversing this territory, discriminating between these two finest capacities and isolating pure consciousness. Yoga philosophy is less interested in enumerating cosmic structural principles. Instead, Yoga uses these principles to build a detailed map of the psychological states that correspond to the progressive isolation of consciousness itself from mental process of any kind. A concrete example makes the nature of this classical yogic mysticism clear. The way will be somewhat indirect, for to penetrate the tradition very deeply we must first explore the nature of meditation.

Although the YS offers a wide variety of choices for inducing mystical experience in the direction of its salvific goal, perhaps the means par excellence is a practice known as *īśvara-praṇidhāna*: "meditation on the Lord."

Meditative Practice: īśvara-praṇidhāna *and* samādhi

Meditation practice, or *yoga*, is defined in the very beginning of the YS:

1.1 Here begins the traditional teaching of Yoga.
(*atha yogānuśāsanam.*)
1.2 Yoga is the quiescence of the operations of awareness.
(*Yogaś citta-vṛtti-nirodaḥ.*)

The text then details and analyzes the various ordinary and nonordinary states of awareness that lead with disciplined practice to the actual quiescence of mental activity. This involves paradigmatically the distinction of two unusual states of experience (called *samādhi*) in which the mental activity becomes *coherent*[49] (i.e., focused, unified):

1. *samprajñāta samādhi*, or *perceptive coherence*, in which the awareness as a whole is entirely fixed upon an object of any kind (YS 1.17)
2. *asamprajñāta samādhi*, or *quiescent coherence* of awareness, in which, relinquishing any kind of object, the mental activity as a whole has entirely settled down, isolating consciousness itself

The consequence of the operations of awareness settling down entirely, the very goal of yoga, is stated in YS 1.3:

1.3 Then the seer abides in its essential nature.
(*tadā draṣṭuḥ svarūpe 'vasthānam.*)

The innate capacity, the essential innate form (*svarūpa*) of that which really *sees* in all seeing, is all that remains: *puruṣa*. Otherwise, there is the confusion, the apparent mixing of the intellectual process and consciousness itself:

1.4 Otherwise [consciousness, the seer] appears to be identical with the operations of awareness.
(*vṛtti-sārūpyam itaratra*)

This apparent mixing of what is truly separate is the Pandora's Box of Sāṃkhya-Yoga. From it come ego, personhood, and the various forms of ignorance whose common consequence is pain and frustration.

The prudent conclusion is that

2.16 Future suffering should be avoided.
(*heyam duḥkham anāgatam.*)

The means of escape is to cultivate the experiential states that result in the discrimination and isolation of the *true* seer, *puruṣa*.

The first and second chapters of the YS refer to a particular meditation process to attain the most quiescent state of awareness and to purify the mind of obstacles along the way. Its central placement and the discussion about it indicate its importance. On the surface it may be seen, interestingly enough, as a kind of theistic "devotion"[50] to the "Lord."

Although the same religious commentators elaborate this so-called "meditation on the Lord," *īśvara-praṇidhāna*, into a kind of devotion (*bhakti*) appropriate to their own time and religious viewpoint, Patañjali's own expressed description in the YS seems to focus more on technical practice (*abhyāsa*) than on piety. In fact, the *sūtras* themselves (apart from later commentaries) actually emphasize meditation on sacred sound (rather than emotional worship with loving devotion, *bhakti*) to bring about (1) the preliminary stages of coherent awareness and (2) the final perfect isolation of consciousness itself in *asamprajñāta samādhi*, the complete quiescence of mental operations:

> 2.45 Coherence is perfected by meditation on Isvara, the Lord.
> (*samādhi-siddhir īśvara-praṇidhānāt.*)

The existence of a sacred seed-sound (*bīja*) for Īśvara (OṂ) and the sound's use as an option for inducing and perfecting coherent states of awareness are logically laid out in chapter 1:

> 1.23 Or by meditation on (devotion to) the Lord.
> (*īśvara-praṇidhānād vā.*)
> 1.27 The sound which expresses Him is the praṇava (OṂ).
> (*Tasya vacakah pranavah.*)
> 1.28 Meditative repetition of it [results in] the realization of its referent.
> (*Tajjapas tad-artha-bhāvanam.*)
> 1.29 From that the consciousness within is attained, as well as the negation of obstacles.
> (*Tatah pratyak-cetanadhigamo 'pi antarāyābhavaś ca.*)

What is the ultimate referent for the *praṇava* OṂ? It is consciousness itself. Puruṣa is referred to as *master* or *owner* (*svāmin*, 2.23) and Lord (*prabhu*, 4.18); the Lord God (Īśvara) is defined in the YS in terms of *puruṣa* (1.24). The YS seems to go out of its way (unlike the SK) to include God, but only as an impersonal cipher whose "name" is particularly suited to isolating consciousness itself.[51]

This yogic means of isolating consciousness itself is by mentally *applying oneself to*[52] the name, the *mantra OṂ* (called *praṇava*), which reduces mental activities to the silence of pure consciousness. To understand this process of using language within the mind to go beyond both language and mind, we must dig more deeply into the history and earlier traditions behind this practice.

Meditation on OṂ

The nature of the practice of *īśvara-praṇidhana* is specified most directly in *sutras* 1.27–8:

> 1.27 The sound which expresses Him is the praṇava (OṂ).
> (*Tasya vācakaḥ praṇavaḥ.*)
> 1.28 Meditative repetition of it [results in] the realization of its referent.
> (*Tajjapas tad-artha-bhāvanam.*)

Patañjali's emphasis on the meditative repetition of the linguistic symbol (*vācakaḥ*) is neither original with him nor out of the mainstream of Indian thought. The religious or ritual use of language as *mantra*, literally a "thought-tool" consisting of a sacred sound or string of sounds, is common in Indian religion. Mantra use ranges from a practical and relatively impersonal repetition to intensely personal devotional prayer. The overall use of mantras as a means to change one's state of experience derives from the ancient Indian conception of the intrinsic correlation of name (*nāma*) and form (*rūpa*), language and reality. Vedic ritual, the earliest stratum of Hinduism, for example, was based on the premise that by manipulating sacred names (irrespective even of the will of the gods), the realities they represent would change in the way desired, since word and referent in magical Vedic language are two forms of the same thing.

The German Indologist J. W. Hauer links OṂ to the groups that practiced the intensive study and recitation of sacred texts (*svādhyāya*).[53] Such absorption in sacred texts through repetition was practiced mentally (*manasā*) in the village and orally (*vācā*) in the forest. It was known from earliest times as *japa* ("murmuring").[54] Repetitive "murmuring" or " humming," which may have been used to aid concentrative absorption, was technically called *praṇava*; later, the term *praṇava* became exclusively identified with the syllable OṂ itself. Hauer notes that such *svādhyāya* or *japa* of OṂ probably brought it to acceptance as a designator of the highest power, *brahman*.[55]

Although the single syllable OṂ seems to be the ultimate in simplicity, much is made of its inner acoustic structure, which is understood to correspond to the structure of the microcosm and the macrocosm. OṂ is understood to be made up of sequential elements (counted variously as three, four, or, more technically, 3½ elements): "A" and "U" (which elide to make "O"); "Ṃ" (*anusvāra*), the nasalization; and the silence ("½") that remains after the hum of nasalization. The three letters and the dichotomy between sound and silence furnish the basis of much analysis and analogy for the linguistically minded philosophers of the later Vedic Upaniṣads.[56] The unfolding sound/silence structure of OṂ parallels the structure of the mind and the universe itself.

The great source of confusion for any interpreter comes from mixing or not continually discriminating between two levels:

1. The *sound* OṂ, which comprises the levels of *relative awareness* from most gross to most subtle
2. The *silence* to which OṂ *points*. This silence correlates with contentless consciousness itself. (In this perspective, silence itself is not real absence of sound but the very quietest "pronunciation" of the cosmic OṂ.)

Though OṂ has been associated with the divine in all Hindu religious sects, it is obviously much more than just a convenient tag for a personal Lord. Names for divinity in Hinduism are innumerable; OṂ is unique.

OṂ is speech par excellence. By linking the mind with the nonlinguistic realities beyond it, OṂ, as speech, acts as a bridge, a means of passing over from the word to the referent. In the case of a referent that is spiritual—that is, *entirely immaterial*—OṂ also functions paradoxically to disjoin what in speech is erroneously linked—the material intellect and consciousness itself. Here language does not function constructively to shape and mold experience; it functions to deconstruct itself, to remove itself from consciousness. The ultimate purpose of ritual murmuring of the OṂ sound is conscious silence. This involves knowledge of a range of progressively more attenuated levels of speech and mental functioning as a whole.

Language, Levels, and Meditation on Īśvara

Some modern constructivists might respond that, while *puruṣa* may be consciousness, still, language must be involved in its production. After all, they might insist, the Sāṃkhya system of thought and the use of mantras are clearly linguistic phenomena. To counter this argument and to clarify this point, I now elucidate how the use of language in Sāṃkhya-Yoga to either describe a nonlinguistic phenomenon or to bring a nonlinguistic experience about does not necessarily imply that we have a linguistically constructed experience in the Sāṃkhya-Yoga PCE.

To help us understand exactly how the tradition is capable of using language to remove language and isolate consciousness itself, we must explore the philosophy of language contemporary with Sāṃkhya-Yoga thinking. An important discourse on philosophy of language that arose at the approximate time of the YS might help us flesh out some of the remaining mysteries behind Patañjali's understanding and use of *praṇava* (OṂ). This work, the *Vākyapadīya* of Bartṛhari, celebrates the nondual Absolute religious ultimate of the Upaniṣads, *brahman*, as *śabdatattva*, "that whose very principle or essence is the word."[57]

The *Vākyapadīya* (VP) goes on to identify this *śabda-brahman* (the Absolute-as-Word, Word-*brahman*) as the seed (*bīja*) of all things, all multiplicity of enjoyer, enjoyed, and enjoyment (1.4) attained and symbolized by the Veda (also one and many) (1.5), the source of conflicting views as dualism and monism (1.8) (Bartṛhari seems to recognize dualism while ultimately preferring monism). Bartṛhari goes on to link the Word-*brahman* with OṂ. Referring to the Vedic tradition, he notes:

> 1.9 The true and pure essence has been taught there, the knowledge capable of being grasped through one word, having the form of Praṇava, and in no way contradicting the different views.[58]

Thus, OṂ is understood here as the very essence of the Veda (the collection of chants that Hindus revere as highest revelation) and as the unitary syllable of *brahman* from which all thoughts, all dogmas or doctrines arise. In a truly conciliatory spirit, the commentary (possibly also by Bartṛhari) adds with respect to OṂ:

> The mystic syllable (Praṇava) allows for all points of view, it is the source of all Scripture, it is the common factor of all original causes, it is the cause of the rise and fall of doctrines, it accepts within itself all mutually contradictory ideas of Brahman or disallows all of them. The object of this allowance or disallowance does not, therefore, vary.[59]

Patañjali's nonsectarian philosophy of meditation, whose prototype is the repetition of OṂ, seems to resonate with Bartṛhari. Although Bartṛhari favors monism and

Patañjali dualism, both rely on OṂ in their parallel quests for universality. Both men reached for common ground in a period that sought to shore up intellectually what their rulers hoped to maintain politically in the face of geographical, ethnic, social, and religious divisions. As meditative discipline, or yoga, appeared as a common theme in Indian religions, so philosophy of language and the "perfected" medium of classical Sanskrit could also provide a common foundation for intellectual life. Both met in the syllable OṂ.

Bartṛhari goes on to link *śabda-brahman* with yoga by underscoring and supporting the supernormal powers (*siddhis*) of perception of those who have purified their minds (1.37) and cognized the eternal scriptures (Veda) and the science of grammar that explicates and preserves the scriptural potency (1.35–43). Such discrimination reveals that language (*śabda*) is to be differentiated into three levels:

> 1.42 This Science of Grammar is the supreme and wonderful source of the knowledge of the threefold word, comprising many paths, of the *Vaikhari*, (the Elaborated), the *Madhyama* (the Middle One), and the *Paśyanti* (the Seeing One).[60]

Here the *vaikharī* level represents the uttered sounds produced by the vocal cords and heard by the ears, the gross level of speech. *Madhyamā* is the subtle, mental level of speech, the verbal thinking level that is the source of gross speech. *Paśyantī*, the "Seeing One," corresponds to the very finest level of intuitive cognition, where name and form (word and material referent) are one in *seed-form*, known in a flash of direct intuition so compact and whole that it is without the usual sequence and distinction of ordinary thought or articulated speech . This most compact seed-level of speech for Bartṛhari points to an underlying monism. This is presumably the level of mental function where the *ṛṣis* and advanced yogins are said to cognize the impersonal acoustic structures of the Veda and the universe as a whole.

The concept of these three distinct, increasingly inward levels of speech is probably not unrelated to the ancient use of Vedic *mantras* in the sacrifice, which also knew of *three* levels of recitation—the loud chanting of the *hotṛ*, the low muttering of the *adhvaryu*, and the silent witness and mental recitation of the *brahmin* priest during the ritual.

The three levels of speech seem to refer to the material universe. Beyond the three material levels of speech there is still a fourth level—the speechless, soundless silence. For example, the Upaniṣads differentiate the level of *śabda-brahman* (Brahman-as-Word) from *aśabda-brahman* (Wordless Brahman), the lower Brahman of activity and mental operation, from higher Brahman, a silent, wordless Absolute beyond thought. Tantric thought, recognizing the same distinction, also characteristically adds a fourth level of speech, the *para*, or transcendental level. We see that the language speculations upon which Patañjali could draw spoke of three levels of sound or word (quintessentially represented by three levels of OṂ) and beyond material vibration, an ultimate level of conscious silence.

Patañjali shows special interest in language in the YS (1.27, 1.42, 3.17), particularly in relation to the ordinary cognitive process that mixes the word-sound, the associated mental concept, and the actual referent. Though this mix may be advantageous for normal language communication, YS 3.17 promises that by applying coherent awareness (*samādhī*) to the discrimination of these levels, the "knowledge of the sounds of all beings" might be gained. Indeed, discrimination of mixed levels is the essential tool for yogic liberation. Although neither Patañjali nor his primary commentator, Vyāsa, specifically mention the three or four levels of speech, the levels of mind and meditation as well as the corresponding levels of matter he delineates seem to correspond.

In Sāṃkhya, to have saving knowledge is to know the structure and composition of life in its twenty-five constituents, especially its duality of consciousness and matter. Yoga philosophy is the form or wing of Sāṃkhya that details practical methods to achieve this nonordinary salvific knowledge. The process of yoga (i.e., meditation) is simply to provide firsthand experience of this Sāṃkhya structure of life, for all its components are available within the meditator. The yogin systematically, gradually, experiences the full range of matter in the form of his own body and mind. As YS 1.40 announces: His mastery ranges from the most minute to the greatest magnitude.[61]

Following the Sāṃkhya scheme, Patañjali lays out the levels of matter from grossest to most subtle (YS 2.19).[62] They present the Sāṃkhya structure (the divisions of the *guṇa*s) from the perspective of a meditator's progressive "deconstruction" of his own mental world—perception of increasingly subtle, increasingly stripped down levels of being:

1. DISCERNED (*viśeṣa*) composed of:
   5 gross elements (*mahābhutas*)
   5 sense capacities (*buddhīndriyas*)
   5 action capacities (*karmendriyas*)
   1 mind (*manas*)
2. UNDISCERNED (*aviśeṣa*) composed of:
   5 subtle elements (*tanmātras*)
   1 ego or "amness" (*ahaṃkāra, asmitā*)
3. BARELY MANIFEST (*liṅgamātra*), that is,
   the intellect (*buddhi*), the first manifestation
4. UNMANIFEST (*aliṅga*), that is,
   prakṛti with three *guṇas* in equilibrium, *unmanifest matter.*

Parallel to these divisions of the basic building blocks of matter and personality, Patañjali lays out levels of meditative process (*samprajñāta samādhi, samāpatti*) (1.17, 1.42). The levels are progressive levels of discrimination that result from increasing focus (coherence) of mind. They are:

1. ORDINARY THOUGHT ABSORPTION (*savitarka samāpatti*)
   This absorption discriminates least—with respect to language it still fails to properly distinguish among word (*śabda*), i.e., the articulated sound); concept (*jñāna*), i.e., the idea known; and *object* (*artha*), the referent
2. SUBTLE THOUGHT ABSORPTION (*savicāra samāpatti*)
   This level transcends language and concepts—here the object of meditation "appearing in the mind as the object alone (*svarūpamātra*)" seems to correspond to the level of the *tanmātra*s, the object directly perceived in terms of its component subtle elements. This is beyond discursive thought or language. One sees the subtle object without mental conversation or thinking about it. The mirror of the mind simply takes the form of the subtle object, without label or comment.
3. BLISS ABSORPTION (*sānanda*[63] *samāpatti*)
   This level seems to correspond to the purest portion of the ego faculty (*asmitā, ahaṃkāra*),[64] the sheer sense of identity that underlies all personal experience.
4. AMNESS ABSORPTION (*sāsmita samāpatti*)
   This level seems to correspond to the *buddhi*, the intellectual faculty. As *buddhi* is the first evolute (*liṅgamātra*) of *prakṛti* (*aliṅga*), it represents the most subtle possible object of the yogin's coherent awareness, bringing him to the farthest extreme of perception of the manifest world.[65]

Perception bereft of ordinary thinking (*nirvicāra*—2–4), conducted at the most delicate and brilliant level of awareness (*buddhi*), is understood to directly reveal truth (*ṛta*, 1.48). The range of matter, however, ends in the unmanifest, imperceptible *prakṛti*.[66] The yogin must transcend all vestiges of *prakṛti* for that which is beyond her and conscious-in-itself, *puruṣa*. The ultimate level of meditation is then without *seed* (*nirbīja*) of any kind and beyond any phenomenal perception (*asamprajñāta*)—it corresponds to the total cessation of the operations of awareness (as *manas*, *ahaṁkāra*, or *buddhi*) and leaves the yogin isolated as impersonal *puruṣa*, consciousness itself.

The yogin's ideal, archetypal vehicle in this meditative journey is the vehicle of *vāk*, speech, which arises mysteriously, spontaneously from deep within him, naturally responds to his will, and corresponds in its levels to the full range of creation. The essence of speech and the mantric vehicle par excellence, as we have seen, is the all-inclusive syllable OṂ.[67]

The method is well known in the Indian tradition: meditative repetition (*japa*). From earliest times the Vedic tradition has accessed holy power and salvation primarily through the recitation of sacred texts (*svādhyāya*). Oral recitation of the Vedic hymns, later internalized in Upaniṣadic meditation, reaches its simplest and most practical form in *OṂ-japa* of the YS. Just as Patañjali strips human personality to its bare core, pure consciousness, he seems to strip down the complicated external paraphernalia of sacrificial rituals and sectarian devotional worship (such as the religious praises of the thousand names of God) to the simple and profound repetition of OṂ.

OṂ, as we have seen, carries the whole Indian tradition on its back, as well as certain associated presuppositions about the interrelated nature of language, reality (*nāma-rūpa*), and human awareness. This understanding of OṂ, admittedly cultural and linguistic, does not stop there; it is presented, as we have indicated, in order to transcend itself. As the proverb goes, it takes a thorn to remove a thorn. How exactly might this work in yogic practice?

The Process of Meditation

The mechanism is relatively simple. Mental repetition of a special "mind-tool" (*mantra*) like OṂ is traditionally taught only in private initiation, where the sacred *mantra* is whispered into the initiate's ear. This already takes the sound in the correct direction—from the external speech to the internal thought. Continued repetition of this single item in face of the diversity of ordinary thought presents the mind with a unique mode of functioning. Such practice of a single principle (OṂ, OṂ, OṂ, OṂ, OṂ, and so on)[68] must give the mind an extraordinary experience of continuity and unity. That in itself is not enough: the skill in repetition demands a counterpart in dispassion as the operations of awareness come to quiescence only "by practice and detachment" (*abhyāsa-vairāgyabhyam*, 1.12). Dispassionate repetition of the *mantra* implies a certain attitude of relaxation and letting go: this mastery cannot be the fanatical intensity with which the West generally caricatures the yogin, for there is not to be any "thirst for objects perceived or those revealed in scripture" (*dṛṣṭānuśravika-viṣaya-vitṛṣṇa* 1.15) or, eventually, for anything of the *guṇa*s (1.16). Such relaxed, unattached, repetition must become steady (1.13). It gains this necessary steadiness and becomes "firmly established when practiced assiduously in the proper way without interruption over a long period of time" (1.14).

Continued practice is particularly necessary in the light of the theory of afflictive impressions (*kleśas*, 2.2–2.17), which holds that the various operations of the awareness, any and all activities of the mind, leave traces. The human mind is simply riddled with such traces or impressions, which together make up our conscious and subconscious memory and which rise and fall from dormancy to activity according to stimulus, context, and association. The collection of such impressions (*saṃskāra*s) make up one's character, personality, and fate: They determine our reactions to events (attachment or aversion) and thus maintain our ignorance, our misidentification of pure consciousness with the mind/body complex (2.13–2.14). Our fate is one of inevitable and continuous frustration (*duḥkha*) (2.15–2.16) unless we can weaken, overpower, and eliminate these impressions from ordinary experience.

Ordinary experience involves an ordinary and relatively scattered pattern of attention that perpetuates itself. The yogin's detached practice of a single *mantra* is just the medicine the mind requires. Mantras themselves are called *pavitrāṇī*, or purifiers. They are understood to have special power (*adṛṣta*) to cleanse impurities from the mind.[69] Even more important, their method of use, as Patañjali describes, makes them ideal objects for creating a new, dominant kind of mental impression that is not only pure (harmonious, soothing, nonobstructing) but also exponentially more influential.[70] This power is due to the relaxed but increasingly focused awareness with which they are entertained. The more coherent the mental function, the more powerful the result.

Ordinary mental process is seen as relatively incoherent—subject to constant distraction, vacillation, and weakness—and incapable of sustained function as a unified, coordinated whole. (Observing your flow of thoughts as you continue to read this might confirm the point.) The yogin's practice of a single syllable creates a one-pointed state of awareness, a state of coherence (termed *samādhi*, literally, "synthesized," "placed or put together"). Coherent impressions accumulate as the yogin practices until the underlying process[71] of the *guṇas* (which compose his mind) is a steady flow of coherent silence (*nirodha*)—the total cessation of ordinary mental operations (3.9–3.15).

This practice of *īśvara-praṇidhāna*, as we noted earlier, is perhaps the chief example of the means to *asamprajñāta samādhi*. This process may sound very technical and exotic. In effect, it means that Patañjali's practice of *īśvara-praṇidhāna*, given enough time, strips ordinary mental activity and ordinary personality to the bone. The practice is analyzed into stages, as we have seen.

1. First, the beginning repetition of OṂ mixed in the yogin's mind with idea (some conception of the personal God, Īśvara) and referent (in my contention, *puruṣa*) is entertained. This is the so-called *ordinary thought absorption* level. This preliminary level of *japa* is sometimes even begun with voiced chanting—(*vaikhari* level)—and slowly diminished to purely mental (*madhyamā*) repetition. It is only at this gross and beginning level that OṂ can be associated with an ordinary word meaning such as *īśvara*. Who or what OṂ refers to as the designator of Īśvara will become apparent in *pure experience* as the meditative process deepens. In any case, we must recall that even this coherence on the level of ordinary thinking must be detached from the personal or dogmatic Lord, since He is an object "revealed [by scripture]" (*ānuśravika-viṣaya*, 1.15). Thus, the concept of *īśvara-praṇidhāna* as a kind of intensification of emotional attachment to the anthropomorphic Lord as the sum of religious imaging and conceptualization seems to be ruled out. In fact, in Patañjali's formulation it would restrict one from further progress in experiencing more subtle, more significant levels of apprehension.

2. As the mind settles with the detached repetition of the OṂ, the more laborious and more energy-consuming association chains of scattered thoughts, definitions,

impressions, and memories drop away. Eventually, as the coherent impressions grow stronger, a new level of coherent absorption arises that is completely free of ordinary mixed thinking and presents the object of awareness without verbal association, judgments, or reasoning. In this *nirvitarka* level the object alone, the sound OṂ in this case, appears in its *svarupa*, its innate essence, as the subtle element of sound (*śabda-tanmatra*). There is no sense that someone is seeing something through the process of perception, only complete identification of awareness with the subtle elemental level. This is subtle thought absorption, the second level of coherent mental functioning. As detached repetition of this level of OṂ continues, awareness eventually slips to an even more subtle and more simple level.

3. The third level involves the dropping away of even the subtle sound element itself—without losing awareness. This leaves the yogin absorbed in the bliss (*ānanda*) of the substrate of subtle experience, the *asmitā* or *ahaṃkāra* level of awareness. Here the previous blending of intellect, egoity, and OṂ-sound, now stripped of the subtle sound, leaves only intellect (*buddhi*) absorbed in its own *amness* (*asmitā*) as the object or content of meditation. This level is very rarified, of course. It would seem to correspond to the extreme limit, the very "bottom" of what Bartṛhari termed the *madhyamā* level of *vāk*.

Identification with the bliss of the *ahaṃkāra* loosens with detachment. The bliss is relinquished for the even more tranquil absorption in the intellect (*buddhi*) alone. In Sāṃkhya-Yoga the faculty of intellect is the most transparent, most pure, and most radiantly desirable material faculty. It is the first manifestation of matter, the most delicate and primal. Here all knowledge is available—the yogin is absorbed in the faculty of knowing in its unhindered clarity and perfection. Impressions on this level are said to be truthful and to block all other impressions (1.48–150.) In a real sense this, too, is a level of OṂ; it is the subtlest level where speech emerges from the unmanifest, or, in Bartṛhari's terms, the "Seeing One," *paśyantī*.[72] This may correspond symbolically to the abstract but completely unified resonant nasalization (*nāda*) of OṂ. From the viewpoint of Sāṃkhya-Yoga, however, even this most subtle and luminous level is relative, conditioned, and material. This is not yet the ultimate nature of the yogin; this is actually understood as the root of all ignorance. Intellect (sometimes also called *mahat*, "great one"), the most transparent and perfect level of awareness, is matter that, due to its transparent purity, mistakenly identifies itself with consciousness itself, an act that creates personal suffering and the need for impersonal salvation.

4. With supreme detachment, this most subtle object or seed of awareness, the *nāda* of OṂ, reduced to a brilliant point (*bindu*), drops as well, leaving the yogin, bereft of operational intellect, at the goal.[73] Speech has returned to its source in conscious silence (*para*). The levels of the mind have been progressively stripped away, merging each effect into its cause, until the awareness (*citta*) itself is dissolved into the unmanifest *prakṛti*. The final act of renunciation (*paravairāgya*, 1.16, 3.50) leaves the mind dissolved in its unmanifest state, while at the same time isolating the inner-

most core, the knower, of human personality, *puruṣa*, consciousness itself. This is the *para* level of speech, the ultimate referent of OṂ, the conscious silence to which it points. This totally silent, totally inactive witness to all levels of *buddhi* is now isolated in its own unthinkable but conscious luminosity. The layers of human personality have been peeled away by following a reducing sound beyond its material source to conscious silence, *quiescent* and seedless *samādhi*, called *kaivalya* (3.55, 4.34).

Conclusion

What is clear from our detailed example of yogic meditation on the sound OṂ is that Patañjali's mysticism intentionally goes beyond intentionality and language by using language to transcend itself. In so doing the yogin not only reduces language from *word* to *sound* to *conscious silence* but also eliminates any possible cultural or conceptual building blocks. The yogic meditator transcends not only concepts and thought itself (even the concepts of his own Sāṃkhya system) but also the very innate intentional structures of the mind. In the final analysis, the yogin gains everything (salvation) by losing every *thing*, deconstructing oneself as a *person* in favor of the nonlinguistic experience of *puruṣa*, an "impersonhood" beyond any possibility of suffering, beyond any possibility of conception or construction. All the meditator's doing is undone: in the conscious silence apart from all objects of thought or perception, the meditator finds his or her innate nature to be simply consciousness itself. This innate capacity to be conscious, this *puruṣa*, is familiar in a sense, as it has been the background and precondition for all previous material experiences; yet it is novel, too, as it has never previously been discriminated from the various constructed levels of experience it has enabled.

However this event may be described later—in poetry or prose, in Sanskrit or English, theistically or atheistically—the experience per se is not that of a yogin, or a Hindu, or a South Asian.[74] The experience belongs to no conceptual identity—no religious, ethnic, linguistic, cultural, or conceptual image. All such things are *objects* of consciousness. The experience of isolation belongs to the capacity to be conscious, pure consciousness, alone.

The conclusion for the study of mysticism is that Sāṃkhya-Yoga philosophy enshrines in *kaivalya* a nonordinary experience that transcends not only Sāṃkhya-Yoga philosophy as a conceptual or cultural scheme but any possible conceptual, linguistic, or cultural structure. The assertion that all mystical experience is necessarily constructed seems incompatible with the evidence. Are the creative activities of the mind, with its cultural shaping, training, and basic presuppositions, responsible for all mystical experiences as the constructivists assert, or is something else responsible? In the case of Sāṃkhya-Yoga, it is the inherent structure of reality that is responsible for mystical experiences. The ultimate mystical experience in Sāṃkhya-Yoga results from the final elimination of all concepts, all thinking, all words, all feeling, all memory, and all perception. What is left, properly termed *innate*, is consciousness. It is not self-conscious and not symbolically conscious—just consciousness itself. While its description, analysis, elevation, and method of attainment are constructed, material processes, the experience of *kaivalya* is something else, something simple, which even in a constructed world puts the mystery back into mysticism.

Notes

Translations are those of the author except where otherwise noted.

1. *Bṛhad Āryaṇyaka Upaniṣad* 4. 3. 6, Hume, tr. p. 133.

2. W. James (1958), *The Varieties of Religious Experience: A Study in Human Nature.* Gifford Lectures on Natural Religion 1901–1902 (New York: New American Library of World Literature), p. 295. James reveals that this revelation was in a letter from Tennyson to B. P. Blood, who further recalled that Tennyson said of this experience: "By God Almighty! there is no delusion in the matter! It is no nebulous ecstasy, but a state of transcendent wonder, associated with absolute clarity of mind."

3. S. T. Katz (1978), *Mysticism and Philosophical Analysis* (New York: Oxford University Press).

4. See, for example, S. T. Katz (1978) and (1983), *Mysticism and Religious Traditions* (New York: Oxford University Press), with special regard to Katz's own essays. See also Wayne Proudfoot (1984), *Religious Experience* (Berkeley: University of California Press), and W. Wainwright (1981), *Mysticism: A Study of Its Nature, Cognitive Value and Moral Implications* (Madison: University of Wisconsin Press).

5. A PCE is an event in which experience is reduced to its pure subjective component, consciousness itself, without content, intention or any kind of object. Its nature is discussed from many viewpoints in R. K. C. Forman (1990) *The Problem of Pure Consciousness* (New York: Oxford University Press), and in this essay.

6. By *orthodox* I mean *āstika*—the Hindu systems that accept in their own way the authority of the Vedic revelation. This excludes Buddhism and Jainism, even though such *nāstika* systems have much in common with many Sāṃkhya-Yoga-positions.

7. The SK is understood to be roughly contemporaneous with its philosophical sister, the *Yogasūtra* of Patañjali (ca. 400–500 CE). Dates are very approximate, but these are the most recent estimations. The SK represents the chief known text of Sāṃkhya, which is likely to have been influential on the final formulation of the YS and its main commentaries. See J. G. Larson and R. S. Bhattacharya (1987), *Sāṃkhya: A Dualist Tradition in Indian Philosophy*, Encyclopedia of Indian Philosophies, vol. 4 (Princeton: Princeton University Press), p. 15.

8. By *suffering and frustration* I am attempting to render the Sanskrit term *duḥkha*, (SK 1), which implies that there is an inevitable and unsatisfactory flaw in ordinary experience—the escape from this ill is the main thrust of South Asian philosophy and religion.

9. Major differences between SK and YS are that the YS includes a concept of God, *īśvara*, whose *mantra*, OṂ, is a chief, even perhaps *the* exemplary medium of meditation (*japa*); a unitary term, *citta*, for the relative, object-related, awareness divided in Sāṃkhya into the threefold inner instrument of *buddhi* (intellect), *ahaṃkāra* (ego), and *manas*; composition in *sūtra*s (dense aphorisms) rather than verses (*kārikās*) as in the SK; and, as noted earlier, an emphasis on practice—the SK as a text seems to be bereft of specific guidelines for any spiritual practice or meditation. The YS supplies these.

10. The analysis is epistemologically grounded on three sources of reliable knowledge: direct perception (including what we might call supernormal perception), logical inference, and authoritative scripture (testimony). (These *pramaṇas*, or sources of reliable knowledge,

are the same in both systems, though different terms are used: in SK 4 *dṛṣṭam anumānam aptavācanam ca*; in YS 1.7 *pratyakṣa-anumāna-āgamāḥ.*) The worldview is essentially logical and empirical, since even scriptural evidence is understood to represent the record of the direct perceptions of great seers.

11. Sāṃkhyan analysis begins with objective material elements which we would tend to see as inner and subjective—the first manifest principle of creation is not the atom, or electron, or photon, but the intellectual capacity (*buddhi, mahat*); from that evolves the ego faculty, thence the mind and senses, and so on.

12. Our physics today clearly recognizes and discriminates many "layers" of reality, from the gross material objects to their less obvious and subtler components, such as chemical compounds, molecules, atoms, subatomic particles, and quantum ground states. The importance of ordinarily invisible components of matter is fundamental, even down to "unmanifest" *virtual* particles, whose fluctuations exert measurable influence on real matter.

13. *Yogi-pratyakṣa*, the direct but supernormally acute perception of the trained meditator.

14. SK 22–41.

15. I use the term "nonconscious" as a gloss for Sanskrit *acetana*, as in SK 11.

16. J. G. Larson (1979), *Classical Sāṃkhya: An Interpretation of Its History and Meaning* (Santa Barbara: Rose/Erikson), translation of SK 59, p. 273:

rangasya darśayitvā nivartate
nartakī yathā nṛtyāt,
puruṣasya tathā'tmanam
prakāśya vinivartate prakrtih

As a dancer ceases from the dance after having been seen by the audience; so also *prakṛti* ceases after having manifested herself to *puruṣa.*

The whole purpose of the evolution and activity of material processes is to be observed by another—the consciousness function. When the material intellect discriminates the fact that it is in itself unconscious matter and that its activity is for "something" immaterial quite beyond itself, something conscious, it dissolves—mission accomplished. This observation, again, is not the deliberative or analytical observation of a critic—critical faculties ore material processes in Sāṃkhya. The observation alluded to is one of pure unjudgmental, uncritical awareness. This is difficult because it is so at variance with the usual way we conceptualize the process of experience.

17. Larson, and Bhattacharya, *Sāṃkhya*, pp. 77–78, SK 3 text:

(I) *mūlaprakṛtir avikṛtir*
(II) *mahadādyāḥ prakṛtivikṛtayaḥ sapta*
(III) *ṣodaśakas tu vikāro*
(IV) *na prakrtir na vikritih purusah.*

The seven referred to are intellect, ego, and the five subtle elements; the sixteen are the ten *indriyas* plus the mind and the five gross elements.

18. The term *atriguṇa*, translated by Larson and Bhattacharya, *Sāṃkhya*, as "without tripartite process," refers to *puruṣa* being entirely different and separate from the three "strands" (*guṇas*) or components of *prakṛti.*

19. Ibid, p. 78.

20. I.e., *SK antaḥkaraṇa,* YS *citta.*

21. The actual term most used is "association," *saṃyoga.* To make the association is to be confused, ignorant of the essential independence and separation of the two wholly other elements.

22. Such mental activities in Sāṃkhya are technically called *antaḥkaraṇa-vṛtti*—i.e., the operations of the threefold "inner instrument," intellect (*buddhi*), ego (*ahaṃkāra*), and mind (*manas*). (In the YS these operations of awareness are simply called *citta-vṛtti.*)

23. Larson and Bhattacharya, *Sāṃkhya*, p. 77.

24. Recall that, as stated earlier, the term *guṇas* refers to the three "strands" of the rope of matter, *prakṛti*—the three functional modes or characteristics of material that explain its evolutionary combinations in the twenty-three principles that make up the world. In general when "the three *guṇas*" appears, you can substitute *prakṛti.*

25. My own translation.

26. The same point is echoed in YS 4.19:

> 4.19 *na tat svābhāsam dṛśyatvāt.*
> 4.19 It is not self-luminous because it is something perceived.

27. Larson and Bhattacharya, *Sāṃkhya*, pp. 79–80. By "tripartite process" Larson refers again to the three *guṇa*s and their interaction. Brahmā is the Hindu creator god himself, in Sāṃkhya, also a material creation of *prakṛti*, illumined by *puruṣa.*

Puruṣa fits into this system as an agent of meaning, a motivation for the "dance of matter" since the very functioning of the material universe is to rectify, as it were, an epistomological mistake that results in conscious awareness of suffering (SK 1). SK 20 clarifies the situation: because of the association (*saṃyogād*) of pure consciousness with the material operations that make up the awareness, a tragic error occurs—the unconscious mental processes appear to be conscious, and the inactive pure consciousness appears to be active. In reality, they are both eternally separate. Liberation, the goal of Sāṃkhya, the goal of the incessantly active combinations and interactions of the *guṇas*, is thus not an ontological problem but a problem of epistemological clarity. To save conscious beings from conscious suffering, the intellect must be brought to the realization of its true status, blind mechanical process reliant on another, *puruṣa*, for its consciousness, and on its lack of discrimination between itself and *puruṣa* for it sense of separate selfhood (*ahaṃkāra*) (SK 24). Conceptual error in the form of the ego principle (*ahaṃkāra*) generates the forms and functioning of creation. When the error is exposed, the forms and functioning vanish (SK 61). The intellect finally discriminates the truth: *nā'smi na me nā'ham*, "I am not [conscious], [consciousness] does not belong to me, the 'I' is not [conscious]" (SK 64) and the further surprising consequences (SK 62) "No one therefore, is bound; no one released, likewise no one transmigrates. (Only) *prakṛti* in its various forms transmigrates, is bound and is released." Thus, it may seem that *puruṣa* is bound and liberated, but it is actually *only a mistake of the intellect* that such a thing happens—the action, the drama of liberation is all on the side of the intellect, but the spectacle is only seen by the passive witness *puruṣa.*

28. To wit, *duḥkham eva sarvam.*

29. The wealth of synonyms may indicate that the YS editor was working to harmonize and unify several different Sāṃkhya-Yoga traditions. See note 31 below for a list of different synonyms.

30. Ilumination, activity, and inertia are English translations of the three "strands," *sattva*, *rajas*, and *tamas*, respectively, the *guṇas* of *prakṛti.*

31. In the YS we see that *puruṣa* and *prakṛti* play the same familiar roles—the chief obvious difference is in terminology: *puruṣa* is represented by a wide range of synonyms in the YS: *draṣṭṛ* 'seer' (1.3; 2.17, 20; 4.23); *dṛg-śakti* 'capacity of seeing' (2.6); *dṛśi* 'seeing' (2.20, 25); *citi* 'consciousness' (4.22, 24); *svāmin* owner, master, lord (2.23), and *prabhu* 'master, king, lord' (4.18).

32. Ego or ego structure is not to be taken as an equation with the Freudian *ich* or 'ego'. It is what I would call the sense of separate identity, the material substance that results from

and represents the mistaken identification of the material intellect with immaterial pure consciousness. Take the term in its more general English sense, not in any technical psychoanalytic way.

Although the relationship between Freudian psychoanalysis and other similar Western approaches and Sāṃkhya-Yoga philosophy is potentially rich and illuminating, it deserves a detailed examination on its own.

33. This may sound impossible. Yet Sāṃkhya would agree with our ordinary experience—the *intellect* does seem to be conscious. The truth, however, is that it merely seems to be conscious—upon examination the intellect can actually sort out the difference between itself and the Other whose consciousness it "borrows." The final stage of intellect, its sharpest and clearest level is this distinction between itself and consciousness. Having made that distinction, it is free to dissolve into its source, unmanifest *prakṛti*, mission accomplished.

34. *Prakṛti's* evolution is technically called *pariṇāma.*

35. Involution (*pratiprasava*) refers to the opposite process of dissolving into unmanifest root-materiality when the material evolution has reached its goal, the knowledge of the difference between intellect and consciousness.

36. The dynamic equalibrium (*pralāya*) is the "original" state of *prakṛti* when the three strands (*guṇas*) balance each other—in this state matter is unmanifest. The universe is understood to rest in such a state between cyclic creations.

37. Western philosophers who have taken an interest in consciousness, such as William James or David Hume, have actually asserted that no such thing exists. See W. James ([1904], 1976, "Does Consciousness Exist?" in *The Writings of William James*, ed. J. J. McDermott (New York: Random House), p. 190, and D. Hume (1898), *A Treatise on Human Nature*, ed. T. H. Green and T. H. Gross (London: Longmans Green), p. 533.

38. The metaphor of light is inescapable. Light needs no external second light to illuminate it, it is self-luminous. Thus, light is the central metaphor, either with reference to visual perception with terms like "seer" or "seeing"—2.20 The seer is simply the seeing, [which] although pure sees the object. (*draṣṭā dṛśimātraḥ śuddho'pi pratyayānupaśyaḥ.*)—or by reference to its radiant or "self-luminous" (*svabhāsa*) property as opposed to that of *prakṛti* (see 4.19 in note 12 above).

39. It is an interesting paradox. Matter, though eternally in motion, is essentially dead; consciousness, though eternally unchanging, is life itself, eternal life—not eternal life for someone, but the elimination of the phenomenal person, in favor of the impersonal core of life as consciousness.

40. SK 19 describes *puruṣa* with the term *sākṣitva*, the state of being a witness (*sākṣin*).

41. Perhaps, if the point still seems obscure, a more mechanical analogy might help. The toothache phenomenon is no more the suffering of a conscious entity than is the needle of a taxi's temperature gauge, moving into the red. Neither the needle, the gauge, nor the radiator knows anything; nor do they suffer. Cars don't feel pain: they are not conscious. The consciousness "belongs to" another who is radically different and separate. The passenger in the car may notice the gauge, but he also does not *feel* the *car's* pain. The car is not a conscious being; it has a gauge and a radiator, but no pain, because no consciousness. If this taxi/car analogy seems far-fetched or excessively modern, the Vedic fondness for chariots should be remembered. *Kaṭha Upaniṣad* 3.3 ff, *Svetāśvatara Upaniṣad* 2.9, *Maitri Upaniṣad* 1.3; 2.6, 4.22 all explain *puruṣa* or *ātman* with reference to a similar analogy of the chariot (sans radiator); today's natural parallel is the automobile.

42. Whether this is true or not need not concern us here. It is enough that in Sāṃkhya this understanding was understood to be rationally established, and I believe, more significant, that (from the viewpoint of Yoga) this doctrine was understood to be empirically, experimentally verifiable. Because yogins trained in the requisite discipline and technical practices

in fact had experiences described as *asamprajñāta samādhi, citta-vṛtti-nirodha, puruṣa,* and *kaivalya,* the YS came about to make the experiences systematically intelligible.

43. It is interesting in this regard that the Sāṃkhya-Yoga term for pure consciousness, *puruṣa,* literally means "person." It relates to the ancient Vedic figure of Puruṣa, in RV 10.90 a primordial giant "Person" whose body is sacrificially dismembered to create the world and the human social structure. Puruṣa is also understood to be connected with Agni, the Vedic god of illumination and fire. For a history of the term see L. Pflueger (1990), *God, Consciousness, and Meditation: The Concept of Īśvara in the Yogasūtra* (Ann Arbor, Mich.: University Microfilms), pp. 13ff., 195ff. For interpretation and translation of the Vedic myth see W. N. Brown (1931), "The Sources and Nature of Puruṣa in the Puruṣa-Sūtka," *Journal of the American Oriental Society* 51:108–118.

Even though the term *puruṣa* starts out meaning a cosmic Person, dismembered into the components of the world and society we know, we should be clear that such personhood is not, even then, entirely personal. In fact, both the anthropomorphic gods and the cosmic *puruṣa* are seen from the earliest texts as ambiguous with respect to their personhood. They are often impersonal symbols, with little in the way of the distinctive personalities or character displayed by their Greek Olympian cousins. The term *puruṣa* in Sāṃkhya-Yoga is a technical usage. By using the term "person" for the philosophical and experiential principle of pure consciousness, the schools emphasize the truly impersonal core of ordinary personhood.

44. A sense of humor, as a human faculty, might be defined as a sense of perspective vis-à-vis the many sharply contrasting oppositions of phenomenal life. All the serious philosophizing in yoga literature might lead one to believe that virtuosos of meditative practice, *yogins,* are a very sour and serious lot. This is far from the case, at least in my experience in meeting such people. Lack of identification with the ego seems to liberate much laughter and a bright sense of humor.

45. The term *karman* or karma (literally "action") refers to the material consequences of action according to the "law of *karman,*" the moral law of cause and effect. Every intentional action entails a morally appropriate consequence—one reaps what one sows, either immediately in this life or in future lives. The *guṇas* are in no particular hurry to deliver one's just deserts. *Karman* operates mechanically as natural law.

46. I.e., *dṛg-śakti,* YS 2.6, *svāmi-śakti, YS2.23*; *citi-śakti,* YS 4.34.

47. I.e., *sva-śakti,* YS 2.23.

48. I.e., *darśana-śakti,* YS 2.6.

49. The chief commentator on the YS, Vyāsa, comments on YS 1.1:

> *Yoga* means *samādhi* 'coherence' [of awareness]; and this coherence is a feature of all levels of awareness:
> 1. *ksipta* 'restless'
> 2. *mudha* 'dull'
> 3. *viksipta* 'distracted'
> 4. *ekagra* 'focused' (lit. "one-pointed")
> 5. *niruddha* 'extinguished'
>
> Of these, in the *distracted* level of awareness, the coherence is subject to distraction and thus is not properly classified as yoga. [The same must undoubtedly be said for the restless and dull levels.]

The question arises as to why coherence is explicitly said to be a feature of all five levels of awareness, when the first three levels are essentially excluded in this statement and its logical extension. Vācaspati gives persuasive reasons as to why the first three levels are not to be considered yoga but never clears up why they were included in the sweeping statement in the first place. Their inclusion may be more significant than their exclusion.

What do these states have in common? Nothing but awareness itself. The implication is that *coherence* (*samādhi*), a coherent, extremely orderly form of awareness, is nothing less than inherent in ordinary levels of restless, dull, and distracted awareness. Perhaps it is the essential form (*svarūpa*) of awareness, underlying the disorderly forms, and clearly apparent only when they are allowed to "quiet down" into a focused or quiescent state. When awareness of any kind is present, coherence is an inherent potential. That is to say, when there is any kind of perception or cognition, there must be some orderliness, even if minimal. This order is the inherent coherence. Even in a "blooming, buzzing confusion," there is a sort of order. There is a structure of perception, there are differentiations, even if incomplete.

Perhaps the analogy of a television screen might help the modern reader relate to this concept. Sheer static would not involve any of these five levels. A flickering, fuzzy, or constantly interrupted transmission might correspond to the first three levels, respectively, while a stable, clear, focused transmission appearing on the screen would correspond to the highest potential for television reception—coherent perception—a precise representation of the object televised. The last state of extinction would correspond to a bright, clear screen without an image. Here the screen is perfectly coherent; yet there is no image, just the essential underlying nature of the screen itself. No image is projected or perceived; yet the set is on: there is coherence, purity, not the utter chaos of static or the "nonexistence" of a dark screen when the set is off. All five states, then, have an underlying coherence that is either obscured to some degree or clearly evident. For knowledge of the screen or knowledge of the programming, only states four or five really apply.

Seen from this angle, the teaching of yoga has a basis in the structure of ordinary awareness, and ordinary humans might thus hope (with proper training and practice) to attain it, just as anyone with a television set might hope to obtain a clear, focused picture. Even so, by comparison with ordinary awareness, coherent awareness (*samādhi* of either kind) is nonordinary. Perceptive coherence is a state of awareness (*citta*); quiescent coherence is not even a state—it is pure consciousness isolated from the material awareness and all its states. It is beyond states and thereby salvific. Our true identity, pure consciousness, is beyond all states.

50. The term *praṇidhāna* itself has many meanings. It derives from verb √*dhā* (place, put) + *pra* (before, in front of) + *ni* (down) (Pāṇini 8.4.17). The simple sense seems to be *to place down and/or in front of*. From this a variety of uses are noted by Monier-Williams, including: deposit, place in, bring in, set (a gem) in, apply, touch, turn or direct eyes or thoughts upon, with mind (*manas*)—to give whole attention to, reflect, consider. See M. Monnier-Williams ([1899], 1979), *A Sanskrit-English Dictionary*, new ed. (Delhi: Motilal Banarsidass).

Buddhists use *praṇidhāna* in the classical period to refer to the "vow, or aspiration" of a new Bodhisattva, subsequent to his accepting the *thought of enlightenment* (*bodhi-citta*), strengthening his resolve to attain enlightenment and free all creatures. . . . See H. Dayal ([1932], 1978), *The Bodhisattva Doctrine in Buddhist Sanskrit Literature* (Delhi: Motilal Banarsidass).

For example, the *Lalita Vistara*, the famous biography of the Buddha, states Siddhartha's early *praṇidhāna* in this way: "I will attain the immortal, undecaying, pain-free bodhi, and free the world from all pain." 161.19; 163.16; 175.13; 361.3, etc. The vow becomes more elaborate in some texts, such as the *Sukhāvatī-vyūha*, and in the *Daśa-bhūmika-sūtra,* where it is tenfold.

This resolve might be seen as a kind of devotion, less to the Buddha as Lord than to becoming liberated and liberating, a devotion to duty. This Buddhist usage is closer to the sense in the YS than to that of sectarian Hindu *bhakti*. In the midst of Buddhist *bhakti*, meditation and impersonal liberation are still in the foreground.

Perhaps L. Freer's explanation of the Buddhist usage comes closest also to the sense of the term in the YS: *Praṇidhana signifie "disposition particuliere d'esprit, application del l'esprit a un objet determine. . . ."* H. Dayal (1978), *The Bodhisattva*, p. 64. Dayal quotes Freer in the *Journal Asiatique*, Paris (1881), p. 476. This puts *praṇidhāna* clearly parallel to the old sense of *yoga* and meditation as a harnessing or disciplining of the spirit for a particular task, especially the task of liberation. Indeed, the meditative sense of *praṇidhāna* is the strongest possibility.Kālidāsa uses the term as "profound religious meditation" or in compounds as "abstract contemplation of" in *Raghuvaṃśa*; see M. Monier-Williams (1979), *A Sanskrit-English Dictionary*, new ed. (Delhi: Motilal Banarsidass), p. 660.

51. So far in the specialized vocabulary of the YS, the term *īśvara* has been equated to pure consciousness (1.23) in which there is transcendental knowledge (1.25), described as the timeless source (*guru*) of traditional wisdom (1.26). The only specific appellation of this Īśvara has not been by personal or individual name, Viṣṇu, or Śiva, but by the "significant sound" (*vācaka*) OṂ (the *praṇava*). If Patañjali had a specific personal deity in mind or an anthropomorphic image, it is not indicated in the YS. In fact, given the significant focus on Īśvara, it would seem that the YS is intentionally going out of the way *not* to personalize the Lord.

Elsewhere I have argued at length that Patañjali's view of Īśvara taken from the YS alone, in contrast with that of most of his commentators, seems to support the wholesale equation of Īśvara with pure consciousness, shorn of any personal attribute. Clearly, the concept of a personal Lord has no place in the strict dualism of the Sāṃkhya and Yoga. Everything said of Īśvara in the YS itself can be fruitfully applied as well to impersonal pure consciousness. I argue that Patañjali actually demythologizes the prevalent devotional understanding of a personal God in favor of pure meditative experience—a deep, universal, innate capacity of consciousness. For detailed arguments see L. Pflueger, *God, Consciousness, and Meditation*. This is soon to be published in revised form by SUNY Press as *The God Within: The Lord of Worship and the Lord of Meditation in Ancient India.*

52. Indeed, Indian medical texts such as *Caraka* and *Śuśruta* used the term *praṇidhāna* in the sense of applying a remedy for a disease, such as mantras for snakebite. See A. Padoux (1989), "Mantras—What Are They?" in *Understanding Mantras*, ed. H. P. Alper, SUNY Series in Religious Studies (Albany: State University of New York Press).

53. See YS 2.1, 32, 34.

54. *Japa* in conjunction with *svādhyāya* and *tapas* (purification practices) appears in the YS. J. W. Hauer (1958), *Der Yoga: Ein indischer Weg zum Selbst* Stuttgart: W. Kohlhammer Verlag), p. 22.

55. Hauer, *Der Yoga*, p. 25: *Das Summen dieser Silbe nannte man praṇava, "das Hervorbrummen oder Vorausbrummen"* (*als Einleitung zum Gesang*). *Bald bedeutete dieses Wort auch die gesummte Silbe selber.*

56. The PU, the MU, and the MAU are among the latest of the classical Upaniṣads connected with the Veda and are generally dated in the period of classical Sanskrit literature ca. 200 BCE to 200 CE. See J. N. Farquhar ([1920] 1967), *An Outline of the Religious Literature of India* (Delhi: Motilal Banarsidass), p. 79, and M. Winternitz (1960–62), *A History of Indian Literature*, trans. S. Ketkar (Calcutta: University of Calcutta) and include more theistic references. Their thinking is, of course, closest of all to the YS.

57.

1. The Brahman who is without beginning or end, whose very essence is the Word, who is the cause of the manifested phonemes [*akṣara*], who appears as the objects, from whom the creation of the world proceeds,
2. Who has been taught as the one appearing as many due to the multiplicity of his powers, who, though not different from his powers [*śaktis*], seems to be so,

3. Depending on whose Time-power [*kālaśakti*] to which (though one) differentiation is attributed, the six transformations, birth, etc., become the cause of all variety in Being.

From K.A.S. Iyer (1965), *The Vākyapadīya of Bhartṛhari with the Vṛtti, Chapter I, English Translation*, Building Centenary and Silver Jubilee Series, 26 (Poona: Deccan College).

58. Iyer, *The Vākyapadīya* (1965), p. 14. The text, in K. A. S. Iyer (1966), *The Vākyapadiya of Bhartṛhari with the Vṛtti and the Paddhati of Vṛsabhadeva*. Deccan College Monograph Series, 32. Poona: Deccan College, p. 36, reads: *satyā viśuddhistatroktā vidyaivaikapadāgamā/ yuktā praṇavarupeṇa sarvavādāvirodhinā //*

59. Iyer, *The Vākyapadīya* (1965), p. 14.

60. Ibid., p. 125.

61. *Paramānu-parama-mahatvānto 'sya vaśīkāraḥ.*

62. Seen as the dispositions of the *guṇas*.

63. This level is not explicitly named as such but can be posited from the terse listing in 1.17: *vitarka-vicārānandasmitānugamāt samprajñātaḥ.*

64. The third and fourth levels here are difficult since Patañjali has not defined them in the YS. The commentaries offer little help since they conflict with each other. The structural demands make Bhojarāja's commentary the most reasonable to me, identifying *ānanda* (3) with the experience of *ahaṃkāra*, and *asmitā* (4) with the experience of *buddhi*. Even so, since the yogic word for *ahaṃkāra* is *asmitā*, thus the *asmitā* level of *samāpatti* is a very reasonable correlate with *asmitā* itself.

If we associate sattvic *ahaṃkāra* as the very substrate of the bliss of the senses (tamasic *ahaṃkara* may be blissful too but due to *tamas* beyond perception or recognition as deep sleep) its assignment to the third level makes some sense and fits the structural overview. By the same token, association of the *amness absorption* with *buddhi*, since it is the substrate of amness (*ahaṃkāra*) and clearly the most "stripped down" level of *asamprajñāta samādhi* bereft of *vitarka*, *vicāra*, and *ānanda* characteristics, seems reasonable. In this way, absorption in the satvic *ahaṃkāra* corresponds to Patañjali's distinction of *samādhi* in the process of perception (*grahaṇa*) and absorption in the *buddhi* corresponds to isolation of the relative perceiver (*grahītṛ*). As interpreters of the YS, Patañjali leaves us here (as in many places) with little choice but to scramble for speculative solution that brings out the perceived unity and underlying meaning of the system.

65. The similarity between Patañjali's four levels here and the first four *jhāna* (Skt., *dhyāna*) levels in Buddhist meditation (*Dhīgha-nikāya* 1.182 ff.) is remarkable. The technical Pāli terms *savitakkam* (Skt. *savitarka*) and *savicāram* (Skt. *savicāra*) occur, here referring to critical thinking and sustained thinking, along with *pīti-sukhaṃ*, happiness and bliss, and unification of mind (*ekodibhava*). In the second *jhāna* the factors of critical and sustained thinking drop away; in the third, happiness drops; and in the fourth and last, bliss drops and only the absolute purity (*parisuddhi*) of one-pointed meditation remains—from here one steps into nirvana. See also the detailed explication in 1.4 of the *Visuddhimagga* of B. Buddhaghosa (1976), *The Path of Purification* (*Visuddhim agga*), vol. 1, trans. Bhikkhu Ñyāṇamol; (Berkeley, Calif.: Shambala), pp. 144–175. Perhaps a contemporary of Patañjali.

66. The yogin whose meditation transcends the *buddhi* for absorption in unmanifest *prakṛti* (*prakṛtilaya*, 1.19) attains a simulacrum of liberation in this "nothingness" beyond all suffering, beyond anything manifest to perceive, but unfortunately this state is "dark" in terms of consciousness. Rather than attaining pure consciousness, it represents pure nonconsciousness, and, perhaps even worse, this "pseudoliberated" nonconsciousness is temporary, when the equilibrium of unmanifest matter is disrupted, the period of nonconsciousness is over as well.

67. Bartṛhari philosophy of speech as *brahman* recognized a method for practically using speech to bring awareness back to its unmanifest source. In this process the meditator relies on Grammar (the "door to salvation") for the correct form of speech, and Grammar relies on yogic perception and experience to "purify" speech by reducing it within the mind to its source. The *Vṛtti* on VP 1.14 states:

> One, who, with previous knowledge of the correct forms of words, realizes the unity of the real word, goes beyond sequence and attains union with it. By acquiring special merit through the use of the correct word, he is united with the great Word and attains freedom from the senses. After having reached the undifferentiated state of the word, he comes to the source of all differentiation: Intuition (*pratibhā*). From that intuition in which all Being is latent and which, due to the repetition of the union (mentioned above) tends to produce its result, he reaches the Supreme Source in which all differentiation is completely lost.

See Iyer, *The Vākyapadīya* (1965), p. 21.

68. Called *ekatattvābhyāsa,* YS 1.32.

69. According to the Indian medical science of the time, Ayurveda, mantras were key components in healing rituals and well known, even to the present day, for their reputed ability to neutralize such concentrated poisons as snake venom. Even later, more "rational" medical methods in later times were recommended to be used "*mantravat,*" "like mantras." See K. G. Zysk (1989), "A Study of the Use of Magico-Religious Speech in Ancient Indian Medicine." In *Understanding Mantras*, ed. H. P. Alper, SUNY Series in Religious Studies (Albany: State University of New York Press).

70. The dramatically increasing power of quieter, more internal levels of sound, reflecting the quieter, more powerful levels of the awareness in which they are entertained, is recognized even in *Manu Smṛti*:

> An offering consisting of muttered prayers is ten times more efficacious than a sacrifice performed according to the rules (of the Veda); a (prayer) which is inaudible (to others) surpasses it a hundred times, and the mental (recitation of sacred texts) a thousand times. Translation from G. Buhler ([1886] 1964), *The Laws of Manu*, Sacred Books of the East Series, 25 (Delhi: Motilal Banarsidass), p. 47.

71. I.e., *pariṇāma.*

72. For Bartṛhari the *paśyantī* is the highest, most subtle level of *vāk*; yet it admits of variation—i.e., forms and formlessness. The formless level, called the supreme (*para*) and characterized as both formless and immortal, might best be thought of due to these differences as a fourth level of speech, *para*, transcending *paśyantī*. This, in any case, is how the Tantric elaborations of the doctrine have conceptualized speech. See, for example, S. Gupta (1989), "The Pāñarātra Attitude to Mantra" in S. Gupta, D. J. Hoens, and T. Goudriaan, *Hindu Tantrism*, Handbuch der Orientalistik, 2.4.2 (Leiden: E. J. Brill) or J. Woodroffe (1963), *The Garland of Letters* (*Varṇamālā*)*: Studies in Mantra-Śāstra,* 4th ed. (Madras: Ganesh and Co.).

73. Woodroffe's explication of the *mantraśāstra* reverses this understanding of *bindu* as the transition point to *para*. He explains the Tantric understanding of *The Garland of Letters* to mean that *bindu* is rather the second emanative state of *nāda*, identical with *śabdabrahman*, giving rise to the third level of *tribindu* or *kāmakalā*. My interpretation of *bindu* is offered as a possible, logical view makes sense in the overall scheme I am introducing. The Yoga Upaniṣads use *nāda* and *bindu* in various ways, showing a not unusual lack of unanimity on technical terminology between and sometimes within texts. In all cases, the main point, that the tradition correlates levels of OṂ with levels of speech and levels of mind/meditation, is supported.

74. The existence of a type of mystical experience that transcends the limits of ordinary experience so completely has important consequences for the question of pluralism, for at least in this one type of experience there could be no difference for the experiencer at the time, regardless of his or her adherence to a particular religious or cultural tradition. As Forman (1990), p. 39, notes:

> Strange to say, but a Ganzfeld would produce an indistinguishable visual experience for Picasso or Monet. Both are without content, image formation, and so on. Similarly, if a buddhist, Hindu, or African was able to forget every thought, sensation, emotion, and so on, for some time, then no historically conditioned idea, form, category, or even sensory information would remain conscious to differentiate the resultant events from one to another. In general if a concept is for a moment truly forgotten, it does not form or cause or mediate or construct an experience. Hence, a formless trance in Buddhism may be experientially indistinguishable from one in Hinduism or Christianity.

Such parallels have led Forman to claim a perennial psychology.

References

Alper, H. P., ed. 1989. *Understanding Mantras*. SUNY Series in Religious Studies. Albany: State University of New York Press.

Āranya, H. [1963] 1983. *Yoga Philosophy of Patañjali: Containing His Yoga Aphorisms with Vyāsa's Commentary in Sanskrit and a Translation*. Translated by P. N. Muckerji. Reprint. Albany: State University of New York Press.

Arya, U. 1986. *Yoga-sūtras of Patañjali with the Exposition of Vyāsa: A Translation and Commentary*. Vol. 1. Honesdale, Pa.: Himalayan International Institute of Yoga Science and Philosophy of the U.S.A.

Brown, W. N. 1931. "The Sources and Nature of *Puruṣa* in the *Puruṣa-Sūkta*." *Journal of the American Oriental Society* 51: 108–118.

Buddhaghosa, B. 1976. *The Path of Purification* (*Visuddhimagga*). Vol. 1. Translated by Bhikkhu Ñyāṇamoli. Berkeley, Calif.: Shambala.

Bühler, G., trans. [1886] 1964. *The Laws of Manu*. Sacred Books of the East Series, 25. Delhi: Motilal Banarsidass.

Coward, H. 1989. "The Meaning and Power of Mantras in Bartrhari's *Vākyapadīya*." In *Understanding Mantras*, ed. H. P. Alper. SUNY Series in Religious Studies. Albany: State University of New York Press.

———. 1990. "Derrida and Bhartrihari's Vākyapadīya on the Origin of Language." *Philosophy East and West* 11: 3–16.

Das Gupta, S. B. 1956. "The Role of Mantra in Indian Religion." *Bulletin of the Ramakrishna Mission Institute of Culture* 7 (3): 49–57.

Dasgupta, S. N. 1924. [1922] 1975. *A History of Indian Philosophy*. Vol. 1. Delhi: Motilal Banarsidass.

———. 1930. *Yoga Philosophy in Relation to Other Systems of Indian Thought*. Calcutta: University of Calcutta Press.

———. 1924. *Yoga as Philosophy and Religion*. Calcutta: University of Calcutta Press.

———. 1955. *A History of Indian Philosophy*. Vol. 5, *Southern Schools of Śaivism*. Cambridge: Cambridge University Press.

———. [1957] 1977. *Aspects of Indian Religious Thought*. Reprint. Calcutta: Firma KLM Private Ltd.

Dayal, H. [1932] 1978. *The Bodhisattva Doctrine in Buddhist Sanskrit Literature*. Reprint. Delhi: Motilal Banarsidass.

Falk, M. 1943. *Nāma-Rūpa and Dharma-Rūpa: Origin and Aspects of an Ancient Indian Conception.* Calcutta: Calcutta University.

Farquhar, J. N. [1920] 1967. *An Outline of the Religious Literature of India.* Delhi: Moltilal Banarsidas.

Feuerstein, G. 1975. *Textbook of Yoga.* London: Rider and Co. Ltd.

———. 1979a. *The Yogasūtra of Patañjali: An Exercise in the Methodology of Textual Analysis.* Delhi: Arnold Heineman.

———. 1979b. *The Yogasūtra of Patañjali: A New Translation and Commentary.* Folkstone, Kent, G. B.: W. & J. Mackay Ltd.

Forman, R. K. C., ed. 1990. *The Problem of Pure Consciousness.* New York: Oxford University Press.

Frauwallner, E. 1953. *Geschichte der indischen Philosophie.* Vol. 1. Salzburg: O. Müller Verlag.

———. [1973] 1984. *History of Indian Philosophy.* Translated by V. M. Bedekar. Reprint. Delhi: Motilal Banarsidas.

Gupta, S., D. J. Hoens, and T. Goudriaan. 1979. *Hindu Tantrism.* Handbuch der Orientalistik, 2.4.2. Leiden: E. J. Brill.

Hauer, J. W. 1922. *Die Anfänge der Yogapraxis im Alten Indien.* Stuttgart: W. Kohlhammer Verlag.

———. 1927a. *Das Laṅkāvatāra Sūtra und das Sāṃkhya.* Stuttgart: W. Kohlhammer Verlag.

———. 1927b. Der *Vrātya.* Stuttgart: W. Kohlhammer Verlag.

———. 1931. Das IV. Buch des Yogasūtra. *Studia Indo-Iranica: Ehrengabe für Wilhelm Geiger.* Edited by Walter Wüst. Leipzig: Otto Harrasowitz.

———. 1958. *Der Yoga: Ein indischer Weg zum Selbst.* Stuttgart: W. Kohlhammer Verlag.

Hume, D. 1898. *A Treatise on Human Nature.* Edited by T. H. Green and T. H. Gross. London: Longmans Green and Co.

Iyer, K. A. S., trans. 1965. *The Vākyapadīya of Bhartṛhari with the Vṛtti, Chapter I, English Translation.* Building Centenary and Silver Jubilee Series, 26. Poona: Deccan College.

———, ed. 1966. *The Vākyapadīya of Bhartṛhari with the Vṛtti and the Paddhati of Vṛsabhadeva.* Deccan College Monograph Series, 32. Poona: Deccan College.

James, W. [1904] 1976. "Does Consciousness Exist?" In *The Writings of William James*, ed. J. J. McDermott. New York: Random House.

———. 1958. *The Varieties of Religious Experience: A Study in Human Nature.* Gifford Lectures on Natural Religion, 1901–1902. New York: New American Library of World Literature.

Katz, S. T., ed. 1978. *Mysticism and Philosophical Analysis.* New York: Oxford University Press.

———, ed. 1983. *Mysticism and Religious Traditions.* New York: Oxford University Press.

Larson, J. G. 1979. *Classical Sāṃkhya: An Interpretation of Its History and Meaning.* Santa Barbara, Calif.: Ross/Erikson.

———. 1983. "An Eccentric Ghost in the Machine: Formal and Quantitative Aspects of the Sāṃkhya-Yoga Dualism." *Philosophy East and West* 33: 219–233.

Larson, G. J., and R. S. Bhattacharya, eds. 1987. *Sāṃkhya: A Dualist Tradition in Indian Philosophy.* Encyclopedia of Indian Philosophies, vol. 4. Princeton: Princeton University Press.

Monier-Williams, M. [1899] 1979. *A Sanskrit-English Dictionary.* New ed. Reprint. Delhi: Motilal Banarsidass.

Otto, R. [1923] 1972. *The Idea of the Holy: An Inquiry into the Non-Rational Factor in the Idea of the Divine and Its Relation to the Rational.* Translated by J. W. Harvey. 2d ed. Reprint. Oxford: Oxford University Press.

Padoux, A. 1989. "Mantras—What Are They?" In *Understanding Mantras*, ed. H. P. Alper. SUNY Series in Religious Studies. Albany: State University of New York Press.

Parpola, A. 1981. "On the Primary Meaning and Etymology of the Sacred Syllable OM." *Studia Orientalia: Proceedings of the Nordic South Asian Conference* (Helsinki, 1980), ed. Finnish Oriental Society, 195–213.

Pflueger, L. 1990. *God, Consciousness, and Meditation: The Concept of* Īśvara *in the Yogasūtra.* Ann Arbor, Mich.: University Microfilms.

Prasāda, R., trans. 1978. *Patañjali's Yoga Sutras with the Commentary of Vyāsa and the Gloss of Vācaspati Miśra.* 2d ed. New Delhi: Oriental Books Reprint Corporation.

Proudfoot, Wayne, 1984. *Religious Experience.* Berkeley: University of California Press.

Śastrī, D., ed. 1982. *Yogasūtram* by *Maharṣipatañjali.* Kashi Sanskrit Series, 83. Varanasi: Chaukhambha Sanskrit Sansthan.

Sastri, P. S. R., and S. R. K. Sastri, eds. 1952. *Pātañjala Yogasūtra-bhāṣya-vivaranam of Śaṅkara-bhagavatpāda.* Madras Government Oriental Series No. 94., T. Chandrasekharan, ed. Madras: Government Oriental Manuscripts Library.

Shastri, M. D. 1935. "History of the Word 'Ishvara' and Its Idea." In *Proceedings and Transactions of the Seventh All-India Oriental Conference*, ed. Benoytosh Bhattacharyya. Baroda: Oriental Institute, Government Press.

Staal, F. 1975. *Exploring Mysticism: A Methodological Essay.* Berkeley: University of California Press.

———. 1989. "Vedic Mantras." In *Understanding Mantras*, ed. H. P. Alper. SUNY Series in Religious Studies. Albany: State University of New York Press.

Wainwright, W. 1981. *Mysticism: A Study of Its Nature, Cognitive Value and Moral Implications.* Madison: University of Wisconsin Press.

Winternitz, M. 1920. *Geschichte der indischen Literatur.* 3 vols. Leipzig: O. F. Amelangs.

———. 1960–62. *A History of Indian Literature.* Translated by S. Ketkar. 3 vols. Calcutta: University of Calcutta.

Woodroffe, J. 1963. *The Garland of Letters* (*Varṇamālā*)*: Studies in Mantra-śāstra.* 4th ed. Madras: Ganesh & Co.

Woods, J. H., trans. 1914. *The Yoga-System of Patañjali.* Delhi: Motilal Banarsidass.

———, trans. 1915. "The *Yoga-sūtras* of Patañjali as illustrated by the Comment Entitled 'The Jewel's Lustre' or *Maniprabhā.*" *Journal of the American Oriental Society* 34: 1ff.

Zysk, K. G. 1989. "A Study of the Use of Magico-Religious Speech in Ancient Indian Medicine." In *Understanding Mantras*, ed. H. P. Alper. SUNY Series in Religious Studies. Albany: State University of New York Press.

THREE

Parables of Deconstruction in the *Lotus Sūtra*

ROGER J. CORLESS

ACCORDING TO Mahāyāna Buddhism, all suffering beings (*sattvas*) are in fact liberated beings (*buddhas*). As *sattvas*, they experience the world as meaningless repetition and circularity (*saṃsāra*); yet they are assured that, in fact, according to Reality as it truly is, the world is open, free, or transparent (*śūnyatā*, "Emptiness"). But *sattvas* can make no sense of this assurance because, Mahāyāna explains, they lack the proper instrument with which to observe, or experience, Reality truly. Or, not quite. There is the "innate capacity" to experience Reality as it truly is, but this capacity is obscured, distorted, or diseased.

This innate capacity is sometimes called, in Mahāyāna, the Buddha Nature. More simply, it is "the mind." In Tibetan, *sattva* is translated *sems can*, which means, "a possessor of consciousness." An entity is recognized as possessing consciousness by its actions: it manifestly seeks to avoid pain and to obtain pleasure. Any such entity has the potential to be liberated, and, indeed, from a certain viewpoint, it is already liberated.

The analogy is given of sky and clouds. Mind (or Reality), as it truly is, is likened to a cloudless sky—that is, to space. Space cannot be defined or limited, it cannot be divided into parts, and it cannot be said to have a beginning or an end.[1] It cannot even be found; that is, it cannot be pointed out as being here or there. Yet, undeniably, space exists. In fact, without space, nothing else would exist. But space is not the *cause* of things existing, nor is it the ontological "ground" (*Grund*) of existence. Space "is," but *how it "is"* is not discoverable by investigation or analysis. This is, according to Mahāyāna Buddhism, the way Reality truly "is."

Beings, however, do not see reality this way. They see "things," including themselves, that appear to have inherent existence (*svabhāva*). These things are like clouds in space or in the sky. They appear to be permanent, solid, and inherently existing;

yet they are not. They "take up" space, restricting and obscuring the innate openness of Reality as it truly is.

The problem for Buddhism in general is how to liberate beings from their suffering within a reality experienced as samsara and to bring them (or allow them) to see Reality as it truly is. For Mahāyāna Buddhism in particular, this problem is seen as one of skillful means (*upāya-kauśalya*), which the Chinese call *fang-pien*, "appropriate method." That is, given a sentient being for whom reality is full of "things" and suffering, what method does a Dharma teacher use that will be appropriate to the particular problem or disease of that particular sentient being?

If liberation, or Reality as it truly is, is presented as a *thing*, a worldview or a metaphysic, it will be reified and become a further source of suffering: this is the only way unliberated, or cloudy, mind can imagine it.[2] Since information is, necessarily, composed of things, information about Reality as it truly is cannot be successfully imparted to *sattvas* by the Buddhas. But, if no information is given, beings will either draw the conclusion that liberation is impossible or that Reality as it truly is is a Void (mistaking or reifying, in its turn, *śūnyatā* or no-thing-ness as Nothingness).

Given all this, Mahāyāna Buddhism comes up with a curious solution: deceit.[3] It promises a "thing" and gives "no-thing." At its most alarming, skillful means in Mahāyāna depicts the Buddhas involved in underhanded bait-and-switch maneuvers.

Skillful means is a form of what literary critics such as Derrida call "deconstruction." Any philosophy, explanatory system, or "viewpoint" (*dṛṣṭi*) is regarded by Buddhism as a construction of cloudy mind—or, in a more frequently used image, a disease. The Buddhas are, then, likened to wise physicians who correctly diagnose and treat the particular confusion of a particular being, employing a method (*fang*) that is appropriate (*pien*) to the case at hand. This accounts for the variety of Buddhist teachings, a variety that is celebrated rather than, as in some other religions, regretted. Non-Buddhist teachers are sometimes accused by the Buddist tradition of prescribing the same treatment for all beings and behaving, therefore, like quack physicians.

This essay examines the Mahāyāna teaching about the Buddha Nature (considered as "innate capacity") and skillful means (considered as "deconstruction") as exemplified by one of the most respected Mahāyāna texts, the *Lotus Sūtra*, which presents its teaching in the form of seven parables. It concentrates on the "bait-and-switch" technique, which is, at first sight, a most inappropriate method for the holy Buddhas to employ. The study suggests that, although Buddhism has indeed a good deal to say about "innate capacity" and "mystical experience," its ultimate goal is the deconstruction of these concepts and the phenomena they imply.

I claim that the parables in the *Lotus Sūtra* speak of deconstruction on two levels. First, they deconstruct the thoughts and systems that constitute ordinary, or samsaric, reality; that is, they sweep away the "clouds" that obscure the "sky" of Reality as it truly is. Buddha Nature is thus exposed. However, Buddha Nature may be mistaken by the evolved but still not fully purified and liberated being as a "thing," as *innately pure mind* rather than *the innate purity of mind* (that is, mistaken for the empty sky rather than the emptiness of the sky); in order to guard against this fatal error,[4] the *Lotus Sūtra* goes on to deconstruct all the Buddha's teachings, including that of the Buddha Nature.

In effect, ordinary reality is first deconstructed so as to expose mystical reality; then, mystical reality is deconstructed, and liberation results.

Seven Parables

For readers unfamiliar with the *Lotus Sūtra*, I now give a brief summary of the parables. Those who know the *Lotus Sūtra* well may skip to the following section, in which I begin my analysis of the parables.

In the Chinese translation of the *Lotus Sūtra* by Kumārajīva,[5] which is the one usually read by East Asian Buddhists,[6] the seven parables[7] are as follow.

1. The Burning House (*chapter 3*)

An old, wise man returns from his travels to his large and crumbling mansion to find that it is on fire and his many sons are trapped inside. He tells them the situation and calls on them to come out, but they do not understand what the statement "the house is on fire" means, and they are absorbed with their playthings. So the father tells them that he has presents outside: goat carts for some, deer carts for others, and bullock carts for the rest. The children then hurry to come out and ask for the carts, but the father does not have them. Instead, he gives each child an enormous and magnificent cart, of a type far beyond any splendor they could have imagined, drawn by white oxen. In modern terms, it is as if the children had expected to receive push-bikes, motor bikes, and automobiles, and each was then presented with a starship. They forget their former expectations and joyfully ride on the marvelous ox carts. The Buddha explains that the father in the story is himself; the house is samsara, which is subject to decay and death and is on fire with the passions; the children are disciples; the promised carts are the various apparent rewards consequent upon following Buddhist teachings and practices; and the ox carts are true liberation.

2. The Lost Heir (*chapter 4*)

A boy leaves home and wanders from place to place, taking poorly paid jobs where he can find them.[8] At age fifty, he enters a certain city and sees a millionaire, who is in fact his father who has moved to this same city and built himself a large mansion. The son does not recognize his father, but the father recognizes his son and sends men to capture him. The son is terrified, and the father orders him released, subsequently sending other men who, abandoning force, entice him to accept the job of cleaning the latrines in his father's house, a work that the son finds appropriate to his low sense of self-worth. Occasionally, the father disguises himself and works alongside his son. He frequently sends servants to encourage him and gradually promotes him to chief steward. On his deathbed the father reveals that his faithful servant is in fact his true son and bequeaths to him all his estate. It is explained that the Buddha is the father; the son is a disciple; wandering in poverty is living in samsara; the menial jobs are the teachings and practices of Buddhism; and the inheritance is the Buddha Nature.

3. The Plants (chapter 5)

The rain from the monsoon cloud (*megha*) falls equally on grasses, shrubs, and trees, and they grow to their respective heights.[9] Just so, the monsoon cloud of Buddhist teachings (*dharma-megha*) is offered impartially to all beings, and they receive it and grow, according to their various capacities.

4. The Phantom City (chapter 7)

A group of people are being led by a knowledgeable guide through a wilderness to a place where, they are told, they will find great treasure. After some time, the group become weary and disheartened and wish to turn back. The guide tells them that, just a short distance ahead, there is a city where they can lodge and refresh themselves. They enter the city, and, when they feel better, the city vanishes. The guide explains that he had created it by magic to satisfy their needs, and, now that it has fulfilled its purpose, he has made it disappear. The treasure, he says, is near, and if they make one more effort, they will find it. We are then told that the guide is the Buddha; the group of people are disciples; the phantom city is Buddhism; and the treasure is the Buddha Nature.

5. The Concealed Gem (chapter 8)

A poor man visits a rich friend, gets drunk, and passes out. The rich man, who has to leave on business, gives his poor man a priceless gem, which he sews into the lining of his friend's clothes. When the poor man comes to, he resumes his life as a vagrant, unaware of the treasure he received during his blackout. Later, he meets the rich man again, who shows him where the gem is concealed, and the poor man realizes his wealth. In the story, the rich man is the Buddha; the poor man is a *sattva*, drunk with the passions; and the jewel is the truth about the Buddha Nature.

6. The Crest Jewel (chapter 14)

A mighty king gives lavish gifts of all kinds to his victorious soldiers, holding back only his crest jewel, which is his personal symbol. At length, however, after their repeated victories, he gives his crest jewel to the entire army. The king, then, is the Buddha; the soldiers are disciples fighting the passions; the gifts are the preliminary teachings of Buddhism; and the crest jewel is the supreme teaching of the *Lotus Sūtra*.

7. The Physician's Sons (chapter 16)

The sons of a wise and competent physician get into his medicine cabinet while he is away and make themselves ill by taking drugs. The physician returns and begins to prepare antidotes. The children who are mildly affected take them and are cured, but the seriously ill children are deranged and will not accept the treatment. The physician goes away again, leaving the remedies with his children, with instructions on how to take them. Later, he sends word that he has died, and the children, shocked with grief and feeling abandoned, take the medicine and are cured. The physician returns, and his children welcome him. Here, the physician is the Buddha; the mildly ill children are disciples; the seriously ill children are nonpractitioners; the drugs are the passions; the antidotes are the Buddhist teachings; and restoration to health is liberation.

Classification of the Parables

Because it is germane to his objective, Michael Pye treats all seven parables as "stories about skilful means."[10] But they are also about the Buddha Nature. For the purposes of this essay, I wish to classify the parables into two groups: those that deal more directly with what the Buddha Nature, or innate capacity, itself is and those that concentrate on the skillful means that uncover the Buddha Nature by the deconstruction of ordinary, or deluded, reality. This classification is porous, and operational only, for all the parables are about *both* the Buddha Nature and skillful means. Finally, I wish to point out how the Buddha Nature itself is deconstructed.

The Buddha Nature

The Parable of the Lost Heir

The son in this parable is always the son, but he forgets his true identity. We are not told why the son runs away from home; we are told only that he does run away. This is consistent with the Buddhist view of unliberated beings as *bāla*, foolish, immature people or children. When the father and the son meet again, the father recognizes the son, but the son cannot recognize his father; he can see only a very rich and powerful man. Feeling himself unworthy of such company, he runs away again. When captured by the father's servants, he assumes he is about to be punished. His father releases him not only because he is sorry for his son but because he "knew that his son's ambitions were mean, and he knew that he himself, being rich and powerful, would be a source of trouble for his son."[11] That is, he sees that the son is not yet ready to hear the truth or, indeed, will not be able to understand it if he does hear it. Subsequently, the father sends men who are dressed in ragged clothes (so that they do not appear threatening) to persuade and entice his son with an offer of a job cleaning out dung, a job suited to his presumed lowly status. Later still, the father himself assumes a disguise of tattered clothing when he works alongside his son. In this way, Buddhas and Bodhisattvas appear as *sattvas* rather than as terrifying super-beings, and *sattvas* feel that they can approach them as equals.

The father tells his son that he is such a good worker that he will adopt him and give him his own name. The son is flattered but still calls himself "a lowly workman from elsewhere."[12] The son is promoted to chief steward and told that he and the father "are now to be no different," and the son administers the estate as if it were his own. Finally, as the father is near death, the son is told the truth: it really *is* his own.

> At this time, the poor son, hearing his father's words, straightway rejoiced greatly, having gained something he had never had before. Then he thought: "Formerly I had no thought of seeking or expecting anything, and now these treasure houses have come to me of themselves!"[13]

So, the being who has thought himself of no account and has had no confidence in his own abilities has gradually been ennobled and emboldened until, at last, he is told that he was really a noble being all along.

This teaches that the Buddha Nature is inherent, but beings do not realize it. When told the truth baldly, they do not believe it, and it frightens them. But, by achieving success in some things (i.e., some success along the Buddhist path to enlightenment), they are prepared to be told who they really are, and at that time they are not terrified but joyful.

There is a problem in that the text clearly says that the son gained something he had never had (*tê mei tsêng yu*). We might at first take this to mean that the Buddha Nature is a gift from the Buddha, not something already possessed. This problem seems to be cleared up when we remember that the son is a simile, not of Mahāyānists, but of Hīnayānists—that is, of Buddhists who had satisfied themselves with the lesser teaching of personal escape from samsara by becoming *arhats*: they say, "we have craved only lesser dharmas."[14] Then, through hearing the *Lotus Sūtra*, these Hīnayānists realize that they are in fact full and complete Buddhas (*samyaksaṃbuddha*). What the Hīnayānists get that they never had before is not the Buddha Nature itself but the *realization* that they have the Buddha Nature.

The Parable of the Concealed Gem

In this story, the gem does not belong to the poor man until it is given to him by his rich friend, but the man is not conscious of his newly acquired wealth and continues to behave as if he were poor. Only when "by chance"[15] he meets his friend again does he discover that he possesses the gem. However, this does not mean that beings do not have the innate capacity for Buddhahood until it is imparted to them by the Buddha: as in the previous parable, riches do not symbolize the Buddha Nature itself. Whereas the lost heir's inheritance is the *realization* of possessing the Buddha Nature, however, the concealed gem is the Mahāyāna teaching *about* possessing the Buddha Nature, which the Hīnayānists had received in the distant past (many lifetimes ago) and had forgotten. Having been reminded of it, they say that they have "gained something [they] had never had before."[16]

Common Features of the Buddha Nature Parables

Although the text of the *Lotus Sūtra* may not be a unity, it is regarded as such by orthodox Mahāyāna. Therefore, it is legitimate, for our purposes, to combine the teaching of the parables of the Lost Heir and the Concealed Gem.

When we do so, we come up with something resembling the Gnostic text known as *The Hymn of the Pearl*.[17] In that story, a child who is the natural son of "the King of Kings"[18] is sent to obtain a great treasure. He disguises himself as a poor man and becomes so involved in his deception that he forgets his mission. He eats too much and falls asleep. His parents send emissaries with a letter reminding him who he is and what he is supposed to be doing. He rouses himself, recalls his true nature, completes his mission, and returns home in triumph.

Rewriting this from a Buddhist standpoint, we have a being who is really a Buddha but who leaves Reality and enters samsara. Wandering purposelessly, barely making a living, he has been given a priceless gem but is unaware of it. Then, by an apparently chance meeting, he comes to realize his true nature.

There is, however, one significant difference between the Buddha Nature parables and *The Hymn of the Pearl*. In the Parable of the Lost Heir, the mind, attitude, or superficial "nature" of the son is transformed. In *The Hymn of the Pearl*, there is an untransformative *discovery* of an unchanging nature—that is, of an "innate capacity." At first glance, untransformative discovery of an unchanging nature may also seem to be the point of the Parable of the Concealed Gem. But it is not. Rather, it is a teaching on inner transformation. This appears probable when we read it in the light of the parables of skillful means, to which we now turn.

Skillful Means

The Burning House, the Phantom City, and the Physician's Sons

In all three of these parables, the alarming and apparently unethical trick of bait-and-switch is prominent. The children emerge from the burning house and find that their father has lied to them about the gifts he has for them; the travelers discover that their way station is an illusion; and the physician's sons learn that their father is not really dead.

The *Lotus Sūtra* itself recognizes the problem here and has the Buddha ask his disciples if he has in fact tricked them unethically. For slightly different reasons in each of the stories, they all reply that he has not. The supreme gift of the teaching about Buddha Nature in the *Lotus Sūtra* is of such value that the end of obtaining it justifies the use of any mens. Or, not quite *any* means: force is never used, and in the parable of the burning house it is explicitly considered and rejected. The father reflects:

> I am a man of great physical strength. I might, in the folds of my robe or on top of a table, take them out of the house. [But he considers the fact that] [t]he children are young and, as yet having no understanding, are in love with their playthings. They may fall victim to the fire and be burnt. I must explain the terror of it to them.[19]

This illustrates that the Buddha, although powerful, is not omnipotent, as a God might be, and that liberation by fiat is not an option for him. It also illustrates that, although the Buddha might rescue beings by magically transporting them out of the house by means of his supernormal powers or *siddhi*, he chooses not to, because it would be dangerous. The parable presents us with the quite bizarre and humorous image of one man trying to collect numerous excited children ("ten, or twenty, or thirty of them"[20]) in his clothes (or, perhaps, a sort of cloth bag[21]) or on a table and to carry them all out safely. Any parent might sympathize with the father's decision, in such a case, to use persuasion and tricks, but the point seems to be that, by the use of skillful means, the children escape *of their own accord.*

In the parables of the phantom city and the physician's sons, also, persuasion and trickery are used rather than force. The travelers are given something that they want and can comprehend: "R & R" in a swinging city. Then, having recovered from their exhaustion and depression, they are open to the idea of moving on in search of the real reward.

The physician's sons who are so seriously ill that they have refused the medicine their father has offered them (because they are insane and believe it to be poison) take the medicine after receiving the invented news of their father's death. The physician, we might suppose, is a specialist in substance abuse and realizes that, by staying around and attempting to rescue his seriously ill sons, he is acting as an enabler. When he goes away, apparently forever, they are left with the alternatives of death or taking the medicine, and they choose the latter.

So, the tricks are intended to *change the minds of* or *transform* those who are being tricked. This transformation is similar to that referred to in the parables on the Buddha Nature, but it is here made more explicit. The children in the burning house do not understand what "the house is on fire" means, but they understand their father's promise that he has little carts for them. The weary travelers have decided that the treasure they are seeking either does not exist or is not worth the trouble, so they accept a lesser, but more immediate, reward. The seriously ill sons of the physician need to be shocked out of their expectation that their father will somehow take care of them before they are ready to take his medicine. In all cases, normal expectations (whether samsaric or dharmic[22]) are broken, transcended, or deconstructed. Three methods of deconstruction seem to be presented:

1. What is expected, or can be imagined, is given but is later found to be an illusion (the magic city).
2. What is expected, or can be imagined, is promised but is not given (the little carts).
3. What is expected, or can be imagined, is taken away, and an alternative that had seemed unacceptable is seen as the only solution (the medicine that earlier had appeared as poison).

The result is always the same: those who have been tricked express gratitude at receiving such a wonderful and formerly inconceivable gift. How they are enabled to receive this gift is dealt with more directly in the parables of the plants and the crest jewel, to which we now turn.

The Plants, and the Crest Jewel

Plants are of different kinds and grow to different heights. The sutra mentions specifically "grasses, trees, shrubs, and forests, as well as medicinal herbs."[23] Each is "produced by the same earth and moistened by the same rain";[24] yet each grows differently. The plants are symbols not of *sattvas* that have *inherently* different natures (for, according to Buddhism, they do not) but of beings in different realms: peaceful deities (*deva*), wrathful deities (*asura*), and humans are explicitly mentioned, but all beings in the six realms of rebirth are implied. Each being is offered the same teaching, but each, because of its form in a particular rebirth, receives it differently.

The parable of the plants, however, takes a twist. Rain falls equally on all plants, without considering what kind of plant is being watered. The Buddha, on the other hand, is aware of whom he is teaching. Although (as we have mentioned) he is not omnipotent, he is omniscient,[25] and so he "observes . . . beings, their keenness or dullness, their exertion or laxity, and in accord with what they can bear, preaches the Dharma to them in an incalculable variety of modes."[26] That is, although the Buddha's message is essentially the same, it is modified by skillful means when it is expressed.

This is the same teaching that is illustrated in the parable of the burning house: different carts are offered to different children, but, in the end, they all get the same thing.

The parable of the crest jewel clearly identifies the lesser gifts (i.e., the rewards that are in accord with what one's [Buddhist] worldview would lead one to expect) as the teachings and practices that have, until the preaching of the *Lotus Sūtra*, been identified as "Buddhism." Just as the great king of the parable confers gifts on his generals, so the Buddha "confers upon [his disciples] the precious [but elementary] Dharma-gifts of dhyāna-concentration, deliverance, faculties without outflows, and powers. He also confers upon them as a gift the city of nirvāṇa, telling them they shall gain passage into extinction."[27] The gift of the crest jewel, then, is the subsequent gift of the *Lotus Sūtra*—that is, the teaching about Buddha Nature.

What is important to note in this story is that it is only after the generals have proved themselves successful in lesser battles that the great king gives them the magnificent jewel as a totally unexpected reward. The recipients of the true teaching, this seems to say, must be properly prepared for it or have gone through some sort of preliminary transformation before they are ready for the transformation or deconstruction that takes them beyond that worthy, but temporary, system we call "Buddhism."

Conclusions

It should now be clear that the *Lotus Sūtra* does regard beings as having an "innate capacity" for (or of) enlightenment. Possessing the Buddha Nature, beings do not need to gain anything. Seen truly, as they really are, the Buddha says, all *sattvas* are Buddhas; yet they do not realize it. This is compared to someone being the son of a millionaire or a person with a priceless jewel who thinks that he is impoverished.

The Buddha deals with this situation by deconstructing the false reality (samsara) in which beings find themselves. The lost heir is gradually shown the wealth that is rightly his, and the drunken man is brought to his senses like the prince in *The Hymn of the Pearl*. The parables of the Lost Heir and the Concealed Jewel speak of the finding of a treasure already possessed, by someone who wakes up and/or remembers, but they have a subtext of transformation, of the making of a new kind of seeing.

Transformation is necessary, for, when *sattvas* are told the truth about themselves and about reality, they do not rejoice. On the contrary, they do not understand what is being said to them (like the children in the burning house) or they reject the teaching, believing that what the Buddha tells them is either a fantasy (like the travelers in the wilderness) or the blandishments of a devil (like those who mistake medicine as poison). The minds of beings are diseased, afflicted with what Buddhism calls the "three poisons" of attachment (*rāga*), aversion (*dveṣa*), and confusion (*moha*).

Because of this disease, the root of which is said to be "beginningless ignorance" (*ādyavidyā*),[28] the Buddhas[29] cannot teach straightforwardly about Reality as it truly is. If, as I explained at the beginning of this essay, the Buddhas say something, it is taken by diseased mind as another "thing" within samsara, and, instead of being a source of freedom, it becomes a further source of entrapment. But if, on the other hand, the Buddhas say nothing, this also is taken by diseased mind as a "thing," for a Nothing is a "thing," comprehensible only within a samsaric, or dualistic, framework in which there might be something but in fact there is observed to be nothing. Therefore, the Buddhas, having deconstructed ordinary (samsaric) reality, go on to deconstruct their own teachings (dharmic reality) by means of "bait-and-switch" skillful means.

The bait they offer is the teaching that there are "things," especially such joyful things as victory over the passions, advanced meditative (or mystical) states, and extinction in nirvana. These are things that *sattvas* can conceive of and intelligibly long for within the framework of their samsaric prison.

Then, they switch: All these "things," it is eventually revealed, are devices that have led beings to the point at which they are able to hear, understand, and rejoice in the true teaching. They find out that, like plants that receive rain differentially or children promised toys, they have been taught only according to their superficial, or undeveloped, faculties. Subsequently, the true prize, which is like the crest jewel of a world emperor, is given to them.

The principle of bait-and-switch skillful means is that *the Buddhadharma is transformation manifesting as information*. It is true to say, to a certain mind at a certain time, that there is an "innate capacity" or Buddha Nature, but this piece of "information" is more than it seems: it not only informs, it transforms. Parables are used in the *Lotus Sūtra* because they are transformative. They evoke, or encourage, a new outlook: "I [the Buddha] shall now once again by resort to a parable clarify this meaning. For they who have intelligence [*chih-chê* 'wise ones'] gain understanding [*chieh*, having the nuance of "release"] through parables."[30] Therefore, to another mind at another time, it would be false to say that there is an "innate capacity" or Buddha Nature.

Skillful means is a *process* that "ain't over till it's over"—that is, until one is no longer thinking in terms of "enlightenment" or "no enlightenment." Samsara is the delusory construction of diseased mind, and so it needs to be deconstructed. But, further, visions, mystical states, Nothing, and whatever else we can imagine or imagine that we could imagine, even "liberation" itself, also must be deconstructed. If skillful means stops before "it's over," it leaves a residue of "religion": Zen masters ridicule this as "the stink of Zen" and contrast it with true enlightenment, which is, when it happens, as ordinary and pure as the taste of (ceremonial Japanese) tea.

The deconstruction of Buddhism itself is only hinted at in the *Lotus Sūtra*; its hints become clear when they are read (according to the Mahāyāna tradition) in the light of the *Perfection of Wisdom* (*prajñāpāramitā*) *Sūtras*. The Parable of the Crest Jewel can be seen as teaching that, as the *Heart Sūtra* (*Prajñāpāramitāhṛdayasūtra*) says:

"In emptiness . . . there is no suffering, no origination, no stopping, no path. There is no cognition, no attainment and no non-attainment."[31]

That is to say, in the final teaching, the Four Noble Truths (suffering, its origination, its stopping, and the path to its stopping), which are the cornerstone of Buddhism, and the possibility of liberation, without which Buddhism would be nonsense, are deconstructed so that beings will not be trapped by "liberation" or any belief in an inherently existing "innate capacity."

Notes

1. It is philosophically puzzling for astrophysicists to say that space-time "began" at the "Big Bang."

2. By "cloudy mind" I intend to represent the Sanskrit *avidyā*, often translated as "ignorance." It is, more precisely, "unawareness," the pervasive dullness to reality as it truly is to which mind is subject when the "clouds" of the passions obscure the "clear sky" of its true nature.

3. In colloquial Japanese, *hōben* (as the Chinese *fang-pien* is pronounced) means something like "a white lie"; see Michael Pye, *Skilful Means: A Concept in Mahayana Buddhism* (London: Duckworth, 1978), pp. 138–141. This book is the best study of skillful means in English.

4. Nāgārjuna says explicitly that Emptiness is "the purgative of all worldviews" (*sarvadṛṣṭīnāṁ niḥsaraṇaṁ*), and those who regard Emptiness as itself as a viewpoint are incurable (Mūladmadhyamakakārikāḥ 13:8).

5. The text is in vol. 9, pages 1–62, of the Taishō edition of the Chinese Tripiṭaka. There are scholarly English translations of Kumārajīva's version by Leon Hurvitz, *Scripture of the Lotus Blossom of the Fine Dharma* (New York: Columbia University Press, 1976; Burton Watson, *The Lotus Sutra* (New York: Columbia University Press, 1993); and Bunnō Katō et al., *The Threefold Lotus Sutra* (Tokyo: Kosei Publishing, 1975; distributed in the United States by John Weatherhill, New York). *Saddharma-Puṇḍarīka or the Lotus of the True Law* by H. Kern (New York: Dover, 1963), a reprint of volume 21 of *The Sacred Books of the East* (Oxford: Clarendon, 1884), is translated from the Sanskrit text, which has significant variations (noted by Hurvitz) from the Kumārajīva version. In this essay I have worked from the Chinese text but have generally cited the English according to Hurvitz's translation.

6. Six translations of the *Lotus Sūtra* into Chinese are recorded, but only three have survived. Hurvitz, *Scripture of the Lotus Blossom,* p. ix.

7. The Chinese term *p'i-yü* is ambiguous and means something like "illustration." As Pye points out, some of these "parables" are "little more than extended simile[s]" (*Skilful Means*, p. 47, et passim).

8. This parable has been confused by Western scholars with the New Testament parable of the prodigal son, with which it has, in fact, very little in common. See Whalen Lai, "The Buddhist 'Prodigal Son': A Story of Misperceptions," *Journal of the International Association of Buddhist Studies* 4:2 (1981): 91–98. For a comparison with a Christian model of "innate capacity," see my "The [*sic*; should be "Two"] Dramas of Spiritual Progress: The Lord and the Servant in Julian's *Showings* 51 and the Lost Heir in *Lotus Sūtra* 4," *Mystics Quarterly*, 11:2 (June 1985): 65–75).

9. The Chinese *yao* and the original Sanskrit *auṣadhī* both carry the nuance of *medicinal* plants.

10. Pye, *Skilful Means*, chap. 3.

11. Hurvitz, *Scripture of the Lotus Blossom*, p. 86.

12. Ibid., p. 88.

13. Ibid., pp. 88–89.

14. Ibid., p. 89. "Dharmas" here means "teachings."

15. Ibid., p. 165.

16. Ibid.

17. The title is a modern invention. It calls itself *The Hymn of Jude Thomas the Apostle in the Country of the Indians*. The most recent translation into English is that of Bentley Layton in *The Gnostic Scriptures* (Garden City, N.Y.: Doubleday, 1987), pp. 371–375.

18. Ibid., p. 373 (verse 41).

19. Hurvitz, *Scripture of the Lotus Blossom*, p. 58f.

20. Ibid., p. 58.

21. *The Wonderful Dharma Lotus Flower Sutra*, with commentary by Tripitaka Master Hua (San Francisco: Buddhist Text Translation Society, 1979), vol. 4, p. 619.

22. A samsaric expectation is one that is concerned with ordinary, deluded, or "worldly" reality. A dharmic expectation is one that is concerned with the teaching of the Buddha and is more sophisticated; yet it is not liberation.

23. Hurvitz, *Scripture of the Lotus Blossom*, p. 101.

24. Ibid.

25. The omniscience of the Buddha is a distinctively Mahāyāna teaching and is usually denied by Theravāda.

26. Hurvitz, *Scripture of the Lotus Blossom*, p. 102.

27. Ibid., p. 218f. Words in square brackets are mine.

28. "Beginningless" does not here imply that (absurdly) linear time spreads infinitely backward but that, when samsaric reality is examined, no beginning can be found. It just goes round and round and on and on, causing and conditioning itself, never getting any simpler or reaching anything like a beginning. The investigation of samsara resembles a phase space map of a complex iterative function such as the Mandelbrot set, which is infinitely deep but bounded, full of self-similarities but never exactly repeating itself. (For an absorbing layperson's introduction to such functions, see James Gleick, *Chaos: Making a New Science* [Penguin Books, 1987].)

29. The plural here is intentional. Although the *Lotus Sūtra* is presented as the teaching of "the" (historical) Buddha, Śākyamuni, it explicitly says that all the Buddhas of the past have taught and all the Buddhas of the future will teach the same Dharma.

30. Hurvitz, *Scripture of the Lotus Blossom*, p. 58. Words in square brackets are mine.

31. Translated by Edward Conze in *Buddhist Wisdom Books, Containing the Diamond Sutra and the Heart Sutra* (London: Allen and Unwin, 1958), p. 89.

FOUR

Between the Yes and the No

Ibn al-ʿArabī on Wujūd *and the Innate Capacity*

WILLIAM C. CHITTICK

Averroes: "How did you find the situation in unveiling and divine effusion? Is it what rational consideration gives to us?

Ibn al-ʿArabī: "Yes and no. Between the yes and the no spirits fly from their matter and heads from their bodies."[1]

SUFISM, SOMETIMES CALLED "Islamic mysticism," has been found wherever there have been Muslims. In general, Sufis differ from ordinary Muslims by stressing inwardness and spirituality rather than activity and Law.[2] Sufis have tried to intensify and perfect their knowledge of God, and one of the natural results of these efforts has been the direct experience of the object of faith. Descriptions of such experiences are always expressed in terminology that is recognizably Islamic, but those who speak of it unanimously assert that they have witnessed the single and unique Reality that underlies all appearances and all experience.

Sufism has an enormous primary literature, most of it unpublished and little of it translated. Writings that have a distinctively Sufi flavor appear in the eighth-century C.E. and have continued to be written throughout the Islamic world down to modern times. Here I can do no more than look at a few teachings of the most widely influential Sufi author since the thirteenth century, Ibn al-ʿArabī (d. 1240), known to the tradition as the "greatest master." It needs to be kept in mind that Ibn al-ʿArabī's writings represent "an ocean without shore," as his foremost student in the West has put it recently.[3] His published corpus includes many thousands of pages at an extremely high level of discourse, and it would be impossible to open any of his books to practically any page without finding statements relevant to the question of mystical awareness and the innate capacity.

Ibn al-ʿArabī is primarily a visionary, but he formulated his visions in keeping with practically every form of Islamic learning. One of the first problems we face in investigating his voluminous writings is how to deal with his interpretative biases. It would be tempting to try to leave aside his theorizing and go straight to his experience. But then we would be forced to interpret his interpretation in terms of our own theoretical categories, and there is no reason to suppose that such an approach would bring us any closer to an understanding of what is at issue.

In what follows, I devote most of the space to bringing out Ibn al-ʿArabī's conceptual framework. It is important to stress, however, that Ibn al-ʿArabī was not an armchair thinker. What he writes, as he often tells us, is the embodiment of his mystical vision in an imaginal mode. His vision is a vision of Being, or of Reality itself. And this Reality is inherently aware. Consciousness is inseparable from Being. In a very real sense, consciousness is being, and being is consciousness. The centrality of this idea means that Ibn al-ʿArabī always focuses not on what we perceive but on what actually is, even if these are two sides of the same coin. Yet he is perfectly aware that presuppositions determine perceptions. This is a major theme of his works: he repeatedly tells us that people relate only to the gods of their own belief. But this is not simply psychological perceptiveness on his part. This idea expresses his vision that the god of belief is itself the merciful self-disclosure of the Real.

Fiṭra

Like Muslims in general, Ibn al-ʿArabī frequently employs the term *fiṭra*, which I have in the past translated as "primordial nature" or "innate disposition" but which I am happy to translate as "innate capacity." The root meaning of the term is to split, break open, bring forth, create, make. The Koran employs various forms from the root in twenty instances. Most significant is the single verse in which the word *fiṭra* itself is used along with a verb from the same root: "So turn thy face to the religion as one with primordial faith—God's innate capacity in keeping with which He brought forth [*faṭara*] human beings. There is no changing God's creation. This is the right religion, but most people know not" (30:30). Here the Koran tells us that the innate capacity of human beings pertains to their creation and that to adhere to this capacity is to follow God's right religion, understood by Muslims, naturally enough, as Islam. However, the Koran uses the term "Islam" in several meanings, one of which is simply "revealed religion," and the passage suggests that this is what is meant here, given the mention of the term *ḥanīf* or "one with primordial faith." The Koran associates this term with Abraham, whom it considers the closest of the prophets to

Muhammad.[4] Muslims in general look back to the religion established by Abraham as the most perfect form of Islam before Islam.

Koran commentators usually say that the innate capacity mentioned in this verse is faith in God or—what amounts to the same thing—the recognition of *tawḥīd*, which is the assertion of God's unity defined by the first Shahadah: "There is no god but God." Ibn al-ʿArabī identifies the innate capacity with the sum of the attributes of perfection possessed by the human spirit at its creation. He writes, "When God created the human spirit, he created it perfect, fully developed, rational, aware, having faith in God's *tawḥīd*, admitting his lordship. This is the innate capacity according to which God created human beings."[5]

A famous saying of the Prophet employs the term *fiṭra* in a way that is especially suggestive: "Every child is born with the innate capacity, but then its parents make it into a Christian, a Jew, or a Zoroastrian." Society's imperfections obscure the innate capacity and make it difficult for people to live in accordance with their original nature. In Ibn al-ʿArabī's terms, people remain imperfect, undeveloped, irrational, and unaware; they deny *tawḥīd* and associate other lords with God (*shirk*).

In short, already in the Koran and the Hadith, we find the idea that human beings are created with an innate capacity that allows them to understand things as they really are, but this capacity is clouded by the human environment. The function of the prophets is to "remind" (*dhikr*) people of what they already know, while the duty of human beings is simply to "remember" (*dhikr*).[6] Having remembered, they return to the innate capacity from which they have never really become separate.[7]

If the human spirit knows God and affirms *tawḥīd* at the moment of its creation, this is because this spirit is not completely separate from God. In describing the creation of human beings, the Koran says that God molded Adam's clay with his own two hands, then blew into him of his own spirit. The spirit is God's breath, and Muslim thinkers were well aware of the implications of the metaphor. Breath is different from the breather; yet it is also the same, since a person without breath is a corpse. The divine breath that animates human clay is not identical with God, nor is it completely different.

Human beings are near to God through their spirits, but they are far from him through their bodies made out of clay. The qualities of spirit and body lie at opposite extremes. The spirit is perfect, luminous, alive, rational, aware, intelligent, powerful, desiring, speaking; in short, it possesses all the attributes of God. But the body displays none of these qualities to any perceptible degree. It is merely earth and water, which represent the lowest of created things.[8]

When God blows the spirit into clay, this gives rise to the soul or self (*nafs*), which is an intermediate reality that possesses qualities of both sides. Hence the soul—which is the level of ordinary awareness—lies between light and darkness, perfection and imperfection, intelligence and ignorance, rationality and irrationality, awareness and unawareness, power and weakness. Within the soul, the innate capacity is represented by the luminous qualities of the spirit that are only dimly present. Actualizing the innate capacity in its fullest measure is seen as the goal of human existence. The soul must be transmuted such that its darkness becomes fully infused with spiritual light. What this actualization entails for human consciousness is suggested in mythic fashion in a Koranic passage about Abraham, the prophet "of primordial faith" who is a model of actualized *fiṭra*:

> We were showing Abraham the kingdom of the heavens and the earth, that he might be of those having sure faith. When night outspread over him he saw a star and said, "This is my Lord." But when it set, he said, "I love not the setters."
>
> When he saw the moon rising, he said, "This is my Lord." But when it set he said, "If my Lord does not guide me I shall surely be one of the misguided people."
>
> When he saw the sun rising, he said, "This is my Lord: this is greater!" But when it set he said, "O my people, surely I am quit of what you associate with God. I have turned my face to Him who brought forth [*faṭara*] the heavens and the earth, with primordial faith; I am not one of those who associate others with God." (6:76–80)

Waḥdat al-Wujūd

Like most Muslim thinkers and sages, Ibn al-ʿArabī grounds his perspective in the only completely certain knowledge available to human beings—that is, *tawḥīd* or the assertion of God's oneness. The meaning of *tawḥīd* is epitomized by the deceptively simple statement "There is no god but God." Without trying to define what Ibn al-ʿArabī understands by the word "God," we can simply say that its closest synonym is the word *al-ḥaqq*, the Real. Hence the Shahadah affirms that there is none real but the Real. In other words, there is nothing truly real but the absolutely real: all relative reality appears in function of a single, absolute reality, known in religious language as God.

The later tradition calls Ibn al-ʿArabī the founder of the school of *waḥdat al-wujūd*, "Oneness of Being" or "Unity of Existence," and this is a fair judgment so long as we recognize that he himself never employs this particular expression. His understanding of reality as *wujūd* can provide a useful key to some of his teachings on the nature of human consciousness and the ability of human beings to actualize *tawḥīd* to the fullest degree and thus to return to their innate capacity.

The word *wujūd* entered the technical vocabulary of the Islamic sciences on the basis of translations of Greek philosophical texts. With this background in view, it can be translated as "being" or "existence." But the literal sense of the Arabic word is "to find," and this meaning is never far from the minds of those Sufi authors who employ it. To speak of finding is to speak of awareness and consciousness; it is to imply that someone finds and something is found. To affirm *waḥdat al-wujūd* is to declare not only that existence is one but also that consciousness is one.

Islamic thought is general asserts that *wujūd* cannot be defined, since it is the most inclusive of realities. All definitions and discussion presuppose *wujūd*. For Ibn al-ʿArabī, *wujūd* is a name of God inasmuch as he is the utterly unknowable and inaccessible ground for everything that exists. *Wujūd* in this sense is nondelimited (*muṭlaq*), while everything other than *wujūd* is delimited, constrained, confined, and constricted. Ibn al-ʿArabī refers to the "other" (*ghayr*) by various terms, such as entity, thing, quiddity, and creature. For him and many other Muslim thinkers, *wujūd* remains the absolute, infinite, nondelimited reality of God, while all others remain relative, finite, and delimited.

Since *wujūd* is nondelimited, it is totally different from everything else. Whatever exists and can be known or grasped is a delimitation and definition, a constriction of the unlimited, a finite object accessible to a finite subject. In the same way, *wujūd*'s self-consciousness is nondelimited, while every other consciousness is constrained and confined. But one has to be careful in asserting *wujūd*'s nondelimitation. This must not be understood as an assertion that *wujūd* is different and only different from every delimitation. Ibn al-ʿArabī is quick to point out that *wujūd*'s nondelimitation demands that it be able to assume every delimitation. If *wujūd* could not become delimited, it would be limited by its inability to become delimited.[9]

When employing the language of Islamic theology, Ibn al-ʿArabī makes a parallel point when he says that God is both transcendent and immanent, or, as I prefer to translate the terms, both "incomparable" (*tanzīh*) with all things and "similar" (*tashbīh*) to all things. The creative tension between these two perspectives—declaring God incomparable and seeing him as similar—is a constant theme of his writings.

Ibn al-ʿArabī refers to the Real inasmuch as it is nondelimited, incomparable, and eternally unknowable as the Essence (*dhāt*), while he refers to it inasmuch as it assumes all limitations and is similar to all things by such terms as the Real Through which Creation Takes Place, the Cloud, or the Breath of the All-Merciful. In function of the All-Merciful Breath, the Real creates the universe, which is to say that *wujūd* manifests itself within the limitations of the others. *Wujūd*'s assumption of limitations is commonly called "self-disclosure" (*tajallī*). In its incomparability *wujūd* stands beyond every limitation, but in its similarity it discloses itself as every form in the external and internal worlds. Everything that "exists" or "is found" (*mawjūd*, the past participle of *wujūd*) displays a modality of *wujūd*. Likewise, every finding—every mode of consciousness and awareness—is a mode of *wujūd*'s own self-finding. *Wujūd* is comparable to light, while the things of the cosmos are comparable to the colors that represent the various modes of luminosity.

Wujūd is unknowable in itself; yet it discloses itself through its self-manifestations. Just as light has modalities of self-disclosure that we call colors," so *wujūd* has modalities of self-disclosure that are called "names" or "attributes" or "relationships." The primary attributes of *wujūd* are designated by the primary names of God. These include life, knowledge, desire, power, speech, hearing, sight, generosity, and justice. Wherever anything is found, these qualities are present, though not necessarily manifest. All colors are found in light, and the presence of light is sufficient to indicate that the colors are to be found in some way, but the colors become manifest only through specific conditions.

When a positive quality appears, *tawḥīd* alerts us to the fact that the quality must belong to *wujūd*. If life is observed, we know that *wujūd* is alive and that "there is no life but real life," the unadulterated, pure, absolute, and eternal life of the Real. Life that is found among the creatures is ephemeral, while permanent and real life is an exclusive property of the Real. In short, to declare that *wujūd* is one is to declare that reality is one, and to declare that reality is one is to recognize that all real qualities are found in their pure and absolute form only in the Real.[10]

Imagination

Ibn al-ʿArabī expresses the basic intuition of *tawḥīd*—that all real qualities can be nothing but pale reflections of *wujūd*—in many ways. One of the more useful of his expressions is the word "imagination" or "image" (*khayāl, mithāl*), which he applies on several levels extending from individual consciousness to everything other than God.[11] In general, he uses the term to refer to anything that has an intermediate and ambiguous status. In the broadest sense, it means that everything in existence hangs between sheer Reality and utter nonbeing. To use Ibn al-ʿArabī's expression, everything in the cosmos is both God and not God, or "He / not He."

As a faculty of the soul, imagination brings together sensory things, which have shapes and forms, and consciousness, which has no shape or form. Its nature can easily be grasped by reflecting on dreams, which for most people provide the most direct experience of imagination's nature and power. Dream images are perceived in sensory form; yet they are animated by a formless awareness. Every image brings together the multiplicity of the external world and the unity of the subject; each is an isthmus (*barzakh*) between the darkness of the bodily world and the luminosity of spirit.

In a slightly more extended sense, Ibn al-ʿArabī employs the term "imagination" to refer to the whole domain of the soul, the intermediate level of consciousness between spirit and body that makes up ordinary awareness. For him as for most Muslim sages, the terms "spirit," "soul," and "body" designate qualitative distinctions, not discrete entities. Thus, to speak of the spirit is to speak of a dimension of the human microcosm that is inherently luminous, alive, knowing, aware, and subtle, while to speak of the body is to refer to a dimension that is almost totally lacking in these same qualities. Hence, in itself—without its connection with the spirit—the body is for all intents and purposes dark, dead, ignorant, unconscious, and dense. The term "soul" or "imagination" then refers to the intermediate domain of the microcosm that is neither luminous nor dark, neither alive nor dead, neither subtle nor dense, neither conscious nor unconscious, but always somewhere between the two extremes.

Consciousness cannot escape the ambiguity of the soul. If we ask the question "Has so-and-so achieved consciousness?," the answer depends on the relationship we have in view. On one level, we may simply be asking if the chloroform has worn off. At the opposite extreme, we may be asking if the person has reached buddhahood.

Consciousness, like all divine qualities, represents a continuum. It has degrees of intensity, and the difference between the highest and the lowest created levels of consciousness is practically infinite. At the same time, the Real's consciousness is infinitely more real than the most intense consciousness possessed by the other, since nothing is real but the Real, and nothing is truly conscious but God.

Can human beings experience the consciousness of the Real, which alone can be called pure consciousness? The answer is always yes and no. *Tawḥīd* means that "there is no consciousness but God's own consciousness." Inasmuch as human consciousness is nothing but nondelimited *wujūd*'s finding of itself, the answer is yes. But inasmuch as a delimited reality—a human being—is involved in this finding, the answer is no. Every mode of consciousness accessible to anything other than the Essence of the Real is both identical with and different from the Real's own consciousness of Self. Only nondelimited *wujūd* experiences identity without difference. As the theological axiom puts it, "None knows God but God."

Knowledge

Wujūd in itself is the Real inasmuch as it is nondelimited, incomparable, and forever undisclosed, while *wujūd* in its self-disclosure is all the "others," all the things that find and are found. *Wujūd* as such cannot be found except by *wujūd*: "None knows God but God." But nothing other than the self-disclosures of *wujūd* can be found by anyone, since nothing else exists. Every "other" is simply a modality of *wujūd*.

Ibn al-ʿArabī employs a large number of terms to refer to different modes of awareness and consciousness, or different kinds of perception of and participation in *wujūd*'s self-disclosure. Most of these terms are rooted in Koranic divine names and represent the identity of *wujūd* with its self-disclosures. Under the most general of names that refer to consciousness—that is, Knowing (*ʿalīm*)—a number of other divine names represent specific modalities of knowledge, including Manifest (*ẓāhir*), Aware (*khabīr*), Seeing (*baṣīr*), Hearing (*samīʿ*), Encompassing (*muḥīṭ*), All-embracing (*wāsiʿ*), Witness (*shahīd*), Subtle (*laṭīf*), Light (*nūr*), Examiner (*raqīb*), Wise (*ḥakīm*), Preserver (*ḥāfiẓ*), Guarder (*muhaymin*), and Faithful (*muʾmin*). Each of these names gives news of one mode of *wujūd*'s knowledge of self and others, and each represents a mode of consciousness that is accessible to human beings. Ibn al-ʿArabī discusses the divine and the human implications of each in detail. *Tawḥīd* demands that in every case, the quality in its real and absolute sense belong only to *wujūd*, while it belong to the self-disclosures of *wujūd*—such as human beings—in an unreal and relative sense.

Other terms employed by Ibn al-ʿArabī stress the human vision of *wujūd* disclosing itself in all things. Among these are gnosis (*maʿrifa*), unveiling (*kashf, mukāshafa*), tasting (*dhawq*), insight (*baṣīra*), and opening (*fatḥ, futūḥ*).[12]

In the present context, it is impossible to provide more than the barest outline of what is implied in the most general of all these terms—that is, knowledge (*ʿilm*). It is typically seen as the primary attribute of *wujūd*. Though *wujūd* in itself is nondelimited and unconstricted, it is aware of itself and of every possible mode of its own self-disclosure. In other words, "God encompasses all things in knowledge" (Koran 65:12). *Wujūd* is one, and *wujūd* is both knower and known.

On the basis of *wujūd*'s knowledge of itself, it discloses itself according to the demands of its own qualities. The result is an infinitely diverse universe that externalizes the contents of *wujūd*'s knowledge. The creatures—the realities, entities, or things—are identical with the knowledge's objects. Inasmuch as they are found in the universe, they have been given a trace of *wujūd*. Inasmuch as they are ephemeral and unreal, they reflect their own realities, which have no inherent claim to *wujūd*. To return to the analogy of light, red and green are possible modalities of light; wherever they are found, they owe their existence to light, though they have no claim upon light. Without light there is no red and green, but the nonmanifestation of red and green in any given circumstances has no effect on light.

If we look at *wujūd* in terms of its own self-nature, we have to affirm that it is a single reality. But if we look at it in terms of its self-knowledge, then we have to say that it knows every possibility of expression that it entails, which is to say that it knows the cosmos in all its infinite spatial and temporal expanse. Hence, *wujūd* is one with a oneness that embraces potential manyness. In Ibn al-ʿArabī's terms, God can be called the One/Many (*al-wāḥid al-kathīr*)—that is, He is "one" in terms of his essence, and "many" in terms of his names, which are the general designations for the possible modalities of *wujūd*'s self-disclosure.

Ibn al-ʿArabī and his followers distinguish two categories of divine names in accordance with the predominance of oneness or manyness. Names that pertain mainly to oneness are called names of mercy, gentleness, or beauty; these are closely associated with God's similarity (*tashbīh*). Names that pertain mainly to manyness are called names of wrath, severity, or majesty; these are closely associated with God's incomparability (*tanzīh*). The first category designates creaturely relations with the Real that necessitate nearness, harmony, equilibrium, wholeness, sameness, and knowledge. The second category designates relations that necessitate distance from God, disharmony with the Real, disequilibrium, partiality, difference, and ignorance. These two categories designate the "two hands" with which God molded the clay of Adam.[13]

When *wujūd* discloses itself, it does so in respect of both God's hands—that is, in respect of both unity and diversity, nearness and distance, *tashbīh* and *tanzīh*. Those things that are more closely connected to *wujūd*'s oneness tend to manifest the qualities of unity, simplicity, harmony, equilibrium, and awareness. Salient examples are spirits, which are noncompound and relatively everlasting. Those things that are more closely connected to the diversity of the objects of *wujūd*'s knowledge display multiplicity, compoundness, disequilibrium, darkness, and unconsciousness. Examples are bodily thing. If God's right hand dominates in the makeup of a human being, the qualities pertaining to self-awareness—which is nothing but *wujūd*'s finding of itself—gain the upper hand. To the extent that God's left hand dominates, the human subject is overcome by dispersion, ignorance, and darkness.

The interrelationship between God's two hands is reflected in that between the macrocosm (the universe as a whole) and the microcosm (the human individual). The universe as a whole, in all its spatial and temporal expanse, displays the infinite diversity of *wujūd*'s possible modes of manifestation. The predominant qualities are difference, lack of integration, dispersion, scatteredness, dimness of light, unconsciousness, ignorance, and passivity. The human microcosm brings together and harmonizes all the diverse qualities of *wujūd* and hence manifests *wujūd*'s oneness and wholeness. To the extent that the microcosm represents a full and conscious self-disclosure of *wujūd*, the qualities that predominate in the human personality are unity, harmony, concentration, luminosity, awareness, knowledge, and activity.

The Unknown Station

Muslim thinkers typically explain the nature of the human microcosm in terms of the biblical saying repeated by the Prophet, "God created Adam in His own form [*ṣūra*]." This is understood to mean that human beings were brought into existence possessing all of God's attributes, which are nothing but the inherent qualities of *wujūd*. In other words, *wujūd* itself designates the innate capacity of human beings. To be human is to manifest *wujūd* as *wujūd*, while to be anything else is to manifest certain qualities of *wujūd* rather than others. Notice, however, that "manifestation" is the issue here, not identity with *wujūd* in every respect. Although identity is the goal, modes of difference always remain. God's two hands retain their rights even in the experience of oneness.

Wujūd's qualities are disclosed in the nonhuman realm in combinations that allow one or more qualities to dominate over others. But human beings concentrate and unify *wujūd*'s qualities such that, in the ideal situation, every quality stands in perfect balance and equilibrium with every other quality. All things in the universe except human beings stand in fixed and known stations (*maqām ma'lūm*), because each of them is colored by certain of *wujūd*'s attributes rather than others. Hence, nonhuman things can never reach an equilibrium of attributes or colors, a balance in which the colors cancel each other out, leaving only the pure, colorless light of *wujūd* itself.

Human beings come into the world without a fixed station, and hence they undergo constant change and transformation until death. They have the potential to manifest every color of light, every quality of *wujūd*. If they develop in harmony with nondelimited *wujūd*, they reach an unknown station rather than a known station, a station that Ibn al-ʿArabī often calls the "station of no station" (*maqām lā maqām*). A person who reaches this station displays every quality of *wujūd* in perfect harmony and balance with every other quality. This is the actualization of the innate capacity of being human, since it is a return to the divine form—or the *wujūd*—from which human beings arose.

If people fail to develop in harmony with uncolored and nondelimited *wujūd*, their divine form unfolds in keeping with certain qualities of *wujūd* rather than others. Hence, they enter into a known station like everything else in the universe. This may be a known luminous station like that of the angels, in which case they dwell in paradise after the resurrection. But there are many other possible known stations, some of them dark, dense, and dispersed, corresponding to various hell worlds.[14]

Human beings play a unique role in the cosmos because they alone allow for the full manifestation of the qualities that bring about integration, harmony, and wholeness. This peculiar human characteristic is typically called "all-comprehensiveness" (*jamʿiyya*). Ontologically, all-comprehensiveness goes back to the fact that God gave human beings an innate capacity that manifests the formless form of *wujūd*, which comprehends all realities. But the term "all-comprehensiveness" is also frequently employed to designate the fruit of meditation, concentration, and remembrance (*dhikr*). It is achieved through gathering together all the dispersed powers of the soul and focusing them on the Real itself, or actualizing *wujūd*'s own awareness of itself.

When discussed in positive terms, human perfection is viewed as the realization of every quality of *wujūd* latent in the divine/human form. Perfect human beings (*al-insān al-kāmil*) are looked upon as God's "vicegerents" (*khalīfa*), since they have brought together all his attributes in a conscious and active manner, and thus they rule the macrocosm in his stead. The innate capacity appears as the possibility to realize the qualities inherent in the divine/human form. Human perfection is viewed as a full affirmation of *tashbīh*, such that all the qualities of *wujūd* are humanly embodied in perfect balance and harmony.

Human perfection is also viewed in negative terms. Difference and *tanzīh* are stressed, rather than similarity and sameness. Since there is nothing real but God, human beings are utterly unreal. Ignorance and deviation result from not recognizing this. From this point of view, human perfection is seen as the stripping away of every claim to *wujūd*'s qualities. Human beings are the utter servants (*ʿabd*) of God, since they have nothing of their own. The path of spiritual growth is pictured as the abandoning of all the dark clouds that conceal the sun of *wujūd*. Only through achieving nothingness can people truly affirm the unique reality of the One (*tawḥīd*). From this standpoint, the innate capacity is to be empty of created qualities, because created qualities are delimitations, and *wujūd* is nondelimited. Emptiness alone allows for the full self-disclosure of *wujūd*. But to be empty of created qualities is to be full of *wujūd*, which alone is uncreated.

Ibn al-ʿArabī's description of perfect human beings as standing in the station of no station combines the positive and negative perspectives. Since perfect human beings have abandoned all qualities, they stand in no quality. But standing in no quality can only mean standing in *wujūd*, which alone is nondelimited by any quality whatsoever. Hence, the perfect human being is *wujūd*'s full self-disclosure, unhampered by any quality or entity, yet in complete control of every quality and entity.

Annihilation and Subsistence

Ibn al-ʿArabī and other Sufis employ many pairs of terms to bring out the complementary functions of servanthood and vicegerency—that is, the human state of actualizing simultaneous *tanzīh* and *tashbīh*, or being fully incomparable with *wujūd* and fully similar to it at one and the same time. One of the most famous of these pairs is *fanāʾ* (annihilation) and *baqāʾ* (subsistence). Western scholars seem to have focused on the term *fanāʾ* because it is reminiscent of terms like nirvana and moksha. But in the texts themselves, *fanāʾ* is always contrasted with *baqāʾ*. The locus classicus for the two terms is Koran 55:27: "All that dwells on the earth is *annihilated*, and there *subsists* only the face of your Lord, the possessor of majesty and generosity." For Ibn al-ʿArabī and many others, the "earth" is the divine/human form viewed in respect of *tanzīh*, while the "face of your Lord" is the divine/human form in respect of *tashbīh*. God's face is *wujūd*'s self-disclosure within the divine/human form.

When human beings affirm *tanzīh*, they negate reality from themselves. The goal of spiritual practice becomes the elimination of every claim to divine qualities. This is the station of "servanthood." Once all trace of self-affirmation has been erased, what is left is *tashbīh*. God is experienced as disclosing himself within the creature in order to bring it into existence. Creaturely attributes have been annihilated, and divine attributes subsist. This is the station of "vicegerency," or acting as God's representative in the cosmos. But in truth it is God who acts, since the servant has been utterly effaced.

It should not be imagined that this negation of self and affirmation of God remains a mental exercise. Quite the contrary, the experience of this reality preceded its formulation. Muslims who lived their faith to the fullest, having actually undergone the annihilation of their selfhood, were able, like al-Hallaj, to say "I am the Real," because the Real's consciousness of itself became actualized within them. This, at least, is the constant claim of all the masters of Sufism, and Ibn al-ʿArabī is no exception.

In a chapter of the *Futūḥāt* devoted to annihilation, Ibn al-ʿArabī points out that the term *fanāʾ* is invariably used in its technical sense along with the pronoun *ʿan* (from). Thus, the Sufis speak of annihilation *from* something. Likewise, the term *baqāʾ* is always employed with the pronoun *bi* (through). Hence one speaks of subsistence *through* something. In all cases, annihilation is lower and subsistence higher. "As for annihilation 'from the higher,' that is not a technical term of the Sufis, even though it is correct linguistically" (II 512.30).

Ibn al-ʿArabī does not provide an exact definition of the term "annihilation" but rather provides examples of what Sufis before him have said about it. They use it to mean "the annihilation of acts of disobedience, . . . the annihilation of the servant's vision of his own acts because God undertakes them, . . . and annihilation from creation" (II 512.27). He says that the Sufis consider *fanāʾ* to have seven levels and explains each in some detail. Already at the third level, seekers are annihilated from the attributes of created things and lose consciousness of their own attributes, since they perceive only God's attributes. The higher levels pertain to various modes of witnessing the Real.

The term "witnessing" (*shuhūd*) provides an important key to what is at issue when annihilation is mentioned. It always calls to mind the divine name Witness (*shahīd*), since "there is no witness but the Witness." In general, witnessing is synonymous with seeing, not only sight with the eyes but also sight with the heart, the inner organ that is the locus of awareness and consciousness. It is often employed as a synonym for "unveiling" (*kashf*), the lifting of the veils between creation and the Real. It demands consciousness of what is witnessed, but it does not demand full self-consciousness, especially if what is witnessed is perceived as light and the self is experienced as darkness.[15]

One of Ibn al-ʿArabī's students asked him why the mind does not stay the same after annihilation, given that annihilation erases the soul's faculties. Since the faculties play no role, they should not be affected. In the process of answering the question, Ibn al-ʿArabī refers to the "witness" (*shāhid*), which he defines elsewhere as "the trace [*athar*] that witnessing leaves in the heart of the witnesser" (*Futūḥāt* II 132.25):

> There is no instance of witnessing without a trace in the one who witnesses it. The trace is what is called the "witness." It brings about the increase that accrues to the rational and other faculties. If this witness is not found after the annihilation, then it was not an annihilation in *tawḥīd*. On the contrary, it was a sleep of the heart, since, in our view, annihilation is of two sorts: When we find the witness after it, then it is correct. When we do not find the witness after it, we call it a "sleep of the heart." It is like someone who sleeps and does not dream.[16]

Thus, Ibn al-ʿArabī recognizes a loss of self-awareness in spiritual experience that has no benefit for those who undergo it, since they remain totally unaffected by it. In another passage, he explains that the annihilation of self occurs because the self is darkness, while the object witnessed is light. When the light shines, the soul disappears.

> Shadows cannot be established when there is light. The cosmos is a shadow, and the Real is a light. That is why the cosmos is annihilated from itself when self-disclosure occurs. For the self-disclosure is light, and witnessing the soul is a shadow. Hence the viewer for whom the self-disclosure occurs is annihilated from the witnessing of himself during the vision of God. When God lets down the veil, the shadow appears, and joy is experienced through the witness. (*Futūḥāt* II 466.23)

Ibn al-ʿArabī seems to be saying here that during the self-disclosure, there is no consciousness of either self or other. It is only after the person returns to self-awareness that he experiences joy through the trace left in the soul by the witnessing. However, in another work he makes clear that the retention of a certain mode of self-consciousness during annihilation is necessary if human perfection is to be achieved. Hence, the annihilation of self that is experienced is not absolute.

> True perfection is found only in the one who witnesses both his Lord and himself. . . . If someone were to witness his Lord while being completely free of witnessing himself—as some people have claimed—he would gain no benefit and be the possessor of imperfection. For then the Real would be the one who witnesses itself through itself, and that is the way things are in any case. So what benefit would accrue to the one who supposes that he was annihilated from himself and witnessed his Lord at the same time?[17]

Ibn al-ʿArabī never lets us forget that annihilation is a relative term. We are always talking about annihilation *from* some specific mode of lower consciousness and a simultaneous subsistence *through* a specific mode of higher consciousness. There is a giving up of one kind of awareness for a higher kind (which may well be perceived as an emptiness—though nothing is absolutely empty but the Real). Annihilation, in other words, is validated through the subsistence that accompanies it. That which subsists is the Real's self-disclosure, and that which is annihilated is the unreal—the limited self-awareness of the individual. Ibn al-ʿArabī explains:

> Subsistence is your relationship with the Real. . . . But annihilation is your relationship with the engendered universe, since you say, "I have been annihilated from such and such." Your relationship to the Real is higher. Hence subsistence is a higher relationship, since the two are interrelated states.
>
> None subsists in this path except he who is annihilated, and none is annihilated except he who subsists. The one described by annihilation will always be in the state of subsistence, while the one described by subsistence will always be in the state of annihilation. In the relationship of subsistence is the witnessing of the Real, while in the relationship of annihilation is the witnessing of creation. For you never say, "I was annihilated from such and such," without conceiving of what you were annihilated from. Your very conception of that is your witnessing it, since you cannot avoid making it present to yourself in order to conceive of the property of becoming annihilated from it.
>
> Subsistence is the same. You have to witness the one through whom you subsist, and in this path, subsistence is only through the Real. Hence you have to witness the Real, since you must have made it present in your heart and conceived of it. Then you will say, "I subsist through the Real." This relationship is nobler and higher, because of the highness of the one with whom it is established. Hence the state of subsistence is higher than the state of annihilation, even if the two necessitate each other and are found in a single person at the same time. (*Futūḥāt* II 515. 24)

Human beings are forms of God. In other words, they epitomize the Real in which are found all the qualities of *wujūd*. However, "normal" people live in disequilibrium and dispersion. The divine attributes are actualized only partially and weakly, and certain attributes dominate over others. The dominant attributes most often pertain to qualities of *wujūd* that necessitate distance, differentiation, otherness, and darkness.

When *tanzīh* is taken into account, the transformation that must take place during spiritual practice involves the affirmation of the exclusive reality of the Real and the negation of every human claim to selfhood. This negation is sometimes called "annihilation." But every annihilation demands a subsistence; *tanzīh* cannot be viewed apart from *tashbīh*. Each of Ibn al-ʿArabī's seven levels of annihilation calls for an affirmation of *wujūd*'s self-disclosure and the reality of the human mode of consciousness that this self-disclosure brings about.

Becoming Human

The conclusions that we can draw from the brief outline presented in this essay can be summarized as follows: in Ibn al-ʿArabī's view, the innate capacity of human beings is established by the fact that they were created in the form of God, which is to say that they alone among all things in the cosmos have the potential to experience the full self-disclosure of *wujūd*. In order to actualize the divine form, however, they have to give up the delimited consciousness that separates them from *wujūd*. Through "servanthood," they must surrender to God's will and return everything to its rightful owner, who is the Real. To be annihilated *from* the unreal is to subsist *through* the Real. This "Real" is precisely *wujūd* inasmuch as it discloses itself to the servant. It is the formless divine form in which human beings were created.

The famous ninth-century Sufi Abū Yazīd Basṭāmī reported that he did not reach God until God said to him, "Leave aside your self and come." Ibn al-ʿArabī explains: "God invited him to come from the form of himself to the form of the Real in which God created Adam. The self is only able to assume that form when it departs from attachment to everything other than the Real."[18]

When we look at human consciousness in the context of actualizing the divine form, we see that consciousness represents the first and most salient quality of *wujūd*. To "leave aside oneself and come" to God is to eliminate the constraints of ignorance and separation and to experience oneself as a face of God turned toward manifestation and undergoing endless and never-repeating self-disclosures. This station is achieved only by a small minority of human beings, those who attain perfection, but it remains the innate capacity of all human beings. In Ibn al-ʿArabī's view, only those who achieve it deserve the name "human" in the full sense. In other people, the dispersive qualities of the macrocosm—represented most graphically by the animal kingdom—retain their ruling property; hence, the self does not fully benefit from the integrating qualities of the undifferentiated divine form.

Having reached pure unity and integration, perfect human beings experience the self-manifestation of nondelimited *wujūd* on the level of delimitation. All qualities of *wujūd* are actualized within such beings exactly as they are found in the Real itself. Hence, no quality can be ascribed to them, since to say that they are *this* would mean that they are *not that*. But they are neither this nor that, or they are both this and that. Not only do they move beyond all created limitations, but they also move beyond domination by either of the two primary qualities of the Real, oneness and manyness, or mercy and wrath, or beauty and majesty, or *tashbīh* and *tanzīh*: "The people of perfection have realized all stations and states and passed beyond these to the station above both majesty and beauty, so they have no attribute and no description" (*Futūḥāt* II 133.19).

This station of no station represents utter undifferentiation, pure unity, sheer consciousness, total freedom, complete lack of delimitation, and identity with the Real's self-disclosures. The nature of the consciousness thereby experienced can be expressed only through analogies and metaphors. It is utterly inaccessible to ordinary language, which is to say that people are blind to the shining of its light. In fact, of course, the light witnessed by perfect human beings is forever shining in the darkness of the cosmos; it is only human incapacity that prevents people from seeing it.

There is only one light, but every vision of that light other than that light's vision of itself is colored by the visionary, whether or not the visionary is annihilated from himself in the vision. No Muslim authority could think of denying that a single reality underlies all reality, a reality that is the root and source of all experience, all existence, all consciousness. This is the perspective of *tawḥīd* itself: none is truly real but God; none is truly conscious but God.

Notes

1. On the famous meeting between Averroes and Ibn al-ʿArabī, see, for example, C. Addas, *Ibn ʿArabī ou La quête du Soufre Rouge* (Paris: Gallimard, 1989), pp. 53ff.; H. Corbin, *Creative Imagination in the Sūfism of Ibn ʿArabī* (Princeton: Princeton University Press, 1969), pp. 41–42; W. Chittick, *The Sufi Path of Knowledge: Ibn al-ʿArabī's Metaphysics of Imagination* (Albany: SUNY Press, 1989), pp. xiii–xiv.

2. On Sufism's role in Islam, see my *Faith and Practice of Islam: Three Thirteenth-Century Sufi Texts* (Albany: SUNY Press, 1992).

3. M. Chodkiewicz, *Un océan sans rivage: Ibn ʿArabī, le livre et le loi* (Paris: Seuil, 1992). English version: M. Chodkiewicz, *An Ocean Without Shore: Ibn ʿArabī, The Book, and the Law* (Albany: SUNY Press, 1993).

4. The root meaning of the term *ḥanīf* is to incline toward or away from something, while the term itself is understood to mean someone who inclines toward the right way. The Koran uses it in twelve verses, and these determine the way Muslims have understood it. It is taken to signify the faith of Abraham and of those who continued to follow him in the Arab milieu, even after most people had become polytheists. Thus, the Prophet is said to have been *ḥanīf* even before he was made a prophet. See the article "Ḥanīf," *Encyclopedia of Islam* (new ed.; Leiden: E. J. Brill, 1954–).

5. Ibn al-ʿArabī, *al-Futūḥāt al-makkiyya* (Cairo: n.p., 1911), II 690.30. Cf. his discussion in II 616.91, quoted by Chittick, *Sufi Path*, p. 195.

6. On this double significance of the word *dhikr*, which arguably sums up Islamic teachings better than any other word, see Chittick, "Dhikr," *Encyclopedia of Religion* (New York: Macmillan, 1987), vol. 4, pp. 341–44.

7. See Ibn al-ʿArabī's comparison of the recovery of *fiṭra* to the appearance of the sun after a cloud passes by (Chittick, *Sufi Path*, p. 195).

8. This is not to suggest that clay is somehow negative or evil. The point is simply that clay represents an opposite extreme relative to spirit. Muslim thinkers, Ibn al-ʿArabī in particular, were well aware of the many virtues of clay, earth, and water. See S. Murata, *The Tao of Islam* (Albany: SUNY Press, 1992), pp. 136–41 and passim.

9. On *wujūd* as nondelimited, see Chittick, *Sufi Path*, pp. 109–12.

10. Evil is not ascribed to *wujūd* because, generally speaking, it derives from those qualities that pertain specifically to the unreal, and the unreal has no existence as such. Cf. Chittick, *Sufi Path*, pp. 290ff.

11. On the world of imagination in its various senses, see Chittick, *Sufi Path*, chap. 7.

12. I provide basic definitions for this second set of terms in *Sufi Path*, chap. 13 and passim. Ibn al-ʿArabī also deals in great detail with a large number of "states" (*aḥwāl*) and "stations" (*maqāmāt*), which represent various psychological and spiritual modalities in which people experience *wujūd*. Likewise, he discusses the faculties of mind, the nature of thoughts, techniques of meditation and concentration, and so on. His *Futūḥāt* alone represents an enormous repository of Islamic learning on the nature of human beings and their interrelationships with the visible and invisible worlds. Modern scholars have barely scratched the surface of his works.

13. On God's two hands and their relationship with these two groups of names as expounded by Ibn al-ʿArabī and his commentators, see Murata, *Tao of Islam*, chap. 3.

14. However, Ibn al-ʿArabī maintains that all things reach their own felicity in the end, since all things are possible modalities of *wujūd*, and *wujūd* is fundamentally mercy and bliss. On Ibn al-ʿArabī's eschatology, see W. Chittick, *Imaginal Worlds: Ibn al-ʿArabī and the Problem of Religious Diversity* (Albany: SUNY Press, 1994), chap. 7.

15. For some of Ibn al-ʿArabī's basic teachings on witnessing, see Chittick, *Sufi Path*, pp. 225–28 and passim.

16. Ibn Sawdakīn, *Wasā'il al-sā'il*, pp. 44–45; edited in M. Profitlich, *Die Terminologies Ibn ʿArabīs im "Kitāb wasā'il al-sā'il" des Ibn Saudakīn* (Freiburg im Breisgau: Klaus Schwarz Verlag, 1973).

17. Ibn al-ʿArabī, *Mawāqiʿ al-nujūm* (Cairo: Maktaba Muḥammad ʿAlī Ṣabīḥ, 1965), p. 27.

18. Ibn Sawdakīn, *Wasā'il al-sā'il*, pp. 38–39.

FIVE

Mysticism, Mediation, and Consciousness

The Innate Capacity in John Ruusbroec

JAMES ROBERTSON PRICE III

> There occurs a meeting and a union which are without intermediary and super natural, and in this is found our highest blessedness.[1]

DURING THE PAST fifty years, philosophers of mysticism have been actively intrigued by the meaning and epistemological status of quotations such as this one by John Ruusbroec, the fourteenth-century mystic from Flanders. An intense and fruitful debate has emerged, one marked by three discernible and ongoing philosophic moments. By briefly sketching this debate, I will clarify my own entry into the discussion, as well as my focus on one of its vexed issues: the relationship of mysticism, mediation, and consciousness.

Beginning in the 1940s, "perennial" philosophers such as Aldous Huxley[2] and Frithjof Schuon[3] accepted at face value claims made by Ruusbroec and others regarding an unmediated mystical experience of transcendent reality. Such statements led perennialists to conclude that there is a "common core" to mystical experience, one that transcends the historical and cultural differences of particular religious traditions. Considerable scholarly effort has been devoted to discerning and cataloguing the common features of this experience.

During the late 1970s, the perennialist position was challenged by a group of philosophers who drew on the insights of Kant, linguistic philosophy, and the sociology of knowledge. This group argued that mystical experience can be neither unmediated nor transcultural—for its texture and content are unavoidably shaped by the cultural, doctrinal, and ascetic context of a mystic's own tradition. Thus, in contrast to the "transcendent unity" of religion affirmed by the perennialists, neo-Kantians maintain that different religious traditions necessarily mediate different mystical experiences to their adherents and that a strong pluralism obtains among the world religions. Neo-Kantian scholars have therefore sought to discern and clarify the differences among the various traditions.[4]

In the past ten years, a third wave of philosophers—who have been called the Perennial Psychologists or Experientialists[5]—has challenged the empirical and epistemological assumption of the neo-Kantians.[6] This group argues that similarities and differences in mystical experiences—whether within or across religious traditions—can and should be determined on a case-by-case basis. Thus, their constructive goal is to establish philosophically rigorous foundations for the cross-cultural analysis of mystical experience. The methodological key to this effort is a shift in the analytical focus that marks both perennialist and neo-Kantian approaches to the issue. The latter focus on what its adherents take to be commonalities or differences in the *content* of mystical experiences. The focus of the Perennial Psychologists, in contrast, is a phenomenologically attentive analysis of the *operations* of mystical consciousness. This distinction will be clarified in what follows. The basic argument, however, is that a capacity for transformation toward the mystical dimensions of consciousness is innate in human beings and that this capacity provides the critical ground for cross-cultural analysis.

In this essay I examine the implications of this methodological shift for the notion of mediation, a concept central to the entire discussion. For in each philosophic moment of the unfolding debate, "mediation" has meant largely what the neo-Kantians mean by it—that is, the shaping of the content of mystical experience by the linguistic and cultural factors of the mystic's tradition. The neo-Kantian understanding of mediation is operative even when the fact of it is denied, as when the perennialists assert that mystical experience transcends the mediated character of religious culture and history. It is also operative when it is refuted, as when Perennial Psychology thinkers argue that neo-Kantian cognitional theory is philosophically invalid or that mystical claims for an unmediated "pure consciousness event" are phenomenologically accurate.[7]

I argue that a notion of mediation adequate for analyzing the operations of consciousness (as well as its content) is necessary to properly understand the relation of mediation and mystical consciousness, to establish constructive, critical grounds for the cross-cultural analysis of mystical experiences, and to explain the relationship between mystical consciousness and the mediated character of more ordinary patterns of consciousness.

First, however, it is important to consider more closely the relationship between mediation and mystical consciousness as understood and developed by neo-Kantian thinkers. To this end, I draw on the work of Steven Katz, who is widely regarded as representative in this regard.[8]

Katz and the Neo-Kantian Position

Katz maintains that mystical experiences, like all other experiences, are mediated: "There are NO pure (i.e. unmediated) experiences. Neither mystical experience nor more ordinary forms of experience give any indication, or any grounds for believing that they are unmediated."[9] He goes on to clarify what he means by mediation: "In order to understand mysticism, . . . [one must acknowledge] that the experience itself as well as the form in which it is reported is shaped by concepts which the mystic brings to, and which shape, his experience."[10]

Mediation, then, consists in the shaping of mystical experience by the conceptual expectations of the mystic. Katz, of course, is not using the term "conceptual" in a narrow, intellectualist sense. It functions as a shorthand for the "images, beliefs, symbols, and rituals [which] define, in advance, what experience [the mystic] want to have, and which he then does have, will be like."[11] Much in the manner of Kant, Katz understands mediation as the conceptual lens or filter that shapes every experience, including mystical ones.

The implication here is that mystical experience is a form of *intentional* consciousness. It is the means by which the mystic "intends" or seeks knowledge of what Katz refers to as the desired "mystical object."[12] Notice that by conceiving of mystical experiences in this way, Katz highlights the "object" or *content* of the mystic's experience: "The Christian mystic does not experience some unidentified reality, which he then conveniently labels God, but rather has the at least partially prefigured Christian experiences *of God, or* [*of*] *Jesus* or the like. . . . It is my view . . . that the Hindu experience *of Brahman* and the Christian experience *of God* are not the same."[13] Again, the point is that such experiences of objects like *brahman* and God are necessarily mediated. for Katz and other neo-Kantians, to claim otherwise is, "if not self-contradictory, at best empty."[14]

In assessing the adequacy of Katz's neo-Kantian account of mediation and mysticism, I turn to the testimony of the mystics themselves. In this, I focus on the writings of the Christian mystic John Ruusbroec. I argue for two points: one, that Ruusbroec maintains explicitly that a mystical experience is *not* intentional and does *not* involve the knowing of a "mystical object"; and two, that as a consequence, there is no basis for the neo-Kantian judgment that mystical claims for unmediated experiences of transcendent reality are either "empty" or "self-contradictory." In making this case I clarify both the nature of mystical consciousness as Ruusbroec describes it and the technical meaning of his statement "There occurs a meeting and a union that is without intermediary and supernatural."

Ruusbroec and Mystical Consciousness

Ruusbroec's account of mystical consciousness is based on describing and relating the various "activities of the mind or spirit"[15] and on the degree of awareness that accompanies them. In doing this, he draws on the traditional Christian distinction among active, spiritual, and contemplative lives to distinguish three basic categories of conscious activity and awareness. I discuss each in turn.

The active life concerns a person's actions in the world and focuses in particular on the moral and religious character of those actions. The goal is a life centered in "good works"—in actions that embody the virtues of humility, compassion, and purity.[16] For Ruusbroec, the distinction between the active life and the spiritual life turns on the degree and quality of awareness that a person brings to his actions. An "active" person is one whose attention and awareness are absorbed in the performance and outcome of the action itself. "Actives" do not consciously attempt to cultivate an awareness of themselves as subject—of their feelings and memories or of the dynamic patterns of sensing, understanding, desiring, and choosing that are the interior, conscious ground of all exterior actions.[17]

In Ruusbroec's view, most people are "actives." A "spiritual" person, in contrast, is one who not only acts but also cultivates a sustained attentiveness to the interior movements and activities of his or her consciousness. Ruusbroec offers a detailed account of the stages that mark the development of spiritual awareness and describes the progressive and linked transformations of the senses, feelings, intellect, and will.[18] For the purposes of this essay, however, it is enough to focus on the goal of the spiritual life, on an experience Ruusbroec refers to as "spiritual union with God."[19] This experience involves a threshold awareness of the divine activity that grounds the activities of the spirit. To cross that threshold and to become aware of the activity of God in God's own terms (i.e., the inner life of the Trinity) is to enter mystical consciousness and the contemplative life. Before discussing mystical consciousness, however, it is necessary to clarify the nature of spiritual union.

To attain the level of awareness associated with spiritual union, the activities of the mind must be completely stilled. Ruusbroec states that the powers of the spirit must be gathered into their source in the individual's consciousness, into what he refers to as "the unity of the mind,"[20] or "the bare (*bloet*) essential being of the spirit."[21] Ruusbroec describes this as a state of awareness that is "unified, empty, and imageless, raised up through love to the open bareness of our mind."[22] In it, he continues, "we transcend all things and die to all rational observation in a dark state of unknowing."[23] "[We] turn inward and fix [our] memory on total bareness, above the impressions of all sensible images and above multiplicity, and possess . . . the unity of [our] spirit as [our] own dwelling place."[24]

Ruusbroec explains that being free of images is necessary because "God is a spirit whom no one can properly represent through images."[25] That is to say, "God" is not an "object" in the normal sense of that term and so can neither be directly known nor experienced through the operations of intentional consciousness. Thus, while spiritual exercises involving reason, imagination, and the other powers of the spirit are good and have their place in the spiritual life, these operations must give way if spiritual union is to be attained.[26]

Spiritual union, then, is based on a nonintentional state of awareness in which all the activities and operations of consciousness are stilled. Into this awareness emerges "a divine stirring or touch in the unity of our spirit."[27] this is the experience of spiritual union. The spirit receives it passively, "for here there is a union of the higher powers in the unity of the spirit . . . and at this level no one is active but God alone."[28] Thus, while the spirit is aware of the "divine touch," the touch itself remains both unknown and unknowable, because the spirit's capacity for knowing has been stilled and because the touch is itself a transcendent act of consciousness, not an object of intentional consciousness.

In this connection, it is important to note that for Ruusbroec, spiritual union is a mediated experience. Despite its nonintentional character, Ruusbroec maintains that the awareness attending spiritual union is itself the most subtle of all mediations. He states that the awareness of the divine touch "is the inmost intermediary between God and ourselves, between rest and activity, between particular forms and the absence of all form, and between time and eternity."[29]

Thus, for Ruusbroec (unlike Katz and the neo-Kantians), it is not conceptual expectations but "the activities of our spirit [that] constitute [the] intermediary between the human and the divine."[30] Whenever the human spirit is active in its own terms, the divine is experienced, to use Ruusbroec's phrase, "with intermediary (*met middele*)." This encompasses the entire range of conscious activities associated with the active and spiritual lives. It includes all religious experiences, including conversions, consolations, ecstasies, visions, auditions, and other transpersonal experiences where the powers of the spirit are operative.[31] Even the simple, nonintentional awareness that characterizes spiritual union is for Ruusbroec an activity of the spirit. For the experience of the divine as an active stirring or touch at the depths of one's spirit is an experience mediated by the quality of the awareness itself.[32] Only when the activities of the spirit are completely transformed is it possible to met God "without intermediary." Only then does an individual enter the contemplative life and open up to mystical states of consciousness.[33]

The contemplative life, as Ruusbroec puts it, is a life lived "in the divine light and after God's own manner."[34] By this he means two things at once: that the activities of the spirit cease to operate in their own terms and that the principle of conscious activity becomes that of the divine consciousness itself.

For Ruusbroec, the defining characteristic of contemplation is that "the [divine] light transforms and pervades our spirit."[35] "It envelopes us and transforms us through its own inmost self, so that our own activity is brought to nought by God."[36] Ruusbroec describes this as a "fall into a modeless state" in which the contemplative "loses the power of observing all things in their distinctiveness and . . . all his activity fails him."[37] From the perspective of the (failed) spirit, this is an experience of "darkness, bareness and nothingness."[38]

Yet it is at the same time an experience of "blissful rest"[39] and "loving immersion."[40] For to be brought to nothing in the activities of the spirit is to become one with the activity that is God. As Ruusbroec puts it, "In the empty being of our spirit we receive an incomprehensible resplendence which envelopes and pervades us in the same way the air is pervaded by the light of the sun. The resplendence is nothing other than an act of gazing and seeing which has no ground."[41] That is to say, the divine light received by the spirit is itself a conscious activity ("an act of gazing and seeing which has no ground"). In mystical consciousness, this act becomes the spirit's new principle of activity, and the experience is one of identity and union. The spirit becomes "ceaselessly active according to God's own manner of acting"[42] and "ceaselessly becomes the very resplendence which it receives. . . . The contemplative feels and finds himself to be nothing other than the same light with which he sees."[43]

Ruusbroec is not saying that human consciousness is by nature divine. He goes to considerable length to clarify his position that human beings are created spirits and remain so even during contemplation.[44] Rather, his account of mystical consciousness is descriptive and phenomenological. The activity that is God "cannot be known except through itself."[45] It must be known without the mediating activity of the spirit, for, as Ruusbroec continues, "if we could know and comprehend it by ourselves it would lapse into some particular form or measure and would then not be able to satisfy us." Performatively, to contemplate is to be in act as God is in act: "To comprehend God as he is in himself, above and beyond all likeness, is to be God with God, without intermediary or any element of otherness which could constitute an obstacle or impediment."[46]

Having clarified Ruusbroec's distinction among the active, spiritual, and contemplative lives, it is important to sum up by pointing to their intrinsic connections. Ruusbroec offers the image of three concentric circles: the inner circle is the active life; it is surrounded by the spiritual life, which is encircled by the contemplative life. The point is that action depends upon and is grounded in the activities of the human spirit. If we are not conscious, we cannot act. Yet consciousness and the activities of the spirit are in their turn grounded by an activity of a consciousness that has no ground—that is, the "activities" of God's own consciousness. Without this Divine Ground, Ruusbroec contends that human consciousness would cease to exist.[47] Thus, action, human consciousness, and divine consciousness are differentiated yet linked, and it is the cultivation of spiritual and mystical awareness that reveals their relations. For Ruusbroec, the activity of our spirit in our work and the activity of God in our spirit are mutually related.

Mediation and Mystical Consciousness

We are now in a position to understand clearly the text with which we began: "There occurs a meeting and a union which are without intermediary and super natural, and in this is our highest blessing." This is Ruusbroec's description of mystical consciousness. It entails "a meeting and a union"—that is, a state in which the consciousness of the mystic operates as one with the "activity" of the divine consciousness. This union is "without intermediary and super natural," because all natural activities of the human spirit have been stilled and transformed, and the principle of activity is God.

Ruusbroec's account of mystical consciousness calls into question the adequacy of the understanding of mysticism and mediation advanced by Katz and the neo-Kantians. The differences between the two accounts are several. The first difference is that whereas neo-Kantians assume that mystical consciousness is a form of intentional consciousness, Ruusbroec offers strong evidence that this assumption is false. The activities of the spirit that make up intentional consciousness—sensing, feeling, imagining, reasoning, evaluating, and so forth—are all stilled in the course of attaining spiritual awareness. As Ruusbroec describes it, mystical consciousness is a dynamic, yet nonintentional state.

The second difference is directly related to the first. Whereas the assumption about the intentionality of mystical consciousness leads neo-Kantians to focus analytically on an "object" or "content" of mystical consciousness, Ruusbroec argues that *there is no intentional object* and develops his account in terms of the operations or activities of the spirit. Indeed, to the extent that the spirit is active in mystical consciousness, it is active not in its own terms but according to the activity of the divine consciousness. Moreover, to the extent that "objects" are known in mystical consciousness, they are known in the manner that the divine consciousness knows them, a knowing that Ruusbroec can describe only by means of negation, as a dynamic yet modeless awareness that transcends form, particularity, and all distinctions of time and place.[48]

The third difference is that whereas neo-Kantians understand mediation as the shaping of mystical experience by the conceptual expectations of the mystic, Ruusbroec understands mediation as the apprehension of God through the various activities of the human spirit. Whenever the activities of the spirit are operative, God is experienced "with intermediary (*met middele*)." When the activities of the spirit are stilled and transformed in mystical consciousness, God is experienced "without mediation."

This shows, contrary to Katz's assertion, that Ruusbroec's understanding of mystical consciousness as "unmediated" is neither self-contradictory nor empty. Neither, however, is it complete. For Ruusbroec, mystical experience of God is unmediated by the activities of the human spirit. It is not dependent on the shaping background of one's learning, language, or sensory experience. Without denying this, one could expand Ruusbroec's notion by articulating the obverse: *in mystical consciousness, human consciousness is mediated by the activity of divine consciousness.*

In my view, this notion of the mediated character of mystical consciousness is far more adequate for the philosophy of mysticism than the neo-Kantian notion. As Ruusbroec's account indicates, the neo-Kantian analysis is based on a category mistake: reducing mystical consciousness to a form of intentional consciousness. This is deeply misleading when it comes to the analysis of mystical texts.

The notion of mediation advanced here has a number of analytical advantages. First, it is consistent with Ruusbroec's account of mystical consciousness, and its adequacy can be critically assessed in light of the accounts of other mystics.

Second, since this understanding of mediation is based on the operations of consciousness, it provides a critically grounded entry into the cross-cultural analysis of mystical traditions. The working hypothesis is simply that, whereas symbol systems and cultural constructs may vary across cultures, the dynamic patterns of human consciousness constitute a transcendental "innate capacity." The hypothesis is that the patterns of consciousness operative in a human being in fourteenth-century Flanders are potentially the same as those operative in a human being in sixth-century India. This hypothesis can and must be critically assessed.

Third, the focus on operations within mystical consciousness opens up an analytical perspective on doctrinal and mystical language considerably different from neo-Kantian assumptions. It is clear from Ruusbroec's account that phrases like "union with God" refer with technical precision to particular states and activities of consciousness and not to mystical or ontological "objects." This means that the doctrinal and symbolic language of the various mystical traditions can be compared on the basis of the dynamics of consciousness that ground them.[49] It need not be assumed, as neo-Kantians urge, that different languages indicate different mystical experiences and that the critical identification of significant commonalities among the mystical traditions is foreclosed. On the contrary, the way to a critical and constructive dialog is now clear.

Notes

1. John Ruusbroec, "The Spiritual Espousals," *John Ruusbroec: The Spiritual Espousals and Other Works*, trans. James A. Wiseman, introduction by James A. Wiseman, preface by Louis Dupre (New York: Paulist, 1985), p. 119.

2. Aldous Huxley, *The Perennial Philosophy* (New York: Harper, 1944).

3. Frithjof Schuon, *L'Unité transcendante des religions* (Paris: Editions Gallimard, 1948). Revised English edition: *The Transcendent Unity of Religions*, trans. Peter Townsend, introduction by Huston Smith (New York: Harper, 1975).

4. For two of the best examples, see Robert M. Gimmello, "Mysticism in Its Contexts," in *Mysticism and Religious Traditions*, ed. Steven T. Katz (New York: Oxford University Press, 1983), pp. 61–88; and Daniel Brown, "The Stages of Mindfulness Meditation in Cross-Cultural Perspective," in *Transformations of Consciousness*, ed. Ken Wilber, Jack Engler, and Daniel P. Brown, (Boston: New Science Library, 1986), pp. 219–284.

5. Robert K. C. Forman called them perennial psychologists in a response to a panel at the American Academy of Religion, November 1992. Charlene Spretnak, a member of that panel, suggested the more neutral term "experientialists."

6. See *The Problem of Pure Consciousness: Mysticism and Philosophy*, ed. Robert K. C. Forman (New York: Oxford University Press, 1990).

7. See Robert K. C. Forman, "Introduction: Mysticism, Constructivism, and Forgetting," in Forman, *The Problem of Pure Consciousness*, pp. 3–49; and James Robertson Price III, "The Objectivity of Mystical Truth Claims, *Thomist* 49 (1985): 81–98.

8. For other, compatible accounts, see William Wainwright, *Mysticism* (Madison: University of Wisconsin Press, 1982), and Jerry Gill, "Mysticism and Mediation," *Faith and Philosophy* 1 (1984): 111–121.

9. Steven Katz, "Language, Epistemology and Mysticism," in *Mysticism and Philosophical Analysis*, ed. Steven Katz (New York: Oxford University Press, 1978), p. 26.

10. Ibid.; emphasis mine.

11. Ibid., p. 33.

12. Ibid., p. 26; cf. pp. 50–51, 63.

13. Ibid., p. 26. Emphasis mine.

14. Ibid.

15. Ruusbroec, "Spiritual Espousals," p. 72.

16. Ibid., pp. 54–64.

17. See, for example, Ruusbroec, "The Sparkling Stone," pp. 165–166, where Ruusbroec distinguishes and assesses the qualities of awareness that attend the active (exterior) and spiritual (interior) lives.

18. See Ruusbroec, "Spiritual Espousals," pp. 71-144.

19. Ruusbroec, "Sparkling Stone," p. 157.

20. Ruusbroec, "Spiritual Espousals," p. 72.

21. Ibid., p. 110. As Ruusbroec explains elsewhere: "The unity of our spirit . . . is the originating source . . . of all creaturely activity . . . , whether in the natural or supernatural order. Nevertheless the unity is not active insofar as it is unity" (p. 118).

22. Ruusbroec, "Sparkling Stone," p. 171.

23. Ibid.; cf. "Spiritual Espousals," p. 72.

24. Ruusbroec, "Spiritual Espousals," p. 99.

25. Ruusbroec, "Sparkling Stone," p. 157.

26. Ibid.

27. Ruusbroec, "Spiritual Espousals," p. 130.

28. Ibid., p. 112.

29. Ibid., p. 131.

30. Ibid., p. 120.

31. Ibid., pp. 86–88, 102–105.

32. "We feel an eternal inclination toward something which is different from what we are ourselves. This is the most intimate and hidden distinction which we can feel between ourselves and God, for beyond this there is no further difference." Ibid., p. 133.

33. For Ruusbroec's most detailed description of the transition from spiritual union to contemplation, see ibid., pp. 113–116.

34. Ibid., p. 116.

35. Ibid., p. 132.

36. Ruusbroec, "Sparkling Stone," p. 174.

37. Ruusbroec, "Spiritual Espousals," p. 133; cf. p. 147.

38. Ibid., p. 133.

39. Ibid.

40. Ruusbroec, "Sparkling Stone," p. 174.

41. Ibid., p. 171.

42. Ruusbroec, "Spiritual Espousals," p. 118.

43. Ibid., p. 147.

44. Ruusbroec, "Little Book of Clarification," pp. 259–260.

45. Ruusbroec, "Spiritual Espousals," p. 146.

46. Ibid.

47. Ibid., p. 118.

48. See Ruusbroec, "Spiritual Espousals," p. 118, and "Little Book of Clarification," p. 260.

49. For a preliminary statement of this methodological approach, see James Robertson Price III, "Typologies and the Cross-Cultural Analysis of Mysticism: A Critique," in *Religion and Culture: Essays in Honor of Bernard Lonergan*, ed. Timothy P. Fallon and Phillip Boo Riley (Albany: SUNY Press, 1987), pp. 181–190.

PART II

PSYCHOLOGY AND THE INNATE CAPACITY

SIX

The Innate Capacity

Jung and the Mystical Imperative

JOHN DOURLEY

JUNG'S UNDERSTANDING OF the nature and dynamic of the psyche is intrinsically religious in that the encompassing process of psychic maturation it seeks to describe has as its foundational *telos*, or intentionality, a movement toward a state of consciousness that can, and perhaps must, be described as mystical. "Mystical consciousness," in this context, is taken to mean the conscious experience, admitting various degrees of intensity, of the unification of the many energies of one's individual humanity, simultaneously informed by the sense of one's continuity with the totality and marked by the expanded empathy such continuity engenders.

A brief examination of certain foundational elements of Jung's understanding of the psyche's movement to maturation reveals the religious implications intrinsic to the process itself. These religious implications are nowhere more evident than in the material Jung presents as the master symbols of the self. When examined closely, the symbols reveal a profound religiosity expressive of the religious intent of the psychic agency that sponsors them. Dwelling on these core themes in Jung's psychology forces the conclusion that in the end Jung functionally identifies the further reaches of maturity with a state of consciousness that can only be called mystical.

Furthermore, Jung's thought on religion and mysticism implies a latent metaphysic that he not infrequently denied existed. The isolation of this metaphysic would contribute to a more adequate understanding of Jung's psychology and help elucidate the contribution of Jung's psychology to a more unified vision of the intimately related but often conflicted worlds of psychology (where it is more than measurement), theology or religious studies, and philosophy. Such a metaphysic and its underlying unitary vision would thus serve to unify in the individual those legitimate but disparate experiences out of which these disciplines are born. As it unified the conflict of absolutes within the individual, it would serve socially to foster a sense of human solidarity beneath and beyond the current and possibly terminal clash of conflicting absolutes, from enmity between academic disciplines to the enmity between differently bonded religious or political communities.

The initial point, then, is that for Jung the psyche is natively religious and moves in accord with its own *telos* to mystical states of consciousness. To make this point, one must deal, however briefly, with what Jung meant by religion and how he relates it to mysticism. Jung's psychology is religious, in a primary and deepest sense, because it claims to identify in theory and to engage in practice the agencies operative in the generation of religion universally. He argues consistently throughout his works that the archetypes, those powerful latencies in the collective unconscious, are vested with so great an energy that when they impact on consciousness they generate a sense of the numinous. This experience of the numinous is the basis of the human experience of the divine in both its benevolent and its malevolent forms.[1] On this interplay of archetypal power with the energies of consciousness Jung grounds humanity's universal consent, the *consensus gentium*, that deity exists as well as whatever truth may attach to the ontological argument—namely, that the immediate experience of God under whatever formality is the only "proof" for God's existence.[2]

Further exploration of Jung's thought on the psychogenesis of religion uncovers the unavoidable implication in his psychology that collective religions arise from the matrix of the deeper psyche to compensate for collective disorder and imbalance in much the same sense that dreams address similar problems at the personal level. This means that the world religions and the nightly dream have the same "author" and serve an analogous function in stabilizing and expanding the consciousness of society and individual. It further implies that dialogue with the dream is dialogue with divinity. This makes the analytic process a sacred process and is the reason Jung defined religion as the careful observation of that which proceeds from the unconscious into consciousness, with a certain preference given to the dream. Such observation is an observation of how the Gods and Goddesses are acting in one's life now, or, at least, during the last remembered dream.

Passing from his understanding of religion to his closely related understanding of mysticism, Jung defines the mystic as one who has had "a particularly vivid experience of the processes of the collective unconscious."[3] He adds, immediately, "Mystical experience is experience of archetypes."[4] In these same passages he confesses that he would have difficulty distinguishing mystical from archetypal forms.[5] By this I take him to mean that symbols or other forms of archetypal expression that bear a highly numinous charge are at once archetypal, mystical, and, needless to say, religious, regardless of the literary genre to which they belong.

Like William James, Jung pays tribute to the unmediated nature of mystical experience—to the fact that mystics personally experience the sources from which all religion arises to consciousness. He writes, "We would do well to harbour no illusions in this respect: no understanding by means of words and no imitation can replace actual experience."[6] This intimate experience of the source of religious vitality, as opposed to a purely formal religious observance based, as it often is, on a life of faith severed from an experiential basis, leads Jung to say of the mystics, "Only the mystics bring creativity into religion."[7]

By this remark Jung means at least two things. At the first level, he means that the mystic, who usually stands in a definite tradition and contacts the common source of all religion through a relationship to one of them, can bring new life and understanding to the traditional symbols and dogmas of an established tradition. The mystic does this through the immediate experience of the basis of the symbol's vitality in the unconscious. There is a sense in which Jung himself did this in his work to retrieve the meaning of major Christian symbols and rites from the state of "sacrosanct unintelligibility"[8] in which he found them. Thus, for instance, in his work on the Trinity,[9] the figure of Christ,[10] and the psychological import of the Catholic Mass,[11] he sought to show how these symbols and rites were expressions of the archetypal movements and energies of the unconscious. The legitimate and significant function of such symbols, both personally and societally, is to lead the believer or participant into an immediate experience of the unconscious from which these symbols are themselves born into consciousness. The mystic could thus revitalize the traditional symbol system by personally experiencing and leading others into the experience of the primordial sources of renewal these systems can mediate when they are not fatally encrusted by the familiarity bred by creed and dogma.

But, at a second level, Jung implies that the mystic, in his or her incursions into the unconscious, can discover there dimensions of the human spirit that are needed for its maturity and that are painfully missing from presiding religious traditions. In this implication, Jung is simply developing one side of his theory of compensation, which the unconscious spontaneously proffers to consciousness on behalf of the latter's wholeness. Thus, the mystic with so immediate, intense, and sometimes prolonged an experience of the unconscious may be put in the position of bringing to the tradition the missing wholeness it may itself need for its own healing. This would effectively elevate mystical experience to the status of a private revelation.

In this context Jung refers to the mystical experience of Nicholas of Flue, a fellow Swiss. Nicholas's mystical experience, as read by Jung, completed the one-sided image of the reigning God as male with that of a goddess.[12] Likewise, Jung valued the mystical experience of Guillaume de Digueville, who saw God as king with earth as queen.[13] To the extent these experiences imply that the collective myth lacks, in the one case, a sense of the divinity of the feminine and, in the other, a sense of the divinity of matter, such mysticism can become prophetic. It can also urge a broadening of contemporary religious consciousness that not infrequently threatens the collective myth and the religious tradition that supports it.

Thus, the suffering of tension with the religious tradition may attend the mystic's return to the collective, just as it afflicts the hero or heroine in so many fairy tales when they bring back the fruit of their arduous adventures to the collective. Meister Eckhart was condemned in 1328 for the sense of his natural divinity and the native intimacy between the divine and the human that his mystical experience brought to him. In the following century Joan of Arc was executed for her fidelity to her voices. In 1988 Mathew Fox, O.P., was silenced, in part for his efforts to revivify the religious thought of his Dominican predecessor, Meister Eckhart. Thus, mystical experience is far from asocial or nonpolitical. Jung's psychology of history, like Hegel's, implies that the appearance of the new in history derives from the dimension of the psyche that the mystics experience immediately. His psychology of history further implies that, since this dimension of the psyche proffers that form of compensation that believers call revelation, it is never without political and social implications for the future.

These, then, are some of the major definitions, descriptions, and implications of Jung's conception of religion and of the primary place of the mystic within it.

Let us move to locate these reflections within the broader framework of Jung's understanding of the psyche and its movement to maturation. Individuation, the process of the realization of the self in consciousness, is central to Jung's psychology and in one way or another touches every aspect of it. Basically, the process describes the propulsion of the ego from the unconscious through the agency of the self and the subsequent incarnation of the self into its own creature, the ego.[14] With Jung the self presides, not without the cooperation of the ego at crucial stages, over the whole enterprise. Once born from its unconscious matrix, the ego becomes the coauthor in cooperation with the self of the self's subsequent progressive incarnation in the ego.

In individual life, this incarnation of the self in the ego is most directly worked by the conversation between the ego and the self. The latter usually expresses itself most explicitly in the language of the dream. As the intent and attitude of the self are perceived and then engaged by the ego, the self is ushered into consciousness, where it becomes a more endemic component of the ego's reality. The authentic coalescence of ego and self carries with it the sense of a balanced inner order, an enhanced vitality resulting from a greater access to libidinal energies and an extended embrace or empathy for the surrounding world. In this manner does Jung understand the emergence of that "more compendious personality"[15] or "supraordinate personality"[16] that comes to birth in every life that suffers the self's ingression.

The process Jung here gropes to describe is admittedly a highly dialectical one. For example, it is true to say that the self, having given birth to the ego, seeks its conscious realization in it. One can rightly say that the self, from its basis in the unconscious, is the creative precedent, the generative source, of the ego, exercising a function not unlike that of the creator in popular Christian imagination. But as the process moves to its culmination, the ego's response to the self becomes crucial in assisting at the self's birth into consciousness. This is why Jung occasionally refers to the self as the *filius philosophorum*, the child or son of the ego, born into consciousness through the conscious efforts of the alchemical philosopher.[17] This process is the opus, the alchemical work of transformation, whose true gold is the realization of the self in consciousness redeemed from the leaden matter of its unconscious existence. If the psychology involved in this side of the dialectic were to be expressed in religious language, it would demand a paradigm that would understand God as creator, necessarily creating consciousness in order to become conscious in the creature with the creature's cooperation. It is this endeavor that Jung would see at the heart of the mystic, whose entry into the Godhead enables the Godhead to become conscious in the consciousness with which the mystic returns to his or her culture.

A further complexity, of interest to the religious mind, that attaches to the dialectic of individuation arises from the organic self-containment of the process. In Jung's psychology, one can speak of the unconscious transcending the ego in such a way that the ego can never exhaust or encompass it. Indeed, Jung describes the unconscious as having no known boundaries and, in so doing, conjures images of its infinity.[18] Yet, each center of consciousness, each finite ego, remains throughout its existence organically and ontologically related to this sea from which it is born. Processes of individuation thus imply the intrapsychic transcendence of the self and of the unconscious as such to the ego but deny the significance of extrapsychic transcendence such as popular religious imagination and official theology would attribute to the various one and only Gods of the currently competing monotheisms. It is theologically difficult to evade the conclusion compelled by this side of Jung's thought—namely, that humanity and divinity are engaged in processes of mutual redemption in an intimacy so real that it cannot accommodate that conception of divine transcendence that would posit a God ontologically independent of created consciousness or wholly other in relation to it.[19]

The question may then be asked, "Why is the process of individuation as the core of Jung's psychology religious, even mystical?" The most adequate answer is that the process is religious because the collective unconscious, as the generator of consciousness, is the creative ground of all consciousness and itself seeks to become conscious in human consciousness. To the extent this intent is realized, this common ground imbues each individual center of consciousness with an experience of its inner unification, accompanied by a sense of universal relatedness. The sense of personal completion and extended empathy are for Jung the hallmarks of the self and of humanity's experience of grace. It is in such experience and the symbols it produces and that help produce it in those open to the symbols that Jung locates the truth of humanity as an image of God. Of the unity of the individual with the unconscious worked by and incarnate in the self, Jung writes, "The self then functions as a union of opposites and thus constitutes the most immediate experience of the Divine which it is psychologically possible to imagine."[20]

In this passage, Jung is no doubt speaking of a consciousness blessed by a profound experience of the self. But Jung, read in his totality, must be understood to insist that it is to such harmonies and wholeness that the psyche is driven by its very nature. He thus describes the direction in which individuation moves as one toward the experience of the near identity of one's personal center with the center of the universe. He writes of the bearer of such consciousness, "He is of the same essence as the universe, and his own mid-point is its center."[21] That Jung considered such consciousness the term of the dynamic of individuation and not an epiphenomenal or freakish event is made as evident as possible in a passage that describes the psychological meaning and functioning of cross imagery. Through the power of such imagery, writes Jung, "the unconscious man is made one with his center, which is also the centre of the universe, and in this wise the goal of man's salvation and exaltation is reached."[22] In this passage Jung equates the fuller realization of the self with that religious and mystical experience of a personal centeredness grounded in and made possible by the approximation of the ego and its consciousness to the center of the totality within the psyche of each individual. In this citation Jung makes it quite clear that this consciousness is at once the goal of psychological maturity and the height of religious experience.

Turning now to Jung's discussion of what he considered the master symbols of the self, it must first be noted that he always emphasized their religious implications. The symbols to be discussed here are the mandala, the *anthropos*, and the alchemical consciousness described in the process that culminates in a sense of the *unus mundus*, the one world, which Jung implicates in the phenomenon of synchronicity and synchronous consciousness.

Jung was particularly attracted to the mandala as expressive of the sense of the sacred that attaches to the experience of the self. Jung attributed to the mandala many meanings, among them its symbolic use as the centering power of the self uniting the opposites on its periphery in a center that is at once divine and in the depth of the psyche of every individual. Yet the center of the mandala, that point in which every existent coincides with God, functions in the psyche in such a way that no ego could totally identify with it and so come to as universal a relatedness and comprehension as an unqualified unity with the center would afford. For Jung such a psychic state describes that psychosis that always follows the soul's falling, through unqualified identification, into the hands of the living God.

Mandala imagery, as Jung interprets it, thus implies that the ego's attraction for its divine center can be neither evaded nor fully realized. Its attempted evasion would mean the aimlessness of a life uprooted from its sacred depth and center. Yet unqualified unity with the center would mean the loss of the ego's freedom to a destructive identity with its divine ground. Indeed, it is this near lust for its sacred origin that prompts Jung to point to the dangers faced by the ego in the journey inward, where the experience of the renewing vitalities of the unconscious can consume as well as revitalize. In their experience of these depths, the mystic, the addict, and the fanatic are equally aware of their possessive allure.[23] Only the mystic redeems the experience by bringing it back to consciousness in the service of humanity.

Jung found much of the psychological and religious truth of the mandala expressed in the idiom that appears in Bonaventure's *Itinerarium Mentis ad Deum* and that has a prior history in medieval and hermetic thought.[24] It states that God is the circle whose center is everywhere and whose circumference is nowhere. The idiom meant to Jung that God is the center and centering power in each psyche, although no individual consciousness could ever exhaustively encompass the circumference or the totality of all that emanates from the center in created reality. Again, such an encompassing would mean an unqualified unity with the center, which would consume the ego.

Let us leave this image with the observation that, for Jung, the closer the ego draws to its divine center, the source of all created opposites, the better can the ego relate to the opposites in its own inner life as the basis for a better relatedness to them in external life. This dynamic may lie at the heart of what is often said about the mystical journey—namely, that the journey inward is the journey outward. This implies that the mystic's inner achievement is never without social consequence. This formulation may explain why mystics who have achieved some high degree of the union of opposites within themselves may then become vehicles for the resolution of social and political conflicts beyond themselves.

The symbol of the *anthropos* picks up this social implication of mystical consciousness. It too rests on the experience of the unification of one's disparate personal energies, coupled with an extended sympathy. But the symbol of the *anthropos* carries with it a heightened sense of the coincidence of one's individuality with humanity universal.[25] Jung sees in such images as the Jewish Adam Kadmon, the Pauline cosmic Christ, and the gnostic experience of an inner and universal Christ, variants on the theme that one's humanity in its depth is at one with humanity universal.

With the demise of specifically religious myth and symbol in contemporary consciousness, in large part due to the self-discrediting literalism of orthodox theologies, one might wonder with Jung if the *anthropos* archetype and the kind of participation mystique it engenders in the construction of community has not passed, thinly disguised, from the religious into the political realm. Here it functions to imbue its adherents with a sense of alignment with a historical process that necessarily moves to a human community of communion as the goal of history. Such a vision seems to have enlivened the thought of the young Marx. It is most evident when he describes as the inevitable goal of history a consciousness that would inform its holders with a concern for the species. Such a concern in itself would generate spontaneous activity on behalf of humanity universally.

In this sense these symbols are bearers of humanity's highest aspirations. Yet Jung is keenly aware that the very power of the ideals they bear can become the psychic foundation for the unconscious communal bonding they also generate. Such energies then produce the psychic epidemics in the form of political ideals that have ravaged the Western twentieth century in the form of politically inspired genocide.[26] Thus, because of their power to render the communities they create unconscious, Jung points consistently to the social and political dangers of what he calls "isms"[27] that attach to the same archetypal energies that empower mystical consciousness.

Within the context of Jungian psychology, the mystical and religious implications of the self are nowhere so well, one might even say, methodically developed as they are in Jung's discussion of the process that leads to the state of consciousness called the *unus mundus*, the one world. His reflections on the processes that lead to this consciousness come at the end of his last major work, *Mysterium Coniunctionis*, and serve as a capstone to this work and to the work of his lifetime.[28]

The term *unus mundus* is taken from Gerhard Dorn, a late medieval alchemist. By appropriating the process Dorn describes to arrive at this consciousness, Jung accepts Dorn's anthropology, which divides the human into the realms of body, soul, and spirit. Again following Dorn, Jung describes an initial psychic ascetic stage, the *unio mentalis*, whose culmination is symbolically depicted as the separation of the soul from the body in a state Jung interprets to mean a freedom from the constrictive powers of instinctual and destabilizing emotionality.[29]

This first stage brings the soul before what Jung calls "the window into eternity."[30] But because Jung's psychology moves from this ascetic stage back into embodiment, it does not allow the soul to step prematurely through this window and away from the confines of finitude. In one of the more radical points in his critique of Christianity, Jung argues that this preliminary and ascetic stage of psychospiritual development is as far as Christian spirituality extends. He thus criticizes official Christian theology for its rejection of a pantheism that would support the sense of the divinity of matter and body. He writes, "And although it was also said of God that the world is his physical manifestation, this pantheistic view was rejected by the Church for 'God is Spirit' and the very reverse of matter."[31] He goes on to attribute this pathologizing removal of the sense of divinity from the physical and incarnate human to the central figure in the Christian myth in these words: "Despite all assurances to the contrary Christ is not a unifying factor but a dividing 'sword' which sunders the spiritual man from the physical."[32]

In Jung's mind and, he implies, in the mind of Dorn the alchemist, this unincarnated spirituality demanded reincarnation if it was to serve the whole person, which would have to include the embodied person in relation to the world. Hence, Jung and Dorn go beyond this first stage to a second in which the soul, united with the spirit and so freed from the compulsions of the body, is reincarnated to effect a spiritualized body or an embodied unity of spirit and soul. Jung writes, "By sublimating matter, he [the alchemist] concretized spirit."[33] The alchemists described this state of consciousness as a "caelum,"[34] a heaven, in which body, soul, and spirit become one. They also related this state to what they called the glorified body. Jung suggests that the alchemists may have understood this state, symbolized by the glorified body, to be an experience equivalent to the experience of resurrection.[35]

Only from this state of a unified personality, firmly embodied in space and time, does the extension of empathy toward an embrace of the whole through unity with the source of all in the ground of the individual's personal being authentically develop. This stage is best described in Jung's own terms as he adapts Dorn to his psychology. He writes, "For him [Dorn] the third and highest degree of conjunction was the union of the whole man with the *unus mundus*."[36] To get at what is involved in the unity of the whole person with the *unus mundus*, Jung draws an analogy with the symbol of the "one day" taken from Bonaventure's *Itinerarium*. Jung understands this day to be the first day of creation, and he equates the consciousness of this first day with the consciousness Dorn seeks to describe with the phrase "*unus mundus*."[37] Jung writes, "By this he [Dorn] meant, as we have seen, the potential world of the first day of creation, when nothing was yet 'in actu,' i.e., divided into two and many but was still one."[38] For Bonaventure this world of the one day refers in symbolic terms to a state "prior to the fall," when creation was fully at one with and transparent to its divine ground. In orthodox thought this describes a prelapsarian state of consciousness when humanity and God were unqualifiedly at one. This state will be recovered in a posttemporal eschaton when God will be all in all.

The amazing claim that Jung is making here in his reading of Dorn is that this consciousness is the goal of the transformation toward which the process of individuation naturally works. This state of consciousness is one in which the individual in unambiguous unity with one's divine ground sees all else as thus grounded in God. To a consciousness transparent to its native divinity all else appears as an epiphany of the divine. In Jung's appropriation of the alchemical tradition, this experience is not only accessible to the natural psyche; it is both demanded and supported by natural processes of a maturing consciousness in time and space as the opus, or spiritual goal, of each individual life. Jung obviously means this when he writes of the alchemical endeavor:

> The creation of a unity by a magical procedure meant the possibility of effecting a union with the world—not with the world of multiplicity as we see it but with a potential world, the eternal ground of all empirical being just as the self is the ground and origin of the individual, past, present, and future.[39]

In the context of this passage, Jung does not understand the consciousness that attaches to the *unus mundus* to be a union with the universal ground of being in any pretemporal or posttemporal state. Rather, it is the natural culmination of maturational processes demanded by the natural working of the psyche itself in the here and now of everyday life.

In this passage Jung clearly affirms that the psyche is driven by its own *telos* toward that consciousness that our still presiding myth locates in the past in Eden and in the future in the New Jerusalem but hesitates to describe as a state of consciousness to be realized in the present as the culmination of the psyche's natural maturation. The implications of this consciousness are made evident in the examples Jung chooses to amplify it. He sees such consciousness depicted in Philos's conception of the individual as a microcosm who realizes consciously "the unity of the psychic man with the cosmos."[40] He sees it in Plotinus's speculation that "all individuals are merely one soul."[41] He see it again reflected in Eastern thought when he writes, "It is the relation or identity of the personal with the suprapersonal atman, and of the individual tao with the universal tao."[42]

Perhaps the most significant amplification of the *unus mundus* is in the manner in which Jung relates it to other master themes in his own work. He writes, "If mandala symbolism is the psychological equivalent of the *unus mundus*, then synchronicity is its parapsychological equivalent."[43] This citation provokes the question "What do the *unus mundus*, the mandala and synchronicity have in common?"

As we have seen, the mandala for Jung points to the universal presence of the divine in the center of each psyche as its ultimate point of consistency, working internally to draw consciousness into its stabilizing influence and so to relate consciousness more adequately to the external world. The experience of the *unus mundus* harmonizes with the imagery of the mandala because it, too, points to the presence of the ground of being in each existent psyche and implies that the movement of the psyche is toward the ego's conscious union with this ground and so with the totality that this ground also sponsors.

Synchronicity as understood by Jung presupposes a common generative substrate that gives rise to all centers of consciousness and, indeed, to non- or prehuman nature.[44] But, with synchronicity, Jung introduces the added note that this common ground can, in effect, intervene in consciousness, usually under stress related to the deeper truth each life seeks. In discrete synchronistic episodes, this substrate dramatically orchestrates events between individuals or between individuals and nature. The individual is so impressed by striking "meaningful coincidence" that his or her consequent life is transformed as the individual moves toward the realization of the deeper truth conveyed by the sense of the event. What can with every justification be dismissed as pure chance by the disengaged observer is perceived as a "providential" intervention in the life transformed by such "chance."

The wealth of such events in his life and in the lives of his clients eventually forced Jung to the conclusion that each center of consciousness continues in its finitude to participate in its prefinite or eternal ground and that this ground could intervene in certain lives to work patterns of meaning in defiance of all statistical probability. More than this, he would argue that this ground was inextricably connected with finite consciousness, which in one sense is its product and in another is the only place where this ground can itself become conscious. Furthermore, the wisdom of this ground that is manifest in the synchronistic event implies a viewpoint superior to that of the stressed ego it addresses. Indeed, this ground can convey its wisdom on occasion through the orchestration of external events both human and natural, with a dramatic impact that surpasses even that of the dream, which manifests the same wisdom internally and usually with intensity.

But more important than discrete synchronistic events is the synchronous consciousness they point to and whose appropriation they in some sense urge. Such a synchronous consciousness is characterized by a residual sense of its possessor's groundedness in the ground of the universe, with the resultant heightened capacity to perceive the sacred in all else as similarly grounded. Though intermittent synchronistic events may aid the traveler toward this consciousness, it is this consciousness as a residual state that seems to be the goal to which the psyche moves with all of its energies.

The following concluding remarks seem to follow from the foregoing. One must assume that Jung took the master images, described earlier, of the movement of the psyche toward its maturation to be in some sense grounded in the nature of the psyche itself. As such, these images, allowing for immense variations of cultural expression, describe a universal process in which every psyche participates. The process he describes as individuation is not atypical, epiphenomenal, or confined to a privileged few. Yet it is equally clear that this process moves inexorably toward patterns of individual wholeness in conjunction with a more universal empathy that Jung equates with the experience of grace and of God, although such experience is a work of nature and nature's goal. In so conceiving of the psyche, Jung identifies without residue psychological maturation with the further reaches of religious and mystical experience. Thus, the goal toward which individuation moves is a state of consciousness that unites the psychological, the mystical, and the religious in a unity that continues to surpass most modes of contemporary perception and, all too often, the self-understanding of those engaged formally in the disciplines of psychology and of theology or religious studies.

More than this, Jung's understanding of the psyche raises the issue of a surreptitious metaphysic operative throughout his psychology. Though Jung is frequently heard to deny the status of metaphysician to the psychologist and to himself as a psychologist, he obviously enters the metaphysical realm when he argues that whatever is known is known through the psyche and that existence itself is psychic.[45] Furthermore, there seem to be metaphysical implications when he dismisses as naive the Aristotelian and Thomistic claim that there is nothing in the intellect except through the senses.[46] To the contrary, Jung claims that the psyche is alive with the God-creating energies of the archetypes even prior to its creation of consciousness and that these powers continue their semiautonomy even after the creation of consciousness and its consequent fascination with the sensible world.

Furthermore, Jung seems to give psychology itself a certain supremacy in the world of metaphysics and, indeed, of all the human disciplines when he argues that even metaphysical statements are statements of the psyche and so are themselves psychological reflections of the complex or complexes dominant in the philosopher's or metaphysician's psyche.[47]

These are metaphysical claims of the first order, which justify the attempt to isolate the metaphysic that is there. Its rudiments may be these. All that is significantly knowable, as well as the possibility of consciousness itself, exists originally in what Jung calls the "matrix" nature of the creative unconscious,[48] the source of all consciousness but in itself wholly undifferentiated. As consciousness proceeds from this seething precedent, it becomes the agent that first perceives, then differentiates, and, finally, under the direction of the self, reunites the antinomies and contradictions of its unconscious generator. Dialectically, this process is initiated and presided over by the self, which seeks conscious realization in the individual and in history through first constellating and then reuniting in human consciousness opposites that remain contaminated or undifferentiated in the unconscious. The philosophy of history and, religiously, the eschatology consistent with this metaphysic is one in which archetypally empowered opposites, usually concretized in communities of conflict, move to their resolution in more inclusive syntheses. On this point, Jung may be closer to Hegel than he himself was aware until very late in life.[49]

When this metaphysic is given its theological formulation, Jung is found to be arguing that God seeks a unity of opposites in human consciousness that defied realization within the Godhead. This ultimately is what demands the creation of consciousness and forces Jung from a trinitarian to a quaternitarian paradigm. In this paradigm, the creative but unconscious One differentiates into its opposites in historical consciousness and then brings the opposites together in the age of the Spirit. The moral imperative that arises out of this metaphysic and its theological equivalent demands that the individual, with the help of the self or diety, bring to consciousness and then, one hopes, to some resolution whatever form of the divine self-contradiction is most operative in that individual's life. In this manner are God and the human, dimly aware of their ontological bond from the outset, engaged in mutual redemption as the deepest meaning of history.

In the final analysis, the philosophical and theological consequences of this paradigm appreciatively undermine current religious configurations of transcendental monotheisms and equivalent absolute monomyths in the political order. Jung's paradigm grants to them all a relative truth based on their archetypal grounding, but it denies to them any finality. In Jung's psychological reflections on twentieth-century political "isms," he argues that the lust for the absolute and its certitude has moved into political configurations, aided to a great extent by religion's theological self-discrediting in its conversation with modernity. Collective humanity is now coming to see that its hope for the future increasingly depends on its loss of its current faiths, political or religious, in favor of a broader human sympathy than those faiths can apparently mediate. Since these faiths owe their origins to the unconscious and since the mystic has some ready access to it, the fostering of such sensitivity, whether by specifically religious or psychological agencies, may make a significant contribution to the emergence of a broader and more encompassing empathy.

This newer sense of our common humanity, at one in its origin and in the common task of the hazardous historical redemption of its origin, may in the end provide an unlikely but powerful alternative to our possibly imminent destruction at the hands of lesser, still-competing Gods. From Jung's perspective, the conscious cultivation of the psychological experience of the mystic would thus become a key in the strategy of surfacing a newer myth whose broader empathy would give greater assurance of a usable future. Such consciousness would foster the vision Jung himself held for the future when he wrote, "The afternoon of humanity, in a distant future, may yet evolve a different ideal. In time, even conquest will cease to be a dream."[50]

Notes

1. All citations are from C. G. Jung, *Collected Works* [CW] (Princeton: Princeton University Press, Bollingen Series 20, 1953–1979), 20 vols., trans. R. F. C. Hull. Citations are listed by title, volume number, paragraph, and page. Cf. "Psychology and Religion" CW 11, par. 3, p. 6; par. 6, p. 7; par. 9, p. 8.
2. *Psychological Types*, CW 6, par. 62, p. 42.
3. "The Tavistock Lectures," CW 18, par. 218, p. 98.
4. Ibid.
5. Ibid., pars. 219, 220, p. 99.
6. "The Philosophical Tree", CW 13, par. 482, p. 349.
7. *Mysterium Coniunctionis*, CW 14, par. 530, p. 375.
8. "A Psychological Approach to the Dogma of the Trinity", CW 11, par. 170, p. 109.
9. Ibid., CW 11, p. 109f.
10. Cf., for instance, "Christ a Symbol of the Self", CW 9ii, p. 36f.
11. Cf. "Transformation Symbolism in the Mass," CW 11, p. 203f.
12. "The Tavistock Lectures," CW 18, par. 221, p. 99.
13. Ibid.
14. Though this dialectic is foundational to an organic reading of Jung, it is very precisely described in "Transformation Symbolism in the Mass," CW 11, sec. 4, "The Psychology of the Mass," p. 247f.
15. "Transformation Symbolism in the Mass," CW 11, par. 390, p. 258.
16. "The Psychological Aspects of the Kore," CW 9i, par. 306, p. 182.
17. Cf. *Mysterium Coniunctionis*, CW 14, par. 290, p. 219; "Transformation Symbolism in the Mass," CW 11, par. 400, p. 263.
18. "Transformation Symbolism in the Mass," CW 11, par. 390, p. 258. Jung writes of the unconscious as "of indefinite extent with no assignable limits."
19. *Psychology and Alchemy*, CW 12, fn. 6, p. 11. Jung writes, "It is therefore psychologically quite unthinkable for God to be simply the 'wholly other,' for a 'wholly other' could never be one of the soul's deepest and closest intimacies—which is precisely what God is."
20. "Transformation Symbolism in the Mass," CW 11, par. 396, p. 261.
21. Ibid., par. 440, p. 288.
22. Ibid., par. 445, p. 292.
23. Cf. *Two Essays on Analytical Psychology*, CW 7, par. 260, p. 169.
24. *Mysterium Coniunctionis*, par. 41, p. 47. Here Jung refers to Bonaventure's *Itinerarium*, chap. 5. He relates this idiom to a religious description of the self in *Psychological Types*, CW 6, par. 791, fn. 74, p. 461. In "A Psychological Approach to the Dogma of the Trinity," CW 11, par. 229, p. 155, fn. 6, he relates the idiom to hermetic and gnostic traditions and to the medieval thinker Alan de Lulle.
25. "Gnostic Symbols of the Self," *Aion*, CW 9ii, pars. 312, 313, pp. 199–202.
26. "Psychology and Religion," CW 11, par. 17, p. 12, and par. 23, p. 14.
27. Cf., for example, ibid., par. 144, p. 88.
28. *Mysterium Coniunctionis*, CW 14, sec. VI, "The Conjunction," p. 457f.
29. Ibid., par. 694, p. 487f.
30. Ibid., par. 670, p. 471.
31. Ibid., par. 773, p. 541.
32. Ibid.
33. Ibid., par. 764, p. 536.
34. Ibid., par. 763, p. 535.
35. Ibid.

36. Ibid., par. 760, p. 534.
37. Ibid., par. 718, p. 505.
38. Ibid., par. 760, p. 534.
39. Ibid.
40. Ibid., par. 761, p. 534.
41. Ibid.
42. Ibid., par. 762, p. 535.
43. Ibid., par. 662, p. 464.
44. Cf. "Synchronicity: An Acausal Connecting Principle," CW 8, sec. VII, p. 419f.
45. Cf. "Psychology and Religion," CW 11, pars. 16, 18, p. 12. Jung writes, "Not only does the psyche exist, it is existence itself."
46. "Psychological Commentary on 'The Tibetan Book of the Great Liberation,'" CW 11, par. 785, p. 492.
47. "Psychological Commentary on the 'The Tibetan Book of the Dead,'" CW 11, pars. 835, 836, pp. 511, 512.
48. "Foreword to Suzuki's 'Introduction to Zen Buddhism,'" CW 11, par. 899, p. 552.
49. Cf. *Letters* (Princeton: Princeton University Press, Bollingen Series 95, 1975), ed. Gerhard Adler, 2 vols., vol. 2, p. 502, where Jung writes in a letter to J. F. Rychlak, April 27, 1959, "There is, of course, a remarkable coincidence between certain tenets of Hegelian philosophy and my findings concerning the collective unconscious."
50. "Psychological Commentary on 'The Tibetan Book of the Great Liberation,'" CW 11, par. 787, p. 493.

SEVEN

The Swami and the Rorschach

Spiritual Practice, Religious Experience, and Perception

DIANE JONTE-PACE

NEARLY A CENTURY after William James initiated the psychological study of mysticism with the publication of *The Varieties of Religious Experience*,[1] Robert Forman has returned to James's project by issuing a call for a *psychologia perennis*.[2] This "perennial psychology" would investigate mystical or nonordinary states of consciousness and the transformative processes that produce them. Whereas James offered a typology of mystical experience structured around the mysticism of the "healthy minded" and the mysticism of the "sick soul," Forman proposes an inquiry that goes well beyond the work of his predecessor. He raises questions not only about types of mystical experience but also about the influence of innate psychological structure and of culture upon mystical experience.

Four central theses structure Forman's argument. First, he differentiates ordinary consciousness from mystical consciousness. Second, he argues that transformative processes like meditation can enact a shift from ordinary to mystical consciousness. Third, he suggests that the transformative efficacy of practices like meditation lies in the stripping away of learned cultural and linguistic categories to expose an underlying "innate capacity" for experiencing mystical "pure consciousness." Fourth, he maintains that this state of "pure consciousness" is cross-culturally and historically stable.

Forman argues, in other words, that *mystical experiences of pure consciousness, made possible by transformative processes like meditation, transcend historical and cultural differences and are in some way "innate."* As he explains in this volume, his approach to mysticism represents a "decontextualist" as opposed to a "constructivist" approach. Decontextualists are universalists who argue for the unity or identity of mystical experiences across cultural and historical boundaries. In their view, which the psychologist of religion Ralph Hood refers to as the "common core theory" of mysticism, "variations in descriptions may mask similar if not identical experiences."[3] "Constructivists" like Wayne Proudfoot and Steven Katz, on the other hand, are pluralists who argue that mystical experiences differ according to cultural and historical context.[4] The focus of the constructivists is on the cultural construction of experience: they argue, in opposition to the decontextualist thesis of an innate capacity for pure awareness, that no unmediated experience is possible and that all experience, including mystical experience, is shaped by culture and language. From their perspective, claims for universality or commonality in religious experience are a result of a cultural hegemony that disregards the differences that are the basis of historical and cultural particularity.

In his call for a perennial psychology and in his articulation of the decontextualist thesis, Forman urges scholars to initiate "comparative work in mysticism, religion, spirituality, and the fundamentals of cognitive psychology . . . (to investigate) deep psychological structures, states of consciousness, as well as transformative processes."[5] I propose that the Rorschach test might serve well as such a method for investigating religion, spirituality, psychological structure, and cognition. In addition, it might bring some clarity to the debate between the decontextualists and the constructivists. In this essay I discuss three unique Rorschach studies that, in my view, represent an important step toward such a psychology of religious experience and examine their implications for Forman's decontextualist thesis.

Why might the Rorschach test represent a valuable method for studying religious experience? The nature of perception is the explicit concern of both the Rorschach test and the texts that describe religious experience. The Rorschach test explicitly deconstructs in order to analyze, understand, and interpret the process of perception while much of the mystical literature similarly describes an explicit deconstruction of the process of perception in order to escape from that process. William Blake's famous assertion, "If the doors of perception were cleansed, everything would appear as it is—infinite," echoes, for example, the Upaniṣadic texts that urge the cessation of "the five sense knowledges" and the Buddhist Abhidamma texts that instruct the meditator in the practice of gaining insight into and detachment from sensation, perception, and judgment.[6]

Forman's attempt to differentiate ordinary consciousness from mystical consciousness similarly focuses on perception. He outlines a tripartite epistemological and perceptual framework that characterizes ordinary consciousness: he describes the perceiving subject, the perceived object, and the process of perceiving or knowing. In mystical consciousness, Forman suggests, a subject no longer perceives an object but perceives or knows consciousness itself.[7] For Forman, the transformations in the perceiving subject, the perceived object, and the process of perception are crucial in understanding the shift from ordinary consciousness to mystical consciousness. What makes the Rorschach test so valuable in this context is precisely its ability to analyze the perceiving subject and the process of perceiving. By offering to the subject an ambiguous object—by removing, in a sense, the "perceived object" from the tripartite epistemological structure of awareness—the Rorschach test makes possible an inquiry into the relationship between the other two components, the perceiving subject and the process of perception. Since the Rorschach test itself is an instrument sensitive to the nature and the process of perception, the test records of spiritual masters can provide insight into perception in nonordinary consciousness.

The Rorschach Test

Primarily a diagnostic tool, the Rorschach, or "inkblot," test has been widely utilized for many decades as a measure of perception and personality. The creator of the test, Hermann Rorschach (1884–1922), was vitally interested in the intersections of perception, cognition, and religion. His work developing the inkblot test was immediately preceded by—and, I've argued, was closely related to—his study of sectarian religious groups in the mountains of Switzerland.[8] After publishing papers on these groups in early psychoanalytic journals, he put aside his research on religion to complete his manuscript on perception and personality, *Psychodiagnostics*.[9] Letters written at this time to Swiss pastor and psychoanalyst Oskar Pfister refer to the psychological analysis of religion he intended to pursue.[10] Plans for this research were cut short by his unexpected death, caused by acute peritonitis, in 1922 at age 37.

In spite of Hermann Rorschach's interest in religion, in spite of what I consider to be the great potential of the Rorschach test for understanding religious experience, and in spite of the fact that the Rorschach is "the most extensively researched projective instrument" in diagnostic testing,[11] only a few Rorschach studies have focused explicitly on religion. Fewer still have explored nonordinary religious consciousness. Typical studies in the field of religion and the Rorschach, for example, have constructed personality profiles of nuns, priests, ministers, and applicants to seminaries.[12] This research has barely begun to explore the potential of the Rorschach test as a method of studying religious experience. Those few studies that have investigated the effects of altered states experience or meditation on Rorschach records have utilized inexperienced or naive subjects—Maupin's study of the influence of Zen meditation practice on college students, for example, involved subjects with fewer than ten hours of meditation practice.[13]

The Rorschach literature, however, contains three remarkable but little-known sets of studies of the spiritually advanced. In the 1950s French psychiatrist Frederick Spiegelberg administered the Rorschach test to an Indian Vedantic master, Swami Sivananda;[14] in the 1960s psychoanalytic anthropologists L. Bryce Boyer and Bruno Klopfer and their associates administered the test to Apache shamans and "pseudo-shamans";[15] and in the 1970s and 1980s psychologists Daniel Brown and Jack Engler conducted a complex study of advanced Buddhist meditators at different stages of progress in the Vipassana tradition of mindfulness meditation. Brown and Engler's study differentiated four groups of Western meditators (a beginners' group, a samadhi group, an insight group, and an advanced insight group) and a "masters' group" that consisted of a single South Asian enlightened master.[16]

The value of these studies of advanced practitioners of spiritual disciplines for the sort of *psychologia perennis* proposed by Forman is immense. Although they cannot offer a literal window into the pure consciousness experience, they do offer an opportunity for cross-cultural comparison into the cognitive and perceptual processes of the religiously and spiritually advanced. In this essay I discuss the Rorschach protocols of the swami, the shamans, and the meditators, demonstrating some remarkable similarities in the Rorschach records of the most advanced masters, similarities that may help lift some of the obscurity clouding the debate between the decontextualists and the constructivists regarding nonordinary experience and the processes that produce them.

Let us examine briefly the rationale and vocabulary of Rorschach test administration and scoring. Hermann Rorschach discovered in his inkblot test a method of measuring the human process of perceiving and creating the world out of the ambiguous sensory stimuli we constantly confront. His central insight concerned the relationship between the structure of perception and the structure of personality: he discovered that when exposed to relatively "unstructured or ambiguous materials (we) organize and interpret them in a manner characteristic of (our) own personalities and perceptions of the world."[17]

In the Rorschach test, the subject is given ten cards, one at a time, and is asked to tell the examiner what each card looks like. The cards are ambiguous, symmetrical inkblots, some nearly monochromatic, others including colors. The examiner records the responses (e.g., "bat," "butterfly," "clouds") and, in a subsequent inquiry, ascertains the perceptual stimulus that produced each response. Later, the "Rorschach test record" (the full set of responses to the ten cards) is interpreted according to a standardized set of perceptual and interpretive scoring categories. While several schools of thought have emerged in recent decades regarding the specifics of interpretation, all are in general agreement with Rorschach's original method and insights.[18]

Responses are classified under two major headings—location and determinant—and two minor headings, content and popularity/originality. Location scores (whole, detail, or small detail) are a measure of cognitive approach: they describe the area of the card chosen in the response and are an indication of style of approach and mental ability to organize. Whole responses reveal a capacity to integrate, organize, and see relationships between disparate parts, while detail responses indicate practicality and a focus on the particular. The sequence of approach (whole to detail or detail to whole) indicates how the subject encounters a task or engages a problem.

The determinant scores classify responses according to four specific perceptual properties: form, color, movement, and shading. Form responses measure the ability to objectify the visual field into definite patterns and objects; they provide an index of ego strength, rationality, and disciplined thinking. Color responses indicate the way one is influenced by one's surroundings and one's emotional state, with high color responsivity interpreted as a sign of impulsivity and emotionality. Movement responses are characterized by the perception of a form combined with the perception of motion in the form. These, especially when the content is human (the Human Movement response), represent a capacity for inner life, fantasy, and a potential for empathy. Finally, the shading, or Chiaroscuro, responses (perceptions, for example, involving clouds, darkness, or smoke) are generally interpreted as a sign that the subject is at the mercy of the environment, beset by undifferentiated moods or depression. Thus, in these two major interpretive categories, location scores and determinants, the formal elements of perceptual structuring are the primary concern. The test provides a measure of how one perceives and what one selects as perceptually relevant.

The other two indices of interpretation turn away from the formal elements of perception to examine aspects of the content of the response. Although Rorschach was explicit in ascribing to the formal features the primary import in his diagnostic method, he acknowledged the subtle significance of content as well. Content and the related measure "popularity/originality" provide an understanding of the associative process and its social context. Attention to the content of Rorschach responses also makes possible a more nuanced interpretation of the formal elements of perception.

Popularity/originality is a specific measurement applied to the content. This measurement functions as an index of conventionality versus independence of thinking. Responses that are given by a statistically high percentage of adults in a culture are scored as "popular" responses. "Original" or rare responses are responses of good form quality (reasonably "realistic" responses) that are given by a small percentage of adults in a culture. Statistical norms for popular and original responses have been established by Rorschach researchers for many cultural groups.[19]

These scoring categories expose the perceptual and associative patterns foundational to consciousness. Rorschach argued that the inkblot test made evident the nonconscious elements of perception and cognitive experience. All perception, he maintained, involved a process of separating a total visual field into distinct percepts: encountering sense data, selecting particular elements of the data as relevant, eliminating other elements as irrelevant, and selecting an associative or verbal label.

Rorschach Test Records of Swamis, Meditators, and Shamans

First, a word about terminology: while Forman's interest is in "the mystic," I hesitate to call the subjects of these studies "mystics." Each is an advanced practitioner of his or her culture's tradition of religious discipline; each is an adept in nonordinary states of consciousness; and each might be called a spiritual master. The term "mystic" would clearly be inappropriate for the shaman; the Buddhist meditators and the Hindu Swami would not call themselves mystics. Thus, I use the term "spiritual master" rather than mystic. Brown and Engler refer to their most advanced subject, an enlightened South Asian woman, as "the master" or as "the single subject in the masters' group." Since my term "spiritual masters" is broader than Brown and Engler's "masters' group," I refer to their most advanced subject as the "enlightened master" to differentiate her from the other advanced Buddhist meditators who have achieved varying degrees of "mastery." In addition, I generally refer to "nonordinary experience" rather than to "mystical experience."

What does the Rorschach test indicate about the perceptual patterns or cognitive styles of spiritual masters? If the nonconscious components of perception and cognition are revealed through the Rorschach test, and if the deconstruction of perceptual categories constitutes nonordinary consciousness, then Rorschach test records of those deeply involved in a spiritual tradition should reveal some important commonalties. I show that this is precisely the case.

In specific responses the Rorschach test records of the spiritual masters differed considerably: there was clearly no universalism of content. Location scores and determinants as well showed a great deal of variation. The masters, in other words, did not see the same shapes and images in the Rorschach cards. However, notable parallels emerge in three particular areas. First, the responses reflect major cultural or religious tenets, rather than individual psychological concerns; in other words, the content is "impersonal" or "culturally embedded" to a degree never recorded in previous Rorschach literature. Second, the masters' test records share an "integrative" approach in which all the inkblot cards are thematically and systematically related to each other in a comprehensive whole. Third, the test records reveal a common cluster of determinants, a grouping I call the "vague and slippery determinant cluster": the masters' records share high shading responsivity, high amorphous form responsivity, and high inanimate movement responsivity.

These three common features of the masters' test records are quite unusual. The integrative style and the culturally embedded content of the responses are virtually unknown in the Rorschach literature, and the elements of the determinant cluster are generally interpreted as an indication of psychopathology. Let us examine these commonalties and the interpretive problems they raise.

Culturally Embedded or Impersonal Content

In the Rorschach cards each spiritual master saw representations of the doctrinal truths of the Apache, Vedantic, or Buddhist doctrines of his or her spiritual tradition. They either did not offer the "personal" responses normally expected in the Rorschach test or their "personal" responses were embedded in a "cultural" meaning or content. The Apache shaman Black Eyes gave responses involving traveling stars, the powers of nature, the energy of lightning, and the sequence of seasonal change on earth as perceived from above—all elements of his spiritual practice and discipline, especially his ecstatic journeys through space.[20] Swami Sivananda perceived symbolic representations of the unity that underlies all diversity, the union of the erotic and divine forces Shiva and Shakti, and the rising of the sun of knowledge behind the clouds and shadows of ignorance—central tenets of the Vedantic tradition. The Buddhist enlightened master saw human and animal forms that represent the causes of suffering; black shapes depicting the entrapment of the human mind in envy, disease, sorrow, and hatred; and temples associated with the freedom of the mind from attachments. Each of these represented teachings central to her Vipassana tradition.[21]

The spiritual masters' responses to Cards V and VI provide dramatic examples of this cultural embeddedness of content. The Apache shaman Black Eyes gave the following response to Card V:

> Well, this one, he travels with no star. Jus' a refleck from daybreak. This is a female. See daybreak is jus' comin' in there. Refleck from the rock bluffs. Female of the thunderwinds. It looks like a bat, but it's not a bat. This is a fas' travelin' jus' like a high wind. You could almos' see the reflection, travel on the Eastern States, way up close to Canada. That cloud is too wide. It covers the star there. This black here, cover the mornin' star. But it don't show.[22]

Swami Sivananda responded to the same card with the following:

> I like this design because it describes very accurately the practice of Radja Yoga. Look at this bat. It is a bird, and also a mammal. It has extended its wings and has taken the role of a bird. The alert ears and the nose like a searcher indicate that the bird is on wings searching for something. Like this creature, humanity has a subordinate nature and a dominant nature. The lower is animal nature and the higher, we say, is divine or human. The lower holds his feet firmly planted on the ground, so he is glued to worldly things. As long as he is concerned with his progeny, his country, and keeps his feet firmly planted on the ground, as long as he is stuck in worldly affairs, he will forget that he possesses wings. The movement which he releases with his wings (*viveka* or discrimination, and *vairagya* or nonattachment for the world . . .) makes his ears lift up with alertness and makes him eager to hear the truth and to pursue the quest for knowledge. He goes beyond the earth. He transcends his inferior nature and flies away as divine or as human, to realize, finally, the will of the soul.[23]

The enlightened Buddhist master saw in Card V the ignorance and craving of the mind and the causes of human suffering. She went on in Card VI to describe how the mind can be used to gain liberation: "A pillar. It has taken the form of truth. This pillar reminds me of a process of getting at or discovering the human mind. Inside there is envy, disease, sorrow, and hatred in the form of black shapes. After conquering truth the mind has become clean and white."[24]

These are unusual and striking responses, quite different from the responses found in typical Rorschach test reports. The masters were enmeshed in their spiritual traditions to such a degree that inner life became indistinguishable from the spiritual teachings. Even their preconscious perceptual selections were congruent with their cultural traditions. The embeddedness of these Rorschach responses must not be misinterpreted as cultural shaping of individual responses within a standard expectable range. All Rorschach records contain, of course culturally influenced responses. Social structure, language, geography, and culture influence the content of Rorschach responses, making some responses unusual for one group but common in another. Norms for all the scoring categories, established for many regions, nations, and cultures, are readjusted periodically.[25] While the Rorschach can be used to measure broad variations *among* cultures, it is most often used to measure individual differences *within* cultures. Given a base level of groundedness in cultural norms, most responses, no matter what the cultural context, reflect the particulars of the individual's personality. Such factors as gender, age, education, intelligence, health, adaptability, and inner conflict influence the style of perception and response. Such individual factors, however, are virtually absent from the records of these spiritual masters, creating test records that stand out as anomalous and differ dramatically, not only from American and European records, but also from Native American, Asian, and South Asian records.

I think we can differentiate three types of cultural embeddedness in these records. In the first type, individual perceptions are expressed but are immediately connected to cultural and spiritual meaning systems. This is the case with the shaman's response of "bat" on Card V, which, as noted, "looks like a bat" but is not a bat. Instead, it's "fas' travelin' jus' like a high wind." In the second type, elements of the card that appear to reflect cultural teachings are selected as a primary percept: the masters perceptually select and organize into responses those stimuli that are congruent with aspects of their spiritual traditions. Illustrative of this type of response is Swami Sivananda's view of the bilateral symmetry of Card V as a representation of unity in duality. In the third type, responses reveal the virtual disappearance of individual perceptions: Brown and Engler found individual responses entirely absent from the Buddhist master's record and argued for an "impersonal" style of response, a response style entirely consistent with the Buddhist doctrine of no-self. Intrapsychic structure, they argue, "has undergone a radical enduring reorganization. . . . There may be no endopsychic structure in the sense of permanently opposed drives and controls."[26]

Other examples of this cultural embeddedness abound in the test records. In Swami Sivananda's record, aspects of the inkblot consistent with Vedantic teachings became the primary focus: for example, the symmetry of Card VIII reflected the duality of the world of appearances and the ultimate unity of true reality:

> Beyond the colors is the Self from which the colors are emanated. The card has two of each color to show that creation is based on defined laws, that the picture has its own soul in its symmetry, and that creation is supported by the pairs of opposites: good, bad, hot, cold, pleasure, pain, etc.[27]

The paucity of personal responses and the preponderance of cultural responses in these records raise two provocative questions. First, do these cultural responses represent a stereotyped social conventionality or an impoverished inner life, devoid of intellectual or emotional richness? Second, might these responses represent a pathological disintegration of the ego? The answer to these questions lies in a "contextual" approach to the material. The test records must be interpreted in the context of both other records from the same culture and the subject's entire set of responses to the ten cards.

The popular/original index of the Rorschach test provides a way of answering the first question regarding conventionality. A record in which "popular" responses predominate might also be considered "culturally embedded," but the responses would be stereotyped or conventional. These masters' test records, however, do not represent "popular," socially stereotyped, or impoverished records. An informal comparison of these test records with test records of others from the same cultures shows the richness of the masters' responses. Many of the responses may, in fact, be "original"—good "form responses" that are statistically rare.

Just one example from the Rorschach literature can vividly demonstrate the fact that these culturally embedded responses are far from stereotyped. Klopfer, Boyer, and their associates contrasted the Rorschach records of Apache shamans with "nonshaman" and "pseudoshaman" members of the Mescalero culture. In the Mescalero Apache society, the "true" shamans were believed to have supernatural powers: they were widely acclaimed as the possessors of the power to heal and the power to control the weather, and they were said to live and travel both in the world of the spirits and in the world of humans. Boyer and his colleagues defined "pseudoshamans" either as those who claimed to possess supernatural powers but were not acknowledged as shamanic healers by other members of the society or as those to whom such powers were attributed but who denied possessing them. The nonshaman group consisted of other members of the Mescalero Apache society. The study found that, in contrast to both the pseudoshamans and the nonshamans, "the shamans have a way of handling objective data with keener awareness of peculiarities and more selective theoretical interest."[28] Shamans were also found to be capable of using "regression in the service of the ego"—a capacity to revert temporarily to earlier forms of thought or behavior in order to make possible a renewed progression or recovery—and to have a greater creative potential, while pseudoshamans, as a group, had impoverished personalities and a lesser capacity for creative regression. Thus, the shaman's responses are creative and unconventional in comparison with the responses of others of their culture—although, paradoxically, the responses are, at the same time, impersonal or culturally embedded. Responses of the shamans, in other words, stand out from their own Apache culture in comparison with those of both nonshamans and pseudoshamans.

The second question—might these records be indicative of pathology—can be answered negatively as well: this culturally embedded style is not a result of ego disintegration or psychosis. The Rorschach record of the master looks entirely different from the record of a psychotic: psychotic records typically contain idiosyncratic, aggressive, and violent associations. The study of Apache shamans, nonshamans, and pseudoshamans addresses this question directly, concluding that the shamans "were not autocultural psychological deviants who had resolved serious psychopathological conditions . . . (such as) schizophrenic illnesses, through assumption of the shamanistic role. . . . The shamans as a group had a high degree of reality-testing potential."[29]

Thus, the contextual approach affirms that the masters' culturally embedded responses are not reflective of cultural stereotypes, mental impoverishment, psychopathology, or ego disintegration. Rather, the culturally defined content of the masters' responses indicates that individual perceptions and associations are embedded in cultural teachings: individual identity is subsumed by spiritual/cultural identity to a far greater degree than the typical cultural shaping of individual consciousness. This feature of the Rorschach suggests that devoting one's life to a spiritual path, focusing constantly on spiritual goals, and being continuously engaged in the spiritual practice have a powerful effect on perception and personality. Individual perceptions take on the cultural content of the teachings; personal identity merges with social role to an unprecedented degree. In the masters' responses, as Buddhist students sometimes say respectfully about enlightened teachers, "There's no one there!"

Integrative Style

In addition to this culturally embedded content, the masters exhibited a highly unusual integrative style, weaving their responses to all ten cards into a comprehensive, systematic, and sequential whole. Standard Rorschach test scoring procedure has no category for this degree of integration and organization, but I believe it is related to the organizational activity Rorschach measured by means of the whole response in his location scores. As noted earlier, the "whole response" represented for Rorschach the capacity to analyze percepts into parts and to integrate them into meaningful wholes; thus, it revealed analytic-synthetic abilities and the capacity for abstraction and generalization. Rorschach himself recognized that there were different kinds of whole responses, differentiated by the degree of organization and the complexity of the response. Subsequent Rorschach theorists have developed additional ways of measuring this capacity, including "organization scores" and "incorporation responses."[30] However, these indices of organization and integration measure perceptual skills *within* individual cards. The masters' organization scores are, in a sense, "off the charts": they integrate all ten cards into a systematic whole in a radical extension of the perceptual and organizational components of the whole response.

This integrative style in the masters' records is characterized by a systematic and sequential approach and by a didactic focus on the central teachings of the tradition. One would almost believe that the masters had been given the Rorschach cards in advance with the request that each prepare a lecture on his or her spiritual tradition based on the sequence and the imagery of the cards. For the enlightened Buddhist master, for example, the Rorschach test situation became an opportunity for a coherent spiritual discourse or "dharma talk." She used the Rorschach test situation to describe the causes of suffering and the way to alleviate suffering through spiritual practice based on nonattachment, closely following the traditional Buddhist teachings regarding the Four Noble Truths and the Eightfold Path. Brown and Engler describe portions of her test record:

> Card I sets the stage with four images of humans and beasts in their everyday life of suffering. Card II depicts a picture of the mind in its angered state, and Card III depicts the creatures of hell, the hellish stage of mind produced by anger in this life or the plane on which an angry person is believed to take birth in a future life, both in accordance with the Buddhist teachings on karmic action based on hatred. Cards IV–V depict the ignorance and craving of the mind, believed to be the two root causes of suffering in Buddhist psychology. . . . The remainder of the cards depict the enjoyment of the perfected practice as well as the consequences of practice that is not perfected.[31]

Similarly, Swami Sivananda created a coherent sequence that portrayed the stages of the spiritual path from a Vedantic perspective. Cards I and II showed devotees of the Lord at worship; Card III portrayed the removal of attachments and desires as one progresses in spiritual practice; Card IV depicted the three elements of ultimate reality experienced by the practitioner and the unity underlying the apparent duality of spirit and matter. Card V showed the lower and higher natures of mankind and the nonattachment possible through the practice of Yoga; Card VI portrayed the symbolism of the union of spirit and matter in the Shiva Linga cult, and Cards VII to X depicted various aspects of Atman, the soul, Brahman, the ultimate source of all reality, and Avidya, the darkness or ignorance that hides the truth. Thus, Swami Sivananda's record offered an organized set of instructions in the doctrine and practice, proceeding from worship to spiritual practice to ultimate reality and the monistic source of all things.

The shaman's record also contains a sequential, comprehensive approach toward cultural teachings. Black Eyes' responses created a description and history of the spiritual reality of the shaman's world. He began with "the old time" when there were "enemies in the clouds"; he shifted in the early cards to a description of the most prominent elements of his shamanic experience (traveling stars, seasonal changes, and views of the earth from far above); and he concluded with descriptions of the vital forces of movement and life (wind, lightning, and water). More specifically, Cards I–IV, for Black Eyes, depicted the traveling stars of summer and autumn (I); the view of Alaska from high above the earth during the early spring (II); traveling stars in the early fall when crops are maturing (III); and the view downward toward the earth in late spring (IV). The dynamic forces underlying all movement and life appeared in Cards V–X. Cards V–VIII showed the "fast-traveling thunderwinds" and the power of lightning "going straight to the earth"; Card IX showed thunder over the crops in late fall "giving them life, giving life again to go on through the winter"; and Card X showed a land underneath the water and a purposeful shaking of water directed by an unseen androgynous "water boss." What emerges is a coherent and sequential progression of spiritual perspective from the "old times" to the star travels to the elements of the cosmos to the life force that underlies the cycles of nature.

For each of these spiritual masters, then, taking the Rorschach test became an opportunity to function didactically as a teacher of spiritual realities and soteriologically as a proponent of the highest truth. The integrative, sequential quality of these Rorschach records represents a considerable accomplishment. Against the varied stimulus-pull of the diverse cards, the masters succeeded at integrating all ten cards into a single body of teaching in an orderly and systematic way, without significant departures from reality testing.[32] The shaman communicated his ecstatic flights through space; the Swami taught the essential elements of Vedantic doctrine; and the enlightened Buddhist master related her knowledge and experience of the means to end suffering. The integrative and unitive styles reveal the masters' remarkable intellectual capacities; the presentations of cultural/spiritual truths support the earlier suggestion that individual perceptions seem to disappear as individual identity is subsumed by spiritual identity, while the didactic style demonstrates a deep embeddedness in the therapeutic and salvific role of master.

Again, it is necessary to raise the interpretive question regarding pathology: Can these integrative records be distinguished from symptomatic and pathological Rorschach records wherein one might also find the ten cards related to a single theme? The record of a delusional paranoid schizophrenic or an obsessive with fixated responses, for example, might show a single-pointed focus. There are several differences, however, in the types of records one would find in these cases. Again, a contextual approach clarifies the issues. First, the highly unique, idiosyncratic, and personalized nature of paranoid delusion or obsessional fixation contrasts sharply with the impersonal, culturally embedded, systematic presentation of a consensual body of teaching established by a tradition. Second, as Brown and Engler note, the decision to use the testing situation as an occasion to teach stands in stark contrast to the guardedness and constrictedness of a paranoid record.[33] Third, the spiritual masters' associations are consistent and integrated across all ten cards, rather than being loosely related from card to card. Finally, the responses show good form quality: percepts are quite realistic. We can conclude that the integrative quality of these records thus does not represent a defensive, obsessive, fixated, or perseverative clinging to fixed concepts.

The Vague and Slippery Determinant Cluster

Although the major scoring determinants (movement, form, and color) in the test reports of the masters showed no uniformity in the masters' Rorschachs, these unique records share high responsivity to the particular cluster of determinants I have called "vague and slippery." This includes shading responses, inanimate movement responses, and amorphously perceived form responses. These are particularly problematic findings, because in standard Rorschach diagnosis they are clear signs of pathology.

Shading can involve the perception of diffuse cloudiness, the perception of darkness in the card, or the perception of discrete nuances of shading. Although theorists debate the scoring and interpretation of shading, it is generally seen as an index of the sense of being engulfed by nothingness, the sense of groundlessness, or the sense of being lost in a world that has no discernible organization. Such responses are usually interpreted as a sign of depression, character disorder, feelings of inferiority, or vague anxiety. They are "more frequent in neurotics than in normals and still more frequent in psychopaths . . . [and] they are always connected with central feeling tones, mostly of a dysphoric nature."[34] In addition, these responses often involve a tendency toward inadequate mood control. The closely related "vague or amorphously perceived form response" is a sign of lack of integrative ability, a noncommittal hold on reality, and weak mental processes.[35] The Rorschach literature thus views the shading and amorphous form responses perceptually as the experience of loss of boundaries, groundlessness, and constant change, emotionally as a manifestation of diffuse anxiety, and diagnostically as signs of depression and weak reality contact.[36]

Typical examples of shading responses to the Rorschach cards are dark clouds or shadows, and such responses were frequent in the masters' records. The most common form of shading among the masters was the perception of diffuse cloudiness. Black Eyes' record contained seven shading responses and four (related) achromatic color responses. These included clouds, reflections of light on clouds, and darkness. Some Rorschach theorists such as Samuel Beck also score three-dimensionality and "bird's-eye views" of landscapes or maps as shading responses.[37] In Beck's system, Black Eyes would have had additional shading responses in Cards II, IV, and V. No matter which scoring system is used, Black Eyes' record reveals very high shading responsivity in comparison with Rorschach test norms. Swami Sivananda's record contains three dramatic shading responses. These include Card VI, "light hidden in darkness, truth buried in false appearances"; Card VII, "Atman hidden under apparent darkness surrounded by mold"; and Card IX, "rising of the sun of knowledge behind the clouds and shadows of ignorance." Similarly, the Rorschach record of the Buddhist master showed "considerable reliance on shading responses and vague and amorphously perceived form."[38] Notably, these features were also present in the Rorschach test records of the "samadhi group" in Brown and Engler's study.

In addition to high shading responsivity, the masters' records revealed a tendency toward inanimate movement responsivity. The inanimate movement response is characterized by a perception of movement in an object in the inkblot. This is differentiated from human or animal movement and is generally interpreted as "infantile intrapsychic tension" or "hostile and uncontrollable impulses."[39] This percept was evident in very high incidence in Black Eyes' record and in Brown and Engler's "advanced insight group" of Western-born students of mindfulness meditation who had attained the first stage of enlightenment.[40]

The Rorschach records of the "advanced insight group" of meditators, otherwise "mundane," showed an extraordinarily high use of inanimate movement responses, alone and in conjunction with color and shading. Brown and Engler note: "10–20% of the total responses were inanimate movement responses for each of the four subjects. No subject's record contained less than a raw count of eight such responses."[41] Typical responses involved content related to energy in motion, such as this response to Card X:

> Sort of like just energy and like molecules . . . something like the energy of molecules. Very much like a microscopic view. . . . In some way there are more patterns of energy. . . . There are different energies in the different colors. It looks like it's a view into the body where there's energy, there's movement, but it's steady because it's guided by a life force. There is a rising and passing away of these different elements.[42]

This determinant is also present in Swami Sivananda's record, notably in Card X: "All these have left the One. There is something beyond. On this side, across from a trunk, or a shadowy passageway . . . diverse objects are falling. Some large, some small, some with many limbs, others with none, with various nuances and forms."[43] Similarly, Black Eyes' "traveling stars" are an excellent example of this response, as are his "lightning power" and "shaking water."

How can the preponderance of shading, inanimate movement, and amorphous form in these records be interpreted? Are these masters depressed, anxious, or unable to control their moods, as the high incidence of shading would indicate? Do they have a weak hold on reality, as the high incidence of amorphous form would indicate? Are they beset by hostile and uncontrollable urges, as the inanimate movement responses indicate? Klopfer and Boyer raise this question pointedly in relation to Black Eyes:

> One of the most damaging aspects of . . . (Black Eyes') record is the prevalence of undifferentiated shading and the inanimate or magic motion throughout the ten cards. . . . The best possible explanation in the given cultural setting for this combination of the deep anxiety connected with the strong and totally unrefined impulsive sensuous reaction, and the identification with the erratic wanderings of the traveling stars, seems to lie in the assumption that he identified his urges with his magic mandate, but is very careful, at the same time, to avoid any ego responsibility for his actions.[44]

Thus, a traditional diagnosis—even from interpreters as sympathetic as Klopfer and Boyer—views Black Eyes' record as pathological. I suggest, however, that in a spiritual rather than a psychological context, the shading responses, the amorphous form responses, and the inanimate movement responses should be interpreted differently. The perception of shadows, vague shapes, or moving fields of energy is not anomalous or pathological for a spiritual adept accustomed to the sense of reality as impermanent and in constant flux, the blurring of self-environment boundaries, and the sense of nothingness or groundlessness. These are experiences often attributed to mystical states, meditative states, or other altered states of consciousness. Buddhist teachings, in fact, are remarkably congruent with the experiential elements of this shared determinant cluster. The constant flux of reality is consistent with the Buddhist teaching of impermanence (*anicca*), the constant change inherent in every aspect of the finite world. The blurring of self-environment boundaries, characteristic of shading percepts, parallels the Buddhist teaching of *anatta*, the lack of intrinsic durable nature of the self. Furthermore, the perceptual experience of nothingness in the shading response echoes the Buddhist view of Nirvana—nothingness, or the void.

Brown and Engler interpret the vague and slippery determinant cluster in the meditators as indications of the achievement of specific levels of meditative progress. In their view, inanimate movement in association with shading is a specific predictor of having achieved "access samadhi,"[45] while the inanimate movement responses, emphasizing the relationship of form, energy, and space as life forces, are predictors of having achieved the first level of enlightenment in "advanced insight."[46] They might suggest that the shaman and the swami had achieved, through their own spiritual practices, the equivalent of the "samadhi" or "insight" levels of advancement. I think, however, that the experience of "perceptual deautomatization" in nonordinary consciousness itself is a more parsimonious—and cross-culturally applicable—way of explaining these patterns.

The notion of perceptual "automatization" and "deautomatization" was developed by A. Deikman in the 1960s in an attempt to understand ordinary and nonordinary or altered states of consciousness.[47] "Automatization" in Deikman's theory is the mental process basic to human consciousness whereby the repeated exercise of an action or a perception results in the disappearance from consciousness of its intermediate steps. In other words, we are not consciously aware of the perceptual process of encountering an ambiguous stimulus, selecting certain features to attend to, ignoring other features, and providing a verbal label. All of these elements contribute to every perception, but the process is "automatized." "Deautomatization" is the undoing of automatization by reinvesting actions and percepts with attention, leading to the breakdown of the psychological structures that organize, limit, select, and interpret perceptual stimuli.

According to Deikman, concentrative meditation is a primary method of attending to and deautomatizing the process of perception. He has suggested that deautomatization is the primary component of all mystical and meditative experience: "Training in contemplative meditation leads to the building of intrapsychic barriers against distracting stimuli. . . . The phenomena described in mystic accounts can be regarded as the consequence of a partial deautomatization of the psychic structures that organize and interpret perceptual stimuli."[48]

In ordinary perception, we select from ambiguous sense data the more stable, firm, clear, or rigid perceptual stimuli. Those who are accustomed to nonordinary states of consciousness, however, are able to perceive the unstable, infirm, unclear, and nonrigid. In the literature we've examined, the masters' achievement of meditative, contemplative, or ecstatic states of consciousness has provided them with expertise in breaking down ordinary perceptual patterns—an expertise that is evident in the Rorschach records.

The Buddhist meditators and the Swami are participants in spiritual traditions that engage the deautomatization of normal perceptual processes. Vedantic meditative practice is a classic example of a concentrative approach, while the Vipassana groups are practitioners of a mindfulness meditation system that emphasizes both concentrative meditation and "insight" (bare awareness of all mental processes). The "samadhi group" of Buddhist meditators, the group that shows the greatest evidence of perceptual deautomatization, is the group that is most diligently practicing concentration. Meditation in both its concentrative and its insight-oriented forms radically slows perceptual processing of stimuli and deconstructs cognitive structures. The shaman's altered state experience, on the other hand, is clearly not meditative or concentrative. Rather, as the work of Eliade and Fisher suggests, shamanic ecstasy is akin to the rapid cognitive processing characteristic of hallucinogenic states.[49] Regardless of the source of the deautomatization or the degree of doctrinal and didactic elaboration on deautomatization, however, the result is a breakdown of ordinary perceptual processing. In Rorschach terms, this breakdown results in a predominance of shading responses, inanimate movement responses, and amorphous form responses. Thus, the deautomatization of ordinary perceptual structures appears on the Rorschach test in the vague and slippery determinant cluster and is indicative of a predictable and regular pattern among spiritual masters.

If these responses are an indication of spiritual progress, why are they understood as an indication of pathology in the psychodiagnostic literature? Shading does provide, in all contexts, an index of the perception of reality as changing and without boundaries. This is an appropriate experience for a practitioner of altered states but an inappropriate or frightening experience for those attached to the firmness and stability of reality in normal waking consciousness. The percepts that reveal anxiety in the Rorschach record of the ordinary subject instead reveal toleration of ambiguity and expertise in the spiritual realm in the Rorschach record of the master.

Thus, although the clearest theological and theoretical reflection of this experience occurs in the Buddhist literature, it is not foreign to the Apache and the Vedantic traditions. Shading, amorphous form, and inanimate movement may be valid indicators of the awareness of subtle internal and external nuances in stimuli that is a result of disciplined exploration of altered states of consciousness.[50] I would predict a high correlation of this determinant cluster with advanced spiritual practice in any tradition involving mystical, contemplative, or altered-states experiences.

Conclusions

I've argued that three dramatic cross-cultural similarities emerge in the Rorschach tests of the spiritual masters. First, the Rorschach responses of the spiritual masters are "impersonal" or "culturally embedded" to a degree far greater than one would expect from previously established Rorschach norms. Second, the masters integrated their responses to all ten cards into a systematic, coherent whole. Third, the masters perceived a great deal of shading, amorphous form, and inanimate movement in the Rorschach test.

These cross-cultural similarities raise several interpretive problems. A preliminary problem, as I've noted, involves the question of diagnosis: Do these Rorschach records indicate spiritual progress or mental pathology? I've shown that the "impersonal" response might be misinterpreted as impoverished; the "integrated" responses might appear fixated; and the "vague" determinant cluster might appear to be signs of depression. I've argued, however, that when the context of the entire record and the norms within a culture are taken into consideration, the responses stand out as nonpathological.

A second major interpretive question raised by this material returns us to the Forman thesis with which we began this discussion. Do the Rorschach records of spiritual masters contribute to the cross-cultural psychological study of nonordinary consciousness proposed by Forman in his call for a *psychologia perennis*? To my mind, there's no question that these Rorschach studies offer a valuable paradigm for a cross-cultural psychology of religious experience. While psychological inquiries into religious experience have a century-long history, much of the research on religious experience remains fairly superficial. Typically, researchers have attempted to create or elicit religious experiences in experimental subjects through sensory deprivation, drugs, ordeals in nature, or suggestion.[51] Predictably, such studies fail to uncover deeper cognitive or perceptual patterns related to long-term religious experience. Forman's proposal represents a significant shift from this earlier approach. His call for a *psychologia perennis*—which I would prefer to rephrase as a call for an investigation of the psychology of spiritual mastery—is well met by the Rorschach studies discussed here, studies that explore perception and cognition in the spiritually advanced. As I've shown, an analysis of these Rorschach studies reveals important commonalities. "Impersonal" responses indicate that the masters are, in a sense, embodiments or carriers of their spiritual traditions; "integrative" responses suggest that the masters utilized the Rorschach test as an opportunity to communicate the essential truths of their tradition; and "vague and slippery" responses indicate a mastery of nuance and a familiarity with nonordinary states of consciousness developed through perceptual deautomatization.

The Rorschach literature thus confirms the first two of Forman's four central theses: there is indeed a difference between ordinary and nonordinary consciousness, and transformational processes like meditation and shamanic training can enact a shift from ordinary to nonordinary consciousness. That shift is visible in the Rorschach test records we've examined. But what of Forman's third and fourth theses—that the transformational power of meditation lies in its ability to strip away learned cultural and linguistic categories, exposing an innate capacity for pure consciousness that is cross-culturally and historically stable? Can the similarities we've seen in the

Rorschach records of spiritual masters be interpreted as evidence of a stripping away of learned cultural and linguistic categories and of an innate capacity for pure consciousness? Brown and Engler would support Forman's thesis. Posing the questions "Does the yogi . . . 'really' reduce thinking and perceptual processes during concentration practice?" and "Does he 'really' become aware of the most subtle workings of his mind and the universe during insight practice?" they answer yes. They demonstrate remarkable congruities between Rorschach records at various stages of advancement and Buddhist teachings about the stages of the path toward enlightenment, arguing that "more complex thinking and perceptual processes are deconstructed during meditation" and that the Rorschach records of meditators at different stages expose this gradual deconstruction of perception.[52] In their view, the Rorschach records validate the truth claims of Buddhist doctrine and practice: they would affirm Forman's view that spiritual practice gradually removes the perceptual veils that obscure pure awareness.

I am hesitant, however, to support this interpretation of the Rorschach material. My reading of the Rorschachs from the swami, the meditators, and the shaman is somewhat different. I see the similarities in the masters' Rorschach records as evidence of the two interrelated factors I've described—a perceptual deautomatization of consciousness resulting from expertise in nonordinary states of consciousness; and a didactic, salvific, or healing stance developed in response to the demands of the social role of shaman, teacher, or master. The vague and slippery determinant cluster illustrates most vividly the effects of perceptual deautomatization, while the impersonal and integrative response styles exemplify the pedagogical and soteriological stance of the masters' style. Let me explain the implications of these two factors for an assessment of Forman's thesis by returning to the debate Forman described between the decontextualists and the constructivists regarding the relationship between spiritual practice and nonordinary experience.

As Forman noted, decontextualists and constructivists disagree about the relationship between meditation and mysticism or other nonordinary states of consciousness. While both groups acknowledge that practice of meditation or other transformative techniques can lead to mystical experience, the constructivist sees the practice as a learned tradition within a particular religious/cultural context that produces, creates, or "constructs" a certain mystical effect, whereas the decontextualist sees the practice as a process of escaping from or eliminating cultural constructs to expose an authentic core of consciousness through an unlearning, deconstructing, or "forgetting" of cultural categories.[53] Those cultural categories, in the decontextualist view, may allow us to function efficiently within the social realm of human interactions in ordinary consciousness, but they obstruct access to an innate capacity to be aware of awareness itself. Thus, according to the decontextualists, spiritual practice gradually removes the cultural and perceptual veils that obscure pure consciousness; according to the constructivists, spiritual practice, rather than lifting veils, creates and constructs religious experience.

Can this debate be resolved? Is it possible to differentiate innate elements from learned elements in religious experience? Can these Rorschach records shed light on the controversy that divides the decontextualists from the constructivists, lifting the veils that obscure the nature of nonordinary consciousness itself? Seeking to resolve this question by controlling for the effects of culture, teaching, and doctrine, Brown and Engler gathered a set of "control" Rorschachs from a group that was familiar with the Buddhist teachings but did not practice intensive meditation.[54] This was the staff at the site of their "Three-Month Study." This group listened to lectures with the meditators and embraced the teachings but, unlike the meditators, did not practice sixteen hours of daily meditation. As Brown and Engler predicted, the staff did not show the dramatic Rorschach results evident among the meditators. They concluded that the Rorschach results are an effect of meditative practice itself. I concur with their conclusion.

The fact that intense meditation results in perceptual changes, however, does not prove that meditation strips away culturally learned perceptual categories, leaving an innate capacity for awareness itself—even though the religious teachings may claim to be doing exactly that.[55] Indeed, members of Brown and Engler's "advanced insight group," who were not practicing intensive meditation at the time of testing, showed very few unusual effects in their Rorschach records. Although Brown and Engler see this as a confirmation of the Buddhist teaching that after first-level enlightenment one regains normal consciousness or "retains his ordinary mind,"[56] this seems to me an indication that the Rorschach effects were directly derived from the (presence or absence of) intensive meditation practice: the vivid effects of the meditating groups were caused by the perceptual deautomatization created through the meditative practice; the paucity of effects of the members of the "advanced insight group" was caused by the fact that they were not, at the time, involved in intense meditation practice. In other words, while the perceptual deautomatization of spiritual practice may create the perceptual changes characteristic of nonordinary consciousness, the question of the stripping away of learned structures and the question of the "innateness" of the nonordinary awareness remain unanswered.

I think that the Rorschach literature sounds a cautionary note. Rather than unambiguously supporting either the decontextualists or the constructivists, it points, in my view, toward the necessity of acknowledging both innate elements and cultural elements in nonordinary experience. The Rorschach studies we examined do not actually differentiate—and perhaps cannot differentiate—between "innate capacities" and culturally shaped experiences, nor can they prove a gradual unveiling of pure awareness through spiritual practice.

We must acknowledge that all human expressions are in some way created or shaped by language and culture: all human products, communications, texts, and behaviors are culturally and linguistically situated. At the same time, there are innate, universal aspects of the human experience: biological and physiological structures, perceptual capacities, capacities for ordinary and nonordinary experiences, and a realm we haven't discussed here, the realm of unconscious fantasy and desire, the territory Freud devoted his life to charting. Indeed, even such radical constructivists as deconstructionist philosopher Jacques Derrida or social historian Michel Foucault, I think, would agree that the capacity to be shaped by language and culture is universal and in some way innate in humans. Historian of religions Catherine Bell articulates with clarity the impact of this paradox for the field of religious studies: "For many scholars who work closely with religious data of one sort or another, there is little confidence in any universal religious dimension, whether it be psychological, sociological, or metaphysical. Yet neither does it seem obvious that there are no commonalties and that what we want to talk about as 'religion' is in fact a matter of fundamental cultural differences."[57]

In support of the decontextualist thesis, we can affirm that humans have an innate capacity for altered states of consciousness. As ethnopsychiatrist George De Vos states, "a psychological universal in human beings is what might be broadly termed the capacity for altered states of consciousness."[58] While not everyone experiences these altered states of consciousness, the basic capacity is widespread, if not universal. In support of the constructivist's view, however, we can also state that those who become masters of these nonordinary states of consciousness, whether through meditation or through other means, exhibit certain perceptual and cognitive changes that are shaped by spiritual practice, language, society, culture, and belief.[59] Decontextualists and constructivists would agree that "perceptual deautomatization" follows a long period of transformative practice, but we cannot finally determine whether or not the practice removes cultural obstacles that previously obscured something hidden and innate. This dilemma remains finally undecidable.

We scholars seem inevitably to frame our debates in terms that require an oppositional other: culture versus nature; universality versus plurality; theology versus religious studies; constructivism versus decontextualism. If William James argued against the "medical materialists" whose reductionistic approaches would pathologize religious experience, and if other generations of scholars argued over whether the mystic vision was attributable to divine or human origination, we argue today over whether mysticism should be traced to innate human capacities or to learned cultural/linguistic categories. What seems to be nearly universal is an "innate capacity"—or, better, an "inescapable compulsion"—to frame our intellectual debates dualistically: in ordinary consciousness or theory-building consciousness, we structure our ideas, experiences, and theories oppositionally in debates that "set up their terms in fundamentally reciprocal or oppositional relationships in which they are foils for defining each other."[60]

It is clear that the contemporary study of religious experience has moved far beyond the collection of spontaneous religious experiences gathered by William James for his 1902 *Varieties of Religious Experience*. The essays in this volume exemplify what might be called, in a paraphrase of James's title, *The Uniformities of Religious Experience*. Yet, paradoxically, Forman's call for a cross-cultural and transhistorical psychology of religious experience is far more diverse, broad, and complex than James's collection of primarily Christian experiences in *The Varieties*. The Rorschach studies of spiritual masters described in this essay provide an opportunity to examine, from the perspective of ordinary consciousness, the cross-cultural uniformities in the perceptual effects of expertise in nonordinary consciousness. I fear, however, that the Rorschach cannot resolve the debate over cultural versus innate experience. A valuable paradigm for understanding mystical consciousness is perhaps to be found in psychoanalyst D. W. Winnicott's formulation of the infant's initial encounter with the world as simultaneously a creation and a discovery. In Winnicott's view, "the infant creates what is in fact . . . waiting to be found. . . . Yet the object must be found in order to be created." He adds, "this has to be accepted as a paradox and not solved by a restatement that, by its cleverness, seems to eliminate the paradox."[61] We would do well to acknowledge the Winnicottian paradox in our attempts to formulate an understanding of religious experience: spiritual masters, we might say, discover an innate "pure consciousness"; at the same time, culturally and linguistically, they create it.

Notes

1. William James, *The Varieties of Religious Experience* (Cambridge: Harvard University Press, 1985). (Original edition 1902)

2. Robert Forman, "Mystical Consciousness, the Innate Capacity, and the Perennial Philosophy," this volume.

3. Ralph Hood Jr., "The Facilitation of Religious Experience," in *Handbook of Religious Experience*, ed. Ralph Hood Jr. (Birmingham: Religious Education Press, 1995), p. 577.

4. Wayne Proudfoot, *Religious Experience* (Berkeley: University of California Press, 1986); Steven Katz, *Mysticism and Language* (New York: Oxford University Press, 1992).

5. Forman, "Mystical Consciousness."

6. William Blake, cited in Aldous Huxley, *The Doors of Perception* and *Heaven and Hell* (New York: Harper, 1963), p. 1. See also R. M. Mishra, *Yoga Sutras: The Textbook of Yoga Psychology* (Garden City: Anchor Press, 1963); T. Narada, *A Manual of Abhidamma* (Kandy: Buddhist Publication Society, 1975); Mahasi Sayadaw, *Practical Insight Meditation* (Santa Cruz: Unity Press, 1972).

7. Forman, "Mystical Consciousness."

8. Diane Jonte-Pace, "From Prophets to Perception: The Origins of Rorschach's Psychology," *Annual of Psychoanalysis* 14 (1986): 179–203. See also D. Jonte-Pace, "Religion: A Rorschachian Projection Theory," *American Imago* 2 (1985): 199–234.

9. Hermann Rorschach, "Einiges über schweizerische Sekten und Sektengründer" (originally published 1917), "Weiteres über schweizerische Sektenbildungen" (originally published 1919), "Sektiererstudien" (posthumously published 1927), in *Gesammelte Aufsätze von Hermann Rorschach*, ed. K. Bash, trans. Paul Lemkau and Bernard Kronenberg (Bern: Huber, 1965); Hermann Rorschach, *Psychodiagnostics* (Bern: Huber, 1975) (originally published 1921).

10. Henri Ellenberger, "The Life and Work of Hermann Rorschach, 1884–1922," *Bulletin of the Menninger Clinic* 18 (1954): 173–219.

11. Stephen W. Hurt, Marvin Reznikoff, and John Clarkin, "The Rorschach," in *Integrative Assessment of Adult Personality*, eds. Larry Beutler and Michael Berren (New York: Guilford Press, 1995), p. 187.

12. See, for example, Melvin Zax, Emory Cowen, and Mary Peter, "A Comparative Study of Novice Nuns and College Females," *Journal of Abnormal and Social Psychology* 66 (1963): 369–375; Philip Helfaer, *The Psychology of Religious Doubt* (Boston: Beacon, 1972); Gotthard Booth, "The Psychological Examination of Candidates for the Ministry," in *The Ministry and Mental Health*, ed. H. Hoffmann (New York: Associated Press, 1960); R. Draeger, "Some Personality Correlates of Religious Atttiude as Determined by Projective Techniques," Ph.D. diss., University of Southern California, 1950.

13. M. Maupin, "Individual Differences in Responses to a Zen Meditation Exercise," *Journal of Consulting Psychology* 29 (1965): 139–145.

14. Frederick Spiegelberg, "Le Protocole du Rorschach du Swami Sivananda Saraswati Maharaj," *Psyche* (Paris) 7 (1952): 598–602.

15. Bruno Klopfer and L. Bryce Boyer, "Notes on the Personality Structure of a North American Indian Shaman: Rorschach Interpretation," *Journal of Projective Techniques* (1961): 170–178; L. Bryce Boyer, Bruno Klopfer, Florence Brawer, and Hayao Kawai, "Comparisons of the Shamans and Pseudo-shamans of the Apaches of the Mescalero Indian Reservation: A Rorschach Study," *Journal of Projective Techniques and Personality Assessment* 28 (1964): 173–80. See also L. Bryce Boyer, George De Vos, and Ruth Boyer, "Crisis and Continuity in the Personality of a Shaman," in *Symbolic Analysis Cross-Culturally: The Rorschach Test*, ed. George De Vos and L. Bryce Boyer (Berkeley: University of California Press, 1989).

16. Daniel Brown and Jack Engler, "The Stages of Mindfulness Meditation: A Validation Study," *Journal of Transpersonal Psychology* 12 (1980): 143–192; Daniel Brown and Jack Engler, "An Outcome Study of Intensive Mindfulness Meditation," *Psychoanalytic Study of Society*, vol. 10, ed. Werner Muensterberger, L. Bryce Boyer, and Simon A. Grolnick (Hillsdale, N.J.: Analytic Press, 1984), pp. 163–225. This research drew upon three independent projects: a study of Western-born meditators on a three-month retreat, a study of advanced Western students of meditation, and a study of South Asian meditators. I am greatly indebted to Brown and Engler for many of the ideas in this paper.

17. Hurt, Reznikoff, and Clarkin, "The Rorschach," p. 187.

18. See Samuel Beck, *Rorschach's Test*, vol. 1 (New York: Grune and Stratton, 1961); Ernest Schachtel, *Experiential Foundations of Rorschach's Test* (New York: Basic Books, 1966); Maria Rickers-Ovsiankina, "Synopsis of Psychological Premises Underlying the Rorschach," in *Rorschach Psychology*, ed. Maria Rickers-Ovsiankina (Huntington, N.Y.: Krieger, 1977); Bruno Klopfer, M. Ainsworth, Walter G. Klopfer, and Robert Holt, *Developments in Rorschach Technique*, vol. 1 (Yonkers: World Book, 1954); John Exner, *The Rorschach: A Comprehensive System* (New York: Wiley, 1974).

19. See A. Irving Hallowell, "The Rorschach as an Aid in the Study of Personalities in Primitive Societies," *Rorschach Research Exchange* 4 (1940): 106; Gardner Lindzey, *Projective Techniques and Cross-Cultural Research* (New York: Appleton-Century Crofts, 1961); Francis L. Hsu, *Psychological Anthropology* (Cambridge: Schenkman, 1972); and George De Vos, "Transcultural Studies: Normative and Clinical," in *Symbolic Analysis Cross-Culturally: The Rorschach Test*, ed. George De Vos and L. Bryce Boyer (Berkeley: University of California Press, 1989).

20. "The basic concept of Apache religion is that of a vague, diffuse, supernatural power that pervades the universe and may enliven inanimate objects. To become effective it must 'work through' humankind." Boyer, De Vos, and Boyer, "Crisis and Continuity," p. 382.

21. The Buddhist meditators all practiced a Burmese meditation technique called Satipatthana-Vipassana, or mindfulness meditation.

22. Klopfer and Boyer, "Notes on Personality Structure," p. 173.

23. Spiegelberg, "Le Protocole," p. 599. Translations are mine. I thank Joann Jonte for assistance with translations.

24. Brown and Engler, "Stages of Mindfulness Meditation," pp. 168–169.

25. See Lindzey, *Projective Techniques*; Hsu, *Psychological Anthropology*; and De Vos, "Transcultural Studies."

26. Brown and Engler, "An Outcome Study," p. 219. Here and in their 1980 essay, they stress that the Rorschach data for the master's record corroborates traditional Buddhist teachings regarding enlightenment: ariyas or "ones worthy of praise" who have attained the ultimate (4th) or penultimate (3rd) stage of enlightenment are said to "no longer be subject to sexual or aggressive impulses or painful affects." The fully enlightened master is alleged to have "perfected the mind and to be free of any kind of conflict or suffering" ("Stages," p. 185).

27. Spiegelberg, "Le Protocole," p. 600.

28. Boyer, Klopfer, Brawer, and Kawai, "Comparisons of the Shamans and Pseudo-shamans," p. 178.

29. Ibid., pp. 175, 179.

30. L. Hemmendinger and K. Schultz, "Developmental Theory and the Rorschach Method," in *Rorschach Psychology*, ed. Maria Rickers-Ovsiankina (Huntington, N.Y.: Krieger, 1977); and Marguerite Hertz, "The Organization Activity," in *Rorschach Psychology*, ed. Maria Rickers-Ovsiankina (Huntington, N.Y.: Krieger, 1977).

31. Brown and Engler, "An Outcome Study," pp. 197–198.

32. Ibid., p. 198.

33. Brown and Engler, "Stages of Mindfulness Meditation," p. 186.

34. Ewald Bohm, "The Binder Chiaroscuro System and Its Theoretical Basis," in *Rorschach Psychology,* ed. Maria Rickers-Ovsiankina (Huntington, N.Y.: Krieger, 1977). p. 315.

35. Martin Mayman, "A Multidimensional View of the Rorschach Movement Response," in *Rorschach Psychology*, ed. Maria Rickers-Ovsiankina (Huntington, N.Y.: Krieger, 1977).

36. Schachtel, *Experiential Foundations*, pp. 246–248; Rickers-Ovsiankina, "Synopsis of Psychological Premises," pp. 13–16. The early literature on the *Helldunkel* (Chiaroscuro, or shading) response contains some hints of euphoric mood quality, subsequently unexplored in the Rorschach literature. See H. Binder, *Die Helldunkeldeutungen im psychodiagnostischem Experiment von Rorschach* (Zurich: Urell Fussli, 1932), and Bohm, "The Binder Chiaroscuro System."

37. Beck, *Rorschach's Test*, 1961.

38. Brown and Engler, "Stages of Mindfulness Education," p. 168.

39. Mayman, "Multidimensional View," p. 240.

40. Brown and Engler, "An Outcome Study," p. 184.

41. Ibid., p. 210; "Stages," p. 163.

42. Brown and Engler, "Stages of Mindfulness Meditation," p. 166.

43. Spiegelberg, "Le Protocole," p. 600.

44. Klopfer and Boyer, "Notes on Personality Structure," p. 178.

45. Brown and Engler, "An Outcome Study," p. 204.

46. Ibid., p. 193.

47. Arthur Deikman, "Experimental Meditation," in *Altered States of Consciousness*, ed. Charles Tart (New York: Doubleday, 1969), pp. 203–223.

48. Ibid., p. 204.

49. Mircea Eliade, *Shamanism: Archaic Techniques of Ecstasy*, trans. Willard R. Trask (Princeton: Bollingen, 1964). See also Roland Fischer "A Cartography of Ecstatic and Meditative States," *Science* 174 (1971): pp. 897–904. However, see De Vos, who argues that ec-

static components are largely absent from Native American forms of shamanism; "Transcultural Studies," p. 379.

50. Cf. Brown and Engler, "Stages of Mindfulness Meditation," p. 186.

51. David Wulff, *Psychology of Religion: Classic and Contemporary Views* (New York: Wiley, 1991), pp. 172–193, See also Ralph Hood Jr., "The Facilitation of Religious Experience," pp. 568–597.

52. Brown and Engler, "An Outcome Study," p. 167.

53. Forman, "Mystical Consciousness."

54. Brown and Engler, "An Outcome Study," p. 167.

55. As Freud shows in *The Future of an Illusion*, religions often make truth claims that fulfill unconscious wishes but are not necessarily factual. Sigmund Freud, *The Future of an Illusion*, in *The Standard Edition of the Collected Works of Sigmund Freud*, vol. 21, trans. and ed. James Strachey (London: Hogarth, 1961).

56. Brown and Engler, "An Outcome Study," p. 211.

57. Catherine Bell, "Modernism and Post-Modernism in the Study of Religion," *Religious Studies Review* 22, no. 3 (1996): 188.

58. De Vos, "Transcultural Studies," p. 47.

59. Ibid., p. 35. Here De Vos also points out that "psychological functioning is governed by a finite number of mental processes . . . involved in the development of affective and intellectual controls. Although influenced differentially by the practices of childhood socialization found in particular cultures, psychological functioning depends upon certain underlying physiological-hereditary structures common to all Homo Sapiens. Universals, therefore, are to be found cross-culturally."

60. Bell, "Modernism and Post-Modernism," p. 187.

61. D. W. Winnicott, *The Maturational Process and the Facilitating Environment* (New York: International Universities Press, 1966), p. 181.

EIGHT

William James and the Origins of Mystical Experience

G. WILLIAM BARNARD

SEVERAL DECADES AGO, Western philosophers of religion frequently claimed that mystical experiences were the result of direct contact with an undefined, but usually vaguely Christian, Ultimate Reality.[1] In recent years, however, a significant philosophical shift has taken place. In most contemporary philosophical discussions of mysticism, it is now almost axiomatic that mystical experiences are not so much revelations of a transcendent Ultimate Reality as they are highly refined, culturally produced, linguistically structured phenomena.[2] Many contemporary scholars of mysticism might, if pressed, admit that it is logically possible to claim that mystical experiences are constituted by something other than *just* the mystic's cultural assumptions; however, even those scholars who are philosophically open to the possibility that mystical experiences might indeed originate from contact with a transcultural reality often claim that this level of reality is beyond the grasp of conceptual categories—an assumption that turns metaphysical formulations into, at best, idle guesswork. Many philosophers of mysticism have therefore tended to avoid pursuing any in-depth explorations of the metaphysical implications of mystical experiences and have, instead, preferred to direct their energies toward categorizing and examining the characteristics of mystical experiences in and of themselves.

William James, a turn-of-the-century American psychologist and philosopher, offers us an alternative to this rather restrictive methodology. A close examination of James's work demonstrates that a full-bodied investigation of mystical experiences can and should wrestle not only with epistemological questions but also with the psychological and metaphysical implications of mystical experiences.[3] Although much of James's work is more than a century old, his philosophical perspective is surprisingly relevant. It can still offer the contemporary study of mysticism challenging and provocative insights into our seemingly innate capacity to have mystical experiences, experiences that can dramatically alter our everyday sense of who we are and radically revise the nature of the world in which we live.

This essay focuses first on James's epistemology and its implications for the study of mysticism and then explores the ways in which James's notions of selfhood and metaphysics can help us understand the origins of mystical experience. In the epistemological sections of the essay, James's theory of knowledge is shown to be directly pertinent to current debates among scholars of mysticism in that it bridges the chasm that separates those philosophers who stress the nonnatural origin of mystical experiences from those who emphasize the vital role played by culture and language. James has an interactive, dialectical understanding of the dynamics of mystical experience in which mystical experiences are understood to be neither the direct, authoritative revelations of a transcendent Absolute nor simply linguistically structured, culturally produced natural phenomena. For James, mystical experiences are best understood as the dynamic fusion of cultural and transcultural components; he views mystical experiences as both natural and transnatural in origin.

The psychological sections of this essay investigate the ways in which James's model of selfhood gives us a persuasive cluster of hypotheses on the psychological processes that are operative during a mystical experience, while the metaphysical sections explore James's complex vision of a world in which our everyday experience is surrounded and interpenetrated by an unseen spiritual dimension of reality that can, and often does, reveal its presence through mystical experience—a level of existence that is not divorced from us but, rather, can be understood as "deeper" or "higher" levels of our own being.

Knowledge-by-Acquaintance and Knowledge-About

Perhaps the best place to begin an analysis of the epistemological framework that informs much of James's investigation of mysticism is with a discussion of his distinction between *knowledge-by-acquaintance* and *knowledge-about*. For James, knowledge-by-acquaintance is immediate or intuitive knowledge; it is that which is directly evident. This type of knowledge is operative, for instance, when we see the color "blue," when we taste the flavor of a pear, or when we make any effort of attention. Knowledge-about, on the other hand, is conceptual or representational knowledge. Knowledge-about is operative when we give the blue that we are seeing or the pear that we are eating a name (let's say "navy" or "Bartlett") and bring to these sensory experiences the wealth of cultural information that we possess about, for instance, colors or fruits.

In James's epistemology, knowledge-by-acquaintance gives us information that is qualitatively different from the information we receive via knowledge-about, even though knowledge-by-acquaintance is always, to a greater or lesser degree, tempered with knowledge-about. James illustrates this distinction with a telling example. As he puts it, "a blind man may know all about the sky's blueness, and I may know all about your toothache, conceptually; . . . But so long as he has not felt the blueness, nor I [your] toothache, our knowledge, wide as it is, of these realities, will be hollow and inadequate."[4]

According to James, knowledge-by-acquaintance cannot be described and it cannot be imparted to anyone who has not directly experienced it. Knowledge-by-acquaintance occurs when, as much as possible, our knowledge of an object is limited to the bare impression that it makes on the senses or, in the case of religious or mystical varieties of this type of knowledge, when we experience or feel something with an immediacy and vividness that is similar to sensory experiences. Knowledge-by-acquaintance is inarticulate; it is a preverbal, unmediated knowledge of the simple "thatness" of something. James argues that we get glimpses of relatively pure varieties of knowledge-by-acquaintance when we become conscious after fainting or when we emerge from the full effects of anesthetics, or when we stare at an object until it loses most of its commonplace associations. Knowledge-by-acquaintance occurs when an object is cognized with a minimum of the "psychic fringes" or "overtones" that are present during knowledge-about—that is, when it is cognized with a minimum of the tacit assumptions, expectations, beliefs, and other preconscious associations that are always linked to this particular object in the background of the field of our awareness.

Knowledge-about, on the other hand, is connected with the "whatness" of something. If we want to know how something came to pass, if we want to understand how something relates to something else, then we have to depend upon knowledge-about. Knowledge-about analyzes, compares, contrasts, explains, and describes the qualities of an object. Knowledge-about is explicit, highly articulate, linguistically structured, and culturally communicated knowledge.

James repeatedly emphasizes that these two types of knowledge always appear together in any concrete moment of knowing. While they indeed represent crucial differences in the ways we apprehend and manipulate our environment and ourselves, "knowledge-by-acquaintance" and "knowledge-about" are relative terms for James. They are hypothetical ending points of a spectrum that ranges from "some imagined aboriginal presence in experience, before any belief about the presence [has] arisen"[5] to our most explicit and abstract constructions.

James is painfully aware that every conscious investigation of moments of knowledge-by-acquaintance automatically introduces knowledge-about into that introspective moment. In other words, as soon as we attempt to become aware of the occurrence of relatively pure moments of knowledge-by-acquaintance within us, we have already brought with that reflective awareness, minimally, a tacit awareness of the self, as well as an underlying awareness of what that self is hoping to experience. In a very real sense, our explicit knowledge of these moments of knowledge-by-acquaintance can occur only in the form of a highly abstract, rarefied version of knowledge-about.

It would seem, then, that all moments of "knowledge-by-acquaintance" are, in actuality, nothing more than modifications of "knowledge-about," and, therefore, it would appear that James fails in his argument that our experience contains immediate and nonlinguistic elements within it.

However, as James is quick to point out, there is an important "difference between the immediate feltness of a feeling, and its perception by a subsequent reflective act."[6] Scholars have to be careful not to make what James calls the "Psychologist's Fallacy."[7] The Psychologist's Fallacy occurs when investigators of states of consciousness confuse the "mental fact" that they are examining with their understanding *of* that mental fact. While it is undeniable that moments of knowledge-by-acquaintance, when studied as objects of reflective deliberation, are indeed instances of knowledge-about, we can still logically hypothesize the existence of moments of awareness that precede any explicit, conceptually based knowledge-about. Furthermore, even if we theorize that a completely "pure" knowledge-by-acquaintance is possible only as the theoretical end point on the spectrum of moments of knowing, even if knowledge-by-acquaintance in all concrete moments of knowing always arrives already "mixed"[8] with knowledge-about, it seems preferable to maintain the distinction between these two types of knowing rather than collapse all knowing into knowledge-about. Knowledge-by-acquaintance provides information that knowledge-about simply cannot replicate; tasting an apple is fundamentally different from knowing-about apples, even if these two processes are fused during each bite. Analogously, seeing and feeling the Hindu God Kṛṣṇa in a visionary experience can be understood to give the mystic a categorically unique type of information, information that could never be gained from years of arduous study of Hindu (or, more specifically, Vaisnava) doctrine, even if Hindu theological concepts, to one degree or another, were inevitably implicated in the structure of the visionary experience itself.

It also seems crucial not to dismiss too quickly the claims made by numerous mystics to have had mystical experiences that, from a Jamesian perspective, could legitimately be understood as completely pure moments of knowledge-by-acquaintance. One type of mystical experience that might indeed qualify as a moment of knowledge-by-acquaintance that is unencumbered by knowledge-about is the experience of perceiving the world *as it is*, the experience of perceiving the *suchness* of life. Much of the spiritual discipline involved in, for instance, Zen sitting or Theravāda Buddhist insight training, is explicitly designed to strip us, bit by bit, of the layers of attachments, desires, fears, conceptual labeling, and so on (all of which are different types of knowledge-about), that, according to their traditions at least, prevent us from experiencing the world as it truly is. The claim often made by these traditions (as well as numerous others) is that through these spiritual disciplines we *can* come to experience the world in its purity, we *can* perceive the world free from our conceptual categorizations.

Some scholars of mysticism would disagree with these claims. For instance, Steven Katz, a contemporary philosopher of mysticism, asserts that "properly understood, yoga, for example, is *not* an *un*conditioning or *de*conditioning of consciousness, but rather it is a *re*conditioning of consciousness."[9] However, while Katz's observation might indeed be a valuable insight into the underlying dynamics of many, if not most, mystical experiences, Katz's Kantian perspective, in which *all* experiences of the world are *always* structured through our categories of understanding, might also keep us from acknowledging that a *de*conditioning of consciousness is a very real epistemological possibility. Simply because all of our everyday moments of experiencing the world are inevitably processed through our implicit knowledge-about is no reason not theoretically to acknowledge the very real possibility that we could, whether through grace or long hours of meditative effort, have moments where "we" (and all our knowledge-about) disappear and only the world remains present as an object of consciousness. To deny this possibility outright seems rash and somewhat culturally and philosophically presumptuous, stating, in essence, that Kant is correct and Dōgen, for instance, is not, without ever overtly addressing *why* the Eastern philosophical perspective is wrong.

Since so many of the contemporary understandings of the dynamics of mystical experience are, on the face of it at least, indebted to Kant,[10] it is important to take a moment to point out that while James's epistemology may appear to be similar to Kant's in that both philosophers emphasize the ways in which our conceptual categories help shape our experiences, there is a crucial difference between their respective epistemologies. According to Kant, we passively receive a formless content from our intuition of the world, a world that is unknowable in and of itself. This formless content is then given a specific form by our conceptual scheme.

James, on the other hand, is not overly concerned with the theoretical existence of a world that exists in and of itself (Kant's numina) but instead focuses his attention on the world that enters into our *experience*. James emphasizes that if we pay attention, we will notice that this world-of-our-experience always comes to us already partially preformed. Even in those moments in which our knowledge-about appears to be reduced to a minimum, certain basic information is present. For instance, a woman might suddenly wake up and for several disconcerting moments not know where or who she is, all the while staring at a variety of forms near to her without any idea of what they are or what they do. Then, in a rapid influx of meaning and memory, the woman regains her sense of self, along with the enormous net of associations that this sense of self implies, and recognizes in a flash that the mysterious forms previously experienced are, in fact, a clock, a bed, sheets, pillows, walls, and so on. In this example, while the woman's knowledge-about who she is and what she is experiencing has momentarily vanished or, more accurately, has been extremely curtailed,[11] the knowledge-by-acquaintance of the sheer "thatness" of what she is experiencing has not: certain clusters of sense data have entered into her awareness (i.e., the "redness" of the bedspread, albeit devoid of the linguistic markers of "red" or "bedspread"). James would stress that these clusters of basic data given via knowledge-by-acquaintance can or should resist inappropriate interpretative glosses by knowledge-about (i.e., if the woman began to think of herself as a cat or thought that the clock was really a pen and so on, this knowledge-about would not "fit" the shapes, densities, textures, and so on that are given to her via knowledge-by-acquaintance).

As Jamesian scholar John Wild perceptively comments, the world that we experience through our knowledge-by-acquaintance is not, as the Kantians might have it, a "mere chaotic manifold" but instead "already contains the germs of meaningful patterns,"[12] patterns that are unfolded and elaborated but *not* created by our knowledge-about.[13] According to James, knowledge-by-acquaintance provides our experience with the "raw material" that our knowledge-about can refine, place in a context, give meaning to, and so on, but the "raw material" provided by knowledge-by-acquaintance is not completely malleable. Instead, it enters our experience with a certain cluster of basic qualities that knowledge-about has to work with, qualities that limit the range of interpretations and meanings that knowledge-about can legitimately superimpose upon it.

In many contemporary epistemologies of mysticism, the contrast that is often drawn between "experience" and "interpretation" mirrors, at least to some extent, the complex interaction that takes place between knowledge-by-acquaintance and knowledge-about. It is instructive, however, to note the differences between a Jamesian understanding of the dynamics of mystical experience and the epistemological assumptions that underlie the ways in which mystical experiences are understood by, for instance, Steven Katz and many of the scholars who have contributed to his various edited volumes on mysticism. These "neo-Kantian" philosophers of mysticism emphasize (correctly, for the most part) that mystics of different traditions do not merely interpret their experiences through the conceptual framework of their culture *after* the experiences themselves; instead, they argue that each mystic's interpretative framework is actively present in every mystical experience at every moment. This otherwise laudable epistemology becomes problematic, however, when examined more closely. As Nancy Frankenberry, an astute contemporary philosopher of religion, notes:

> A critical issue in this discussion is whether and to what extent the data of experience exercise any influence on the interpretations. If there is no self-evident, uninterpreted datum of any sort of experience, is there, nevertheless, a distinctive otherness or objectivity to the data? Is interpretation *derived* from experience as much as it is *added* to it? How far can we assume that human interpretations provide evidence of the actual nature of things? . . . Are our theories constructed only to satisfy our intellectual and emotional demands or do they in some sense, however problematically, "fit" the nature of the reality they claim to render intelligible?[14]

A Jamesian epistemological analysis of mystical experience offers us an opportunity to resolve these important questions by positing a dialectical relationship between experience and interpretation. In a Jamesian mystical epistemology, the knowledge-by-acquaintance aspect of experience maintains a degree of theoretical autonomy and coerciveness and is not pushed out of the picture by the jostling insistence of the mystic's culturally based interpretative framework. According to James, experience is fueled by an engagement with an irreducible facticity—it is driven by an encounter with a basic givenness. Although James recognizes that tacit belief structures are interwoven with each and every experience, he nonetheless stresses that there is something in the heart of every experience that comes to us unbidden, something that initiates changes in our assumptions and actions, something that refuses to be coerced. In *religious* experiences, that "something" is that which allows itself to be clothed in the metaphysical and theological garb of different cultures, yet which nevertheless frequently manages to transform, often radically, the very culture by which it is partially shaped and molded.

From a Jamesian epistemological perspective, we can theorize that a mystical experience is formed in roughly the following way: a preexisting, partially structured, nonverbal "something" appears within the consciousness of the mystic.[15] This knowledge-by-acquaintance aspect of experience, however, does not appear alone but rather comes into consciousness fused with the mystic's knowledge-about, structured by the mystic's cultural and psychological categories. Furthermore, this mystical experience is not a static moment frozen in time but, rather, shifts and reforms, with different "percentages" of these two types of knowledge prevalent at different moments in the process. Let us envision, for example, a Hindu yogi immersed in an ecstatic meditation on the form of Kālī. Over a period of time, this meditation becomes so profound that the form of Kālī disappears. Meanwhile, the yogi's sense of identity also begins to dissolve, and only an ineffable sense of unity and oneness remains. If we analyze this process using James's epistemological categories, we could say that during the time that this yogi was meditating on the form of Kālī, he or she had an experience that was a fusion of knowledge-by-acquaintance and knowledge-about. The knowledge-by-acquaintance components of the experience were those elements of the experience that entered the yogi's awareness with a high degree of objectivity, that came without the conscious instigation of the mystic, that shone with what James calls "immediate luminosity." And yet, this mystical experience also possessed important elements of knowledge-about. For instance, knowledge-about was present in the cultural constructs that helped to create a visionary form of Kālī instead of Jesus or Muhammad, or in the tacit egoistic identifications present within the yogi during this experience, or in the yogi's preconscious understanding of the functions and goals of meditation, and so forth. However, when the visionary form of Kālī disappeared and the yogi's experience shifted to a nondual state of oneness, it could be theorized that the "percentage" of knowledge-about that was previously present during the yogi's mystical experience was significantly lowered. It is even possible, if we accept the claims made by the yogic tradition, that during these moments the yogi's egoistic identification completely disappeared, his or her conceptual activity totally ceased, and there was a radical disappearance of any sense of separate existence. If these claims can be taken seriously, then we would have to say that knowledge-about disappeared altogether during these moments of mystical union. However, to describe what remains during these nondual experiences as knowledge-by-acquaintance is perhaps philosophically imprudent, since the category of knowledge depends upon an implicit duality of the knower and the known, and it is this very duality that has purportedly disappeared during unitive mystical experiences.[16]

Mystical Discoveries

James's epistemological perspective revolves around a seemingly inescapable paradox. For James, the world of our experience is both something that comes into existence as the result of human effort *and* something that is found—that is, something that seemingly exists prior to its discovery. James points out, for instance, that our knowledge of the Big Dipper constellation has, in one sense, always been true, in that the reality that our knowledge "agrees with" has existed long before the birth of any human beings. Yet, in another sense, because it is human beings who decide that those seven stars, out of all of the mass of stars in the sky, form the shape of the dipper, "something comes by the counting that was not there before. . . . In one sense [we] create it, and in another sense [we] find it."[17]

James's epistemology is, therefore, double edged and dialectical. As he puts it, "we add . . . to reality. The world stands really malleable, waiting to receive its final touches at our hands."[18] But the world, according to James, is not *completely* malleable. James stresses that even though "we carve out everything, just as we carve out constellations, to suit our human purposes,"[19] we are always given something to carve; we discover the world as much as we create it. According to James, "there is something in every experience that escapes our arbitrary control. . . . There is a push, an urgency, within our very experience, against which we are on the whole powerless."[20] From James's perspective, we *find* the world as much as we *make* our experience of that world, and what we find is a world that is not completely chaotic, as the Kantians would hold, but, rather, only a "quasi-chaos." James admits that we can never be certain what shape this world might possess apart from our conceptually altered experience of it, and he concedes that "reality *per se* . . . may appear only as a sort of limit";[21] but James also emphasizes that, within our own experience, we do discover that the world seems to come to us containing certain inherent tendencies, patterns, and consistencies.

James's epistemological stress on this preexisting, partially formed world-of-our-experience that can at times resist our attempts to encapsulate it arbitrarily within our conceptual framework has important implications for our understanding of the dynamics of mystical experience. For instance, the neo-Kantian "complete constructivism" posited by Katz and others aligned with his perspective, which insists that mystical experiences are inevitably and completely structured by the mystic's cultural and linguistic categories, has difficulty accounting for any mystical experiences that appear to contradict the mystic's theological and cultural assumptions. James's "partial constructivism," however, can easily account for mystical experiences that contradict the mystic's theological and cultural background, since it postulates the existence of an extra "something" that is operative within mystical experiences in addition to the mystic's psychological and cultural categories—"something" that the mystic finds (or that finds the mystic), "something" that is not under the volitional control of the mystic's ego, "something" that has an integrity of its own, "something" that has sufficient power not only to coerce the mystic's attention but also to transform the mystic's self-understandings and tacit worldviews. This "something" is malleable; it can and does appear to mystics in forms that they can most easily comprehend, but it also can and often does appear to mystics in ways that they never imagined, in ways that confound their personal expectations and cultural assumptions, in ways that surprise and disturb them.

By way of illustration, I would like to narrate a personal experience that I believe supports James's mystical epistemology. But, beforehand, because I am acutely aware that personal testimony is often frowned on in academic philosophical discussions, it seems vital that I take a moment and attempt to justify this transgression of academic orthopraxy.

I begin by arguing that attempts to "ghettoize" the religious experiences of scholars of religion to the safely guarded parameters of their private lives, cut off from any explicit contact with the public arena of their academic enterprises, is overly restrictive and methodologically unsound. While a fervent proselytizing missionary zeal is obviously misplaced within the academy, the endeavor to emulate the natural science paradigm of complete neutrality and objectivity is equally misguided. I believe that James is correct: we inevitably approach any philosophical project, including the study of religious phenomena, guided and empowered by our passions, our personal interests, and our idiosyncratic perspectives. Pretending that this is not the case is not only impractical but also leads to an impoverishment of our grasp of the material we are studying, since a study of that which we have experienced and which passionately concerns us will arguably produce more fruitful and nuanced observations than a study of that which we only observe from a disinterested distance.

Aligning myself with James once again, I believe that the study of religious phenomena needs to be broadly empirical; personal religious and mystical experiences, if examined with appropriate rigor, can and should become a rich source of empirical data for further philosophical reflection. If we become overly dependent upon texts to provide all of our data about mystical experiences and overlook or, more seriously, censor the information available through personal introspective work (or through even careful, in-depth discussions with living mystics), then it is perhaps inevitable that we will be tempted to reify mystical experiences—that we will forget the very real limits to the accuracy and completeness of retrospective, textual accounts of mystical experiences, limits that are often overlooked when, as has become fashionable, we restrict our sources of information on mystical experiences to narratives written by mystics who lived in centuries and cultures that are far removed from our own. If we focus our attention to such an extent on the substantive, more apparent aspects of the experiences that are encoded within the words of historical narratives, we will quite possibly overlook the less obvious, but equally tangible, elements of the experiences that might well exist in the interstices and margins of the verbal formulations. If we are not careful, an overreliance on descriptions of mystical experiences neatly packaged in precise, beautifully crafted phrases can lead us to imagine that mystical experiences really do have such carefully delineated borders, really are something static and frozen in time. Including personal mystical experiences within our methodological parameters, we are less likely to forget that mystical experiences are actually dynamic, ongoing, subtly shifting, complex, and often obscure processes of awareness that, instead of being completely constituted by our concepts as the "full constructionists" would have us believe, can often shatter the rigidities of our previously held conceptual framework—can expose us to something novel, something unexpected, something not captured in the web of our words.

Keeping the points raised in this methodological digression in mind, it seems useful here to demonstrate the ways in which at least one personal experience of my own leads me to support James's hypothesis that not all mystical experiences are created from previous theological assumptions.[22]

When I was thirteen years old, I was walking to school in Gainesville, Florida, and, without any apparent reason, I became obsessed with the idea of what would happen to me after my death. Throughout that day I attempted to visualize myself as not existing. I simply could not comprehend that my self-awareness would not exist in some form or another after my death. I kept trying, without success, to envision a simple blank nothingness. Later, I was returning home from school, walking on the hot pavement next to a stand of pine trees less than a block from my home, still brooding about what it would be like to die. Suddenly, without warning, something shifted inside. I felt lifted outside of myself, as if I had been expanded beyond my previous sense of self. In that exhilarating and yet deeply peaceful moment, I felt as if I had been shaken awake. In a single, "timeless" gestalt, I had a direct and powerful experience that I was not just that young teenage boy but, rather, that I was a surging, ecstatic, boundless state of consciousness.

In relating this description of my experience, I am conscious of the fact that my narrative is itself a reification of the experience; yet, at the same time, I argue that this awareness of the difference between the verbal narrative and the experience itself is highlighted precisely because it *was* my own experience. I am vividly aware of the vast difference between what I experienced and what I have just described, and my awareness of this difference can then itself become the basis for theoretical observations that would be problematic, if not impossible, if I was simply reading a preexisting narrative written by a mystic who lived hundreds of years ago. For instance, I suggest that the difference between my experience as a thirteen-year-old boy and my narrative of that experience is not simply due to the difficulties inherent in describing any mystical state of awareness. As a child of thirteen, I had no words with which to make sense of this experience, no "knowledge-about" with which to give my "knowledge-by-acquaintance" a context or even to give this knowledge-by-acquaintance a specific, describable shape. I just knew that "something" profound had occurred. What little religious training I had been exposed to during my brief and, to me, incredibly boring Sundays in church did not help me in my subsequent attempts to come to grips with this mysterious and yet powerful event. It was not until many years later, after several years spent practicing meditative disciplines and studying Eastern philosophical scriptures, that I was able to give this experience a viable interpretative structure. The "thatness" of the experience was always there, but this "thatness" was primarily operative as a goad prodding me to find some philosophical framework that could do justice to the inchoate content that had been so powerfully present to me in that brief, but transformative, moment.

I argue that an epistemology of mystical experience that is based on "complete constructivism" does not adequately reflect the dynamics of this experience. My previous religious and cultural conceptual background was not sufficiently dense and nuanced to constitute completely this experience. Instead, I first had an experience, without any real religious preparation, that possessed inherently "mystical" qualities; then, *after* having this experience (because it was sufficiently puzzling), I began to search for an intellectual framework that could accurately reflect the content that was latent in that experience. Undeniably, at thirteen years of age, I was not a completely blank slate: I knew that the experience had something to do with awareness (and I knew enough to remain quiet about this experience with my parents and even friends). But to claim, as complete constructivists would, that this highly rudimentary conceptual framework created that experience seems woefully inadequate.

It seems clear that a Jamesian "incomplete constructivism" is better equipped to handle the dynamics of this experience. James's willingness to claim that we discover the world as much as we create our experience of it, his theoretical openness to a preexisting, partially formed, autonomous "otherness" appearing within experience, can account for the fact that I did experience "something" that came to me possessing certain specific and inherent "mystical-like" qualities (i.e., loss of personal boundaries, feelings of extreme joy and peace, vivid and convincing metaphysical knowledge), even though I possessed no prior religious or cultural preparation. However, James's corresponding emphasis on the ways in which our tacit interests, assumptions, and intellectual constructs continually shape our experience in specific ways can theoretically justify why my initial experience was so inchoate and vague, as well as why that vagueness differs from the current, highly polished, intellectually informed nature of my memories of that experience. A Jamesian epistemology, however, would not be forced to claim that this difference is radical, since it could legitimately affirm that my current memories of that experience are still, in some very real sense, faithful to the initial experience itself.

The Shifting Contours of the Unseen World

Although James's interactive, dialectical epistemology was not developed specifically in response to his exploration of mystical states of awareness, it is clear that James was not reluctant to apply this epistemological perspective to a deeper understanding of mystical experiences. In a letter written in 1904 to James Henry Leuba, an American psychologist whose work James periodically refers to in his now classic text, *The Varieties of Religious Experience*, James explicitly utilizes his epistemological understanding of the relationship between the senses and an individual's intellectual background to comment on the nature of mystical perceptions:

> Just as the foundation of "natural" knowledge is sensation due to immediate non-rational influence of either body on body (or if you are an idealist, of mental fact on mental fact), so there might be a similar direct influence from God, and our knowledge might be partly at least founded thereon. . . . The mystical and the rational spheres of life are not absolutely discontinuous. It is evident that our intellectual stock in trade plays a suggestive part in our mystical life, and that this suggestive part changes with the progress of our thoughts, so that Vedantic and Christian mysticism have slightly different forms.
>
> If mystical states with all their differences have a common nucleus, then this nucleus should be reckoned a coordinate factor with reason in the building of religious belief. The intellect is interpretative, and critical of its own interpretation, but there must have been a thesis to interpret, and that thesis seems to me to be the non-rational sense of a "higher" power. Religious men largely agree that this sense has been that of their 'best' moments—best not only in passing, but when looked back upon. The notion of it has leaked into mankind from their authority, the rest of us being imitative, just as we are of scientific men's opinions. Now may not this mystical testimony that there is a God be true, even though his precise determinations, being so largely "suggestive" contributions of our rational factor, should widely differ? It seems to me that to throw out, as you do, the whole mystical life from a hearing, because of the facility with which it combines with discrepant interpretations, would be like throwing out the senses, for a similar reason.[23]

In this letter, James makes it clear that while he would agree that the cultural and psychological background of a mystic is an inevitable and important factor in the construction of that mystic's experiences, he would also argue that every authentic mystical experience has a "core" of "raw material" that the intellect operates "upon." According to James, this undefinable, but directly felt, "'higher' power" will always be perceived differently, but "its" energy is what catalyzes every mystical experience; "its" presence is what informs every mystical experience.[24]

It is necessary to be careful at this point, however. By using such a concrete metaphor, it is almost not possible to avoid imagining that this "higher power" is something objective, something definable, something that is a transcendent, unchanging foundation for every mystical experience. However, simply because James does not reduce all mystical experiences to natural causes and is willing to admit a sense of a "higher power" into his epistemology, this does not imply that James is an advocate of what has recently come to be known in philosophical circles as "objectivism." Richard Bernstein, a contemporary philosopher, defines objectivism as "the basic conviction that there is or must be some permanent, ahistorical matrix or framework to which we can ultimately appeal in determining the nature of rationality, knowledge, truth, reality, goodness, or rightness."[25] James was an early and powerful opponent of any and all such attempts to ground the knowledge or the claims to truth in any indubitable, unchanging metaphysical foundation.[26] But, at the same time, James was not a relativist or an advocate of skepticism. He never argued that all knowledge and claims to truth are simply variations of competing, humanly created, linguistically based webs of beliefs. For James, our concrete experience in the world is a rich and important testing ground for knowledge claims. While never static or clear-cut, and always interwoven with human desires and beliefs, our concrete experience in the world provides us with a nonhuman, partially objective referent that often stubbornly refuses to mold itself into the shapes that we might desire. Therefore, in many ways, it can be said that James is interested in articulating a position that avoids the rigidity and dogmatism of an objectivist perspective, while at the same time he wants to leave a space in his philosophical model for the existence and power of the translinguistic and transcultural modes of reality that relativism denies.

James most certainly believes in the existence of an unseen spiritual world, but he also adamantly resists any temptation to describe its contours conclusively or to ground the legitimacy of particular beliefs on a dogmatic affirmation of its existence, even if that affirmation emerges out of a powerful mystical experience of that spiritual level of reality. Although James occasionally does imply that he believes that there is a single source to all mystical experiences, he is just as likely to claim that the "unseen world" is at least as pluralistic and complex as the world we experience in our everyday life. In addition, contrary to the assumptions of some theorists, James is most certainly *not* an advocate of the "common core theory." This theory claims that although the mystics of different traditions interpret their experiences differently according to the religious and cultural environment in which they live, the mystical experiences in and of themselves are basically the same. While James most certainly does believe that powerful religious experiences and saintly actions are often strikingly similar from one cultural system to the next, and while James does work hard to articulate some basic commonalties between different mystical experiences, he also emphasizes that each mystical experience is unique. As he says in the *Varieties*: "I imagine that these experiences can be as infinitely varied as are the idiosyncrasies of individuals."[27]

This emphasis on the continual variety and plurality of mystical experiences reflects James's emphasis on the ever-changing nature of experience in general, a position first clearly expressed in his seminal text, *The Principles of Psychology*. For

James, consciousness is dynamic, ever new, perpetually in motion. No state of consciousness ever repeats itself or is ever identical to what came before. According to James, we mistakenly think that we hear the same sounds or see the same sights simply because we confuse the apparent "sameness" of the objects (e.g., blades of grass) with our *perceptions* of those objects (e.g., the colors and feel of the grass). Even if the objects themselves managed somehow to remain completely static (which James would deny is actually possible), the ways in which we perceive them inevitably change from moment to moment since every new perception changes the mass of memories, expectations, and so forth that form the background context that surrounds and suffuses our perception and understanding of these objects. As James puts it: "experience is remoulding us every moment, and our mental reaction on every given thing is really a resultant of our experience of the whole world up to that date."[28] In a similar way, if these observations were extended to mystical states of consciousness, it would be possible to come to realize that, from a Jamesian perspective, no two mystical experiences will ever be the same, even though it is quite possible that all of these different experiences do come from the same transnatural catalyst.

A "Mother-Sea" of Consciousness

Since James was convinced that an "unseen world" or "higher power" existed that was, in part at least, the catalyst for mystical experiences, he was determined to explore the psychological and metaphysical ramifications of such an assumption. Therefore, much of James's later career can be seen as a concerted attempt to answer the following types of questions: What sort of personality structure is most open to mystical experiences? What do mystical experiences tell us about the nature of selfhood? How does this "higher power" interact with individual selves? What would count as a reasonable, yet open-ended, description of this higher power? What sources of information can we draw upon to formulate this metaphysical account?

In the early part of James's career, however, these types of questions appear to have been rather peripheral, since during this time period, James was only marginally concerned with the psychological and metaphysical implications of mystical experience. For instance, when James wrote the *Principles*, he went out of his way to argue that there was an "absolute insulation" and "irreducible pluralism"[29] between individual minds. Nonetheless, even this early in his career, he was still willing to admit that the evidence of "thought-transference, mesmeric influence and spirit-control" was so persuasive that it was perhaps safer to conclude that "the definitively closed nature of our personal consciousness is probably an average statistical resultant of many conditions, but not an elementary force or fact."[30] In the years after the *Principles*, James's cautious openness to deeper levels of consciousness slowly shifted to a full-fledged endorsement of a nonmaterialistic vision of the universe—a universe consisting of a complex, multilayered plurality of existents that, ultimately, were part of a deeper, unseen world. In the conclusion of "Confidences of a 'Psychical Researcher'," James acknowledges:

> Out of my experience, such as it is (and it is limited enough), one fixed conclusion dogmatically emerges, and that is this, that we with our lives are like islands in the sea, or like trees in the forest. The maple and the pine may whisper to each other with their leaves, and Conanicut and Newport hear each other's fog-horns. But the trees also commingle their roots in the darkness underground, and the islands also hang together through the ocean's bottom. Just so there is a continuum of cosmic consciousness, against which our individuality builds but accidental fences, and into which our several minds plunge as into a mother-sea or reservoir. Our 'normal' consciousness is circumscribed for adaptation to our external earthly environment, but the fence is weak in spots, and fitful influences from beyond leak in, showing the otherwise unverifiable common connexion.[31]

Gerald Myers, a noted Jamesian scholar, underscores the significance of James's shift toward a more "mystical" understanding of the self:

> A world of individual and substantial selves, each private and irrevocably removed from its neighbor, was not an attractive idea for James. He preferred to believe in a world where continuity prevails, including that between individual streams of consciousness; to the extent that the concept of a substantial self encourages the belief in metaphysical discontinuity between individual selves, he opposed it. It is a common judgement that James's *Anschauung* was excessively individualistic and ignored the role of community; on the contrary, he sought notions of self and reality that permit communality of the profoundest sort—in the depths of the most intimate personal experience.[32]

When James was writing the *Principles*, he pledged to restrict his observations on the nature of the self to that which is immediately perceptible; after finishing this massive work, he was willing to speculate in more detail on the possibility that there are dimensions of the self that transcend personal levels of consciousness and the physical body. Increasingly, James expressed his conviction that the self is not limited to the confines of our psychophysical components but, rather, extends outward (and inward) in the form of broader and deeper levels of consciousness, levels of consciousness that can easily be understood as the source of mystical experience.

James's first detailed metaphysical ruminations on the likelihood of our connection with a universal soul appeared in his 1887 Ingersoll lecture, "Human Immortality: Two Supposed Objections to the Doctrine." He begins his essay with a nod toward the prevailing materialistic understanding of the interaction between the brain and the mind. He readily concedes that drugs can alter our state of awareness and admits that stimulation of different parts of the brain can also provoke changes in our consciousness. For James, it is clear that "thought is a function of the brain."[33] However, he insists that it is not equally clear that consciousness inevitably disappears with the brain's death and decay. James points out that there are several ways in which the relationship between the brain and consciousness can be understood.

First, the brain itself could produce the "stuff" of consciousness in much the same way that steam is produced by a kettle or light is produced by an electric circuit. From this perspective, which James calls the "productive" theory, consciousness is created by the various complex chemical interactions that take place inside the brain, and consciousness ceases when the brain stops working at the moment of death.[34] He notes that there is, however, another alternative. It is also possible that consciousness preexists the brain and that the role of the brain is to mold that preexistent consciousness into various forms (a possibility that has profound implications for the innate capacity of human beings to have mystical experiences).

James goes on to point out that there are two variations of this second alternative. The first version of the preexisting consciousness theory states that consciousness exists in a scattered, particlelike form. Seen from this perspective, the job of our brain is to concentrate this "mind-dust" into usable, personal forms. James, however, does not spend much time developing and refuting this theory, since he believes that his discussion of the mind-stuff theory in the *Principles* has already performed this task.

Instead, James is much more interested in the second variation of the preexistent consciousness theory. This variation of the theory claims that the hypothetical preexisting consciousness already possesses a unified structure, perhaps that of an "absolute 'world soul,' or something less,"[35] in which case the brain's task is to receive and transmit limited forms of this consciousness in much the same way as, to use an anachronistic example, a radio receives portions of preexisting radio waves and then transmits them through the air as sound waves. James refers to this relationship between the brain and a preexisting larger consciousness as the "transmissive function" and points out that this transmissive function is operative "in the case of a colored glass, a prism, or a refracting lens," when "the energy of light, no matter how produced, is by the glass shifted and limited in color, and by the lens or prism determined to a certain path and shape."[36]

James insists that it is just as logical and scientific to postulate that the brain receives, limits, directs, and shapes preexistent states of awareness as it is to postulate that the brain produces different states of consciousness. Both theories, in fact, have philosophical and scientific difficulty accounting for how the brain and the mind, which are completely heterogeneous, interact at all. James believes that "the theory of production is . . . not a jot more simple or credible in itself than any other conceivable theory. It is only a little more popular."[37] Indeed, James claims that, in some ways, the transmissive function has certain theoretical advantages over its more popular competitor. For instance, if the transmissive theory of consciousness is accepted, then consciousness "does not have to be generated *de novo* in a vast number of places. It exists already, behind the scenes," intimately connected with this world.[38] In this way, the transmissive theory not only avoids "multiplying miracles"[39] but also aligns itself with quite respectable philosophical systems, such as transcendentalism and idealistic philosophy.

James points out another apparent advantage of the transmissive theory of consciousness over the productive theory: the transmissive theory is able to coherently account for a wide variety of phenomena that the productive theory has difficulty explaining. Phenomena such as "religious conversions, providential leadings in answer to prayer, instantaneous healings, premonitions, apparitions at time of death, clairvoyant visions or impressions, and the whole range of mediumistic capacities" are all more easily understood with the transmissive theory of consciousness.[40] James notes that the productive theory of consciousness is intimately linked with sense perceptions, but in the case of many of these less orthodox phenomena, "it is often hard to see where the sense-organs can come in."[41] For instance, as James mentions, a psychic might have knowledge of the personal life of his or her client that would be impossible to obtain from the senses, or a person might see a vision of someone who, hundreds of miles away, is at that very moment dying. James points out that it is difficult to see how the productive theory of consciousness can explain how these bits of knowledge were produced within a single brain. But if the transmissive theory is accepted, the answer is apparent: "they don't have to be 'produced'—they exist ready-made in the transcendental world,"[42] so that in "cases of conversion, providential leadings, sudden mental healings, etc., it seems to the subjects themselves . . . as if a power from without, quite different from the ordinary action of the senses or of the sense-led mind, came into their life, as if [their life] suddenly opened into that greater life in which it has its source."[43]

James believes that psychologists and philosophers choose between the transmissive theory and the productive theory on the basis of what type of world they are willing or able to accept (i.e., their metaphysical assumptions). If these thinkers are limited to a purely materialistic or naturalistic perspective, then the productive function of the brain will be all that they will acknowledge as valid. If, however, these thinkers assume that "the whole universe of material things . . . [is] a surface-veil of phenomena, hiding and keeping back the world of genuine realities," if they believe that life resembles Percy Shelley's image in his poem "Adonais," in which "Life, like a dome of many-colored glass, Stains the white radiance of eternity," then they will acknowledge that the transmissive function of the brain is a legitimate possibility.[44] Utilizing Shelley's simile, James theorizes that our brains might indeed be places in this "dome" where the "beams" of consciousness could most easily enter into our realm of experience. In that case, as the "white radiance" of that larger preexisting consciousness enters our brains, then a type of refracting and "staining and distortion" will naturally occur, shaping that greater consciousness into the personal, imperfect, and unique forms that consciousness takes inside "our finite individualities here below."[45]

James then goes on to point out the implications for human immortality if this transmissive theory of consciousness is basically accurate:

> According to the state in which the brain finds itself, the barrier of its obstructiveness may also be supposed to rise or fall. It sinks so low, when the brain is in full activity, that

> a comparative flood of spiritual energy pours over. At other times, only such occasional waves of thought as heavy sleep permits get by. And when finally a brain stops acting altogether, or decays, that special stream of consciousness which it subserved will vanish entirely from this natural world. But the sphere of being that supplied the consciousness would still be intact; and in that more real world with which, even whilst here, it was continuous, the consciousness might, in ways unknown to us, continue still.[46]

James realizes that if this "more real world" is one in which our individual consciousnesses merge into Oneness after death, then this loss of our personal boundaries conflicts with the desires of many individuals to retain the "finiteness and limitations" that appear to be the very essence of their being.[47] However, as he insightfully goes on to comment, it is an open question as to "how much we may lose, and how much we may possibly gain, if [the] finiting outlines [of our individual consciousness] should be changed."[48]

James attempts to garner support for the transmissive theory of consciousness by drawing upon the work of Gustave Fechner, a German psychologist and philosopher who lived from 1810 until 1887. James is especially interested in Fechner's conceptualization of the "threshold" of consciousness. Fechner postulates that consciousness can appear only after a particular psychophysical level of activity has been reached—that is, consciousness can become manifest only after it has passed over a mental or physical "threshold." But, as James notes, "the height of the threshold varies under different circumstances: it may rise or fall. When it falls, as in states of great lucidity, we grow conscious of things of which we should be unconscious at other times; when it rises, as in drowsiness, consciousness sinks in amount."[49] James offers a diagram to illustrate Fechner's theory. The diagram shows a wavy line (looking somewhat like a child's drawing of three mountains) bisected by a straight horizontal line. The three sections of the wavy line above the horizontal line represent three apparently separate individual consciousnesses, whereas the parts of the wave under the threshold (the horizontal line) represent that which is unconscious in each of the three individuals. From the point of view of the three individuals, their respective consciousnesses (the peaks of the waves) are separate from one another, but underneath the threshold of consciousness, all three waves are united in a common "ocean" of awareness. As James, quoting Fechner, points out, if "we should raise the entire line of waves so that not only the crests but the valleys appeared above the threshold, then [the valleys] would appear only as depressions in one great continuous wave above the threshold, and the discontinuity of the consciousness would be converted into continuity."[50]

Fechner himself appears to be quite dubious about our ability to bring about this awareness of our connection with an underlying, preexisting ocean of awareness, but, depending upon one's understanding of the relationship between grace and self-effort, it seems quite legitimate to postulate that the spiritual disciplines in various mystical traditions function to bring about exactly this sort of recognition of our inherent connection with the deeper source of our being. It could be argued that the various chanting, fasting, and meditative practices are techniques that serve to lower the threshold of consciousness, thereby revealing to the mystic his or her underlying connection with this "ocean" of awareness. Reverting to the earlier simile, it could also be postulated that these spiritual disciplines expand the brain's capacity to hold increasing amounts of the light of this preexisting consciousness, while simultaneously minimizing the distortion and refraction of that light typically caused by the individual's psychological and cultural background.

James, for one, believes that mystical and psychical experiences can easily be accounted for by postulating "the continuity of our consciousness with a mother-sea, [which permits the] exceptional waves occasionally pouring over the dam."[51] However, influenced by his Protestant background, James attempts to make it clear that this belief in our connection to the "mother-sea" of awareness does not have to be interpreted in a purely monistic fashion. He clarifies his position in a footnote:

> It is not necessary to identify the consciousness postulated in the lecture, as pre-existing behind the scenes, with the Absolute Mind of transcendental idealism, although, indeed, the notion of it might lead in that direction. . . . [Alternatively] there might be many minds behind the scenes as well as one. All that the transmission-theory absolutely requires is that they should transcend *our* minds,—which thus come from something mental that pre-exists, and is larger than ourselves.[52]

James's critics were not satisfied with this metaphysical flexibility, however, and accused James of advocating pantheistic ideas of immortality (i.e., an absorption into a higher consciousness after death), rather than the Christian idea of personal survival after death. Therefore, in the preface to the second edition of "Human Immortality," James attempted to mollify his critics, admitting that while he did "speak of the 'mother-sea' in terms that must have sounded pantheistic," nevertheless, "one may conceive the mental world behind the veil in as individualistic a form as one pleases" without reducing the viability of the transmission theory of consciousness.[53] James points out that, if this individualistic perspective on the unseen world is adopted, then "one's finite mundane consciousness would be an extract from one's larger, truer personality, the latter having even now some sort of reality behind the scenes."[54] Understood from this point of view, the experiences of one's mundane personality would register in the consciousness of one's larger personality, perhaps leaving a collection of memories that would, in effect, constitute a type of personal survival after death.

"A Suggestion about Mysticism"

In many ways, James's belief in a "mother sea" of cosmic consciousness links his interest in psychical research to his philosophy of mysticism. For instance, the notion of an ocean of cosmic consciousness appears in "A Suggestion about Mysticism," an important essay on mysticism that James published in 1910 (the year of James's death). In this essay, James hypothesizes that perhaps "states of mystical intuition" are actually "very sudden and great extensions of the ordinary 'field of consciousness'" in which the "margin" of the field expands to such an extent that "knowledge ordinarily transmarginal would become included" within it.[55] Drawing once again on Fechner's work, James speculates that one way to picture a person's present moment of awareness is to imagine it as a wave in an ocean—a wave that, while perhaps momentarily rising above sea level, also remains in its depths connected with the ocean (and with all the other "waves" of awareness). James suggests that "sea level" in this model can be seen as the base level of human consciousness, the "threshold" of waking awareness. A person's moment-to-moment "wave" of conscious awareness includes everything that appears above this threshold, while below it there exists the oceanic depths of "subliminal" awareness—depths not normally conscious to the person but that nonetheless contain an enormous amount of psychic activity. James's hypothesis is that in mystical states of awareness, the threshold is lowered, producing surprising results. James writes:

> A fall of the threshold, however caused, would, under these circumstances, produce the mental equivalent to what occurs in an unusually flat shore at the ebb of a spring-tide. Vast tracts of what is usually covered are then revealed to view, but nothing rises more than a few inches above the water's bed, and great parts of the scene are submerged again whenever a wave washes over them.[56]

In this hypothesis, mystical awareness is viewed as a sudden and dramatic opening of ordinary consciousness to the vast quantity of information in the subconscious[57]—a powerful influx of previously hidden data breaching the seemingly secure boundaries of the self.

However, James would say it is not just in moments of mystical ecstasy that these boundaries shift. According to James's field conception of consciousness, our awareness is *always* in a state of flux. James summarizes this theory when he asserts:

> The field is composed at all times of a mass of present sensation, in a cloud of memories, emotions, concepts, etc. Yet these ingredients, which have to be named separately, are not separate, as the conscious field contains them. Its form is that of a much-at-once, in the unity of which the sensations, memories, concepts, impulses, etc. coalesce and are dissolved. The present field as a whole came continuously out of its predecessor and will melt into its successor as continuously again.[58]

In this continuous ebb and flow of our awareness, the "horizons" or "margins" of consciousness lack specific boundaries; furthermore, what is central in consciousness can rapidly shift to the margins and vice versa. According to James, this shifting of our field of consciousness is "like the field of vision, which the slightest movement of the eye will extend, revealing objects that always stood there to be known."[59] James suggests that these shifts in our field of consciousness are very similar to the lowering of the threshold of consciousness that occurs in mystical experience, but in a mystical experience, new sensations do not enter into consciousness. Instead, what is revealed is another, larger "much-at-onceness" of previously hidden memories, impulses and beliefs that have always been operative either on the margins of our awareness or within our "transmarginal" awareness. James concludes:

> If this enlargement of the nimbus that surrounds the sensational present is vast enough, while no one of the items it contains attracts our attention singly, we shall have the conditions fulfilled for a kind of consciousness in all essential respects like that termed mystical. It will be transient, if the change of the threshold is transient. It will be of reality, enlargement, and illumination, possibly rapturously so. It will be of unification . . . [because the enlargement of consciousness unites normally unaccessible psychic elements within one field of consciousness]. Its form will be intuitive or perceptual, not conceptual, for the remembered or conceived objects in the enlarged field are supposed not to attract the attention singly, but only to give the sense of a tremendous *muchness* suddenly revealed.[60]

In "A Suggestion about Mysticism," James attempts to create a viable model of the processes active below the surface of consciousness that help catalyze a mystical experience. Yet, at the same time, James realizes that his model is tentative at best and that many mystics might well have problems with his psychological theories on the underlying dynamics of mystical experience. It is highly probable that this cautious assessment is correct. For instance, James's theory does not seem particularly helpful when it is applied to mystical experiences that are apparently devoid of objective content (for instance, the *nirvikalpa samādhi* of the Hindu *yogi*). It is difficult to see how getting flooded with information from the subliminal depths of one's consciousness could produce the acute awareness, profound stillness, and apparent lack of mental activity that characterize the "pure consciousness events"[61] so often described in different mystical traditions.

However, certain types of mystical experiences do appear to lend themselves particularly well to James's "suggestion" about the psychological processes that may generate a mystical expansion of consciousness. Mystical transfigurations of nature, for instance, seem particularly amenable to this level of explanation. Typically, in these types of mystical experiences, the mystic is swept up by the beauty of nature and perceives with great joy his or her union with the natural world. The "outer" scene is unchanged; it is still the same trees, ocean, mountains, sunset, and so on that the mystic sees, hears, smells, touches and tastes; however, he or she experiences this outer beauty in a radically new way. If we use James's hypothesis to help us understand the underlying dynamics of this experience, then two different, yet interrelated possibilities present themselves.

First, the transfiguration of nature can be seen as the result of previously inaccessible emotions, memories, and beliefs that surge up from the transmarginal areas of the mystic's psyche and superimpose themselves upon the mystic's more commonplace perceptions of the external world. According to this hypothesis, during moments of mystical awareness, the mystic's sensory data remains roughly constant, but that data is perceived very differently since it is "filtered" through an enormously expanded gestalt of a newly felt emotional and cognitive "lens."

The second, less prosaic, possibility is that in the transfiguration of nature the mystic not only is flooded with newly felt *personal* memories and impulses but also experiences a joyous recognition of a *transpersonal* underlying connection with nature, a connection that already existed in the mystic's subliminal depths.[62]

If James's "suggestion" about mystical experience can be seen to include an openness to transpersonal input, then the ability of his hypothesis to account for other types of mystical experiences, such as highly detailed visionary experiences, is enormously strengthened. In other words, if the mystic's transmarginal awareness could be understood to contain not only personal memories and buried emotions but also transpersonal or transnatural "raw material" ("raw material" that is, inevitably, molded by one's psychological and cultural background), then James's hypothesis could easily account for the powerfully felt, intricately detailed sense of the "otherness" and "newness" inherent in many visionary experiences. According to this reading of James's hypothesis, if the mystic's psychic threshold suddenly lowers, it will uncover and release into awareness preexistent, highly structured "gestalts" of psychologically and culturally shaped, but transpersonally generated, information—gestalts of information that will then catalyze and form the mystic's numinous visionary experience.

Unfortunately, in this essay, James's hypothesis suffers from an overly sparse depiction of the nature of the contents of the mystic's subliminal awareness. It seems, at first, as if James depicts the subliminal or transmarginal awareness in strictly personal terms, as if it were only an amalgam of each particular individual's unavailable memories, beliefs, and impulses. But James's conception of our subliminal awareness is typically not so circumscribed; in fact, it is specifically constructed in such a way as to allow for both psychological and theological interpretations of the dynamic processes that underlie mystical states of consciousness. James did believe that each person's transmarginal awareness contains transpersonal as well as personal "contents"; however, this expanded understanding of the nature of each individual's transmarginal awareness is not readily apparent in this essay.[63]

The Subliminal Self

In the *Principles*, James had spent considerable time demonstrating how we are all "surrounded" by a vast complex nexus of tacit memories, habits, and cultural assumptions that subtly and yet continuously influence the perceptions, thoughts, and feelings that take place within our present sphere of awareness. He pointed out that we usually do not notice this "margin" of awareness, even though it is "ready at a touch to come in" and itself in turn become the present center of attention.[64] All that remained for James was to admit that beyond "the consciousness of the ordinary field, with its usual center and margin," there exists "a set of memories, thoughts and feelings which are extra-marginal," and yet which are "conscious facts of some sort, able to reveal their presence by unmistakable signs."[65] These "transmarginal" levels of consciousness are present, James suggests, in the subliminal self.

James's notion of the subliminal self grew out of his conviction that a person's typical waking consciousness is perhaps best understood as "only a small segment of the psychic spectrum."[66] The subliminal self, for James, is "the enveloping mother-consciousness in each of us" from which our everyday consciousness "is precipitated like a crystal."[67] Existing outside of most individuals' conscious awareness, the subliminal self, in James's view, often acts as a type of doorway by which the unseen "spiritual world" can enter into, and profoundly affect, ordinary awareness. For instance, James theorizes that many positive psychological transformations, such as "the reparativeness of sleep, the curative effects of self-suggestion, the 'uprushing' inspirations of genius, the regenerative influences of prayer and of religious self-surrender, the strength of belief which mystical experiences give" are made possible only by the subliminal self's connection with the "dynamogeny" of this unseen, but powerfully felt, spiritual level of existence.[68]

Conservative psychologists in James's time (as well as, in later years, Freud and his orthodox disciples) were quick to claim that James's understanding of the subliminal self incorporated too much dubious material within its boundaries. According to James, traditional psychologists willingly accepted the existence of "a dissociated part of the normal personality" linked to "experiences forgotten by the upper consciousness," which may "still lead a parasitic existence" and "may interfere with normal processes"; however, they were unwilling to accept those " 'evolutive,' 'superior,' or 'supernormal' phenomena" that were supported by evidence from psychical research.[69] James criticized this methodological rigidity, noting that the phenomena investigated by psychical research (such as telepathy, clairvoyance, trance states, and so on) "have a right to definite description and to careful observation."[70]

James claimed that conservative philosophers and psychologists rejected the "evolutive, superior or supernormal" aspects of the subliminal self not because of any intrinsic faults in the model itself; rather, according to James, these philosophers and psychologists refused to accept the possibility of transpersonal aspects of the subliminal self because they were clinging to one side of a historically defined aesthetic battleground: the clash between "the classic-academic and the romantic type of imagination."[71]

According to James, the classic-academic imagination "has a fondness for clean pure lines and noble simplicity in its constructions. It explains things by as few principles as possible and is intolerant of either nondescript facts or clumsy formulas."[72] This type of imagination lives on "a sort of sunlit terrace" populated only by that which is either clearly visible or logically pleasing—that is, by the "brain and other physical facts of nature on the one hand and the absolute metaphysical ground of the universe on the other."[73] In contrast, the romantic imagination possesses a more gothic sensibility; it acknowledges the existence of levels of reality that transcend the natural world and yet abhors the abstraction and sterility of a logically derived Absolute. This romantic vision of the self and the universe is willing to peer into the shadows beyond the sunlit terrace of discursive rationality. Regarding this romantic vision, James writes:

> A mass of mental phenomena are now seen in the shrubbery beyond the parapet. Fantastic, ignoble, hardly human, or frankly non-human are some of these new candidates for psychological description. . . . The world of mind is shown as something infinitely more complex than was suspected; and whatever beauty it may still possess, it has lost at any rate the beauty of academic neatness.[74]

James's own aesthetic preference is clear. According to his vision, even the universe of our quotidian experience "is everywhere gothic, not classic . . . [it] forms a real jungle, where all things are provisional, half-fitted to each other and untidy."[75] For James, it is unlikely, therefore, that the spiritual world revealed by our more extraordinary experiences is classically formed. He noted that psychical research, psychopathology, and investigations of religious experiences demonstrate that the unseen aspects of our being that lie beneath the surface of our experience do not exist in a "realm of eternal essences, of platonic ideas, of crystal battlements, of absolute significance"[76] but, rather, take place in a complex, multitextured, intricately detailed, frustratingly confusing level of reality that transcends the boundaries of our personality, while simultaneously touching the depths of our being. According to James, the subliminal self is not clear; it is not pure; it is not simple. Instead, it is full of strange, unexpected shapes and mismatched combinations of utter nonsense and lucid inspirations. As such, the subliminal self denotes "a region, with possibly the most heterogeneous contents": some of the subliminal region is "rubbish" (e.g., scraps of "lapsed" memories, the "stuff that dreams are made of," odd bits of ingrained habits, and so on), while some of it is "superior and subtly perceptive" (e.g., the insights of trance mediums, the creative inspirations of artists, the revelations of mystics).[77]

In the *Varieties*, James retains the "gothic" contours of this "transmarginal or subliminal region."[78] He does not attempt to tone down its rough edges or deny its ability to contain both mental trash and psychological gems. Instead, this "area of the personality," which he terms the "B-region" (as opposed to the A-region of "full sunlit consciousness"), becomes the location of almost everything that is not immediately and easily available to our conscious attention. In the following passage, James seems to revel in the range of phenomena that he claims are located within this mysterious and subterranean expanse within ourselves:

> It is the abode of everything that is latent and the reservoir of everything that passes unrecorded or unobserved. It contains, for example, such things as all our momentarily inactive memories, and it harbors the springs of all our obscurely motived passions, impulses, likes, dislikes, and prejudices. Our intuitions, hypotheses, fancies, superstitions, persuasions, convictions, and in general all our non-rational operations come from it. It is the source of our dreams. . . . In it arise whatever mystical experiences we may have, and our automatisms, sensory or motor. [It is also the source of hypnosis,]

> our delusions, fixed ideas and hysterical accidents [as well as] our supra-normal cognitions, if such there be.[79]

It is evident to James that certain people are more fully in contact with this subliminal self than others. Psychics, the mentally ill, geniuses, saints, and mystics are all understood by James to be individuals with a strong "ultra-marginal life," individuals who are frequently subject to unexpected invasions from their subliminal region that take "the form of unaccountable impulses to act, or inhibitions of actions, of obsessive ideas or even of hallucinations of sight or hearing."[80] James uses the term "automatism" to designate those mental or physical activities that seem to take place without the individual's conscious instigation. James considers hallucinations, automatic writing, the utterances of trance mediums, religious visions, and the involuntary body movements seen during revivals to be the effects of these invasive "'uprushes' into the ordinary consciousness of energies originating in the subliminal parts of the mind."[81] Unlike many psychologists of his time (and ours as well), James insists that these automatisms are not necessarily evidence of psychopathology, pointing out instead that "the whole array of Christian saints . . . the Bernards, the Loyolas, the Luthers, the Foxes, the Wesleys, had their visions, voices, rapt conditions, guiding impressions, and 'openings.'"[82] For James, these automatisms are, at times, crucial to a powerful and personally transformative religious life in that they help to convince the saints, mystics, or converts that their previously held beliefs are indeed authentic. He notes:

> Incursions from beyond the transmarginal region have a peculiar power to increase conviction. The inchoate sense of presence is infinitely stronger than conception, but strong as it may be, it is seldom equal to the evidence of hallucination. Saints who actually see or hear their Saviour reach the acme of assurance. Motor automatisms, though rarer, are, if possible, even more convincing than sensations. The subjects here actually feel themselves played upon by powers beyond their will. The evidence is dynamic; the God or spirit moves the very organs of their body.[83]

For the saint, the mystic, and the convert, the spiritual world is not a matter of speculation. They see spiritual beings; they hear the angelic voices; they feel the divine touch within them. More open to information from the transmarginal region than the average person, these "religious geniuses" touch "the fountainhead of much that feeds our religion. In persons deep in the religious life . . . the door into this region seems unusually wide open; at any rate, experiences making their entrance through that door have had emphatic influence in shaping religious history."[84]

James is convinced that contact with this transmarginal region is to be found at the heart of a salvific nucleus that is present within every religion. James boils this salvific nucleus down to "two parts: 1. An uneasiness; and 2. Its solution."[85] The uneasiness, in essence, "is a sense that there is *something wrong about us* as we naturally stand," while the solution is "a sense that *we are saved from the wrongness* by making proper connexion with the higher powers."[86] James argues that, from a psychological perspective, the experience of salvation occurs when a person "identifies his real being with the germinal higher part of himself [the "evolutive" or "superior" aspects of the subliminal self]" and then "becomes conscious that this higher part is conterminous and continuous with a *more* of the same quality, which is operative in the universe outside of him, and which he can keep in working touch with, and in a fashion get on board of and save himself when all of his lower being has gone to pieces in the wreck."[87]

James is convinced that, as psychological phenomena, these salvific experiences are extremely valuable; in these experiences, "spiritual strength really increases in the subject when he has them, a new life opens for him, and they seem to him a place of conflux where the forces of two universes meet"; nonetheless, James is also aware that each one of these dramatic experiences could conceivably be nothing but the individual's "subjective way of feeling things."[88] What is needed, therefore, is an assessment of the truth-status of this "more" that is the source of these experiences, this "more" that exists within us and yet that is also somehow beyond us. As James puts it: "Is such a 'more' merely our own notion, or does it really exist? If so, in what shape does it exist? Does it act, as well as exist? And in what form should we conceive of that 'union' with it of which religious geniuses are so convinced?"[89]

James notes that these questions are answered by theologians within the different religious traditions, but unfortunately, although they all agree that this "more" does exist and that it actively works for our benefit, they have vastly dissimilar understandings of the nature of our connection with this higher power. What James attempts to do is to use the concept of the subliminal self in a way that not only reconciles these opposing theological perspectives but that also connects them with psychological theories of the subliminal forces associated with conversions and other religious experiences.

James points out that while both psychology and theology "admit that there are forces seemingly outside of the conscious individual that bring redemption to his life," psychology understands these forces to be *merely* subconscious and assumes that these forces do not exist beyond the boundaries of the individual's psyche, whereas theology insists that experiences of salvation are the "direct supernatural operations of the Deity" and are not the results of the individual's efforts.[90] James is convinced that this opposition between psychology and theology can be overcome via the mediation of the concept of the subliminal self. According to James, if there are indeed spiritual forces that are working for our salvation and healing, then it is quite possible that these "higher powers" produce their salvific effects primarily by entering into our life through "the subliminal door."[91] James hypothesizes "that whatever it may be on its *farther* side, the 'more' with which in religious experience we feel ourselves connected is on its *hither* side the subconscious continuation of our conscious life."[92]

In this formulation, James pictures the self as a series of overlapping, interpenetrating, ever-shifting, and dynamic dimensions of awareness, in which the conscious aspects of the self merge into the subconscious, which in turn shades off imperceptibly into a spiritual source of vast and beneficent power—the "more." By envisioning the self in this manner, James aligns himself with the scientific authority and respectability of a psychological understanding of the subliminal origins of religious experiences, while simultaneously siding with the theological conviction that the "higher power" that is contacted during salvific experiences is objective and external to the individual. For James, the evidence in the fields of psychopathology, psychical research, and religious studies strongly suggests that there are dimensions of our being beneath the level of our conscious awareness that can operate independent of our conscious instigation, dimensions of our being that are, in a very real sense, simultaneously self and other.[93] Therefore, when we feel that something "more" is in control of the salvific process, we can legitimately claim to be united with a "power beyond us,"[94] even if that power is ultimately best understood to be deeper dimensions of the self.

The bottom line for James is that it "is literally and objectively true as far as it goes" that what is "common and generic" to every religion is "the fact that the conscious person is continuous with a wider self through which saving experiences come."[95] However, as James points out, as soon as we "ask how far our transmarginal consciousness carries us if we follow it on its remoter side,"[96] then we once again run into the cacophony of conflicting theological opinions:

> Here mysticism and the conversion-rapture and Vedantism and transcendental idealism bring in their monistic interpretations and tell us that the finite self rejoins the absolute self, for it was always one with God and identical with the soul of the world. Here the prophets of all the different religions come with their visions, voices, raptures, and other openings, supposed by each to authenticate his own peculiar faith.[97]

James refuses to endorse any of these theological perspectives, but he *is* willing in the *Varieties* to confess publicly his own theological predilections:

> The further limits of our being plunge . . . into an altogether other dimension of existence from the sensible and merely "understandable" world. Name it the mystical region, or the supernatural region, whichever you choose. So far as our ideal impulses originate in this region (and most of them do originate in it, for we find them possessing us in a way for which we cannot articulately account), we belong to it in a more intimate sense than that in which we belong to the visible world, for we belong in the most intimate sense wherever our ideals belong.[98]

Although in the *Varieties* James does not yet think that he is philosophically prepared to muster a strong defense for this vision of the intimate interaction between the self and the "mystical region," he is personally convinced that we are not confined to the apparent boundaries of our physical and psychological being. James believes that in some fashion we exist as well on other levels of consciousness, levels of consciousness that primarily operate independently from our everyday sense of ourselves as individuals but that, nonetheless, from another perspective, can be best understood as "deeper" or "higher" aspects of our own being. On the final page of the main text of the *Varieties*, James forcibly sums up his position:

> The whole drift of my education goes to persuade me that the world of our present consciousness is only one out of many worlds of consciousness that exist, and that those other worlds must contain experiences which have a meaning for our life also; and that although in the main their experiences and those of this world keep discrete, yet the two become continuous at certain points, and higher energies filter in.[99]

In the postscript to the *Varieties*, James offers some tantalizing hints as to how he would articulate the connection between this unseen world and our "higher" or "deeper" self. After arguing that religious experiences unequivocally testify only that "we can experience union with *something* larger than ourselves and in that union find our greatest peace," James states that, from a practical standpoint, a religious individual needs only believe that "there exists a larger power which is friendly to him and to his ideals," a power that is both beyond the boundaries of the individual and yet "in a fashion continuous with him."[100] This power does not have to be "infinite, it need not be solitary. It might conceivably even be only a larger and more godlike self, of which the present self would then be but the mutilated expression, and the universe might conceivably be a collection of such selves, of different degrees of inclusiveness, with no absolute unity realized in it at all."[101]

In this passage, James is returning to the speculations that he began in "Human Immortality," playing once again with notions of a substantial, cosmic self that transcends the limitations of the physical form, a self that is neither a ghostly reproduction of the individual (like the soul) nor an all-pervasive, omniscient Absolute Self. However, as James seems quite aware, at the end of the *Varieties*, numerous questions about the relationship between the self and the "mystical region" remain unanswered. While these questions are not specifically addressed in James's next works (*Pragmatism* and the essays that were ultimately published in *Essays in Radical Empiricism*), in *A Pluralistic Universe* James finally returns to the task of exploring the interaction between the self and the unseen world, marshaling considerable energy in order to explicate and defend his creatively vague vision of a spiritual realm populated by a multitude of cosmic selves.

Earth Angels and Cosmic Selves

James's primary job in *A Pluralistic Universe* is to provide a philosophical understanding of the relationship between the self and the divine that is a viable alternative to the choices that were prominent at the time: traditional theism and neo-Hegelian monism. In an effort to muster support for his cause, James returns, once again, to the work of Gustave Fechner.

Fechner's work is appealing to James because, in contrast to the "shiveringly thin wrappings" of the logically derived justifications of the Absolute offered by James's neo-Hegelian opponents (Josiah Royce and F. H. Bradley in particular), Fechner bases his religious speculations on the "intense concreteness" of sense data as well as on the "fertility of detail" inherent in everyday experience.[102] Fechner's central contention is "that the whole universe in its different spans and wavelengths . . . is everywhere alive and conscious."[103] Fechner elaborates this panpsychic view of the universe by hypothesizing that, in the same way that consciousness is linked to the human body, a corresponding level of consciousness may be associated with the earth, stars, and galaxies. James explains Fechner's position in more detail:

> The vaster orders of mind go with the vaster orders of body. The entire earth on which we live must have, according to Fechner, its own collective consciousness. So must each sun, moon, and planet; so must the whole solar system have its own wider consciousness. . . . [In the same way, the universe as a whole] is the body of that absolutely totalized consciousness of the universe to which men give the name of God.[104]

James realizes that, strictly speaking, Fechner is, like James's philosophical adversaries, a monist. But unlike neo-Hegelians, such as Royce and Bradley, Fechner focuses most of his attention on the levels of consciousness that might conceivably bridge the gap between humanity and God. For James, Fechner's vision is thus much more aesthetically appealing than the "thinnest outlines" given by the neo-Hegelians:

> Ordinary monistic idealism leaves everything intermediary out. . . . First, you and I, just as we are in this room; and the moment we get below that surface, the unutterable absolute itself! Doesn't this show a singularly indigent imagination? Isn't this brave universe made on a richer pattern, with room in it for a long hierarchy of beings?[105]

James is especially pleased with Fechner's richly nuanced depictions of the "earth-soul," which Fechner believes to be a "guardian angel" that "we can pray to [just] as men pray to their saints."[106] In a way that anticipates much of the current speculations by contemporary environmentalists and theologians, Fechner notes numerous ways in which the earth could indeed be the body of a sentient being.[107] He posits that the earth, like the body of any organism, is a complex unity. It contains a teeming abundance of life-forms within itself, and yet, seen as a whole, it displays a simple, contained grace. Like a sentient being, the earth also changes from within. Unlike a piece of clay, which has to be molded by an external agent, the patterns of the earth's rhythms and historical development appear to be self-propelled and governed. Yet, as Fechner points out, the earth is not identical in structure to its constituent organisms. In many ways, the earth is actually superior to human beings and other creatures, both in complexity and in self-sufficiency. Unlike human beings, the earth does not depend upon other organisms for its life: the air, water, animals, and plants that sustain us are simply constituent components of the earth's body. The earth has no need for limbs to move, no need for hands with which to grasp anything, no need for eyes with which to see, since in a very literal sense the earth moves and grasps with the fins, paws, hands, and feet of every organism and sees through the eyes of every creature. The earth does not need a heart and blood vessels when it has the showers of rain and the flow of tides and rivers. Similarly, the earth has no need for lungs when it is in constant and intimate contact with the atmosphere itself. As James puts it, because "we are ourselves a part of the earth, so our organs are her organs. She is, as it were, eye and ear over her whole extent, seeing and hearing at once all that we see and hear in separation."[108]

For Fechner, the earth is the physical instantiation of the angels that are described in numerous myths of different cultures: beings that live in the light, beings that fly effortlessly, beings that are "intermediaries between God and us, obeying his commands."[109] The earth, as an angel, is understood by Fechner to be the physical body of a higher and wider awareness that lovingly looks after our best interests. This theological understanding that the earth is a manifestation of an angel apparently was aroused within Fechner as a result of "moments of direct vision of this truth," moments such as the following:

> On a certain spring morning I went out to walk. The fields were green, the birds sang, the dew glistened, the smoke was rising, here and there a man appeared; a light as of transfiguration lay on all things. It was only a little bit of the earth; it was only one moment of her existence; and yet as my look embraced her more and more it seemed to me not only so beautiful an idea, but so true and clear a fact, that she is an angel, an angel so rich and fresh and flower-like, and yet going her round in the skies so firmly and so at one with herself, turning her whole living face to Heaven, and carrying me along with her into that Heaven, that I asked myself how the opinions of men could ever have spun themselves away from life so far as to deem the earth only a dry clod, and to seek for angels above it or about it in the emptiness of the sky.[110]

The primary difference between the angels commonly portrayed in different religious mythologies and Fechner's earth-angel is that this great and benevolent consciousness is not a spiritual entity that is ontologically separate from human consciousness. Instead, the earth-angel or earth-soul is a dynamic gestalt of each of the unique and apparently separate consciousnesses that populate the earth. The perceptions of each person, animal, and plant—along with the hypothetical perceptions of the seemingly inanimate levels of being, such as rocks and rivers—combine to form the unitary, yet collective, consciousness of the earth. Fechner hypothesizes that in the same way that a leaf can be understood as having a separate existence from other leaves and from the branch to which it is connected, in the same way, each individual consciousness momentarily perceives that it is cut off from other individual consciousnesses and from the underlying earth-soul. However, just as the leaf is, in actuality, never separate from the branch, and just as the health and vitality of each leaf has repercussions for the tree as a whole, Fechner proposes that each seemingly separate consciousness is, on a deeper level, connected to all other individual consciousnesses through their collective integration as aspects of the earth-soul, and the earth-soul itself is affected by the numerous experiences of each seemingly separate individual consciousness.

For Fechner, the earth-soul and thus, by extension, the soul of the universe as a whole, or "God," is not a static, unchanging reality but, rather, a dynamic awareness that has an inner life that is enriched and altered by the countless experiences and ideas of the individual consciousnesses that are, so to speak, its "eyes." According to this theory, the experiences and ideas of each individual consciousness are preserved in the greater memory and awareness of the earth-soul and, in a sense, take on a life of their own, combining and interacting outside the individual's conscious awareness with the ideas and memories of other human and nonhuman individuals. For Fechner, the physical death of any individual is, therefore, nothing more than a closing of one of the earth's "eyes" in which, at the moment of death, the individual's awareness neither disappears altogether nor is absorbed by the larger earth-soul but, rather, survives as a preexisting, relatively independent but radically freer and more expansive grouping of ideas and memories. This cluster of ideas and memories that is the individual's awareness after death maintains a degree of integrity, but it also possesses a new and expanded awareness of its connection both with the earth-soul and with the memories and ideas of other individuals. After the death of the individual's physical body, the individual's consciousness remains, but since it now identifies less with the physical body, its boundaries are more porous, and it is therefore more capable of freely interacting with other fields of consciousness, including those of the living. This increased freedom, fluidity, and expansiveness allow the individual's life to continue in unexpected ways, since it can now combine with other dynamic fields of consciousness to generate novel ideas and to create new and ongoing experiences.

James's discussion of Fechner's theories is always rhetorically presented in such a way as to imply that these theories are simply fascinating possibilities that are offered up to the reader as one of many alternatives. James never goes out on a limb and embraces Fechner's ideas as his own. Nonetheless, it is clear that James is implicitly giving a muted endorsement to Fechner's ideas; his reluctance to more actively defend Fechner's position seems to stem primarily from James's desire to maintain a theoretical openness on metaphysical speculations that, by their very nature, cannot be empirically confirmed or denied. James never expresses any serious qualms about Fechner's hypotheses, and, in fact, Fechner's scheme is closely aligned with James's own radical empiricism, especially James's attempts to articulate a theory of reality that would allow for a maximum of diversity and plurality while simultaneously permitting a maximum of unity and connectedness.[111] Fechner's earth-soul can be seen as different from a person's individual consciousness. This difference leaves theoretical room for genuine personal autonomy; yet, the earth-soul can also be seen as intimately connected to the individual's consciousness to the extent that it is, in some sense, the individual's deeper, truer, and wider self (ideas that are also highly congruent with James's conception of the subliminal self).

In his discussion of Fechner's ideas, James frequently draws upon explicit parallels in his own work to strengthen Fechner's analogical arguments. By far the most important of these parallels is James's depiction of the dynamics of our individual consciousness. James's psychology stresses that our consciousness always has a "hot spot," a center of gravity, a focus of attention. Surrounding this central focus of our awareness, however, is a vaguely felt but crucially significant penumbra of tacit assumptions, memories, hopes, and prejudices that operates below the surface of our conscious awareness and strongly influences how we perceive and interact with the world around us. In addition, encircling this fairly accessible preconscious background, there is another, deeper level of subconscious awareness, an awareness that appears to be extremely active below the surface boundaries of our consciousness and that occasionally erupts into our lives with powerful and undeniable force.

Our attention, moment to moment, is, by definition, on the hot spot of our consciousness. According to James, this hot spot often becomes such a central part of our experience that the surrounding background of our awareness fades from view. However, in a split second, our consciousness can expand to include within its active purview material belonging to this background (e.g., vivid memories of early childhood), making the background, for the moment, the foreground—that is, the new hot spot. James beautifully describes this inherent complexity and fluidity of our inner life:

> My present field of consciousness is a centre surrounded by a fringe that shades insensibly into a subconscious more. I use three separate terms here to describe this fact; but I might as well use three hundred, for the fact is all shades and no boundaries. Which part of it properly is in my consciousness, which out? If I name what is out, it already has come in. The centre works in one way while the margins work in another, and presently overpower the centre and are central themselves. What we conceptually identify ourselves with and say we are thinking of at any time is the centre; but our *full* self is the whole field, with all those indefinitely radiating subconscious possibilities of increase that we can only feel without conceiving, and can hardly begin to analyze.[112]

For James, in the same way that we are "co-conscious" with the margin of our tacit background awareness, perhaps our individual consciousnesses form a collective pool of awareness present in the margins of a more central self that is "co-conscious" with each of us. Extending this metaphor, the deeper or more extensive self that is the core reality of each of our beings would be the "hot spot" of the earth soul's consciousness that is surrounded and interpenetrated by a collective field of less extensive personal consciousnesses. Thus, for James, the dynamics of our personal consciousness can be understood as mirroring the dynamics of the relationship between each individual consciousness and the greater, more encompassing consciousness of the earth-soul. James emphasizes that if this hypothesis is accurate, if indeed "every bit of us at every moment is part and parcel of a wider self," then, while our individual consciousnesses may not be cognizant of our connection to this vaster awareness and while we may feel that we are insulated from other individual consciousnesses as well, it is still quite possible, indeed, likely, that, on a deeper or higher level of our being, we are "conscious, as it were, over our heads"[113] of this underlying connection with other individuals and with this wider self. From this more encompassing perspective, we may have a much broader range of knowledge and experiences than we presently realize; we may be intimately aware of other individual consciousnesses; we may be initiating an enormous amount of activity that has a tremendous impact upon the world, all with only the slightest hint of awareness from our present, more limited perspective.

The Compounding of Consciousness

James's willingness to accept hypothetically the possibility of a wider or deeper consciousness that is, in part at least, constituted by our less extensive individual consciousnesses was rooted in an earlier important philosophical shift: James's decision that the compounding of consciousness is possible. In the *Principles*, James had argued that a complex unit of consciousness is not just a simple combination of different simpler states of consciousness but something entirely new. A complex state of awareness is not, for instance, twenty-five separate simpler awarenesses added together. Instead, this complex state of awareness is itself a simple, whole, new awareness *of* these twenty-five seemingly separate awarenesses; it is a single unit; it is not made of parts; it is not a compound. However, even as early as 1895, in the President's Address before the American Psychological Association, James had publicly admitted that his prior opposition to the compounding of consciousness was perhaps ill founded. His change of heart came about when he realized that there is an inner complexity to experience that *can* be introspectively analyzed. For instance, as he mentioned in the lecture, "in a glass of lemonade we can taste both the lemon and sugar at once. In a major chord our ear can single out the c, e, g, and c' if it has once become acquainted with these notes apart."[114] Unlike the psychology of the *Principles*, which insisted that each moment of consciousness was an indivisible, simple unity of perception, by the 1895 lecture James had come to see that within our consciousness, unity does not have to exclude diversity. Gerald Myers underscores this shift in James's thought:

> Here we come upon a favorite idea of James's, one that especially intrigued him during his later years: unity need not be simple, unanalyzable, or utterly homogeneous. Our own experiences are unities that are also diversities. Our "knowledge of things together" is an instance: there are different things to see on the beach; of themselves they represent merely a multitude, but when we perceive them simultaneously we group them as the contents of a single state of perceptual consciousness. A state of mind such as this is not homogeneous but is rather a synthetic union of diverse elements. It is unlike anything in the physical world (James had not in 1895 eliminated psychophysical dualism) because in that world the parts of a so-called whole are separable; in a mental unity such as a state of perceptual awareness, on the other hand, the parts are distinguishable but not separable, for if any are detached, the unity which they help to constitute immediately collapses.[115]

James's willingness in *A Pluralistic Universe* to accept that the compounding of consciousness takes place moment to moment within the awareness of each individual had important metaphysical ramifications. James realized that a willingness to admit that the dynamic stream of our individual consciousness, when examined closely, is a seemingly contradictory diversity-within-unity, permitted him to extend metaphorically this diversity-within-unity to Fechner's metaphysical proposals. Because in *A Pluralistic Universe* James was willing to accept that within our own consciousness it is possible to observe that different "parts" of our awareness are conjoined within our awareness as a whole, James was also willing to accept that perhaps Fechner was correct that our individual consciousness is itself a constituent part of a larger consciousness:

> In ourselves, visual consciousness goes with our eyes, tactile consciousness with our skin. But altho neither skin nor eye knows aught of the sensations of the other, they come together and figure in some sort of relation and combination in the more inclusive consciousness which each of us names his *self*. Quite similarly, then, says Fechner, we must suppose that my consciousness of myself and yours of yourself, altho in their immediacy they keep separate and know nothing of each other, are yet known and used together in a higher consciousness, that of the human race, say, into which they enter as constituent parts.[116]

However, even though in *A Pluralistic Universe* James is willing to accept certain aspects of the doctrine of the compounding of consciousness and its analog, the compounding of individual consciousnesses within a larger, cosmic self, he has more difficulty completely discarding the idea of God as "a distinct agent of unification"[117] of these separate consciousnesses—an idea that is similar to his prior psychological conviction that the higher, complex level of awareness of an individual is something new, something different from just a combination of other awarenesses. For James, even the earth-soul is not just a simple combination of the multitude of our awarenesses:

> As our mind is not the bare sum of our sights plus our sounds plus our pains, but in adding [this sense data] together also finds relations among them and weaves them into schemes and forms . . . of which no one sense in its separate estate knows anything, so the earth-soul traces relations between the contents of my mind and the contents of yours of which neither of our separate minds is conscious.[118]

According to James, the earth-soul is not a simple combination of our consciousnesses, even though our consciousnesses are co-conscious with it. It has knowledge that we, as individuals, do not have access to, except during rare moments of mystical insight. James argues that "we are closed against its world, but that world is not closed against us. It is as if the total universe of inner life had a sort of grain or direction, a sort of valvular structure permitting knowledge to flow in one way only, so that the wider might always have the narrower under observation, but never the narrower the wider."[119] James wants a divine being who is intimately connected with us, but he does not wish to reduce that divine being to a simple combination of the totality of consciousnesses in the universe. Although James claims that his theology in *A Pluralistic Universe* is pantheistic, in actuality it is closer to being pan*en*theistic. For James, God is found *within* the universe, but God is not reduced *to* the universe.

A Pluralistic Universe is a snapshot of James himself in flux. He is attempting to jettison years of theological and psychological assumptions in order to construct an alternative psychological and theological vision, but he has difficulty completely making the transition. For many years in his career, James was an ardent opponent of philosophers who argued that our individual consciousnesses are one with a monistic Absolute. He, instead, advocated the idea that our individual consciousnesses are separate from, but known and loved by, a theistic personal God. From this earlier theological perspective, God was understood to be a separate being who reacts and responds to our experiences, which are known within God as a totality, a oneness of experience. This earlier Jamesian theology had claimed that just as a constellation is not merely a simple collection of stars but, rather, is the result of a separate being who views those stars as a related unit, in the same way God, unlike the Absolute, does not simply consist of a combination of all of our seemingly separate awarenesses but, rather, is an "independent higher witness" of our experiences.[120] In *A Pluralistic Universe*, James changes his theology: he no longer conceives of God as an ontologically separate knower of our individual consciousnesses, but he still fights to maintain the distinctiveness and uniqueness of God's awareness.

As a result of his acceptance of important aspects of the doctrine of the compounding of consciousness, James realizes that he has to formulate a new theological doctrine of God, but he is still extremely reluctant to accept one obvious possibility: the monistic understanding of God as the Absolute. However, as we have seen, since James wants to accept a religious vision almost identical to Fechner's, he is forced, fighting all the way, to accept that the Absolute might indeed exist:

> The self-compounding of mind in its smaller and more accessible portions seems a certain fact, . . . [therefore] the speculative assumption of a similar but wider compounding in remoter regions must be reckoned with as a legitimate hypothesis. The absolute is not the impossible being I once thought it. Mental facts do function both singly and together, at once, and we finite minds may simultaneously be co-conscious with one another in a superhuman intelligence.[121]

Nonetheless, James remains more open to Fechner's monistic vision of reality than to Royce's or Bradley's, not only because, unlike these neo-Hegelians who claim that we are forced by logical necessity to believe in the Absolute, "Fechner treats the superhuman consciousness he so fervently believes in as an hypothesis only," but also because Fechner's vision is much more concretely and thickly articulated than the abstract conceptual system of the philosophers of the Absolute.

Nonetheless, James is not completely happy with Fechner's theological vision. He still does not agree with the monistic implications of Fechner's conception of God as the hypothetical end of the hierarchy of larger consciousnesses enveloping smaller consciousnesses. James claims that, "as we envelop our sight and hearing, so the earth-soul envelops us, and the star-soul the earth-soul, until—what? Envelopment can't go on forever . . . so God is the name that Fechner gives to this last all-enveloper.

But if nothing escapes this all-enveloper, he is responsible for everything, including evil."[122] James prefers to "assume that the superhuman consciousness, however vast it may be, has itself an external environment, and consequently is finite."[123]

This concept of the "finite God" is a puzzling irritant within James's basically promising theometaphysical hypothesis: pluralistic pantheism.[124] Pluralistic pantheism (admittedly, an apparent contradiction in terms) is James's attempt to avoid the rigid, static, completely monistic "block universe" that he claims is portrayed in the various neo-Hegelian philosophies of the Absolute. At the same time, pluralistic pantheism is James's attempt to align himself with the understanding that the divine is constituted, at least in part, by our own finite individual consciousnesses. James's religious impulses want a God that is extremely intimate, so much so that he understands God to be, from a certain perspective at least, our deepest self; yet, James's ethical needs mandate that this God not be all-pervasive in order to allow real moral choice for each individual. Unfortunately, James never adequately harmonizes these often contradictory temperamental requirements, leaving his finite God to end up at times looking suspiciously like a weaker, younger brother of the older theistic God and his alleged pantheism looking very much like a revamped version of polytheism.

Arguably, James never adequately reconciled the contradictory images of the divine that are contained within *A Pluralistic Universe*; nonetheless, it is at least clear that, for James, an unseen spiritual world exists that is not ontologically separate from human consciousness—a realm of existence that is intimately linked with the deeper selves of every individual. If this hypothesis of our subconscious connection with a deeper and wider spiritual level of existence is accepted, then coherent explanations of psychical and mystical phenomena begin to take shape. For instance, it is reasonable to suggest that telepathy, clairvoyance, and other psychical experiences occur when the limitations inherent within our present level of personal identity momentarily dissolve and our awareness expands and embraces within itself the knowledge possessed by other individual consciousnesses. In the same way, mystical experiences could also be seen as a letting go of our identification with our present level of consciousness in order to unite with deeper or wider dimensions of our being. Nature mysticism, from this perspective, would imply an experiential connection with the awareness of the earth-soul, while unitive, interior mystical experiences might well be catalyzed by a powerful sense of our underlying oneness with the universal soul itself.

While James does not explicitly develop this argument in *A Pluralistic Universe*, his position points in this direction. For instance, James notes that Fechner's hypothesis has enormous potential to help us comprehend psychical and psychopathological phenomena:

> I doubt whether we shall ever understand some of [these phenomena] without using the very letter of Fechner's conception of a great reservoir in which the memories of earth's inhabitants are pooled and preserved, and from which, when the threshold lowers

> or the valve opens, information ordinarily shut out leaks into the mind of exceptional individuals among us.[125]

James also thinks that the religious experiences that he described in the *Varieties* supports Fechner's ideas, claiming that "they point with reasonable probability to the continuity of our consciousness with a wider spiritual environment from which the ordinary prudential man (who is the only man that scientific psychology, so called, takes cognizance of) is shut off."[126] These religious experiences show us that our naturalistic ideas of selfhood are insufficient; they demonstrate that there are "possibilities that take our breath away, of another kind of happiness and power, based on giving up our own will and letting something higher work for us"; they "suggest that our natural experience, our strictly moralistic and prudential experience, may be only a fragment of real human experience. They soften nature's outlines and open out the strangest possibilities."[127] In James's opinion, profound religious experiences give rise to religious beliefs that are "fully in accord with Fechner's theory of successively larger enveloping spheres of conscious life"; furthermore, as James notes, Fechner's theory is congruent with James's own conception developed in the *Varieties* that "the believer is continuous, to his own consciousness, at any rate, with a wider self from which saving experiences flow in."[128]

James points out that those who have had such profound religious experiences "are quite unmoved by criticism . . . they have had their vision and they know—that is enough—that we inhabit an invisible spiritual environment from which help comes, our soul being mysteriously one with a larger soul whose instruments we are."[129] On the basis of experiences such as these, James is willing to state that Fechner's ideas have a modicum of empirical verification. In addition, he asserts that these ideas offer us a viable explanatory model that naturalism or certain varieties of theism cannot, since naturalism assumes "that human consciousness is the highest consciousness there is," while theism, although willing to posit the existence of a "higher mind," nonetheless asserts that this higher mind "is discontinuous with our own."[130]

Interestingly, despite James's caution in the *Varieties* that we need not uncritically accept the testimony of mystics, by the time of *A Pluralistic Universe*, he is convinced that the weight of the evidence provided by psychopathological, psychical, and mystical experiences "establish, when taken together, a decidedly formidable probability in favor of a general view of the world almost identical with Fechner's," even though "the outlines of the superhuman consciousness thus made probable must remain, however, very vague;" when all is said and done, James comes down forcefully in favor of Fechner's vision of the universe:

> The drift of all the evidence we have seems to me to sweep us very strongly towards the belief in some form of superhuman life with which we may, unknown to ourselves, be co-conscious. We may be in the universe as dogs and cats are in our libraries, seeing the books and hearing the conversation, but having no inkling of the meaning of it all.[131]

A Field Model of the Self and Reality

Unlike many contemporary philosophers of mysticism, James is unwilling to simply describe the phenomenological characteristics of mystical experiences or to merely detail the religious beliefs and practices of mystics from other cultures and traditions (although he is convinced that this is an important first step). Instead, James emphasizes that it is crucially important to sift through the accounts of the beliefs, practices, and mystical experiences of other places and other times in order to construct "our more or less plausible pictures" of our world and our place within it.[132] Although James stresses the plurality and cultural specificity of different mystically inspired claims to truth and refuses to put his stamp of approval on any metaphysical system simply because it arose out of deep mystical experiences, James *is* willing to defend the importance and legitimacy of using descriptions of the beliefs and experiences of mystics as resources from which to construct one's own metaphysical vision of reality.

James acknowledges that his own "metaphysical myths,"[133] filled as they are with references to mother seas of awareness, earth souls, and hidden depths of cosmic consciousness, are speculative, at least to the extent that they cannot be readily verified through the everyday experience of most human beings. However, James goes out of his way to insist that these metaphysical speculations are not just nicely phrased, and yet ultimately unverifiable, hypotheses unconnected to anything substantial. Instead, from James's perspective, his metaphysical ruminations are reasonable, coherent, and empirically grounded attempts to draw out the ontological and psychological implications of a wide range of experiences that many philosophers were, and are, overly quick to dismiss.

Furthermore, James argues convincingly that metaphysical speculations, if taken seriously, are not innocuous, relatively idle, academic musings unconnected to the rest of reality but, rather, are frequently a vital component of an individual's moment-to-moment experience of, and response to, life itself. James points out that our metaphysical beliefs are often an important element of the tacit, typically unexamined gestalt of assumptions, interests, and cultural conditionings that not only continually shape our daily experience but also influence how we choose to respond to the world around us. Therefore, from James's perspective, our metaphysical assumptions have the potential, not only to mold our day-to-day experience, but also, at their best, to encourage an energized and engaged response to life. However, James is not naive. He also acknowledges that, at their worst, certain metaphysical beliefs have the potential to create a wide array of negative psychological repercussions: moral collapse within an individual, a sense of meaninglessness and nihilistic futility, or dogmatic rigidity and intolerance of novelty.

James argues that we will never be entirely free from a certain degree of internalized metaphysical assumptions. Therefore, instead of blindly accepting the unexamined, taken-for-granted materialism and determinism that frequently underlie many scientific and philosophical perspectives, James prefers to bring his own metaphysical assumptions out into the light of public scrutiny. James's intention is to create a defensible metaphysical model that is nonnaturalistic, open ended, and more adequate to the full range of experience, as well as one that can serve as a catalyst for increased personal and social well-being. From the perspective of James's pragmatic understanding of truth, any metaphysical model that is rooted in empirical observations, that provides solutions to tough philosophical dilemmas and that, on the whole, helps to transform individuals and the communities in which they live is not only philosophically, psychologically, and culturally helpful but is also quite possibly true. It is crucially important, therefore, to pause for a moment to examine the general contours of James's model of the interaction between the self and the divine in order to determine what might make this model such an enormously suggestive and appealing candidate for James's pragmatic vote of confidence.

Eugene Fontinell, a creative and careful Jamesian scholar, suggests that we might best envision James's model of the self and reality as "fields within fields within fields."[134] This field model sees individual selves not as self-contained monads with an unchanging, essential core but as swirling vortices of interpenetrating, interdependent fields whose boundaries are, according to Fontinell, "open, indefinite, and continually shifting such that other fields are continually leaking in and out."[135]

From the perspective of the *Principles*, which primarily focuses on the observable components of the individual, these fields can be seen as the continually shifting elements of the empirical self: our moving, breathing, eating, excreting body in continuous interaction with the surrounding environment; our ever-changing emotional bond to our possessions, friends, and family; the different degrees of social approval and rejection superimposed and churning within us as we play the numerous roles thrust upon us by our social circumstances; as well as the slowly shifting background of our memories, hopes, dreams, and cultural assumptions, the surging tides of our emotions, and the sharp influx of unexpected inspirations or volitional decisions.[136]

The *Varieties* depicts a world in which these fields within fields not only take the form of our ongoing stream of consciousness but are themselves surrounded by another whirling miasma of interpenetrating fields: the subliminal self, that bubbling cauldron of intuitions, passions, delusions, fantasies, paranormal cognitions, and mystical ecstasies that from time to time spills over into our consciousness and yet which, in many ways, appears to have a dynamic life of its own above, or below, our conscious awareness.

Finally, a still further extension of this field vision of reality is dealt with in *A Pluralistic Universe* with James's qualified acceptance of the compounding of consciousness. Here we find a hierarchy of different interpenetrating fields of awareness: not only the collective fields of our conscious and subliminal selves, but also the earth-soul, the solar-soul, the galaxy-soul, and so on—a veritable pantheon of cosmic consciousnesses that are not ontologically separate divine beings but, rather, are our very own deeper and wider selves.

Ignoring for the moment the problems inherent in James's conception of the finite God, it seems that Fontinell is essentially correct when he claims that this field model of the self and reality provides a coherent, persuasive vision of a world in which, although "all fields are 'incomplete' and continuous with others, they are not so continuous that reality is reduced to an undifferentiated monistic flux"; a vision of reality that provides "ground for the recognition of individuals while avoiding any atomistic individualism or isolating egoism."[137] This field model of reality has enormous metaphysical and ethical advantages in that it posits a self that is connected with the divine, with the selves of others, and with nature, without allowing that self to be swallowed up into an unchanging, all-pervasive Oneness. In this vision of the self and of reality, the individual is seen as deeply connected to the divine and yet also able to maintain a very real degree of autonomy. In similar fashion, the divine is understood to be neither purely other nor purely the same as the self. The divine is seen as intimately united with humanity and nature but not so closely united as to dissolve operative, if not ontological, distinctions between humanity and the spiritual world.

Unlike the purely logical justifications of the Absolute, and unlike the dogmatic denial of anything beyond the senses that is insisted upon by materialism, this field understanding of reality can be seen as offering a hypothetical, yet coherent and reasonable extrapolation from the concrete experience of life itself, buttressed by the data gathered from psychical and mystical experiences.[138] If James is correct and the diversity-within-unity that appears to be present within our conscious experience of reality is also the structure of reality itself, and, furthermore, if the existing accounts of mystical and psychical experiences are reasonably trustworthy, then this model appears to offer a relatively secure starting point for extremely productive philosophical work.

Even though I recognize that it is impossible, within the confines of the present context, even to begin the detailed and careful work that is necessary to support any of the claims that I might make about this field model's alleged philosophical advantages, I believe that it is legitimate, and necessary, to indicate the valuable contributions that a revised Jamesian field model of the self and reality could make to several contemporary philosophical discussions. Therefore, bearing in mind that in the future I intend to amplify and support the following set of philosophical proposals, I ask that they be seen, for the moment at least, as intriguing suggestions that bear careful consideration.

To begin with, I propose that we modify Fontinell's field model in a nondualistic direction,[139] in order to make the claim that the overlapping, ever-changing fields of reality and the self consist of different vibratory rates of conscious energy.[140] If we do so, then a number of provocative possibilities for philosophical reformulation offer themselves to us.

First, modifying the model in a nondualistic direction opens up the possibility that the model can be aligned explicitly with James's radical empiricism, which is also a nondual metaphysical position. James's radical empiricism posits that the commonsense separation between mental and physical reality is a postpartum functional distinction, not an ontological chasm. From the perspective of James's radical empiricism, our mental and physical spheres of experience, which on the surface seem so heteronomous, actually emerge from a prior, nondual "pure experience" that is neither physical nor mental but potentially both.[141]

Second, a nondual reworking of this field model of the self and reality creates numerous points of connection between James's work and several other nondual metaphysical systems (of which the Tantric metaphysical understandings, with their focus on unity-within-diversity and the vibratory nature of reality and consciousness, are perhaps the best "match").

Third, using an energetic metaphor for consciousness underscores James's claim that consciousness is not static, empty, unchanging, and devoid of contents but, rather, a dynamic, rich, mutable flux (a notion that, once again, aligns quite nicely with Tantra's own emphasis on the creative and fluid nature of consciousness).

Fourth, because this nondual field model of the self and reality posits that the mind, body, and spirit are not heteronomous substances but, rather, are mutually interacting and interdependent fields of energetic awareness, then the mind/body interaction itself is much easier to account for and justify than if reality is understood to consist of a mysterious fusion of opposing mental and physical substances.

Finally, a field model of the self and reality in which everything and everyone is understood to possess individual integrity and yet is also understood to be intimately connected and interdependent offers a persuasive and valuable framework for cultivating a reverent respect for all of nature and for each other.[142]

This neo-Jamesian field model of the self and reality also has important implications for the philosophy of mysticism. To begin with, it often appears as if each of the reigning theological paradigms (monism, theism, and polytheism) has difficulty accounting for a particular range of mystical experiences.[143] For instance, any theism that posits a God who is totally Other than humanity often has to contort itself into numerous uncomfortable and awkward theological positions in order to accommodate mystical experiences of complete identity with the divine. (Christian devotional mystics, for instance, frequently extol their union with God, while simultaneously insisting that God and the soul are completely different substances. This claim is perhaps legitimate, but most Christian mystics rarely address the philosophical issue of how two heteronomous substances can interact at all, preferring instead to rely upon evocative metaphors—for instance, the image of the iron bar thrust into the fire, which takes on the qualities of fire, while remaining different from the fire itself.) Similarly, any polytheistic position that considers the gods or spirits or ancestors to be ontologically separate beings from humanity appears to have the same kind of problems accounting for unitive mystical experiences as a theistic stance that insists on the complete Otherness of the divine. (It is rare to see shamans philosophically address, for instance, how their souls are both united with, yet distinct from, their totem or power animal during shamanic out-of-body journeys.) On the other hand, any monistic worldview that denies the reality of diversity and of the individual often has to resort to a type of metaphysical sleight-of-hand to account for why the mystical experience of unity is not our universal and perpetual experience. (Advaita Vedānta's reliance on the concept of māyā seems particularly dubious in this regard, in that māyā, as the illusory source of separation from *brahman*, is itself seen to be both real, since it projects the changing world of appearances, and unreal, since it does not exist separate from *brahman*.)[144]

A field model of reality, however, could conceivably accommodate our everyday experience of alienation and separation as well as mystical experiences of oneness with the divine. If reality indeed is a network of overlapping, shifting vortices of conscious energy vibrating at different rates, then we could easily picture our normal awareness of separation from the divine as an identification with those fields that vibrate within a rather narrow portion of the entire spectrum of energy. These fields might include especially dominant and taken-for-granted cultural assumptions, such as "I am a physical body"; "I am completely separate from other human beings and from the world around me"; and "reality is nothing more than matter in different combinations." These fields might also consist of the individual's internalization of, and response to, the traumatic events that every person endures in the process of maturation—internalizations that tend to manifest as defensive and painfully contracted self-perceptions, such as "I am unloved and unlovable"; "The world is an untrustworthy place"; and "I am weak and alone." Mystical experiences of oneness with the divine, however, could be pictured as moments when, for a variety of reasons, our self-identification suddenly opens up to a broader spectrum of the fields of energy and awareness that are always present and operative within us, thereby catalyzing an experience of joy, freedom, expanded vision, and fulfillment.

These unitive mystical experiences (as well as the perhaps more common "visionary" experiences) would naturally vary from person to person and from moment to moment, because within a field model of reality, nothing is static, including the deeper, broader fields of our being that constitute the different dimensions of spiritual reality. Therefore, each mystical experience would take on a unique, culturally and psychologically appropriate shape, since it would be formed by the interaction of the ever-changing fields that create our quotidian awareness and the ever-changing fields that create the deeper levels of our being. The differences from one mystical experience to the next could therefore be understood as coming from both "directions": these differences would emerge either because different "strata" of the deeper fields of our being were contacted or because there were alternations in the fields that constitute our individual sense of ourselves, or, more likely, because both of these alternations took place simultaneously. From this perspective, mystical experiences could be understood as catalyzed by a variety of interrelated causes: the disciplined, steady transformations in our ego-sense that are nurtured by an immersion in various spiritual practices, or the violent, sudden alternations of our quotidian awareness that lead to a collapse of ego boundaries and the individual will, or the spectacular "subterranean" initiatives of the deeper strata of our being that are experienced as unforgettable, wondrous moments of grace, compassion, and unasked-for spiritual openings.

Furthermore, even though several philosophical and theological perspectives would have difficulty coexisting with this field model of the self and reality, this model could easily be aligned with a broad range of other spiritual traditions. Although a field model would conflict with any theistic claim that the divine is totally Other than humanity or with different varieties of naturalism, or with certain versions of monism in which the reality of the individual is completely denied, there is still room under its extremely flexible roof for a multitude of mystical and visionary experiences: becoming lost in the nondualistic flashes of *satori*, perceiving the radiant manifestations of Christian and Islamic angels, experiencing the gracious presence of the celestial *bodhisattvas* of Mahāyāna Buddhism, hearing the sacred words of the spirits and ancestors of tribal peoples, or having the beneficent visitation of the Taoist and Hindu gods. Each of these spiritual experiences would have a legitimate and understandable place within a field model, as long as the levels of reality apprehended within these experiences were not seen as completely ontologically distinct from human consciousness.

As Fontinell points out, a field model of the self and reality is eminently congenial with a perspective that emphasizes the worth of a plurality of religious traditions:

> The divine life, understood as the widest field, enriches and is enriched by the variety of fields with which it is related. Thus, the plurality of religions may not be a necessary evil to be endured until the one true religion is formed; rather this plurality may be the necessary and only means by which the richness of the divine life can be lived and communicated.[145]

A field model of the self and reality could actually go further and say that, while important, practical, and fascinating differences can be observed from one religious tradition to the next, from one religious person to the next, and from one religious experience to the next, these traditions, people, and experiences are not hermetically sealed off from one another but, rather, overlap and interact with one another. From this perspective, personal and cultural identity would be understood not as any sort of static, indivisible essence but as a relatively stable, yet complex, cluster of dynamically interrelated experiences that is open to, and affected by, other clusters of experiences. If a field model of the self and reality were accepted, it would be impossible to claim that there is any such thing as a purely "Hindu" mystical experience or a purely "Jewish" mystical experience. Instead, as scholars of mystical experience, we would be forced to undertake the much more complex task of describing and assessing the numerous vortices of influences present within each mystical experience (whether psychological, physiological, historical, cultural, linguistic, or economic), while remaining open to the very real likelihood that each mystical experience is also shaped, in ways that we may never be able to determine, by a wide variety of transcultural and transnatural influences as well. A field model of the self and reality could, therefore, be receptive to, and even encourage, a wide variety of theoretical approaches to mystical experiences, respecting and valuing the countless different ways in which we each choose to explore the unseen worlds that surround and interpenetrate our being.

Notes

1. While it is always problematic to group together scholars, as this tends to imply that they are in fundamental agreement on every issue, I argue that investigators of mysticism such as Baron von Hugel, Evelyn Underhill, Joseph Marechal, W. T. Stace, and Rudolph Otto are, on the whole, representatives of this understanding of mysticism. See, for instance, Baron Friedrich von Hugel, *The Mystical Element of Religion* (New York: Dutton, 1923); Evelyn Underhill, *Mysticism* (New York: Dutton, 1911); Joseph Marechal, S. J., *Studies in the Psychology of the Mystics*, trans. Algar Thorold (Albany: Magi Books, 1964); W. T. Stace, *Mysticism and Philosophy* (Los Angeles: Jeremy P. Tarcher, 1960); and Rudolph Otto, *The Idea of the Holy* (New York: Oxford University Press, 1958).

2. Once again, groupings such as this are perilous, but I argue that, for the most part, scholars such as Steven Katz, Wayne Proudfoot, Robert Gimello, and Hans Penner are representative of this perspective on mystical experience. See, for instance, Wayne Proudfoot, *Religious Experience* (Berkeley: University of California Press, 1985), and the volumes edited by Steven Katz (in which the work of Gimello and Penner appears): *Mysticism and Philosophical Analysis* (New York: Oxford University Press, 1978) and *Mysticism and Religious Traditions* (New York: Oxford University Press, 1983).

3. When depicting James's thought, it is important to remember that terms such as "metaphysical" or "epistemological" or "psychological" do not necessarily denote exactly the same meanings that they do in contemporary philosophical discussions. While James's earlier work (in particular, *The Principles of Psychology*) does tentatively accept the commonsense division between subjective and objective "realms" of inquiry, James's later work (from *The Varieties of Religious Experience* on) begins to dismantle the dualist separation between inner and outer, mental and physical, or subjective and objective that the terms "epistemological" (or "psychological") and "metaphysical" typically imply. In this essay, therefore, the epistemological discussion focuses primarily on James's earlier work, which accepts a dualistic separation between the knower and the known, while the psychological and metaphysical sections, on the whole, explore James's later work, in which "psychological" discussions of the nature of selfhood almost inevitably fuse with "metaphysical" ruminations on the contours of nonnatural levels of reality.

4. William James, *The Principles of Psychology*, 3 vols. (Cambridge: Harvard University Press, 1981), p. 656.

5. William James, *Pragmatism* (Cambridge: Harvard University Press, 1975), p. 119.

6. Ibid., p. 189.

7. Ibid. , p. 195.

8. This metaphor of two elements combining into one is dubious from a Jamesian perspective, but it will have to suffice for the moment.

9. Steven Katz, ed., *Mysticism and Philosophical Analysis* (New York: Oxford University Press, 1978), p. 57.

10. Anthony N. Perovich Jr. argues quite persuasively that the positions taken by "complete constructivists" like Katz and Proudfoot are based on a misreading of Kant. See his chapter, "Does the Philosophy of Mysticism Rest on a Mistake," in Robert K. C. Forman,

ed., *The Problem of Pure Consciousness* (New York: Oxford University Press, 1990), p. 237–253.

11. In this example, the woman might still, for instance, retain the underlying sense that she has a body that is separate from the other forms that are sharing space with her or still possess the terrifying feeling that she should know more than she does, and so on. James, for one, doubts whether it is ever possible to experience moments of sheer knowledge-by-acquaintance, completely devoid of knowledge-about, but he nonetheless argues that a retrospective analysis of our experience (especially out-of-the-ordinary experiences such as this example) reveals a qualitative difference between knowledge-about and knowledge-by-acquaintance.

12. John Wild, *The Radical Empiricism of William James* (Garden City, N.Y.: Doubleday, 1969), p. 52.

13. Admittedly, it is relatively easy to claim that meaningful patterns are already present in our knowledge-by-acquaintance. It is much more difficult to account for the *origin* of these patterns.

14. Nancy Frankenberry, *Religion and Radical Empiricism* (Albany: State University of New York Press, 1987), p. 67.

15. The term "something" is placed in quotes to emphasize that the "otherness" that sometimes appears to the mystic is not necessarily an object separate from the mystic's consciousness.

16. Robert Forman has proposed that for these types of unitive experiences we might well use another term: "knowledge by identity." See, for instance, Robert K. C. Forman, "Mystical Knowledge," *Journal of the American Academy of Religion* 61, 4 (Winter 1993).

17. William James, *The Meaning of Truth* (Cambridge: Harvard University Press, 1981), p. 56.

18. James, *Pragmatism*, p. 123.

19. Ibid., p. 122.

20. James, *The Meaning of Truth*, p. 45.

21. Ibid., p. 115.

22. I make no claims here that anecdotal evidence is binding on others, but I do claim that it can become part of a cumulative argument in favor of specific metaphysical/theological truth claims. For a further discussion of the concept of the cumulative argument, see Caroline Frank Davis, *The Evidential Force of Religious Experience* (New York: Oxford University Press, 1989).

23. Ralph Barton Perry, *The Thought and Character of William James*, 2 vols. (Boston: Little, Brown; 1935), 2: 349–350.

24. The quote marks around the word "it" indicate that "it" is not necessarily an object separate from the perceiver.

25. Richard J. Bernstein, *Beyond Objectivism and Relativism* (Philadelphia: University of Pennsylvania Press, 1985), p. 8.

26. It might appear that James's stress on the given, preexisting nature of knowledge-by-acquaintance contradicts this position. However, the "raw material" that is received via knowledge-by-acquaintance is extremely mutable and open to a wide range of interpretations and understandings.

27. William James, *The Varieties of Religious Experience* (Cambridge: Harvard University Press, 1985), p. 324.

28. James, *Principles*, p. 228.

29. Ibid., p. 221.

30. Ibid., p. 331.

31. William James, *Essays in Psychical Research* (Cambridge: Harvard University Press, 1986), p. 374.

32. Gerald Myers, *William James: His Life and Thought* (New Haven: Yale University Press, 1986), p. 350.

33. William James, *Essays in Religion and Morality* (Cambridge: Harvard University Press, 1982), p. 81. James emphasizes that during this essay he is only provisionally using dualistic terminology to describe the realm of "mental facts" and the realm of "physical facts."

34. Ibid., p. 84.

35. Ibid., p. 83.

36. Ibid., p. 86. In an earlier lecture, "The Knowing of Things Together," James points out that transcendentalism could use physiology to support their own thesis of the "oversoul," using a similar example: "As the pipes of an organ let the pressing mass of air escape only in single notes, so do our brains, the organ pipes of the infinite, keep back everything but the slender threads of truth to which they may be previous. As they obstruct more, the insulation increases, as they obstruct less it disappears." William James, *Essays in Philosophy* (Cambridge: Harvard University Press, 1978), p. 86.

37. James, *Essays in Religion*, p. 89.

38. Ibid.

39. Ibid.

40. Ibid., p. 92. Obviously, a wide range of mystical experiences could also be included in this list, as could near-death experiences (a tip of the hat to Bob Forman for that last insight).

41. Ibid., p. 93.

42. Ibid.

43. Ibid.

44. Ibid., p. 86.

45. Ibid., p. 87.

46. Ibid.

47. Ibid., p. 95.

48. Ibid., pp. 95–96.

49. Ibid., p. 90.

50. Ibid., p. 92.

51. Ibid., p. 94.

52. Ibid., p. 89.

53. Ibid., pp. 75–76.

54. Ibid., p. 76.

55. James, *Essays in Philosophy*, p. 157.

56. Ibid., pp. 157–58.

57. The term "subconscious" is not Freudian. Freud used the term "unconscious" to refer to the repressed contents of the mind or to indicate the locus of conflicting mental forces that are hidden from our consciousness. James preferred to use the term "subconscious" because he did not believe that anything mental could be simultaneously mental (a form of consciousness) and unconscious (not experienced). James argues that the mental processes of the subconscious *are* experienced, but only on a deeper level of the person's being, by the "wider" or "higher" self.

58. *Essays in Philosophy*, p. 158.

59. Ibid., pp. 158–59.

60. Ibid., p. 159.

61. I first encountered the term "pure consciousness event" in an article by Robert K. C.

Forman, in the book he edited, *The Problem of Pure Consciousness*: (New York: Oxford University Press, 1990), p. 8.

62. The term "transpersonal" in this essay is not meant to be an unqualified statement of support for the positions held by the different theorists in what has come to be called "transpersonal psychology" but rather is meant to be a neutral word that designates something beyond the boundaries we normally associate with the realm of the personal (and yet that may also become manifest in and through the personal realm).

63. It is also perhaps important to clarify the distinction between James's use of the term "transmarginal" and my use of the term "transpersonal." "Transmarginal" is typically a more inclusive term in that for James, transmarginal aspects of consciousness can be *either* "personal" (i.e., the hidden memories, desires, prejudices, and so on, of an individual) *or* "transpersonal" (i.e., those areas of awareness that are not limited to the confines of an individual's psyche but, rather, are rooted in "wider" or "deeper" levels of existence). James tends to use "transmarginal" and "subliminal" as equivalent terms.

64. James, *Varieties*, p. 189.

65. Ibid., p. 190.

66. Ibid., p. 196.

67. Ibid.

68. James, *Essays in Psychical Research*, p. 207.

69. Ibid., p. 204.

70. Ibid., p. 195.

71. Ibid., p. 193.

72. Ibid.

73. Ibid.

74. Ibid., p. 194.

75. Ibid., p. 201.

76. Ibid.

77. Ibid., p. 199.

78. James, *Varieties*, p. 381.

79. Ibid.

80. Ibid., p. 191.

81. Ibid.

82. Ibid., p. 377.

83. Ibid.

84. Ibid., p. 381.

85. Ibid., p. 400.

86. Ibid. There are interesting parallels between this understanding of salvation and Fredrick Streng's notion of religion as "ultimate transformation," in which "an ultimate transformation is a fundamental change from being caught up in the troubles of common existence (sin, ignorance) to living in such a way that one can cope at the deepest level with those troubles. That capacity for living allows one to experience the most authentic or deepest reality—the ultimate." Frederick Streng, *Understanding Religious Life* (Belmont, Calif.: Wadsworth, 1985), p. 2.

87. James, *Varieties*, p. 400.

88. Ibid., p. 401.

89. Ibid. In the *Varieties*, James has not yet fully embraced his later pragmatic understanding of truth, although he is, almost unknowingly, already moving strongly in that direction. From a pragmatic perspective, truth is not an objective quality of something (for instance, the "More"), rather, truth is contingent on that thing's ability to produce observable

effects that can be communally assessed. From the point of view of James's later pragmatism, his apparent opposition in sections of the *Varieties* between the psychological value and the objective truth of the "More" becomes a false dichotomy, since value itself becomes the index of truth.

90. Ibid.

91. Ibid., p. 198.

92. Ibid., p. 403.

93. The experience of this paradoxical union of self and other is perhaps most accented during unitive mystical experiences, a fact that James is quick to underscore, noting the comment by a French author that "when mystical activity is at its height, we find consciousness possessed by the sense of a being at once *excessive* and *identical* with the self: great enough to be God; interior enough to be *me*. The 'objectivity' of it ought in that case to be called *excessivity*, rather, or exceedingness." (Récéjac, *Essai sur les fondements de la connaissance mystique* 1897), p. 46, quoted in James, *Varieties,* p. 401.

94. James, *Varieties*, p. 403. James also recognizes, however, that he does not discuss the "practical difficulties" connected with how someone can come to a direct realization of his or her "higher part," or how that person can manage to maintain an exclusive identification with that "higher" aspect of the self, or, finally, what that person can do to experience this higher aspect of the self as identical with the "more" that exists outside, or beyond, the individual's personality structure. See *Varieties*, p. 400.

95. Ibid., p. 405.

96. Ibid., p. 404.

97. Ibid.

98. Ibid., p. 406.

99. Ibid., p. 408.

100. Ibid., p. 413.

101. Ibid.

102. William James, *A Pluralistic Universe* (Cambridge: Harvard University Press, 1977), p. 64.

103. Ibid., p. 70.

104. Ibid., p. 71.

105. Ibid., p. 81.

106. Ibid., p. 72.

107. See, for instance, Matthew Fox, *Creation Spirituality* (San Francisco: Harper San Francisco, 1991); Thomas Berry, *The Dream of the Earth* (San Francisco: Sierra Books, 1988); J. E. Lovelock, *Gaia* (New York: Oxford University Press, 1987); and Pierre Teilhard de Chardin, *Hymn of the Universe* (New York: Harper and Row, 1965). Henry Corbin also discusses in intricate detail various Persian and Islamic ideas of an earth-angel. See Henry Corbin, *Spiritual Body and Celestial Earth* (Princeton: Princeton University Press, 1977).

108. James, *Pluralistic Universe*, p. 74.

109. Ibid., p. 76.

110. Ibid., pp. 76–77.

111. In fact, James explicitly notes the correspondence between his thought and Fechner's in *Essays on Radical Empiricism*, where he says that since "a pure experience can be postulated with any amount whatever of span or field . . . speculations like Fechner's of an Earth-soul, of wider spans of consciousness enveloping narrower ones throughout the cosmos, are, therefore, philosophically quite in order, provided they distinguish the functional from the entitative point of view, and do not treat the minor consciousness under discussion as a kind of standing material of which the wider ones *consist*." William James, *Essays in Radical Empiricism* (Cambridge: Harvard University Press, 1976), pp. 66–67.

112. James, *Pluralistic Universe*, p. 130.
113. Ibid.
114. *Essays in Philosophy*, pp. 71–72.
115. Myers; *William James*, p. 357.
116. James, *Pluralistic Universe*, p. 72.
117. Ibid., p. 91.
118. Ibid., p. 78.
119. Ibid.
120. Ibid., p. 90.
121. Ibid., p. 132.
122. Ibid., pp. 132–133.
123. Ibid., p. 140.
124. The term "theometaphysical" is meant to refer to formulations that are simultaneously theological and metaphysical in nature.
125. James, *Pluralistic Universe*, p. 140.
126. Ibid.
127. Ibid., p. 138.
128. Ibid., p. 139.
129. Ibid.
130. Ibid.
131. Ibid., p. 140.
132. *Essays in Philosophy*, p. 142. For a detailed account of the methodology that James advocated for the study of religions, see *Varieties*, p. 359.
133. I borrow this term from Eugene Fontinell, an insightful Jamesian scholar. Fontinell uses this term in *Self, God, and Immortality* (Philadelphia: Temple University Press, 1986), p. 10.
134. Ibid., p. 27. This field model of the self and reality is "Jamesian" in its approach, rather than a literal reiteration of every aspect of James's philosophical perspective.
135. Ibid., p. 154.
136. Fontinell stresses that, although it might appear that any sense of personhood would be lost in this onrushing flux, personhood and individuality are possible within this model. Since these fields shift and change at different rates, enough stability and cohesiveness remain in the flux to legitimately speak of individuals, even if we can no longer speak of individuals as self-contained atomistic egos. However, much further philosophical work needs to be done to justify how these different physical, emotional, and mental levels of experience can all be legitimately considered interactive fields. A good start in this direction would be an attempt to reconcile James's radical empiricism with this field notion of the self and reality.
137. Fontinell, *Self, God, and Immortality*, p. 27.
138. Although Gerald Myers claims that James fails to establish the validity of his analogy between the compounding of consciousness in our individual states of consciousness and the conflux of consciousnesses within the cosmic self since "there is no experience that indicates that we can literally experience ourselves being at once both ourselves and others," he is either unaware of the numerous accounts of mystical experience that make just this very claim, or he discounts their validity. See Myers, *William James*, p. 360.
139. "Nondual" does not mean "monistic." Nonduality is more apophatic than monism; that is, a nondual understanding of the self and reality claims that all metaphysical proposals, including its own, are invariably metaphorical, unlike monism, which typically argues that its claims about the oneness of existence are literally true.
140. This nondual Jamesian field model of the self and reality has much in common with Ken Wilber's notion of holons. For more details on Wilber's controversial yet intriguing

perspective, see Ken Wilber, *Sex, Ecology, Spirituality* (Boston: Shambhala Publications, 1995).

141. Fontinell brings up many thoughtful comments on the tensions between a Jamesian field model of the self and reality and James's doctrine of pure experience. While appreciative of the subtlety of many of Fontinell's observations, I am more optimistic about the possibility of a philosophical reconciliation between James's notion of pure experience and a Jamesian field model (a reconciliation that James himself never explicitly attempted). See Fontinell, *Self, God, and Immortality*, pp. 32–43.

142. I explore some of the ethical implications of this field model of the self and reality in chapter 4 of *Exploring Unseen Worlds*: *William James and the Philosophy of Mysticism* (Albany: SUNY Press, 1997).

143. I recognize that the categories of "theism," "monism," and "polytheism," are overly simplistic, but these remarks are meant to be suggestive, not comprehensive. Furthermore, I take the coward's way out and simply refuse to discuss several other viable philosophical alternatives such as numerous Buddhist options, as well as the contributions of numerous psychoanalytic, sociological, and economic theories. I suggest, however, that a field conception of the self and reality could be harmonized with important aspects of each of these philosophical alternatives, but such an endeavor, even in its broadest outlines, would take us far afield from our present discussion.

144. For an illuminating discussion of the role of māyā in Advaita Vedānta, as well as a thoughtful discussion of the philosophical implications of different Eastern nondual systems of thought, see David Loy, *Nonduality* (New Haven: Yale University Press, 1988).

145. Fontinell, *Self, God, and Immortality*, p. 137.

PART III

THE PHILOSOPHY OF THE INNATE CAPACITY

NINE

Innate Mystical Capacities and the Nature of the Self

ANTHONY N. PEROVICH JR.

"SHUT YOUR EYES, and change to and wake another way of seeing, which everyone has but few use."[1] Plotinus, understood in the context provided by the spiritually charged atmosphere of Neoplatonism and of his own writings, here endorses the idea that an innate capacity for mystical union is possessed by all of us. (He sounds as well the frequently accompanying note in mystical writers decrying the neglect of this capacity's development.) It is an idea that was to be repeated by an imposing succession of spiritual authors in the West, and by comparable authors elsewhere.

To speak of such an innate capacity is to enter the realm of what might be called "mystical anthropology." Unlike an account of the object of the mystic quest, mystical anthropology aims at offering a description of the human subject insofar as he or she is fitted for carrying out this endeavor. It is a commonplace that the mystic encounter with its object[2] has been described differently in different firsthand reports, resulting in various efforts to classify the different types of encounter. One may dismiss, as adopting a too simplified account of the relation between experience and the conceptual framework associated with a particular religious tradition, the scholarship that suggests a separate type of encounter for each mystico-religious community or approach.[3] Even so, there remain more substantive attempts to offer a typology that distinguishes the different sorts of object that mystics seem to have engaged.[4] Expressions like "*the* innate capacity" suggest that similar questions need to be raised in the realm of mystical anthropology. And once we ask them, we shall find that the writings of the mystics also generate the need for a typology that distinguishes among different accounts of the mystical subject and of its capacities for union. Moreover, we shall also find it useful to raise questions, corresponding to concerns about the proper understanding of the varying descriptions of the mystical "object," about whether the different accounts of the subject spring from genuinely different experiences of the self or from different interpretations of the same experience.

Writers on the topic of mysticism have often been taken to task for too quickly identifying what may be distinct sorts of experience of the mystical "object." However, students of this subject area are often ready to suggest a uniform account of the subject as well. For example, corresponding to W. T. Stace's well-known view that different instances of "introvertive" mysticism are all fundamentally alike is his endorsement of an account of the self that holds constant for all such instances. In the introvertive mystical experience, the empirical content of the empirical ego is stripped away, revealing a pure ego, which Stace identifies both with the Kantian transcendental unity of apperception and the Universal Self of the Upaniṣads. He subsequently concludes that this self may appropriately be identified with God.[5] This view that the mystical experience of the self is uniformly that of a deeper self, always there yet often hidden by the superficial empirical self, is certainly not unique to Stace but is found in the writings of both earlier and later students of the mystics as well, although some stop short of identifying this deeper self with God and limit themselves to the claim that this is the point in the soul where God dwells. Thus, Louis Dupré offers a similar view of the self as belonging to the essence of (religious) mysticism, while suggesting that, for the Christian at least, this self is to be understood only as our point of contact with the divine:

> For the mystical consciousness, at least implicitly, assumes that, underneath the familiar succession of sensations and reflections, a more permanent self rests in which space and time are transformed into vistas of an inner realm with its own rhythms and perspectives. Full self-knowledge must reach to that deeper dimension hidden below the ordinary consciousness with which we work, talk, and study. . . . To this deeper self the mystical experience gives access.
>
> For the Christian it is the point where God and the soul touch, the divine basis on which human selfhood rests.[6]

Hence, while Stace exhibits monistic and Dupré theistic tendencies, their conceptions of the self have much in common: there is a permanent, though typically obscured, aspect of ourselves that is revealed to the mystical consciousness in an experience that introduces us not just to our authentic selves but to God as well.

Such claims about the mystical "subject" call for the same sort of investigation as do those concerning the mystical "object." Just as we can ask whether different descriptions of the encountered object of the mystical quest are best interpreted as descriptions of different experiences of the object of that search or indeed as accounts of entirely different "mystical objects," so we can ask whether different descriptions of the subject of that quest are best interpreted as descriptions of different experiences of that search's subject or, indeed, as accounts of entirely different "mystical subjects." I suggest that, while the accounts of Stace and Dupré capture *one* view of the self encountered in some mystical texts, there are also incompatible views of the self that are encountered in the writings of other mystics, incompatible views that seem to be rooted in quite distinct experiences.

The classificatory scheme I offer is not comprehensive in the sense that it will illuminate all mystical writings. To begin with, there are traditions that do not take the self to be real in the way that is presupposed in the following discussion. My typology offers nothing more than a preliminary framework for understanding views that are advanced in some of the texts that are committed to the reality of the self. Indeed, my examples are more limited than even these remarks suggest and are drawn for the most part from the Christian mystical tradition. I do not presume to exhaust all that can be said even here but intend simply to draw some distinctions that seem to me to be helpful for making sense of what some different mystics have had to say about the nature of the self. It does seem to me, however, that this outline of mystical anthropology, however sketchy and incomplete, is of some use in clarifying the idea of an innate human capacity for mystical experience.

There are two points on which our attention to the conceptions of the innate mystical capacities of the self shall focus: the characterizations of the self uncovered in descriptions of the transition from ordinary to mystical consciousness and the characterizations of the self uncovered in descriptions of mystical union. We may think of the former as the "capacity *by* which," focusing on the ability of the self to achieve this transition, and of the latter as the "capacity *for* which," focusing on the sort of enjoyment of the mystical "object" of which the self is capable. The former concerns the capacity that enables the self to approach and unite with its goal, whereas the latter concerns the sort of enjoyment of the goal the self is capable of achieving. It should be understood that throughout the course of my discussion, when I speak of mystical experience I have in mind what has come to be called (following Stace, who in turn is influenced in his terminology by Underhill and who influences Wainwright and numerous others) "introvertive" experience.

1. "*The innate capacity by which*" Mystical consciousness, however else it may be characterized, is strikingly different from ordinary awareness. Thus, mystical experience requires a transition from our everyday forms of experience, and it is perhaps unsurprising that this transition is thought to disclose not only new objects of awareness beyond the ken of more mundane experience but also new aspects of the self as well. I call those transitions "revelatory" in regard to the self when they are thought to reveal a self that existed in the past (although perhaps hidden for long stretches of our conscious life) as the current (mystical) experience now shows it to exist. Such a transition does not change the character of the self but, rather, reveals its true nature by stripping away an obscuring surface. The self revealed has been there all along. (Indeed, if we took seriously Stace's identification of the pure ego with Kant's transcendental unity of apperception, the self revealed would have been tacitly present in or presupposed by all experience, even the most humble, as its

necessary precondition.) The transition means only that what was formerly concealed is now made manifest but not that what was formerly concealed has altered in becoming manifest. Because this deeper self is typically alleged to stand in an intimate connection with God,[7] a connection that is thought by some to constitute identity, the revelation of it constitutes an important stage on the mystical path. On this view of things, the "innate capacity by which" mystical union becomes possible resides in the access every person has to a deeper self, which in turn permits access to God (if the deeper self is not regarded as itself divine).[8]

On the other hand, I call those transitions "transformative" in regard to the self when they are thought to involve a transformation of the self in the course of the shift from ordinary to mystical consciousness. The self is itself in a process of becoming, and mystical experience marks its development, so in a very real sense the self as it is encountered there has come into being along with the experience itself. Indeed, it may be the case that here "the transformation of the self" and "the mystical experience" simply are alternative ways of describing the same phenomenon. This, then, is a case not of the hidden revealed but of the metamorphosis of what was already present. In this case, the "innate capacity by which" mystical union becomes possible resides in the ability that all of us have to transform ourselves or to be transformed and by this transformation to gain access to God.

2. "*The innate capacity for which*" The mystical life is typically thought to involve a sequence of stages, although accounts of the pathway vary, of course. However, it is also typical for the mystical life to be viewed as culminating in a highest level, although again there are disagreements about how what is taken to be the ultimate phase is most accurately to be described. I want to focus on that ultimate condition (which, following tradition, I call "mystical union") only as regards the self and, moreover, to ask only one question regarding it: Is it characteristic of the self to find the highest level of mystical fulfillment and satisfaction in rest and attainment or in growth and activity—that is, is its supreme condition to be understood in terms of finality or of dynamism?

In the one case, the state of union is that of repose in an attained goal, a state that is frequently taken to involve the absence of any of those qualitative characteristics whose variation seem to be a prerequisite for any experience of change. Moreover, the often-remarked-upon lack of temporality in such states apparently makes it impossible for the self involved in such union to be engaged in any sort of development whatsoever. In this case, then, the ultimate unitive condition is one of attainment by the self at the endpoint of its journey: having achieved union, perhaps by an arduous ascent, the soul goes no further because there is nowhere further for it to go. It has reached its goal, the state of final satisfaction for a self of its character, and thus its desire is not to travel on but to rejoice over what it has attained. The self's "innate capacity for" finding in this sort of mystical state its ultimate fulfillment can be termed its capacity for "final union."

In the other case, union is thought to consist not in repose and attainment but in continuous development and progress: the condition of union is a dynamic one in which the mystical life is not thought to have an end-point in the sense of a place where the soul is ultimately at rest, but, rather, union is compatible with and even involves the perpetual growth of the soul. Selves with an "innate capacity for" supreme fulfillment in this type of ultimate mystical experience I call selves subject to "dynamic union."

Of the four possible combinations of types of innate capacities—(1) by a revelatory transition to a final union, (2) by a revelatory transition to a dynamic union, (3) by a transformative transition to a final union, and (4) by a transformative transition to a dynamic union—I am unfamiliar only with instances of the second combination. While such a case may be possible, revelatory transitions so typically uncover a self and a God freed from the temporal constraints of the ordinary self that a dynamic union is not perhaps to be expected here. In any case, I limit my discussion to the other three combinations of mystical capacities of the self, which do seem to be represented in the literature.

1. *The self as subject to a revelatory transition and a final union.* This, as earlier comments suggested, is the account of the self that philosophers like Stace regard as the uniform experience of introvertive mystics. While I argue that some descriptions of introvertive mystical experience suggest other views of the self, I do believe that this version is very widespread among Western and non-Western mystics alike. It is, for example, the view that I believe is encountered in Śankara. Indeed, what is called "mysticism of the soul"[9] (of which Śankara is thought to be a leading representative) is in many ways an especially clear version of the conception of the self under discussion here, although perhaps the condition described by "union" could in pure mysticism of the soul be more aptly characterized by a different term. "Union" becomes a more appropriate term when an effort is made to distinguish between God and the soul, even when by "soul" we mean this deeper, true self. Whether such a distinction is made sharply enough or is even made at all is a question that arises for a Christian mystic like Meister Eckhart, in whose writings, to use Otto's phrase, mysticism of the soul is overlaid by the mysticism of God. Without focusing on such issues, we can in Eckhart find an account of the self that combines what I have called a revelatory transition with final union.

Only by annihilating the empirical self through detachment do we discover our true self, to which Eckhart refers by means of a set of related terms ("the ground of the soul," "the spark," "a light in the soul"); otherwise, this deeper self can remain unknown. "In the nobleman, just as in God's image, God's son, the seed of divine nature can never be destroyed in us though it may be covered up. . . . The true light shines in the darkness though we may be unaware of it (cf. John, 1:5)."[10] Becoming aware of one's true or deeper self does not amount to bringing it into being or even producing any change in it, for Eckhart's Neoplatonism led him to affirm the virtual existence of the ground of the soul in God Himself.[11] Thus he affirms the eternal character of the true self: "But in my breaking-through, where I stand free of my own will, of God's will, of all His works, and of God Himself, *then* I am above all creatures and am neither God nor creature, but I am that which I was and shall remain forevermore."[12] Of course, God's ground is not left behind, for, as already stated, mysticism of the soul is here overlaid with the mysticism of God, and indeed Eckhart identifies God's ground and the soul's ground.[13] However, as regards the character of that ground, it is clear that the experience of a timeless self that is revealed as it "was and shall remain forevermore" is an experience describable in terms of what I have called a revelatory transition. This first aspect, the mystical revelation of a deeper self, has been well captured by Otto in his account of Eckhart's mysticism of the soul: "Deeply hidden 'within' is something ultimate, pure, inward, entirely separate from all that is outward. . . . It is a 'Self'. . . ." Only when the superficial ego "is brushed aside as alien and false" does one "attain the selfhood of the soul."[14] Further, by means of our innate capacity to uncover this true self, we are able to attain to a final union with God in "eternal rest and bliss":[15]

> Therefore, I say, if a man turns away from self and from all created things, then . . . you will attain to oneness and blessedness in your soul's spark, which time and place never touched. . . . This light is not content with the simple changeless divine being which neither gives nor takes: rather it seeks to know whence *this* being comes, it wants to get into its simple ground, into the silent desert into which no distinction ever peeped, of Father, Son or Holy Ghost. In the innermost part, where none is at home, *there* that light finds satisfaction, and there it is more one than it is in itself: for this ground is an impartible stillness, motionless in itself. . . .[16]

It is worth noting, in preparation for the accounts to come, that the revelatory transition to a final union presupposes a distinction between at least two "selves": the deeper self and the self that is the locus of consciousness. (If we admit an "empirical self" as what is stripped away to reveal the "true self" [e.g., the "turning away from self" in the passage just cited], there may be a need to posit yet a third self.) The conscious self needs to be distinguished from the deeper self if the latter is frequently hidden from and inaccessible to the former. This is at least implicit in the writers we have looked at and is quite explicit in an author like Teresa of Avila. In memorable fashion she describes the deeper self, which at its heart is in contact with God, by asking us to "consider our soul to be like a castle made entirely out of a diamond or of very clear crystal, in which there are many rooms, just as in heaven there are many dwelling places," and urging us to look "toward the center, which is the room or royal chamber where the King stays."[17] Completing this standard picture, Teresa insists that the interior castle of our soul is often hidden from us: "For there are many souls who . . . don't care at all about entering the castle, nor do they know what lies within that most precious place, nor who is within it, nor even how many rooms it has."[18] In this passage, and throughout the rest of the book as well, Teresa then proceeds to speak of the soul as something that enters into these dwelling places, and it is clear that in this usage she is identifying the soul not with the deeper self ("the interior castle") but with the conscious self. Her usage of the term "soul" for both perplexes even her ("It seems I'm saying something foolish. For if this castle is the soul, clearly one doesn't have to enter it since it is within oneself"[19]), but it is a usage that this view invites by its need to distinguish the doctrine of the deeper, hidden self from the conscious self. The views to be considered next, by attributing a transformational capacity to the self, avoid this distinction and regard the individual's mystical life simply in terms of developments involving the conscious self.

2. *The self as subject to a transformative transition and a final union.* This is a self that must continually transform itself on its route to the goal that it aspires to but whose self-transformation halts on attainment of union. Plato Mamo suggests that an example of the conception of the mystical self as moving toward mystical union by means of what I have called an innate capacity for "transformative transition" can be found in Plotinus.[20] According to such a view, the ego is to be described as "polyvalent," as "endlessly oscillating," as a "fluctuating focus."[21] On this view, the ontological status of the ego is determined by the "object" of awareness. Thus, the ego, in leaving the Plotinian soul behind and successively contemplating the Intellect and the One, becomes each in turn. As Plotinus writes, "different souls look at different things and are and become what they look at."[22] Consequently, in writing of the ascent of consciousness from the level of soul to that of the Intellect, Mamo states,

> The soul is not an individual thing having a stable nature. "Soul" is a label for a variety of psychic and intellectual activities characterized by a "scattering" in time. When consciousness returns to the stage of pure *noesis* it is no longer soul, it has become *Nous*. The nature of the subject is precisely determined by the noetic stage. Having been established in the divine *Nous* we are no longer men.[23]

And the ego's subsequent transition from the Intellect to the One exhibits the same characteristic: "His experience defines the level of his existence and now, when he sees the formless, he becomes another and not himself. . . . The self is obliterated."[24] Statements to the effect that the nature of the subject itself, its very level of existence, is determined and defined by the level of the Plotinian universe to which it has ascended are common enough in Plotinus[25] and offer us a very different conception of the mystical self from what we encountered earlier. Here we find a self that may accurately be characterized as fluctuating in its very nature. No longer are we dealing with the revelation of what I truly am and forever have been at a deep, if formerly hidden, level. On the contrary, we are to understand here the ascent of a mobile, changeable self that becomes what it comes to know as it comes to know it. As the self comes to know the Intellect, it is no longer soul but has itself become Intellect instead, and as it comes to know the One it is no longer Intellect but has itself become the One. The self is not here discovering truths about itself that were formerly obscured but is the witness to the coming into being of new truths about what it itself is or, better, about what it has become.[26]

It should perhaps be noted in passing that, just as the prior category admitted both monistic and theistic versions, there is nothing about this category that demands a monistic position. For example, Augustine perhaps represents a theistic position that combines a transformative transition with a final union.

If the self of Plotinus is mobile and changing, if the transition from ordinary to mystical consciousness (a transition that can, as seen from this example, be a complex development) is one that involves an innate capacity for self-transformation, it is also the case that the self of Plotinus is one that does not find its highest satisfaction in alteration itself. On the contrary, it is the nature of the Plotinian self to rest once the goal is attained. The self that attains the Neoplatonic goal is not one to whom change is intrinsic but one that develops only because it is far from its source and seeks to return home. Once home, become the One, the self is changeless, for change could only lead it away from what it has sought and at last has found.

The culmination of the mystical life is a "pressing toward contact and rest," a possibility only for the self whose innate capacity is for what I have called a "final union." The mystic who has achieved this union

> was one himself, with no distinction in himself either in relation to himself or to other things—for there was no movement in him and he had no emotion, no desire for anything else when he had made the ascent—but there was not even any reason or thought, and he himself was not there [i.e., the self had undergone a transformative transition], if we must even say this; but he was as if carried away or possessed by a god, in a quiet solitude and a state of calm, not turning away anywhere in his being and not busy about himself, altogether at rest and becoming a kind of rest.[27]

3. *The self as subject to a transformative transition and a dynamic union.* The third view of the self is the most thoroughly dynamic one. Not only does the transition from ordinary to mystical consciousness signal a transformation of the conscious ego rather than a revelation of a deeper self, but also the self is so constituted as to find supreme mystical fulfillment in its continued transformation, rather than the enjoyment that comes with final attainment, the stillness that accompanies repose. A representation of this self, whose innate capacities exhibit a double dynamism, is found in the writings of Gregory of Nyssa.

According to Gregory, it belongs to our very nature to change, and the whole of our spiritual life is to be understood in terms of perpetual transformation. As Daniélou writes, this transmutation effected by the Spirit "is not only a decisive factor, but is constitutive of man's very being. For him [Gregory] the *physis*, the 'reality' of man is not to *be* spiritual, but continously to *become* so. In this sense *Wandlung* is the very reality of man."[28] If change is intrinsic to human nature, not only should the "innate capacity by which" mystical union is achieved involve transformation, but we might also expect ourselves to possess an "innate capacity for" a mystical union that is transformative as well. We should then expect to find that Gregory follows the account just offered of Plotinian transformative transition but that he deviates from Plotinus by depicting an unresting self whose spiritual life is one of endless growth. Indeed, this is precisely what Gregory reports.

The soul is by nature changeable because it is a living mirror that receives the likeness of whatever it looks upon, becoming substantially transformed in the process.[29] In terms that recall Plotinus's essay on beauty, Gregory urges us to remove the grime from the soul.[30] The cleansed soul then becomes able to reflect and thereby to be transformed into the Divine:

> Our souls cannot be united with God in any other way than by purity and incorruptibility. For the soul in that state is truly like God; and she will be able to attain to Him Whom she resembles by placing herself, like a mirror, beneath His purity; then will she transform her own beauty by a participation and reflection of that archetypal Good.[31]

On this view, mystical technique aims not at revealing a deeper self but at purifying our only self—the changeable self—so that our likeness to ultimate reality can come about. Like Plotinus in emphasizing the transformation of the self, Gregory nevertheless differs from him in terms of the explanatory principles adduced, at least in his later writings. For Plotinus, purification is a process of simplification and unification; as these are achieved, the two principles of "like knows like" and "knowledge (experience) defines the level of existence" come into play, bringing about the transformation without requiring any involvement on the part of what is known. For Gregory, purification is a matter of self-cleansing that (rather than triggering our transformation into the One or revealing a deeper self where God resides) is part of the act of divine grace whereby God allows Himself to be reflected in us. In the passage from the early *On Virginity* just quoted, the principle of "like knows like" can be seen to be still operative, but, as Endre von Ivánka has pointed out, in Gregory's more mature thought our transformation includes our achievement of likeness, an achievement that is only realized through divine involvement:

> Therefore, as far as the knowledge of God is concerned, the old principle, "Like is known by like," which was still employed in *De virginitate* in the sense of the purified soul's natural similarity to God . . . is thus reinterpreted in the sense that it is grace, i.e., the activity of the Holy Spirit, that first *makes* the soul similar to God. . . . When the soul turns into itself it therefore sees God not because he dwells essentially in it and is visible in its essence as soon as the latter is purified of everything foreign, but rather therefore because turning away from the external and toward the spiritual is itself already love of God and similarity to God, because it comes from God, and because that love makes the one who loves similar to the beloved object.[32]

Whatever differences there may be from Plotinus in terms of the factors governing the change, be they divine grace or more anonymous laws of mystical anthropology, Gregory and Plotinus are at one in their affirmation of a dynamic conception of the self that is transformed as it grows in knowledge of and union with the divine. As Gregory writes,

> So too now, when the Word calls a soul that has advanced to come unto Him, it is immediately empowered at His command and becomes what the Bridegroom wishes. It is transformed into something divine, and it is *transformed from the glory* in which it exists to a higher glory by a perfect kind of alteration.[33]

As alike as Gregory and Plotinus are in sharing a view of what we are here calling capacities of "transformative transition," they nevertheless differ in their accounts of the capacities of the self in regard to its highest condition. We have seen that for Plotinus, the self undergoes transformation as the only way of returning home, but, once home, its development ceases as it seeks and finds only repose in its proper resting place: to paraphrase Augustine only slightly, the self is restless and changing only until it finds rest and an end to transformation in the One. Here Gregory differs quite strikingly, for in his view human nature is mutable and prone to change and is indeed ever changing.[34] This evokes Gregory's doctrine of the spiritual life as a life of unceasing progress, of perpetual growth. While participation in the divine nature is possible for us, God's transcendence means that sharing, while real, leaves God unencompassed: "The soul grows by its constant participation in that which transcends it; and yet the perfection in which the soul shares remains ever the same, and is always discovered by the soul to be transcendent to the same degree."[35] This is a comment not so much on God's unwillingness to share Himself with us as a comment on our finitude; of greatest interest here, however, is the notion that each level of our fullest sharing in the divine engenders an increased capacity in us for participation. As Daniélou remarks,

> The soul's desire is at each moment fulfilled. The soul is a potency; and this potency is fulfilled by its participation in God, and in this way it attains some perfection, some completion. . . . But this participation expands the soul further and makes it capable of a still higher degree of participation.[36]

Thus, union for Gregory is never final but a life of perpetual change and development. This means for him that it belongs to the character of the self to find not rest in God but only ceaseless growth, for, as we have seen, it belongs to human nature to be ever changing. In this context, what is being affirmed is that the mystical life involves a transformation of the self not only in its transitional phase but in its unitive phase, or, as Daniélou writes, "every stage of spiritual growth is another creation accomplished by the Spirit."[37] And this view produces yet another distinctive mystical conception of the innate capacities of the self—a view, incidentally, that in positing the eternal transcendence of God is compatible only with an experience that is theistic (or at least dualistic), never with one that is monistic.

One question to which distinguishing among these three different conceptions gives rise is whether they help us distinguish among different types of mystical experience. The distinction between experience and its interpretation has, of course, dominated much philosophical discussion of mysticism, and I now briefly discuss a few cases that may suggest where my attempted typology of the mystical self may be helpful in differentiating among types of experience.

Let us begin with a comparison of different views of the experience of Plotinus and Gregory and relate our distinctions concerning the nature of the self to the dispute. E. R. Dodds has maintained that Gregory was familiar with at least some of Plotinus's writings and found in them a descriptive vocabulary that he himself subsequently employed. However, he also believes that Gregory found the Plotinian vocabulary apt because he had shared the Plotinian mystical experience. Their main difference, he thinks, is the theoretical one that we have already mentioned: that for Gregory active divine involvement is required for the possibility of our spiritual life in a way that it is not for Plotinus.

> This insistence on the intervention of grace seems to be the main feature which distinguishes Gregory's mysticism from that of Plotinus. In their account of mystical union the two writers agree closely, and I find it hard to accept Daniélou's claim that this agreement in language "conceals wholly different realities." Like Plotinus, Gregory describes it as an awakening from the body, or an ascent to a place of watch; as in Plotinus, it is less a vision than an awareness of the divine presence; as in Plotinus the soul becomes simple and unified, and takes on the quality of light, being identical with what it apprehends. I think Gregory had enjoyed the same experience as Plotinus.[38]

On the other hand, C. W. Macleod, in calling attention to some characteristics that led us to distinguish Plotinus's and Gregory's conceptions of the self, insists on the fundamental dissimilarity of their experiences:

> The mystical teaching of these two writers is thoroughly different. Plotinus' way culminates in a supreme intuition (*hypernoesis*, as he once calls it in *Enn*. vi. 8.16) of the One where all duality is done away with: Gregory's has no summit at all, it is an ever more rigorous striving after (*epektasis*) a God whose infinity sets him beyond intuition no less than beyond knowledge; in so far as Gregory conceives of a consummation, it is God-likeness, not union or vision.[39]

Some of our prior discussion can help lessen the distance between these two positions. Insofar as the topic concerns the self's capacity for transformation as it ascends to the Divine, we have seen that the experience of the two is very much alike and that this similarity in characterization of the transition may be behind some of Dodd's perceived similarities, such as the shared awakening from the body, the ascent to a place of watch, and the being (for both Plotinus and Gregory, the preceding suggests that we should replace "being" here with "becoming") identical with what the self apprehends. Insofar as the topic concerns the self's capacity for union with the Divine, we have seen the views of Gregory and Plotinus diverge, and this difference in the characterization of union may be behind some of Macleod's perceived distinctions, such as the lack of duality in the case of Plotinus in contrast to the constant awareness of God's transcendence leading to endless striving on Gregory's account. (Macleod finds even the expression "union" inappropriate in Gregory's case, but if Gregory is speaking of genuine participation in the divine nature, "union"—though not, of course, Plotinian union—seems to me entirely apt.) Thus, some of the difference of opinion between Dodds and Macleod may be due to their focusing on different aspects of the self's mystical life related to different mystical capacities that the above account helps distinguish; if so, we may see how the account offered here may help reconcile some clashes over the issue of sameness of experience. The difference between Plotinus and Gregory that remains concerns the conceptions of the highest condition of which each self is capable, and a difference here does seem to entail experiential differences. This is so because being subject to "final union" and being characterized by perpetual change and consequently subject to "dynamic union" are characteristics of the self that have distinct phenomenological consequences. Thus, it seems clear that at least one of the distinctions I have drawn points in its instances to different sorts of mystical experience.

By contrast, it does not seem so clear that the other distinction has such clear experiential import. One must be careful here to remember that the focus of our discussion has been on alternative *conceptions* of the self. The difference between the revelatory and the transformative transition does not lie in the fact that in the former case we are speaking about some deeper aspect of one's being, ordinarily hidden to consciousness, whereas in the latter case we are speaking of consciousness itself. After all, the mystic of the revelatory transition certainly does not ignore consciousness or its mystical development. But granting that all mystics acknowledge a transition in states of awareness in the course of mystical experience, we have considered here how mystics have used different conceptions of the self to understand that transition. What we have seen is that some understand that transition as the emergence from obscurity of a self that stands in contrast to and lies behind the self of ordinary consciousness; others understand it as the growth, development, and transformation of the self that is found in ordinary consciousness, behind which no hidden self lurks in obscurity. These are fundamentally different conceptions of the self, and it has been part of my aim to try to draw a distinction between them.

Nevertheless, an interesting question that arises here is whether the different conceptions of the self found in the revelatory and transformative transitions relate to different experiences or simply to differing interpretations of an identical phenomenological datum. I see no reason to assume that, in the mystical sphere, wherever alternative conceptual structures are brought to experience, they necessarily result in distinct experiences.[40] Thus, there is no a priori reason that the different conceptions of the self's transitions identified here must correspond (experientially) to different sorts of "mystical self-awareness."

It is not as easy to settle this question as it was the corresponding one asked in regard to the self and its capacities for mystical union. In that case, a self destined for a final union and a self that is changeable and ever changing by nature seemed to require different sorts of experience in which to realize their highest condition. The former self experiences fulfillment in attainment and repose, whereas the dynamic union of the latter is impossible to conceive in these terms. The difference between these two conceptions of the self seemed to have phenomenological consequences.

Still, might not the experience described by one mystic as the emergence of the hidden, true self be identical to that described by another as the self becoming something it formerly was not? After all, it does not seem that the formerly hidden state of the self could itself be a phenomenological feature of the experience. So might not the experience here be the same in both cases? Perhaps. If it is, the *conceptual* distinction between selves subject to revelatory transitions and those subject to transformative ones is not a distinction that carries phenomenological import. On the other hand, Western mystics of the revealed, deeper self regularly affirm an intimate connection[41] between that self and God: Eckhart asserts that the soul's ground and God's ground are the same, Ruusbroec that our innermost essence is in God, Teresa that God resides in the central dwelling place of the interior castle. If the transition to this sort of mystical consciousness involves a "double transcendence" (such that one's awareness of the deeper self is not merely coupled with an awareness of God but such that one becomes aware of a deeper self that is intrinsically bound up with God, for example, via the exemplarism of Ruusbroec), then there may well be good sense in the notion of experiencing the revelation of a deeper self. God presumably is not experienced as one whom our new awareness brings into being, and if the self is experienced as sufficiently close to God, then it will not be experienced as brought into being with our new awareness, either. The self of the transformative transition does not seem to be so closely connected with God or the awareness of God, and uncovering such a connection does not seem to be an intrinsic part of the experience.[42] Such considerations suggest that there may be an experiential difference at the root of this distinction after all.[43]

The fundamental conclusion regarding the innate capacity to draw from my attempt to formulate some distinctions among mystical conceptions of the self is that there is no single teaching from the mystics about a capacity for mystical union. Insofar as the self is differently conceived, the human capacity for such union is going to be differently conceived as well. The capacity of a self subject to a revelatory transition and a final union will be an ability to reestablish conscious connection with one's deeper self and, via that self, to find rest in union with God. The capacity of a self subject to a transformative transition and a final union will be an ability to become what it contemplates, its highest state being achieved when it contemplates what is highest; final union is possible because its capacity for self-transformation is unlimited. The capacity of a self subject to a transformative transition and a dynamic union will be an ability to become what it contemplates, with one proviso: it is never able to lose its finitude, and, thus, its capacity to "become the infinite" is always partial and its life an unexhausted expansion into the unlimited. In short, the way in which any innate mystical capacity is to be conceived is definitely relative to the conception of the self that has the capacity.

As these types show, it is useful to distinguish different capacities in each self. For each conception of the self, we have attended to features connected with the transition from ordinary to mystical consciousness, as well as to ones connected with the ultimate unitive stage that the self attains. It seems that we are drawing attention to different capacities, or at least to different aspects of the same capacity. For example, the capacity for a transformative transition is a different capacity from that for a final union. (Indeed, we have seen the former combined with a capacity for dynamic union in the case of Gregory of Nyssa, so the two must be distinct.) However, it seems that both are required for such a self to attain its mystical goal. This suggests that discussions of the "innate capacity" must recognize that such an idea denotes a complex of capacities in each self.

Finally, one should not conclude that difference of capacities necessarily translates into difference of techniques for the activation of these capacities. All the figures discussed in any detail in this essay belong in some sense to the Neoplatonic tradition, and in all of them standard themes of withdrawal and purification are found. But, of course, what our discussion suggests is that the techniques accomplish something different in each case.

Notes

1. Plotinus, *Enneads*, trans. A. H. Armstrong, rev. ed., 7 vols. (Cambridge, Mass.: Harvard University Press, 1966–1989); I.6.8., vol. 1, p. 259. Plato had already insisted (*Republic*, 518c) that the ability to gaze on the higher, nonsensible realm of the Forms is the birthright of all. Plotinus, of course, includes not only the capacity to ascend to this level in his account of the self but also the capacity to go beyond it. Standard accounts of Plotinus's thought, such as Émile Bréhier (*The Philosophy of Plotinus*, trans. Joseph Thomas [Chicago: University of Chicago Press, 1958]), and John M. Rist (*Plotinus: The Road to Reality* [Cambridge: Cambridge University Press, 1967], acknowledge his mysticism as integral to Plotinus's thought. For a recent, nonmystical account of Plotinus's philosophy, see Lloyd P. Gerson, *Plotinus* (London: Routledge, 1994), especially chap. 10, sec. 3 ("Mysticism and Philosophy"), pp. 218–224.

2. Linguistic convenience favors the use of the intentional idiom—for example, "the mystical 'object,'" "objects of awareness"—even where it may not be strictly appropriate, but it is perhaps sufficient to acknowledge this fact without undertaking the exertions required to avoid in every case possibly misleading locutions.

3. The reference, of course, is to a view most recently and prominently exhibited in the writings of Steven Katz. See the collections edited by him—*Mysticism and Philosophical Analysis* (New York: Oxford University Press, 1978), *Mysticism and Religious Traditions* (New York: Oxford University Press, 1983), and *Mysticism and Language* (New York: Oxford University Press, 1992)—and in particular Katz's own articles in these volumes. For a discussion of the problems inherent in this position, see the articles collected in Robert K. C. Forman, ed., *The Problem of Pure Consciousness* (New York: Oxford University Press, 1990). In addition to my contribution to this volume, I have also criticized this approach in "Mysticism and the Philosophy of Science," *Journal of Religion* 65, no. 1 (1985): 63–82, and in "Mysticism or Mediation: A Response to Gill," *Faith and Philosophy* 2, no. 2 (1985): 179–188.

4. Important older accounts that undertake such a typology are R. C. Zaehner, *Mysticism: Sacred and Profane* (London: Oxford University Press, 1957), and W. T. Stace, *Mysticism*

and Philosophy (London: Macmillan, 1960). A valuable recent effort is William J. Wainwright, *Mysticism: A Study of Its Nature, Cognitive Value and Moral Implications* (Madison: University of Wisconsin Press, 1981), and some useful brief remarks can be found in the section "The 'Object' of Mystical Awareness" in Paul Mommaers and Jan Van Bragt, *Mysticism: Buddhist and Christian. Encounters with Jan van Ruusbroec* (New York: Crossroad, 1995), pp. 45–49. While I have raised some questions about the project of developing such typologies in "Fichte and the Typology of Mysticism" in *Fichte: Historical Contexts/Contemporary Controversies*, ed. Daniel Breazeale and Tom Rockmore (Atlantic Highlands, N.J.: Humanities Press, 1994), pp. 128–141, it is certainly a worthwhile undertaking, and Wainwright seems to me to do the job most satisfactorily. In any event, I will bracket those reservations in this paper, for they do not affect the typological points about the self that I discuss.

5. For the identification of the pure ego with the transcendental unity of apperception, which is normally hidden and which holds together the manifold of the stream of consciousness (i.e., the empirical ego), see Stace, *Mysticism and Philosophy*, p. 87; for its identification with the Universal Self, see p. 90; for its identification with God, see p. 182. I return to some of these points—the distinction between the subject of consciousness and the deeper self and the relation of that deeper self to God—later.

6. Louis Dupré, *The Deeper Life: An Introduction to Christian Mysticism* (New York: Crossroad Publishing, 1981), p. 24. See also chapter 8 ("The Mystical Experience of the Self") of Dupré's *Transcendent Selfhood: The Loss and Rediscovery of the Inner Life* (New York: Seabury Press, 1976), pp. 92–104. For earlier statements of a similar view, see Evelyn Underhill, *Mysticism* (New York: E. P. Dutton, [1911] 1961) and Aldous Huxley, *The Perennial Philosophy* (Cleveland: World Publishing, [1944] 1962).

7. Because most of my examples come from Christian theists (or from Plotinus, where the terminology at issue still fits fairly comfortably) and for the sake of simplicity, I speak of that with which the mystic achieves union as "God." While I do not mean to suggest that the distinctions drawn here have no application outside the theistic context, that sphere does constitute the focus of this discussion and explains the lack of qualifications in my references to God.

8. Thus, Alois M. Haas usefully draws attention to the fact that for the theist there is here a "double . . . transcendence, of the soul becoming interior to itself, and of the deity personally presenting and opening itself therein." ("Transzendenzerfahrung in der Auffassung der deutschen Mystik," in Gerhard Oberhammer, ed., *Transzendenzerfahrung, Vollzugs-horizont des Heils* [Vienna: Institut für Indologie der Universität Wien, 1978], pp. 179–180, quoted in Mommaers and Van Bragt, *Mysticism: Buddhist and Christian*, p. 82.) For the monist, of course, there is only a single transcendence involved here.

9. For an account of Śankara's mysticism of the soul (in comparison with the similar view of Meister Eckhart), see Rudolf Otto, *Mysticism East and West*, trans. Bertha L. Bracey and Richenda C. Payne (New York: Macmillan, 1932), pp. 98 ff. Mysticism of the soul is also discussed in Zaehner's *Mysticism: Sacred and Profane*, e.g., p. 128, and in chap. 1 of Wainwright's *Mysticism*.

10. Meister Eckhart, *Sermons and Treatises*, trans. and ed. Maurice O'Connell Walshe, 3 vols. (Longmead: Element Books, 1979–1987), vol. 3, pp. 109–110.

11. See Bernard McGinn's "Theological Summary" in Meister Eckhart, *The Essential Sermons, Commentaries, Treatises, and Defense*, trans. Edmund Colledge, O.S.A., and Bernard McGinn (New York: Paulist Press, 1981), pp. 40, 42.

12. Meister Eckhart, *Sermons and Treatises*, vol. 2, p. 275.

13. Ibid., vol. 2, p. 53.

14. Otto, *Mysticism East and West*, pp. 98, 100.

15. Meister Eckhart, *Sermons and Treatises*, vol. 3, p. 108.

16. Ibid., vol. 2, p. 105. Similar teachings can be found in other writers who belonged to or who were decisively influenced by the Rhineland school. For example, the exemplarism of Ruusbroec provides a clear framework for the statement of this general type of view of the self:

> Since the almighty Father has perfectly comprehended himself in the ground of his fruitfulness, the Son, who is the Father's eternal Word, goes forth as another Person within the Godhead. Through this eternal birth all creatures have gone forth eternally before their creation in time. God has thus seen and known them in himself—as distinct in his living ideas and as different from himself, though not different in every respect, for all that is in God is God. . . . In this divine image all creatures have an eternal life apart from themselves, as in their eternal Exemplar. It is to this eternal image and likeness that the Holy Trinity has created us. God therefore wills that we go out from ourselves into this divine light, supernaturally pursuing this image which is our own life and possessing it with him both actively and blissfully in a state of eternal blessedness. (John Ruusbroec, *The Spiritual Espousals and Other Works*, trans. James A. Wiseman, O.S.B. [New York: Paulist Press, 1979], pp. 35 and 42)

Ruusbroec further combines this doctrine of the eternal life of our deeper self that resides in God with a conception that corresponds to what I have been calling "final union"—that is, a union "above all activity . . . ; a quieted rest in inactivity . . . ; above all holy living and practice of virtue: simple blessedness . . . ; and above hunger and thirst, love and longing for God: eternal satiety" (*The Seven Enclosures*, quoted in Mommaers and Van Bragt, *Mysticism: Buddhist and Christian*, p. 166). Plotinus may or may not have a doctrine of individual Forms, but if he does it certainly does not figure centrally in a Plotinian account of the mystical life; thus, the exemplarism of Ruusbroec, while rooted in the Neoplatonic tradition, represents an approach to the mystical self different from the one we discuss in connection with Plotinus himself.

17. Teresa of Avila, *The Interior Castle*, trans. Kieren Kavanaugh, O.C.D., and Otilio Rodriguez, O.C.D. (New York: Paulist Press, 1979), pp. 35 and 42.

18. Ibid., p. 37.

19. Ibid.

20. Plato Mamo, "Is Plotinian Mysticism Monistic?" in R. Baine Harris, ed., *The Significance of Neoplatonism* (Norfolk, Va.: International Society for Neoplatonic Studies, 1976), pp. 199–215. Some scholars prefer to regard Plotinus's experience as exhibiting the revelatory transition we have just been considering, rather than the transformative one offered here. See, e.g., A. H. Armstrong, "The Apprehension of Divinity in the Self and Cosmos in Plotinus," also in Harris, *The Significance of Neoplatonism*, pp. 197–198, and Louis Bouyer, *A History of Christian Spirituality*, vol. 1, "The Spirituality of the New Testament and the Fathers," trans. Mary P. Ryan (New York: Seabury Press, 1982), p. 365. Scholars also disagree about whether the final union to be attributed to him is best understood in terms of monism or theism. For Plotinus as a monistic rather than a theistic mystic (to use Zaehner's distinction), see, e.g., Bréhier, *The Philosophy of Plotinus*, esp. chap. 7, pp. 106–131; philosophers of mysticism, e.g., Stace and Wainwright, often categorize his experience as monistic as well, meaning thereby to rule out any dualism and intentionality in its character. For Plotinus as a theistic mystic, see Rist, *Plotinus: The Road to Reality*, chap. 16, pp. 213–230, and Wayne Teasdale, *Essays in Mysticism* (Lake Worth, Fla.: Sunday Publications, 1982), pp. 97–98, both of whom draw on René Arnou, *Le Désir de Dieu dans la philosophie de Plotin*, 2d ed. (Rome: Presses de l'Université Grégorienne, 1967), especially chap. 6, section II.1, pp. 243–252.

21. Mamo, "Is Plotinian Mysticism Monistic?" pp. 203 ("poly-valent" and "oscillating") and 205 ("fluctuating focus").

22. Plotinus, *Enneads*, IV.3.8, vol. 4, p. 57.

23. Mamo, "Is Plotinian Mysticism Monistic?" p. 205.

24. Ibid.

25. Sometimes the transformative capacity of the self is asserted unqualifiedly (e.g., in addition to the passage from IV.3.8 already cited, cf. *Enneads* V.8.7, vol. 5, p. 261), sometimes with less sureness (e.g., *Enneads* VI.9.10, vol. 7, p. 341). Obviously, one's interpretation is going to be affected by which sort of passage one emphasizes.

26. It is, incidentally, only in this sense of our becoming the One, Mamo believes, that we can characterize Plotinus as a monist:

> The texts [of the *Enneads*] themselves create a strong monistic impression; although it is true, of course, that the extreme identity phrases, e.g., "I am God," are lacking. But the reason for this is not that Plotinus was a theist; rather, these phrases would strike him as too crude and inaccurate in view of his own sophisticated notion of the self that can *become* the One only after the most arduous purification and only at the last moment, as it were, of the expansion and simplification of the soul. (Ibid., pp. 209–10; italics in the original)

27. Both quotations come from *Enneads*, VI.9.11, pp. 341, 343.

28. Jean Daniélou, "The Dove and Darkness in Ancient Byzantine Mysticism," in *Man and Transformation: Papers from the Eranos Yearbooks*, ed. Joseph Campbell, vol. 5 (Princeton: Princeton University Press, 1964), p. 280. I have latinized the Greek in the quoted text.

29. Gregory of Nyssa, *From Glory to Glory: Texts from Gregory of Nyssa's Mystical Writings*, selected and with an introduction by Jean Daniélou, S. J., trans. and ed. Herbert Musurillo, S. J. (Crestwood, N.Y.: St. Vladimir's Seminary Press, 1979): "by nature changeable," p. 216; " a living mirror," p. 282; "receives the likeness of whatever it looks upon," pp. 172, 184; "substantially transformed," p. 154. All these passages are found in Gregory's *Commentary on the Song of Songs*.

30. See ibid., p. 101, from the sermons *On the Beatitudes*. Gregory's language can sometimes suggest the view of the hidden, true self that is revealed, and it does so here:

> For, when God made you, He at once endowed your nature with this perfection: upon the structure of your nature He imprinted an imitation of the perfections of His own nature, just as one would impress upon the wax the outline of an emblem. But the wickedness that has been poured all over this divine engraving has made your perfection useless and hidden it with a vicious coating. You must then wash away, by a life of virtue, the dirt that has come to cling to your heart like plaster, and then your divine beauty will once again shine forth.

It is only in the broader context of Gregory's writing that it is repeatedly made clear that our "divine beauty" does not lie hidden as a deeper self continually in touch with the divine and only waiting to be revealed but that our "divine beauty" is something that is produced, coming into being through our growing participation in God. For example, he writes in the *Commentary on the Song of Songs* (*From Glory to Glory*, p. 186), "Now, how can you see a beautiful image in a mirror unless it has received the impression of a beautiful form? So it is with the mirror of human nature: it cannot become beautiful until it draws near to the Beautiful and becomes transformed by the image of the divine Beauty."

31. Ibid., pp. 110–111. This passage comes from Gregory's *On Virginity*.

32. Endre von Ivánka, "Vom Platonismus zur Theorie der Mystik (Zur Erkenntnislehre Gregors von Nyssa)" in *Scholastik* 11 (1936): 189.

33. Gregory of Nyssa, *From Glory to Glory*, p. 217, from the *Commentary on the Song of Songs*.

34. "Mutable and prone to change," ibid., p. 83 (*On Perfection*); "ever changing," p. 103 (*On Virginity*).

35. Ibid., p. 190 (*Commentary on the Song of Songs*).

36. Ibid., p. 62. This introduction by Daniélou is very helpful in general and is very useful for understanding Gregory's conception of a "dynamic union" in particular.

37. Ibid., p. 67.

38. E. R. Dodds, *Pagan and Christian in an Age of Anxiety: Some Aspects of Religious Experience from Marcus Aurelius to Constantine* (Cambridge: Cambridge University Press, 1965), pp. 98–99.

39. C. W. Macleod, "Allegory and Mysticism in Origen and Gregory of Nyssa," *Journal of Theological Studies* 22 (N.S.), Pt. 2 (October 1971): 363. Again I have latinized what is Greek in the text.

40. See note 3.

41. The limit of an "intimate connection" would be identity between God and the self; while I am not considering such cases here, they would only reinforce the point.

42. Indeed, Gregory of Nyssa suggests transitions that move in a direction away from the divine: "Indeed, man was once created in God's image, but became a wild beast, transformed into an irrational creature, becoming a lion and a leopard by reason of his sinful ways" (*From Glory to Glory*, p. 215; from the *Commentary on the Song of Songs*).

43. In considering what the mystics experience, Nelson Pike's distinction between the "discernable given" and the "theoretical given" is useful (*Mystic Union* [Ithaca: Cornell University Press, 1992], p. 142). Phenomenology concerns what is intuited without inference, without any derivation by judgment, not what epistemology might regard as basic. A question about whether a description goes beyond (and interprets) the given may thus elicit different answers from the phenomenologist and the epistemologist.

TEN

Postconstructivist Approaches to Mysticism

R. L. FRANKLIN

The Setting of the Debate

The classic approach to mysticism emphasizes its unity. It points to striking parallels in the language used by mystics from different cultures who were unknown to each other and concludes that they describe the same experience. Hence, it presents mysticism as involving a state of consciousness found in virtually all religions, recognizably the same in each, and acknowledged by those who have eyes to see as the highest goal of the religious quest.

Today that view is challenged by what may be called constructivism.[1] This new point of view developed because, in field after field, scholars realized that our culture shapes all our mental activity; that not only what we think but even what we experience is conditioned by our total belief system. Thus: I now see a metal paper clip. In what sense is my experience the same as that of a New Guinea tribesman looking at the same object if he knows nothing of paper or of metal? Do we even see "the same thing"?[2] However we answer this fundamental question, surely in *some* important sense we construct our world and see what we have learned to see. Constructivism has weaker versions, which merely stress the contribution that our belief system makes to the world as we know it, and stronger ones, which suggest that—at least in such contexts as interpreting texts—we essentially create our reality. But all versions insist that no experience is what we may call *unmediated*, in the sense of being free from determination by our whole belief system.

Applied to mysticism, this argument presents a major challenge to the classic view. If our experience, as well as our understanding, depends on our whole belief system, and if the latter depends on our culture, then how could there be an identical mystical experience that is detectable across diverse cultures? Rejecting this possibility, constructivist views develop a series of attacks on the classic approach. They may reinterpret texts to emphasize their diversity and cultural embeddedness, which they claim the classic view has unduly minimized. Or they may argue that apparent similarities are superficial and misleading, for the meanings of words ramify throughout our belief systems, and mystics who make similar-sounding statements can mean only what their traditions allow them to conceive. Finally, they may claim that the classic approach is conceptually incoherent, for there simply cannot be such a thing as a pure experience, unmediated by our belief system, that can be identical across varying cultures.

I believe that constructivism, despite its insights, cannot do full justice to mysticism.[3] But that is a negative point, and those who accept the need for some postconstructivist view may well differ from me in what they concede to constructivism or put in its place. Such differences are healthy, for with these vast issues many paths should be explored.

Postconstructivism

Undeniably, as constructivism emphasizes, we are historical beings; we are fundamentally conditioned by the belief system inherited from our culture, as modified by our individual history. Without this we would not be human, but it presents reality to us in a preformed way, which both makes understanding possible and yet restricts it. Surely, too, our belief system mediates not only our thinking but also our experience itself. Yet the relation between them is a two-way process in which each continually affects the other. Our whole belief system is potentially involved in our judgment about what we see in front of us. But an experience we do not expect may challenge the beliefs that produced the expectation; proverbially, the exception proves (i.e., tests) the rule. As a result, when complex issues are to be settled, we have debates in which "empirical" and "conceptual" issues, or matters of "fact" and "theory," continually interact.[4] Hence, we cannot say, with the classic view, that whether unmediated mystical experience actually occurs is a sheer matter of fact, to which theoretical considerations are irrelevant. But neither can we decide the issue by a mere appeal to constructivist theory, as though that were independent of experience.

In this discussion I single out two issues. The first is the claim that unmediated mystical experience occurs. Elsewhere I have rejected the constructivist claim that the concept of such experience is conceptually incoherent;[5] but this does not show that it actually occurs, and the general mediation of our thought raises a presumption that postconstructivism must rebut. I now try to take the debate further by considering some central types of mystical experience and asking in what, if any, sense they are unmediated. The second issue is whether any such experience, which *ex hypothesi* is exceptional, is a mere, brute exception, or whether there is a broader picture that makes sense of its occurrence. If the former, claims that it occurs are easily (though not necessarily correctly) dismissed; if the latter, then the new picture can stand as a coherent rival to constructivism. In each of these issues, both conceptual and empirical considerations intertwine.

No one can deal with such matters without assumptions, but I try to make ones that beg no questions against opponents. "Mystical experience" is often extended to cover intense experiences that come to people unexpectedly. However, I am concerned with such phenomena only when they occur within a religious tradition. Each great religion tells how we may surmount the barriers of ignorance, sin, and finitude to reach an ultimate reality of God, *brahman*, or nirvana. Mystics may share the goal with their coreligionists, but are distinguished by the practices they adopt, and by the striking experiences that result. The practices may include music, dance, or the ritual ingesting of drugs, but, like most discussions, I focus on disciplines of meditation or prayer and on the resulting experiences. These experiences have three characteristics. First, they involve passing beyond the distinctions and boundaries of ordinary discursive thought. Second, this unbounded state is also one of intense stillness. It is totally conscious, with an intensity that comes from a sense of reaching a deeper reality, and yet it has a stillness because discursive thought has ceased. Third, it has a feeling-tone—often a most powerful one—of bliss, or joy, or rapture. These elements together amount to an intense, still, blissful passing beyond conceptual distinctions, which I shall call a state of *nonseparateness*. Bypassing other vital elements, such as the impact on the behavior and ethics of the mystic,[6] I focus on these features. They are a deliberately vague starting point, which my discussion aims to clarify.[7]

The Flavors of Nonseparateness

As constructivism emphasizes, mystical traditions are highly diverse. The first issue is how far they control or produce the resulting experience and whether they converge on a common result. To emphasize the diversity, I consider theistic, advaitan, and Buddhist mysticism, though I present only rough sketches of some typical features. They differ in their concept of the goal, in their evaluation of the stages along the way, and in their practices for reaching the goal. As for the goal, theists do not seek to merge with *brahman*, advaitans do not yearn for God, and Buddhists speak merely of extinguishing the self rather than of yearning for or merging with anything. As for stages of the journey, when, for example, ordinary discursive thought ceases, it may be followed by a vision or by a silent dialogue.[8] Theism may see this as a central paradigm of the relation of the soul to God, while other views may treat it as a lower stage in the transforming of our consciousness. As for practices, theism typically moves from intense devotion into nonseparateness in the presence of God, while advaita and Buddhism seek through meditation an awareness of the nature of being that sees God as at best an inadequate representation of the One.

As a final reminder of the variety of mystical traditions, we also find in Buddhism meditative practices that seek not a cessation of the stream of consciousness but a new sort of awareness of it. Thoughts and experiences are to be witnessed as rising and passing away, but we are to be without attachment to them. Here mental content does not cease; it merely ceases to matter. This practice links up in complex ways with those mentioned earlier. Here I need only note that the elements of nonseparateness—the intensity, the stillness, and the bliss—remain and that the goal of the witnessing is again to produce an awareness of not being separate from other beings.

Such differences surely show that mystics' beliefs shape their experience more than the classic view can allow. The nonseparateness of theism is a dualist, I-Thou relationship of total love; it is a being-there-*with*, for both the soul and God remain. The advaitin goal is a monistic merging, a *just*-being-there in which we find we *are* the One. And Buddhism, with its intense sense of the inadequacy of language here, rejects all talk of a self, even of One Self. To try to capture these differences, I introduce a concept that concedes to constructivism more than some postconstructivists might like: that there are *flavors* of nonseparateness, such as theistic, advaitin, or Buddhist ones. Flavors have an incipiently conceptual aspect, because they derive from how the experience would be expressed if the mystic thought about it. They also affect the feeling-tone of joy or bliss; for example, theistic ones have a larger element of devotion. Yet "conceptual"and "feeling" are too gross to capture the subtlety of a flavor. There is an incipient conceptualization that shapes the feeling-tone, but the experience remains one of nonseparateness beyond discursive thought.

What are the implications? If constructivism says merely that different traditions have different flavors and so shape mystical experience, it leaves open the question of how far the experiences do or might converge. This touches on the central issue of the relative importance we should give to the similarities and the differences among different mystical traditions in achieving an adequate overall understanding of mysticism. On these points, I shall say something at the end of this essay. Constructivism may, however, make the stronger claim that all mystical experience is mediated as ordinary thought and experience are; in particular, that it is intentional, in the technical sense of being *about* something. But the notion of a flavor gives no support to that view. Nonseparateness is beyond the intentionality of discursive thought, and a flavor is not *about* anything as a sound is *of* something.[9] Even when the experience is of an I-Thou relation, mystics insist that ordinary boundaries dissolve and that there is no "I" or "other" as in discursive thought.

Pure Consciousness Events

I must now relate my view to an important claim made by many postconstructivists: that "pure consciousness events" (PCEs) are central to understanding mysticism. Such events consist of a "wakeful contentless consciousness," which occurs in mystical contexts.[10] Clearly, this is a form of nonseparateness, where discursive thought ceases. The anticonstructivist implication of PCEs is that, since they are contentless, they must be the same for all who experience them across different cultures. Elsewhere I have argued that these events do occur and that the anticonstructivist implication holds.[11] But whatever their importance in the case against constructivism, they are only one form of nonseparateness, and they do not occur in all types of mysticism.

The obvious way to fit PCEs into my position is to treat them as one possible flavor of nonseparateness. But, it may be objected, if flavors have incipient conceptualization and blissful feeling-tone, which seem to be mental contents, and if pure consciousness is contentless, then it cannot have, or be, a flavor. In reply, the point about incipient conceptualization is, I think, easily met: potentiality is not actuality. How the mystic *would* conceive the experience is not a conception of it; in nonseparateness, including pure consciousness, it is only discursive thought, and not the later possibility of it, that dies away. But the problem about feeling-tone remains. One possible reply is that PCEs do have a feeling-tone, for both in my experience and in descriptions by others they are immensely attractive. Moreover, they range from a quiet, though still attractive, experience to a much more intense bliss,[12] and this seems very like a difference in flavor *within* pure consciousness. But this would need a long further discussion.[13] My question now is this: If we do concede that PCEs may have no feeling-tone, must we then say they have no flavor?

To discuss this, I draw an analogy from the theory of motion. Aristotelean-medieval mechanics, based on ordinary experience, held that the natural state of an earthly body was to be at rest. A body moved when a force was impressed on it and stopped when the force was exhausted. Rest needed no explanation, whereas motion did. The Galilean-Newtonian theory introduced a profound revolution. Defining motion in terms of velocity, it held that rest was merely a special case of motion—namely, the case where velocity was zero. To ears steeped in the old tradition, "zero velocity" might sound as self-contradictory as "motionless motion," but the change allowed all the phenomena to be mathematicized, and so began modern mechanics.[14] Analogously, even if we say pure consciousness has no feeling-tone, we may treat it as a special case where the flavor is flavorless. "Flavorless flavor" may seem an oxymoron, but no more so than "zero velocity" seemed to the seventeenth century. In each case, the feeling of paradox arises because our initial paradigms—the movement of a body, or a feeling-tone—normally have something we could notice, even if in mystical experience we do not attend to it. When there is no movement or quality of experience to notice, the paradigm seems inapplicable. But if we define a sense in which absence is only a special case of presence, we might obtain a more powerful theory for understanding mysticism, as we did with mechanics.

This does not weaken the earlier point—that if PCEs occur, they are incompatible with constructivism. For not only must contentless consciousness be nonintentional, but the argument still holds: PCEs, being contentless, must be the same across any culture, whether within or outside some appropriate mystical tradition. That point remains, no matter how much of mystical experience is mediated by tradition. Moreover, it would not be weakened if we accept what I earlier refused to assume: that PCEs have a flavor of bliss and that this flavor varies in intensity. The variations cannot be culturally mediated, since the pressure in any mystical tradition that expects PCEs will be to have them as intensely as possible. Rather, the bliss, and the variations in it, are also a cross-cultural phenomenon: that the cessation of thought in pure consciousness inherently leads to a nonseparateness that can be more or less intense.

I have not, however, started my argument from the occurrence of PCEs. For if we start with a concept that is not adequately neutral between conflicting views, our formulation of the issue may beg the question. PCEs most commonly occur in a monistic, just-being-there tradition, which aims at merging into a universal consciousness. If we start from PCEs, rather than from the broader notion of nonseparateness, a suggestion easily arises, already half made in speaking of pure consciousness, that PCEs are the uncontaminated paradigm of mysticism. "Pure" may function, not with a descriptive meaning about the PCE content, but with the evaluative one of their being the ideal case, which others approximate. That would be to assume that mystics asymptotically approach an ultimate state that manifests only a vanishingly small element of their historical being. Yet if every flavor, including any flavorless one, involves an incipient (though not actual) conceptualization, then if there *is* any supreme form of mysticism (see later), it will be, not the "purest," but rather that which derives from the best conceptualization. So if, for example, the true relation to ultimate reality were a dualistic being-there-with between a soul and God, then that would be the ideal nonseparateness.

In short, insofar as PCEs are presented as one type of mystical experience that highlights the inadequacy of constructivism, I endorse the argument. But if they are presented as the clue to the true nature of mysticism, they beg the question in a way that the general notion of nonseparateness does not. The anticonstructivist implications, however, remain. What we need is a perspicuous view of mysticism—one that captures its underlying unity while doing justice to its diversity. In speaking of flavors, I emphasize the diversity more than did the classic view, but I see nonseparateness as a central part of the unity that enables us to speak of mysticism at all. If this is true, then whatever we finally say about pure consciousness, we will need a view that gives more weight to the unity than constructivism wishes to do.

The Forgetting Model, Consciousness, and the Self

I turn to the second issue foreshadowed at the beginning: whether we can make sense of nonseparateness by seeing it not merely as an anomalous exception to mediated consciousness but as part of a coherent picture. Here we meet the important notion, defended elsewhere, of the "forgetting model."[15] It sees mysticism as a process of deconditioning of experience. While it agrees that mystical traditions, like all learning, are mediated, it claims that they aim to pass beyond themselves by stripping off or forgetting ordinary consciousness. What emerges from the stripping is, our title suggests, an innate capacity of the human mind to reach nonseparateness, a capacity that, far from being a mere anomaly, is a contact with the deepest reality. This has been presented in defense of the possibility of PCEs, but it applies equally to the more general notion of nonseparateness. For even if the flavors remain as a residue of the original learning, the significance of the innate capacity remains.

I endorse the forgetting model. But it demands reflection on two basic and linked notions: those of the self and of consciousness. Western philosophy has long wrestled with the notion of the self and has related it to consciousness through the question What makes my experiences *my* experiences? Hume, it is often said, could not observe any common element in all his experience; so, driven by his epistemology to deny whatever could not be experienced, he concluded that there was no common element, no real self, at all.[16] Kant agreed that there was no common experiential element but insisted that the self must be in some sense a unity that *has* experience.[17] The unifying element was, he concluded, not anything experienced but a purely formal "transcendental unity of apperception": the sheer fact that these are all *my* experiences. Philosophical ingenuity has developed more complex accounts, but debates about the self and consciousness must still decide between these views.

How might the forgetting model affect on this debate? A first proposal might be that mystics, in their state of nonseparateness, have become aware of just that unity that makes my experiences mine. Have we here something like an awareness of consciousness, and of the self, as such? This proposal is not to be confused with the forgetting model but is one possible way of applying that model to our ordinary understanding of ourselves. Thus it might offer something like an empirical solution to what had seemed a baffling conceptual problem: that what Hume said could not be there *because* it could not be experienced, and what Kant said must be there *although* it could not be experienced, actually *can* be experienced, though only in a special state of consciousness.

However, though I believe the forgetting model has profound philosophical implications, I think this initial proposal does not question deeply enough the presuppositions of the debate that it aims to transform and so is a false trail. As it stands, could it explain, let alone endorse, the value that mystics place on nonseparateness? Would not the appropriate reaction simply be: "So that's what the self is like—how interesting!"? Furthermore, does it really answer the problem of the self and of consciousness? The standard objection to Hume is that an experienc*er* is logically prior to experience. Even if we perform the second-order act of introspecting our experience, we still remain distinct from that introspection. And if we attempt the contorted third-order act of introspecting our introspection, we end only with an infinite regress. Always, the presupposed but unexperienced experiencer remains. How could the proposal avoid this regress? Even an awareness of nonseparateness would not be awareness of the experiencing self, for, if the regress holds, the self cannot be experienced.

These comments from within the Western philosophical tradition are no doubt too cursory to be convincing, but a further difficulty arises within mysticism itself. Surely it is precisely over the nature of the human self and its relation to the One that theistic retentions of the soul, advaitan mergings with the one Self, and Buddhist no-self doctrines most sharply differ in their understanding of nonseparateness. Hence, it seems that, on this point, secular philosophy and mystical interpretations of nonseparateness may both be in the same, rather unseaworthy boat. Thus we must be meeting one of the deepest problems that the human mind can face. But that does not mean that we cannot make progress, still less that mysticism has nothing to contribute. I have suggested that, if we try to use it merely as the source of a neat philosophical move *within our ordinary concepts of the self and consciousness*, then the difficulties are formidable. We may, however, see it as inviting us to *transform* these ordinary concepts in the light of its experience. If we accept the invitation, we may not find a final solution, since the issues reoccur within mysticism itself. And of course, as constructivism insists, any results will be mediated by the process that has led to them. But we might still achieve new insights that present a deeper understanding of ourselves. In doing this, we might also make sense of nonseparateness by making it the central clue to what we are. I now try to bridge the gap between ordinary thought and mysticism from both ends. I first suggest that current views may need modification in the light of neglected factors within ordinary experience. Then I suggest how the mystical sense of nonseparateness may help us in such modification.

The Self, Consciousness, and Identification

In our culture, a widespread starting point is that, whatever else we are, we are material beings.[18] A natural thought, then, is to locate our self where our body is and to think of ourselves as isolated, atomic entities, each as distinct from others as pebbles on a heap.[19] This is at its most persuasive with sensory experience: my pain occurs where my body is harmed; my visual field extends from my eyes. Philosophical doctrines may reinforce this view. Materialism suggests that there is nothing but the body that could be the self. Empiricist epistemology focuses on how we move from sensory information to more abstract beliefs and so takes as basic the perceiving self that is linked to the body. Other cultural factors reinforce the view. Social alienation suggests a sense of an isolated self, and even our hard-won political and moral emphasis on the value of the individual may encourage us to see persons as isolated units.

Yet this picture of an atomic self, which often operates as a powerful background assumption, cannot survive examination. Even at the material level, a living body is not an isolated entity. If we do not breathe, drink, eat, and evacuate, we die. The body is more like a waterfall than a pebble: a *flow* of matter that persists only as a pattern that continually recreates itself. In other contexts the point is even clearer. Thoughts may, but need not, be about bodily stimuli; actions may, but need not, arise as reactions to surroundings. Or consider ordinary, intentional feeling-tone. If I feel elated, what I am elated about may have nothing to do with my body, or even my achievements: it may be because my child has had a child, because my football team has won, because I am proud of my country.[20] The importance of these undeniable facts is easily overlooked. We need to explore how, in a far deeper sense than we usually allow, our self extends to *whatever we identify with*, in the sense of taking its fortunes as our own. Consider: if someone were to murder your child, it is yourself (among others) who would be shattered, as kidnappers well know when they seize the children of the rich. For the murderer to say, "I didn't harm *you*; I killed only your child" would be as far beyond comprehension as it is beneath contempt.

I have spoken of the self, but similar points apply to consciousness. My consciousness of sensation centers on my body, but consciousness of thoughts and feeling-tones need not. I may be more aware of the pain or pleasure of others than I am of my own. And in the grim example just given, my grief at the loss of my child would be indissolubly linked to my sense of the suffering of others bound up in the tragedy.

So we need to explore in what sense our concepts of the self and of consciousness extend to whatever we identify with, but here I make only two points. The first is a negative one: that the concept of an isolated, atomic self cannot survive examination. The second is this: of course we say, from our ordinary standpoint, that identification is not identity. I am not my child, my team, my country, however much I identify with them; others' experiences, of which they are conscious, cannot be mine, of which I am conscious. But still we begin to touch here some themes that arise within mysticism. However far our ordinary concepts of self and consciousness may be from unbounded nonseparateness, the phenomenon of identification shows they are less bounded than we usually allow. Hence, identification might be the site for a bridge from ordinary thought across a gulf of incomprehension to the mysterious territory of mysticism.

Consciousness, the Self, and Mysticism

Identification with child, team, or country may point to the nonatomic nature of the self, but it is still part of the contents of mental activity. When that activity ceases in nonseparateness, we meet a deeper challenge to accustomed notions of the self and consciousness. Ordinarily, we locate these in the world as follows. Of the innumerable objects in the universe, some, such as human beings, are conscious, and others, such as stones, are not; somewhere on the scale of life between chimpanzees and bacteria, consciousness dwindles into unconscious reaction. So consciousness is a feature of some objects, or a property of entities. I shall call a conscious entity, which need not be a human one, a self. Selves can exist without being conscious, as in deep sleep, but we could no more have consciousness without selves than redness without red things. In philosophical terms, the self is ontologically prior to consciousness; this is the standard critique of Hume. Even contemporary views that regard a person as a collection of conflicting discourses rather than a unity still share the picture of consciousness as a property of an entity.

Hence, with mystical experience, we naturally ask, "What entity is in this state of nonseparateness?" We answer, "The individual self, of course." But when boundaries disappear in nonseparateness and yet intense consciousness remains, mysticism concludes that, rather than consciousness being a property of bounded entities like ourselves, all such entities, including ourselves, are structures within a universal consciousness—one that is itself unbounded and that we meet in nonseparateness. This profoundly challenges constructivism, along with our ordinary self-understanding.[21] That is why I can agree that constructivism has such penetrating insights into ordinary consciousness, while denying its adequacy for interpreting mysticism.

This, however, emphasizes the unity of mysticism, and I now turn to the diversity. If we ask how universal consciousness is related to our ordinary self, then theism, advaita, and Buddhism present deeper and deeper challenges to ordinary thought. Theism retains a pluralism of selves, so that while in some sense we are "in" the unimaginable divine consciousness, nonseparateness is communion between the soul and God.[22] Advaita sees an individual self and consciousness as a mere structure within a universal one. Our bounded consciousness, like everything else, is part of the universal Self, though it is not usually conscious of being so. But while these two conceptions leave consciousness dependent on a self, even if in advaita there is only the One Self, Buddhist *anatta* or no-self doctrine rejects not only selves but the Self, leaving only the blissful cessation of selfhood in nirvana. Yet ultimate reality is still conscious, or at least not unconscious, so this view sees consciousness as *ontologically prior to the self.* To some Western thinkers, that may seem as absurd as "zero velocity" seemed to the opponents of modern mechanics. But though much needs to be debated here, my concern now is only to connect these views to the forgetting model and to identification.

The forgetting model asserts that there is a stripping off of boundaries in nonseparateness. On this point the three traditions would agree. But when we strip them, theism says that we discover intense communion with God; advaita, that we discover our true self to be the Self; and Buddhism, that we pass beyond any concept of self altogether. The link with identification lies, I suggest, in what mystics, in conceptualizing nonseparateness, *speak of as their real self.* In theism, the self is seen as that-which-is-drawn-to-the-One, so the language of nonseparateness is dualistic and the experience is a being-there-with. In advaita, the real self *is* the One, though we inevitably begin by believing that we are a separate self, so the language is monistic and the experience is a just-being-there. But Buddhism rejects any extended identification; it sees the self as *inherently* bounded, as our ordinary thought does. So it conceives unboundedness as passing beyond the very notion of self, while still agreeing with all mysticism that consciousness does not cease.

Of the three traditions I have sketched, we could oppose theism, as being personalist, to advaita and Buddhism as impersonalist ones. But the earlier contrast between Hume and Kant, and the question of ontological priority of consciousness or the self, place the divide between the first two, which assume with Kant that consciousness needs a self, and the third, which uses a Hume-like view that it need not.[23] No doubt there are other approaches, for we cannot foreclose how people may struggle to conceive the inconceivable. And, as their efforts stretch language to the breaking point, formulations that to some represent experienced truth are to others simply incoherent. I shall suggest what might be the outcome of the debate.

Prospects

Starting from the current conflict involving the classic view of mysticism, the constructivist critique of it, and the search for a postconstructivist model, my argument has been as follows. First, the flavors of nonseparateness show that mystics' beliefs permeate their experience more than the classic view allowed. Second, though constructivism rightly insists on this mediation, it misses the deeper challenge: that mysticism seeks to strip off mediated consciousness and to transform our ordinary concepts of consciousness and the self. So, third, a postconstructivist view is needed. I endorsed the forgetting model, which suggests that the stripping reveals an innate capacity to reach a state of nonseparateness. But that claim is often presented in terms of the occurrence of PCEs, and to assume that these events are the central paradigm of nonseparateness would beg vital questions. So, I believe, we can see common elements among traditions but have as yet no perspicuous overall theory of mysticism. How might we go beyond that situation?

Any attempt to do so meets two great and opposite challenges. One is within dominant intellectual trends, and the other opposes them, but both center on the concept of change. First, the continual impact of new data and critical reflection in all areas often leads us to take for granted that current theories will one day be superseded. This is what it means to see ourselves as historical beings in a changing culture. Hence arises the postmodernist challenge to all intellectual synthesis.[24] It sees all overall theories, about mysticism or anything else, as forcing phenomena into preconceived and static patterns that distort reality, so it finds in intellectual activity nothing but restless and unceasing change. The second great challenge resists the whole contemporary attitude that takes change for granted. For when we apply that attitude to mysticism, it clashes with many of the data that give birth to the inquiry. Mystical traditions are embedded in religions that control their understanding of the phenomena, and for them it is a very serious question how far this might be open to change. Each sees itself as the guardian of truths that are not a human invention and that it has no right to question or alter.[25] Typically, they either present themselves as *the* true path or, even if they acknowledge other ones, still assess the value of those others in terms of how far they conform to their own position.

Much Western scholarship will not take such views seriously. Of course, it says, traditions may in fact resist all change, but rationally the issue is simply whether such conservatism can bear to open itself to critical reflection. Yet in saying this it begs the question, just as I have suggested that constructivism does in relation to mysticism. For the reply, which may itself be rationally argued, is that change is permissable only insofar as the purported truths really are a merely human construction, and we have no right simply to assume this without argument.

Yet despite postmodernist rejections of all overviews and traditional religious resistance to change, I believe there can be a dialectic of development by which we may achieve a better grasp of conflicting positions and perhaps eventually find a deeper understanding. For this we need, as always, an interplay of theory and practice. This dialectic of development is best found between those who can feel the force of other traditions but who are bound in loyalty to their own experience to protest that *that* is not how they would put it. The others, in turn, explain why they value their approach. Ideally, the power of each viewpoint may eventually be so felt by the other that the conflict is internalized within each of them so that they embark on a joint search for a deeper expression of the truth. Then our differences as historical beings cease to be barriers but can even be used to increase our understanding. Contrasts that at first seem unavoidable may eventually be reconciled, and such concepts as the self, consciousness, and identification may be transformed. There is room here both for detached academic study of mystical traditions and for affirmations coming from experience, as we assess but also learn from the practices. Such a dialectic might eventually show some existing tradition to be the best, but it would, I think, be more likely to result in a metatheory about the least inadequate way to conceptualize the inconceivable One. The theory might increasingly hope to explain why traditions, given their starting point, conceive the One as they do. "In a given cultural setting," it might predict, "you will normally get this version of nonseparateness, and hence that flavor of it." Thus, the setting would shape the practice, as constructivism insists, but passing beyond discursive thought into nonseparateness would remain a transcultural phenomenon.

I cannot adequately defend this hope here. But, as against postmodernism, I would plead that, if we set out to take seriously the others' viewpoint, then, although we may never reach a final end, we may still find genuinely deeper insight. To preservers of tradition who deny the legitimacy of change, I would urge that an acknowledgment of suprahuman authority is compatible with the Socratic challenge to follow the wind of the argument wherever it blows. Critical inquiry need not exalt human judgment over God's, or mere intellect over the enlightenment of the seer; it might be seen, at least in retrospect, as a process, stemming from the One, by which new insight comes to humanity.

A true dialectic of development would involve much more than a mere new intellectual synthesis. Its interaction of theory and practice would point toward a transcending of traditions, which would influence our understanding of nonseparateness and so our experience, too. Insofar as we accepted all traditions as comprehensible alternatives, producing mystics of high rank, then those who remained within one path would still know there were others, and many might explore more than one. This would *create its own flavor*; nonseparateness would be conceived, and therefore experienced, as a state that could properly be conceptualized, as communion, as merging, or as passing beyond self altogether. That, in turn, would reflect back on the theory as it further transformed our understanding of the experience. Whether we could or should transcend traditions in this way is a far greater debate than the one about constructivism and its rivals with which I began, but I think it is that to which we will finally be led.

Notes

1. Forceful expressions of constructivism are found particularly in S. T. Katz, ed., *Mysticism and Philosophical Analysis* (Sheldon Press, 1978) and *Mysticism and Religious Traditions* (New York: Oxford University Press, 1983).

2. Traditional empiricist epistemology would answer: "You both have the same sense data." In rejecting this, constructivism is part of a widespread reaction against the postulation of simple, uninterpreted data of sensation as a foundation for knowledge.

3. In R. K. C. Forman, ed., *The Problem of Pure Consciousness* (New York: Oxford University Press, 1990, cited as PPC), the arguments for constructivism, particularly in the Katz volumes, are discussed in more detail. My contribution to PPC, "Experience and Interpretation in Mysticism," I cite as EIM. I there used "the diversity view" to refer to what I now call constructivist interpretations of mysticism. The former name, though less apt, had the advantage of bringing out that constructivism followed and reinforced earlier views, such as those of R. C. Zaehner, *Mysticism Sacred and Profane* (Oxford, Clarendon Press, 1937), which had stressed the diversity of mysticism without any specifically constructivist arguments.

4. Broadly, I believe, these notions are context-dependent. When we have a sufficient common background of beliefs, we can reach agreement on what is to count as a fact, even if the specific fact is in dispute. Without such a background, the dispute becomes a conceptual one about how the issue should be posed. Cf. my discussion in R. L. Franklin, *The Search for Understanding* (New York: Peter Lang, 1995).

5. See EIM, and also PPC passim.

6. Since nonseparateness involves a sense of oneness with all creation, it points toward an all-inclusive compassion for all other beings. This often clashes with the mystic's tradition, which may reject certain people or phenomena as evil or unclean. So strong tensions may arise, which different mystics solve in different ways.

7. My views have two sources. Partly they are an intellectual interpretation of what I have heard or read. But partly they are based on my own small experience of nonseparateness, which has come from practices in different traditions that are not often combined. These sources, as always, interact; understanding encourages deeper experience, and experience suggests further insight.

8. Consider the visions of Ezekiel, or the "still small voice" that spoke to Elijah (I Kg. 19).

9. If, as many argue, not all *ordinary* consciousness is intentional (though most undoubtedly is), the antimystical assumption is further weakened.

10. PPC, p. 21 and passim. For some of the conceptual problems involved in understanding them, cf. R. K. C. Forman, "Mystical Consciousness, the Innate Capacity, and the Perennial Philosophy," in this volume (cited as MC).

11. See EIM. I was then only groping toward what I now call the flavors of nonseparateness.

12. Forman, MC, and in private communication. I have in mind here the meditative technique of Transcendental Meditation, from which the phrase "pure consciousness" is drawn.

13. Some might further argue that if pure consciousness is inherently attractive (though in differing degrees), it must have some feature that makes it so; hence, it cannot be a featureless experience. However, we can be attracted or repelled without experiencing anything, as most of us suppose to be the case with lower life forms. We need suppose only that our central nervous system is inherently attracted to pure consciousness, whatever feeling-tone may or may not be involved.

14. There is an important methodological shift here. Aristotelean mechanics was based on a classification of paradigm cases into genus and species, but modern mechanics has no special paradigms. *Any* case illustrates it equally well or badly: equally well, because the same laws apply to all; equally badly, because it deals with ideal conditions (e.g., the absence of friction) that may never be realized in experience. Today the use of "ideal types" in sociology seeks to make a similar transition from paradigm examples to abstractly defined cases.

15. Cf. Forman's Introduction to PPC, and his MC.

16. Hume, *Treatise of Human Nature* (Oxford: Selby-Bigge, 1888), particularly Appendix, pp. 633–636. For a radically different, and more sympathetic, view of Hume, cf. Amelie Rorty, "'Pride Produces the Idea of Self': Hume on Moral Agency" (*Austrailian Journal of Philosophy* 68 (1990): 255–269).

17. Kant, *Critique of Pure Reason* A95 et seq., esp. A107–108; B129 et seq., esp. B131–135.

18. Differing approaches are found in philosophy, literary criticism, psychology, and sociology. Furthermore, religious thought, quite apart from mystical traditions, has often seemed to speak of an *intra*human multiplicity. Thus, much Western theology has spoken as if body, mind, and soul were distinct entities. Again, e.g., Bhagavad Gita 7:4 offers an eightfold division of reality—five physical elements, then lower and higher mind and self-sense—which are listed as if they were ontologically separate. Today such language is under attack, not from constructivism—though there may be subterranean links—but from developments in many fields that emphasize the essential unity of the person or self. I, in my own way, endorse a unitary view, but I must bypass this whole area of debate.

19. Postmodernist views often emphasize our fragmentedness, even to the extent of denying any unitary self whatever. Yet such denials are often combined, however uneasily, with a sense of the self as a single physical entity. Here there are, I believe, complex forces that pull contemporary Western thought in divergent directions.

20. Of course, as materialism insists, my feeling of elation has, or is, a physical state in my central nervous system, but that captures only one aspect of my being elated. The same point applies to consciousness, discussed later.

21. So much so that many who have genuine mystical experience may not see the implications and may continue to hold a more standard worldview.

22. This is not confined to mysticism but extends to orthodox theism.

23. I owe this comparison to Robert Forman.

24. Constructivism has affinities with this view but is not committed to the implication I mention.

25. Personalist approaches usually conceive their tradition as a God-given and, hence, unalterable revelation. Impersonalist ones typically see theirs as cognized by seers who were totally enlightened. The practical result in each case is normally that the tradition is taken to be infallible.

DATE DUE
